HOLDING CHINA TOGETHER

Despite many predictions of collapse and disintegration, China has managed to sustain unity and gain international stature since the Tiananmen crisis of 1989. This volume addresses the "fragmentation – disintegration thesis" and examines the sources and dynamics of China's resilience. Through theoretically informed empirical studies, the volume's authors look at several key institutions for political integration and economic governance. They also dissect how difficult policies to regulate economic and social life (employment and migration, population planning, industrial adjustment, and regional disparities) are designed and implemented. The authors show that China's leaders have retained authoritarian political institutions but have also reinforced and modified them and constructed new ones in the light of changing circumstances. In policy implementation, China's leaders have learned by doing and made significant adaptations to improve the effectiveness of socioeconomic policies. Institutional and policy adaptations together have helped shore up political authority and create an environment for rapid growth while accommodating growing diversity.

Barry J. Naughton is an economist who specializes in China's transitional economy. He has written on economic policy making in China and issues relating to industry, foreign trade, macroeconomics, and regional development in China. Naughton teaches at the Graduate School of International Relations and Pacific Studies of the University of California at San Diego. In 1998, he was named the first So Kuanlok Professor of Chinese and International Affairs. His study of Chinese economic reform, *Growing Out of the Plan: Chinese Economic Reform, 1978–1993* (Cambridge University Press, 1995), won the Masayoshi Ohira Memorial Prize. His research on economic interactions among China, Taiwan, and Hong Kong, focusing on the elections industry, led to the edited volume *The China Circle: Economics and Technology in the PRC, Taiwan and Hong Kong* (1997).

Dali L. Yang is Associate Professor of Political Science and Director of the Committee on International Relations at the University of Chicago. He has also served as a Distinguished Visiting Professor at Nankai and Tsinghua Universities in China. He is the author of *Calamity and Reform in China* (1996), *Beyond Beijing: Liberalization and the Regions in China* (1997), and *Remaking the Chinese Leviathan: Market Transition and the Politics of Governance in China* (2004).

Holding China Together

Diversity and National Integration in the Post-Deng Era

Edited by

BARRY J. NAUGHTON

University of California, San Diego

DALI L. YANG

University of Chicago

CAMBRIDGE
UNIVERSITY PRESS

PUBLISHED BY THE PRESS SYNDICATE OF THE UNIVERSITY OF CAMBRIDGE
The Pitt Building, Trumpington Street, Cambridge, United Kingdom

CAMBRIDGE UNIVERSITY PRESS
The Edinburgh Building, Cambridge CB2 2RU, UK
40 West 20th Street, New York, NY 10011-4211, USA
477 Williamstown Road, Port Melbourne, VIC 3207, Australia
Ruiz de Alarcón 13, 28014 Madrid, Spain
Dock House, The Waterfront, Cape Town 8001, South Africa

http://www.cambridge.org

First published 2004

Printed in the United States of America

Typeface Times Ten Roman 10/13.5 pt.   *System* LaTeX 2_ε [TB]

A catalog record for this book is available from the British Library.

Library of Congress Cataloging in Publication Data
Holding China together: Diversity and national integration in the post-Deng era /
Edited by Barry J. Naughton, Dali L. Yang.
p.   cm.
Includes bibliographical references and index.
ISBN 0-521-83730-8
1. China – Politics and government – 1976–   2. China – Economic policy – 1976–2000.
3. China – Social conditions – 1976–   I. Title: Diversity and national integration in the
post-Deng era.   II. Naughton, Barry.   III. Yang, Dali L.
DS779.26.H65   2004
951.05 – dc22   2003065616

ISBN 0 521 83730 8 hardback

Contents

List of Figures and Tables   *page* vii

List of Contributors   ix

Holding China Together: Introduction   1
Barry J. Naughton and Dali L. Yang

PART ONE. THE INSTITUTIONS FOR POLITICAL AND ECONOMIC
CONTROL: ADAPTATION OF A HIERARCHICAL SYSTEM

1. Political Localism Versus Institutional Restraints: Elite
   Recruitment in the Jiang Era   29
   Cheng Li

2. The Institutionalization of Elite Management in China   70
   Zhiyue Bo

3. The Cadre Evaluation System at the Grass Roots: The
   Paradox of Party Rule   101
   Susan H. Whiting

4. Economic Transformation and State Rebuilding in China   120
   Dali L. Yang

PART TWO. CASE STUDIES OF POLICY IMPLEMENTATION

5. Policy Consistency in the Midst of the Asian Crisis: Managing
   the Furloughed and the Farmers in Three Cities   149
   Dorothy J. Solinger

6. Population Control and State Coercion in China   193
   Yanzhong Huang and Dali L. Yang

v

7.   The Political Economy of Industrial Restructuring in China's
     Coal Industry, 1992–1999   226
     Fubing Su

8.   The Western Development Program   253
     Barry J. Naughton

Index   297

Figures and Tables

FIGURES

6.1. TFR, 1978–1998.   *page* 198
6.2. China's birth control structure.   202
6.3. Number of birth control surgeries (in thousands), 1971–1991.   207
6.4. Composition of the contraception rate, by method,
     1987–1999.   209
6.5. Bureaucratic capacities and prevalence of sterilization, 1997.   214
7.1. Share of coal production by ownership, 1976–1997.   228
7.2. Energy consumption in China, 1953–1996.   230
7.3. Growth rates of coal mines in China, 1981–1996.   232
8.1. Western Development Program.   256
8.2. Provincial disparities: GDP pcr capita coefficient of variation.   258
8.3. Budgetary revenues and expenditures.   260

TABLES

1.1. Provincial Leadership Experience of Full Members of the
     1992, 1997, and 2002 Politburos   33
1.2. Distribution of Birthplaces, by Province, of Full Members of
     the 1992, 1997, and 2002 CCs   36
1.3. Members of the Shanghai Gang on the 16th CC   42
1.4. Top Officials in Shanghai (April 2003)   47
1.5. Distribution of Provincial and Municipal Leaders Who Work
     in the Same, Neighboring, or Distant Province or City   50
1.6. Tenure of Top Provincial or Municipal Leaders (2003)   54
1.7. The Average Length of Tenure of Provincial Party
     Secretaries and Governors During the Reform Era   55
1.8. Tenure of Current Positions of Provincial Leaders
     (September 2002)   56

1.9. Age Distribution of Provincial Leaders (September 2002) 58
1.10. Provincial Leaders Holding Full or Alternate Memberships on the 15th and 16th CCs 60
1.11. Promotion or Transfer Patterns of Provincial Leaders (September 2002) 64
2.1. Party Secretaries as Chairmen of the CP PPC (1983–2003) 76
2.2. Transfers Between Provinces (1990–2002) 87
2.3. Transfers from the Provinces to the Center (1990–2003) 91
2.4. Transfers from the Center to the Provinces (1990–2002) 95
3.1. National Guidelines for Performance Criteria of Local Party and Government Leaders 105
3.2. Performance Criteria for Township Government Executives and Party Secretaries, Jiading County, Shanghai, 1989 107
4.1. PBOC Regional Branches 132
5.1. Population of Municipality and Urban Districts 157
5.2. Size of Municipal Economies, 1997 160
5.3. Market Development, 1997 161
5.4. Employment in Private Enterprises 162
5.5. International Economies, 1997 162
5.6. Unemployment 163
5.7. Laid-off SOE Workers 163
5.8. Average Arable per Capita Acreage, Urban Areas 163
5.9. Average Arable per Capita Acreage, Provincial 163
5.10. Migrants: Rural Labor 164
6.1. Provincial Policy Variation in Population Control 200
6.2. Institutional Building for Program Structure, 1987, 1991, and 1995 203
6.3. Patterns of Contraceptive Method Use, by Provinces 210
6.4. Determinants of the Rate of Sterilization and IUD, 1997 213
6.5. Determinants of the Fine for One Extra Child (in logged form), 1991 216
7.1. Energy Comparison between China and the World 230
7.2. Losses of State Key Local Mines in China, 1962–1998 233
7.3. Revenue Breakdown of Small Coal Mines in Ningwu County, Shanxi Province, 1996 242
8.1. Budgetary Revenues, Expenditures, and Balance 261
8.2. Composition of Labor Force 278
8.3. Change in Provincial per Capita GDP Rankings 280
8.4. Composition of Industrial Output, 1998 283

Contributors

Zhiyue Bo is Assistant Professor and Chair of the Department of International Studies at St. John Fisher College in Rochester, New York. Widely published in the areas of local governance and provincial leadership in China, he is the author of *Chinese Provincial Leaders: Economic Performance and Political Mobility since 1949* (Sharpe, 2002).

Yanzhong Huang is Assistant Professor of Political Science at the John C. Whitehead School of Diplomacy and International Relations at Seton Hall University and Inaugural Director of its Global Health Studies Center. He has published a variety of studies on China's public health.

Cheng Li is the William R. Kenan Professor of Government at Hamilton College. He is the author of *Rediscovering China: Dynamics and Dilemmas of Reform* (Rowman and Littlefield, 1997) and *China's Leaders: The New Generation* (Rowman and Littlefield, 2001). He was a fellow at the Woodrow Wilson International Center for Scholars during the 2002–2003 academic year. He is working on a book on Chinese technocrats. Li thanks the United States Institute of Peace and the Chiang Ching-kuo Foundation for International Scholarly Exchange for their generous support of the research in his chapter.

Barry J. Naughton, an economist, is the So Kuanlok Professor of Chinese and International Affairs at the Graduate School of International Relations and Pacific Studies of the University of California at San Diego. His study of Chinese economic reform, *Growing Out of the Plan: Chinese Economic Reform, 1978–1993*, won the Masayoshi Ohira Memorial Prize. He edited the 1997 volume *The China Circle: Economics and Technology in the PRC, Taiwan and Hong Kong*, and he has published extensively on China's economic transition, regional development, and foreign trade.

Dorothy J. Solinger is Professor of Political Science in the School of Social Sciences at the University of California, Irvine, and Senior Adjunct Research Scholar at the Weatherhead East Asian Institute at Columbia University. Her current work is on unemployment and economic reform in China, and her most recent books are *Contesting Citizenship in Urban China* (University of California, 1999) and a coedited volume, *States and Sovereignty in the Global Economy* (Routledge, 1999).

Fubing Su is the Joukowski Post-Doctoral Fellow in Political Science and East Asian Studies at Brown University. His research and publications have been on China's political economy, with a special interest in regulation.

Susan H. Whiting is Associate Professor of Political Science at the University of Washington in Seattle. Among her publications is *Power and Wealth in Rural China: The Political Economy of Institutional Change* (Cambridge University Press, 2000).

Dali L. Yang is Associate Professor of Political Science and Director of the Committee on International Relations at the University of Chicago. His books include *Calamity and Reform in China* (Stanford University Press, 1996), *Beyond Beijing: Liberalization and the Regions in China* (Routledge, 1997), and *Remaking the Chinese Leviathan* (Stanford University Press, 2004).

Acknowledgments

This project has been made possible by generous support from the Smith Richardson Foundation. We wish to thank Susan Shirk for her leadership in initiating this project, and consistent support over the years. The Institute for Global Conflict and Cooperation of the University of California supported the organization of conferences and other work on this project. We would especially like to thank Ron Bee for his help. Earlier versions of the papers were presented at two workshops held in San Diego. We thank all the participants at those workshops for stimulating commentary and conversation, but especially those who contributed papers or comments that we were unable to include in this volume: Max Auffhammer, Richard Carson, Dru Gladney, Yasheng Huang, Li Shantong, Melanie Manion, Kevin O'Brien, Ed Winkler, and Zhai Fan. Anna Corfield and Kourtney Heintz provided valuable assistance in seeing the project through to fruition. At Cambridge University Press, Scott Parris was a wonderfully supportive and helpful editor. We are grateful to four anonymous reviewers for Cambridge University Press for their comments and suggestions. Michie Shaw of TechBooks handled the production with aplomb. The editors would especially like to thank our contributors for their patience with the project and their good cheer in meeting tight production deadlines.

Holding China Together: Introduction

Barry J. Naughton and Dali L. Yang

During the 1980s, China experienced a steady decline in central government control over the economy, the political system, and society as a whole. Economic reforms emphasized decentralization of resources and decision-making authority, which empowered local governments and enterprises at the expense of the national government. Economic liberalization fostered the creation of literally millions of new economic entities, combined with new market rules and incentives. Rapid economic growth not only led to a much larger and more complex economy but also greatly expanded regional diversity. Government demands for conformity receded, allowing a more relaxed and diverse society to develop. Although conservatives sought to roll back some of these reformist changes after the Tiananmen massacre, they were unable to reverse the most fundamental changes. Indeed, there is universal agreement that the 1980s witnessed a historic retreat of the Chinese central government. Given breathing space by the rollback of the Chinese state, Chinese society and the Chinese economy came alive.

Nevertheless, the decline in the authority of the Chinese state was not a smooth or trouble-free process. Like governments in all transitional economies, China's leaders abandoned crude but powerful tools of government resource allocation before market-friendly indirect and regulatory institutions were available. Inevitably, government effectiveness declined and the central government's financial prowess steadily eroded. The Chinese government simply seemed ill equipped to carry out the tasks demanded of it in the new economic environment. Even more troubling, the Chinese government frequently seemed unable to override particularistic, regional, and sectional interests. While decentralizing reforms moved forward, other reforms that required an authoritative state to

1

impose uniform, equitable rules on many different groups – such as fiscal and tax restructuring, or administrative and regulatory reforms – consistently failed. Concerns began to be raised regarding the overdecentralization of power and the maladaption of the Chinese government to the new demands placed upon it.

At such a pivotal time in the process of economic restructuring came the Tiananmen crisis of 1989. The profound political crisis into which the Chinese regime was plunged revealed disarray at the center. Moreover, in the aftermath of the government's deployment of massive brutal force against unarmed civilians, the ruling elite seemed to have lost the ability to use remuneration or legitimacy to govern and was left only with raw coercive power. China seemed to be on the verge of unraveling. Following the Tiananmen crisis, the collapse of the Soviet Union, the fall of other communist governments, and the disintegration of Yugoslavia all highlighted the shaky ground on which China's ruling elite stood, lending plausibility to scenarios of collapse or disintegration in China.

In the wake of these events, and throughout the 1990s, an influential literature developed that saw China as being undermined by centrifugal forces, in danger of coming apart or collapsing in on itself. This "disintegration" literature was a reaction both to the trends of the 1980s and to the shock of Tiananmen. Focusing on the fissiparous forces that had developed in China following more than a decade of decentralizing reforms, this literature extrapolated from the trends of the 1980s in order to look into the future, and it predicted an increasingly decentralized, unregulated, and ultimately uncontrollable society. At the same time, under the influence of the harsh crackdown that occurred at Tiananmen, these authors tended to be profoundly pessimistic about the ability of the Chinese government to adapt to and cope with these trends. In this view, a series of increasingly complex social and economic problems were poised to overwhelm a government that was incapable of mobilizing the social resources or the political will necessary to confront them.

This disintegration view has had a remarkably broad and enduring influence. Authors ranging from political dissidents to Chinese neoconservatives suggested that China faced the prospect of fragmentation or collapse. Various scholars, particularly those with a Taiwan background, began to note parallels between the rise in regionalism in contemporary China and the dynamics of fragmentation in Chinese history. They contended that rising regionalism would lead to the disintegration of the Party-State.[1] In Japan, Kenichi Ohmae went so far as to suggest that eleven Chinese republics might emerge out of China's breakup and then form a loose "Federal Republic of China."[2] The disintegration thesis gained special prominence within China in 1993, when two scholars noting parallels between China and Yugoslavia warned of China's possible disintegration. In their view, although the decentralizing reforms were enabling economic growth by devolving economic management authority and resources to enterprises and local levels of government, the reforms also served to undermine the fiscal foundations of the state. They foresaw that the fiscally enervated central government might not be able to hold the country together, and China might suffer the same fate as Yugoslavia.[3]

By the mid-1990s, the disintegration thesis was making major inroads. *China Deconstructs*: This was the witty and evocative title Goodman and Segal gave their edited volume on national and regional trends.[4] In the United States, the Pentagon's Office of Net Assessment convened a thirteen-member panel to assess China's future and found that a majority predicted disintegration.[5] In the summer of 1995, the journal *Foreign Policy* printed a major article boldly titled "The Coming Chinese Collapse." In this article, Professor Jack Goldstone of the University of California drew on his formidable knowledge of comparative history and sociology to predict "a terminal crisis [for the Chinese ruling regime] within the next 10 to 15 years." According to Goldstone, "China shows every sign of a country approaching crisis: a burgeoning population and mass migration amid faltering agricultural production and worker and peasant discontent – and all this as the state rapidly loses its capacity to rule effectively"

[1] Cheng Chu-yuan, *Behind the Tiananmen Massacre: Social, Political, and Economic Ferment in China* (Boulder, CO: Westview, 1990), pp. 196–7; Maria Hsia Chang, "China's Future: Regionalism, Federation, or Disintegration," *Studies in Comparative Communism*, 30, No. 3 (September 1992), pp. 226–7.

[2] Kenichi Ohmae, *The Borderless World: Power and Strategy in the Interlinked Economy* (New York: Harper Business, 1990).

[3] Wang Shaoguang and Hu Angang, *Zhongguo guojia nengli baogao [Report on China's State Capacity]* (Shenyang: Liaoning renmin chubanshe, 1993). For an English version of the main arguments, see Wang Shaoguang and Hu Angang, *The Chinese Economy in Crisis: State Capacity and Tax Reform* (Armonk, NY: Sharpe, 2001).

[4] David Goodman and Gerald Segal, eds., *China Deconstructs: Politics, Trade and Regionalism* (London: Routledge, 1994).

[5] Eduardo Lachica, "Hedging Bets for China's Post-Deng Era," *Wall Street Journal*, February 21, 1995, p. A20.

because of leadership conflicts and fiscal weakness.[6] Other commentators highlighted the dramatic differences between a capitalist South and bureaucratic–authoritarian North or contended that the Indonesian collapse during the Asian financial crisis might be a harbinger of China's fate.[7] More recently, Gordon Chang, in his best-selling *The Coming Collapse of China*, bemoaned the weakness of China's economic institutions and claimed that China's entry into the World Trade Organization would prove to be the proverbial straw that broke the camel's back.[8]

Ironically, while the disintegration thesis spread broadly in the 1990s, an alternative assessment emerged that stressed China's irresistible emergence as a great power. Drawing on the other set of key trends in the 1980s – namely the early success of economic reform and the rapid growth of the economy – this literature discussed ways to deal with a rising China. Fueled by the International Monetary Fund and the World Bank's purchasing power parity estimates of the size of China's economy and sustained by China's ability to weather the Asian financial crisis relatively unscathed, this view has extrapolated growth into the future, assuming that no domestic problems or external shocks will seriously disrupt China's rise. This second image has been seized on both by boosters of China touting its economic and business importance and by Cold Warriors who see China replacing the former USSR as an emerging threat to the United States.[9]

These two contrasting assessments of China, despite their apparently opposite natures, are like twins separated at birth. Both draw on the distinctive experience of China in the 1980s and early 1990s and extrapolate

---

6   Jack Goldstone, "The Coming Chinese Collapse," *Foreign Policy*, No. 99 (Summer 1995), pp. 35–52, quotes on pp. 51–52.
7   Edward Friedman, "China's North–South Split and the Forces of Disintegration," *Current History* 92(525), (1993), pp. 270–4; Minxin Pei, "Will China Become Another Indonesia?" *Foreign Policy*, No. 116 (Fall 1999), pp. 94–109.
8   Gordon Chang, *The Coming Collapse of China* (New York: Random House, 2001).
9   For one side, see William Overholt, *The Rise of China: How Economic Reform Is Creating a New Superpower* (New York: Norton, 1994); for the other side, see Richard Bernstein and Russ Munro, *The Coming Conflict with China* (New York: Knopf, 1997). For an anthology of debate on China as a strategic threat, see Michael Brown, Owen Coté, Jr., Sean Lynn-Jones, and Steven Miller, eds., *The Rise of China* (Cambridge, MA: MIT Press, 2000). The rise of China has even become the preoccupation of fiction writers, who produced titles such as *The Bear and the Dragon*, by Tom Clancy, *China Attacks*, by Chuck Devore and Steven Mosher, and *Dragon Strike*, by Humphrey Hawksley and Simon Holberton.

from there into the future. Both raise important questions but do so in an alarmist and one-sided fashion. One sees only the problems and assumes the achievements are fragile; the other sees only the achievements and assumes the problems will be overcome. Neither takes adequate account of the extent to which the achievements and problems are intertwined, with the achievements possible only because certain problems could be left unaddressed, deferred to an uncertain future. Neither perspective seems to appreciate the extent to which its own conclusions should be modified by the insights of the other perspective. China is indisputably becoming a more diverse society, with a much larger economy, greater regional diversity, and many areas of social life slipping out of government control. At the same time, China has thus far managed to sustain national unity, and the government has proven itself remarkably resilient while its counterparts in many other transitional countries have fallen apart. What are the forces holding China together? Which institutions are most important and most likely to reinforce national unity? Can we expect Chinese leaders to formulate effective policies and maintain national unity as the country undergoes massive social, economic, and political transitions?

FRAMEWORK OF THE VOLUME

The present volume is the result of a multidisciplinary, collective effort to examine some of these questions. It was initially conceived in 1996, as an effort to analyze more carefully the impact of greater regional diversity and openness on national unity, national integration, and the capacity of the national government to adopt policies in the national interest. It was begun with an attitude of skepticism toward some of the more extreme claims of the "deconstruction" literature. At that time, it appeared to us that the "fragmentation" view of China was mistaken because advocates of this view failed to take into consideration the strength of some of the essential institutions holding China together, and they misunderstood the key adaptive processes in which economic transition reshaped state and society relations.[10] Since that time, as China has continued to change and evolve and as our knowledge has deepened, some of the deeper flaws

---

[10] Dali Yang and Houkai Wei, "Rising Sectionalism in China?" *Journal of International Affairs*, 49, No. 2 (Winter 1996), pp. 456–76; Barry Naughton, *Growing Out of the Plan: Chinese Economic Reform, 1978–1993* (New York: Cambridge University Press, 1995).

of the fragmentation perspective have become obvious. Not only has China not blown apart, it has in many respects succeeded in remaking institutions and reshaping policies in ways that enhance institutional integrity and strengthen national unity. However, few observers have taken note of the breadth and depth of the Chinese response. Since 1994, important changes in the administrative and political system have become increasingly manifest in the policy arena. In that sense, institutions fostering national unity existed in the 1980s, but their impact was obscured by problems of economic transition and a breakdown of political cooperation within the Communist Party elite. The potential effectiveness of those national institutions, which have also undergone adaptations and transformations, has become more evident during the 1990s.

The volume addresses questions of national unity and diversity from a variety of different vantage points, and from each it shows that the fragmentation thesis is inadequate to encompass China's development. The chapters in Part One examine the national political and administrative system. The authors analyze the manner in which political elites are rewarded and monitored, and the way government has been reorganized to perform new functions and strengthen regulatory capacity. The common finding is that the political system has made significant adaptations to the challenges of an increasingly diverse and marketized society. These adaptations, on balance, have tended to shore up political authority and national unity, even as they have created new problems for the future. The chapters in Part Two are case studies of the implementation of central government policies. In four different issue areas – birth control, internal migration and urban employment, coal production, and regional development – the authors analyze the way in which central government mandates are shaped to local conditions. Elucidating the interaction between central and local authorities, and between state and society, the authors show that a diversity of policy outcomes is not equivalent to political fragmentation.

The contributors to this book approach diverse subjects by using a variety of analytic methods; their chapters also reflect their own individual viewpoints. Nevertheless, a common view emerges from this volume. Without doubt, increasing diversity and a larger society create centrifugal forces in China that undermine the traditional monolithic state structure. However, there are also important political, economic, and cultural forces that tend to reinforce national unity and integration. These "centripetal forces" imply that diversity and integration in China develop in a kind of dynamic tension. The fragmentation literature on China is misleading – and ultimately simply wrong – because it examines only one side of this tension and fails to see the forces working against fragmentation. In fact, many of the examples of increasing diversity pointed out by the fragmentation literature are simply that – examples of increasing diversity. There is no evidence that this diversity cannot be accommodated within the framework of a growing and developing China. At the same time, the "China threat" literature seems to willfully ignore the evidence of increasing diversity in China and the enormous domestic challenges China still faces. These challenges significantly constrain the Chinese leadership, making it extremely difficult for them to simply impose solutions on a complex domestic society, and limit their ability to project influence internationally. A dynamic tension between increasing diversity and national unity may not be a bad thing: at a minimum, it is preferable to either of the twin extremes of an all-powerful central government or a society in disintegration. Indeed, it is even possible that this tension may provide just the kind of creative pressure that helps keep China's social and economic transformation moving forward.

In this volume, we seek to provide a more coherent and realistic account of the resilience of the Chinese state. The authors represented herein share a conviction that the fragmentation view of China was mistaken. It was mistaken *at the time* because those observers failed to understand the strength of some of the key institutions holding China together, and they misunderstood the crucial processes of economic transition reshaping state and society relations. Moreover, in the years since 1990, Chinese leaders have undertaken an impressive effort to rebuild central government authority in the wake of further stages of economic transition. Therefore, the fragmentation literature was additionally mistaken because it *failed to predict* the ability of the Chinese government to reformulate power relationships and rebuild institutions on an altered basis. This failure to predict also rests on a failure to appreciate the Chinese leadership's command of crucial institutional resources.

Finally, the contributors to this book describe policies and implementation in their areas of specialization by using the language of principal-agent analysis. However, the "principal" in almost all cases refers to the top leadership of the Communist Party and government of China; it almost never refers to the people of China. The people of China lack institutions to exercise their choice, or even a modest oversight over the top leadership. In this respect, China in the twenty-first century is not further advanced than it was in 1989, and, indeed, it may have slipped backward. Thus, despite the relatively positive appraisal of the strength and resilience of Chinese national unity, the authors in this volume share a realistic assessment of the defeat of, and retreat from, the potentially democratizing reforms of the 1980s. The 1980s policies of separating Communist Party from administration and reducing the scope of Party interference in management died during the 1990s. Despite its increasing diversity and the growing scope for civil society, China remains autocratic. This autocracy, in turn, influences the perspective of the volume, which tends to be from the top down, because many of the changes we describe have been driven from the top down.

Indeed, during the 1990s, rather than the Communist Party being removed from other administrative hierarchies, the reality was that the Communist Party was more tightly integrated into other chains of command. The hierarchical relationships in the government and Communist Party were more clearly specified, monitored more effectively, and tied more closely to material rewards. Administrative capability was increased, and there was a general trend toward professionalization. At the same time, the Communist Party also stepped up its involvement with the other administrative hierarchies. These changes are described in Part One of this volume; it is apparent at the outset that change of this type creates tensions and conflicts that must be resolved in the future. Meanwhile, the trend of change has shifted dramatically away from continuous decentralization and weakening of government power and toward a clearer division of responsibilities among governmental levels, with a tendency toward moderate recentralization in certain areas.

PART ONE. THE INSTITUTIONS FOR POLITICAL AND ECONOMIC
CONTROL: ADAPTATION OF A HIERARCHICAL SYSTEM

The first part of the book analyzes the Chinese political and administrative structure. The first three chapters give primary attention to the vertical dimension of the political structure. They examine the incentives at work in the hierarchy through the patterns of promotion and reward, and the rules that govern this process. Because these processes ultimately determine who exercises power, these "vertical" analyses include the stuff of daily politics, the competition among different factions, and the tensions between center and province and between institutionalization and arbitrary power. Chapter 4 gives primary attention to what we might term the "horizontal" dimension of the political and administrative structure. As the government develops more professional capabilities, it develops new functions and abandons some old issue areas. This reorientation is essential to the movement in the direction of a regulatory state, and the issues are also central to the argument in Chapter 3. Together, these vertical and horizontal approaches permit us to draw a comprehensive picture of the evolution of China's political and administrative hierarchy since the beginning of the 1990s.

An important factor in the evolution of the Chinese administration is that decentralization in China was never what it became in the former Soviet Union – a disintegration of central power and the seizure of power "lying in the streets" by the local authorities.[11] In contrast to Yeltsin's Russia, where regional governors gained power and autonomy at the expense of the center, China has retained a core element of central control: the *nomenklatura* system of personnel management. Under this system, higher-level leaders determine the appointment of lower-level officials, and they also structure the incentive systems that apply to the entire hierarchy. In short, unlike in Russia, China has retained a personnel system that gives the central leadership enormous power vis-à-vis local authorities.[12] This nomenklatura personnel system is the most important institution reinforcing national unity.

The fact of a unified national personnel hierarchy is at the core of the analysis in each of the first three chapters. The central government has much greater control over local decision makers than is initially apparent, simply because personnel power is hierarchically organized. Personnel officials at the central level have the authority to appoint and remove officials at local levels: Even when not actually utilized, this power remains

---

[11] Steven Solnick, *Stealing the State: Control and Collapse in Soviet Institutions* (Cambridge, MA: Harvard University Press, 1998).

[12] John P. Burns, "China's Nomenklatura System," *Problems of Communism*, 36 (September 1987), pp. 36–51; idem., *The Chinese Communist Party Nomenklatura System: A Documentary Study of Party Control of Leadership Selection* (Armonk, NY: Sharpe, 1989). Yasheng Huang has emphasized the importance of the nomenklatura system in understanding central-local relations. See his *Inflation and Investment Controls in China* (Cambridge, England: Cambridge University Press, 1996).

latently available to central officials, making the Chinese political system far more unitary than it might otherwise appear.[13] Moreover, the personnel function is a monopoly of the Communist Party. It is one of the most important bases – perhaps the ultimate foundation – of Communist Party power. But Party decision making is not exposed to public scrutiny, and it is forbidden to publicly discuss personnel decisions or decision making.[14] Therefore, it is easy to underestimate the degree of hierarchical control and overemphasize the degree of effective local autonomy.

The era of economic reform has fundamentally altered the environment in which government officials operate. Economic changes – and especially state enterprise restructuring – have created massive opportunities for private gain. Officials have numerous alternatives to commitment to government-mandated tasks. They can neglect government duties and go into business; they can become corrupt; and they can mix public and private interests through complicated intermediate strategies. With the sources of wealth diversifying, it is now impossible to monitor consumption and simply insist that officials live frugal lifestyles. In and of themselves, these changes tend to undermine the authoritativeness of the government and Party hierarchy: With the onset of economic reforms, the party lost its monopoly over reward and remuneration.

If central policy makers did nothing in response to these trends, they would inevitably watch the commitment to national goals of local officials gradually erode. If they act, they must increase the rewards given to government officials for compliance with their objectives (personal or programmatic) and increase the monitoring of officials to restrain their desire to deviate from central goals. In fact, steadily throughout the reform period, the Chinese government has increased both rewards and monitoring. It has responded and adapted to the challenges of the reform environment by altering the incentive environment that cadres face. The general theory of incentives proposes that, in designing optimal incentives for an agent with multiple tasks, one must consider both rewards for

---

[13] This criticism applies not only to proponents of the disintegration view, but also to theories of "market-preserving federalism" in China. See Barry Weingast, Gabriela Montinola, and Yingyi Qian, "Federalism, Chinese Style: The Political Basis of Economic Success in China," *World Politics*, 48, (October 1995), pp. 50–81.

[14] Yan Huai, "Organizational Hierarchy and the Cadre Management System," in Carol Lee Hamrin and Suisheng Zhao, eds., *Decision-Making in Deng's China: Perspectives from Insiders.* (Armonk, NY: Sharpe, 1995).

engaging in a task and the agent's opportunity costs of committing effort to the task.[15] In the reform environment, the proliferation of competing tasks and options for officials means that the government must step up its rewards and monitoring in order to elicit the effort and commitment it desires. This is exactly what has happened in China, resulting in a kind of rough institutional equilibrium in which the continuing survival of the administrative hierarchy has thus far been ensured.

The common argument of Part One of the volume thus comprises four points: First, the national administrative and personnel system makes an important contribution to national unity by its very existence. Second, that hierarchical system has been significantly adapted over the past decade, in ways that tend to strengthen it. It is not simply or primarily that the system has been "recentralized," although that is sometimes the case. Rather, the hierarchical structure has been strengthened by stronger incentives that more consistently align the interests of local politicians with central government. Third, the hierarchical system has become more regularized, or rule driven. Fourth, the administrative system has been reoriented, and it has developed stronger resources, more capabilities, and more differentiated capabilities. In some cases, this means that administration has become more professional and more transparent, but not always. These four points together imply that the national government, in reformulating itself, has become a potent force for national integration and unity.

Cheng Li, in Chapter 1, describes the interplay of central and local politics in redefining the political hierarchy. Li describes a process in which locally based political forces are more powerful, but also more regularized and legitimate, than ever before. Each province now has two "seats" on the Communist Party Central Committee, and a large majority of Central Committee members have provincial power bases. Moreover, local politicians are encouraged to establish their careers in their local area and to identify their own personal success with the economic progress of their locality. Finally, success in provincial posts is becoming a near prerequisite for success at the national political level. These facts would seem to indicate an unambiguous increase in local power at the expense of the center, but the reality is more complex.

---

[15] Bengt Holmstrom and Paul Milgrom, "Multi-Task Principal Agent Analysis: Incentive Contracts, Asset Ownership, and Job Design," *Journal of Law, Economics, and Organization*, 7, special issue (1991).

In the first place, the center uses its nomenklatura power to rotate the top provincial leaders, the party secretaries. By 2003, only three out of a total of 31 provincial party secretaries were natives of the province they led. Furthermore, a system of term limits and age limits – described more fully in Chapter 2 – ensures that no provincial leader can remain indefinitely in charge of his local power base. Finally – and most importantly – the national leaders who had previously served as provincial chiefs had been posted to the provinces by their patrons in the national government. Although provincial leadership is increasingly an indispensable prerequisite to national power, provincial leadership is also a stage through which potential national leaders are rotated to demonstrate their mettle. Provincial leadership is part of a unified national pattern in which the career paths of the most prominent candidates for leadership run through the provincial capitals and back to Beijing.[16] Provincial power is stronger, but it is also more systematically integrated into the national political system.

Li also describes the interplay between factionalism and professionalization in the bureaucratic hierarchy. Clearly, the top-down, personality-driven hierarchical system allows central leaders enormous discretion in shaping the careers of their underlings. Li uses a wealth of data and anecdotal information to show that, although the national leaders have issued various regulations to curb localism in personnel appointments and institutionalize the personnel selection processes, they have never let process stand in the way of their efforts to strengthen their own personal power and influence. From the time Jiang Zemin moved from Shanghai to become Party General Secretary in 1989 to his retirement from that post at the end of 2002, he promoted many of his friends from Shanghai to important national leadership positions. Continued favoritism and factionalism characterize the political process in China, and this factionalism now has a stronger regional component. At the same time, new rules shape the process of political competition, and contenders use whatever rules are available to enhance their own prospects. As Li writes, the "new leaders are far more interested than their predecessors in seeking legitimacy through institutional channels" rather than ties of blood, native place, and

---

[16] Benedict Anderson attributed a key role to the rotations of elites through a single "capital" in the gradual constitution of a unified national narrative, which he in turn saw as pivotal in the development of the imagined solidarity central to modern nationalism. See his *Imagined Communities: Reflections on the Origin and Spread of Nationalism* (New York: Verso, 1990).

common service. However, they will not hesitate to use whatever means are available to them in the struggle for power.

Zhiyue Bo, in Chapter 2, examines the national political hierarchy and the personnel system, just as Cheng Li did in the previous chapter. However, Bo stresses two different themes that make his chapter complementary to Li's. First, Bo stresses the position of the Communist Party among the other political hierarchies in China. As Bo explains, there are several overlapping hierarchical systems in China, which can be grouped into party, government, and military hierarchies. The party hierarchy is the most powerful because of its personnel and ideological powers. The basic thrust of political reform during the 1980s was to "separate party from government," allowing the governmental hierarchy to be more professional and ultimately, perhaps, more democratic. However, when Deng Xiaoping turned against first Hu Yaobang (in 1987) and then Zhao Ziyang (in 1989), political reform on these terms was aborted. In the more than 10 years since, political reform according to this model has not been revived. Indeed, as already stated, the ability of the party to influence and control outcomes in the other hierarchies has been given renewed "legitimacy," in the sense that it has been explicitly warranted and justified by party documents and policies. Thus, the actual movement of political change in the 1990s has been precisely the opposite of that envisaged by political reform of the 1980s.

However, in China's increasingly diverse and articulate society, the Communist Party cannot simply assert its dominance over the other hierarchies. The government administrative systems have become more professional, and they have developed their own institutional, financial, and information resources. Most tricky is the relationship with the people's congresses – the legislative branch of government – at the national and provincial levels. As Bo notes, the people's congresses have formidable institutional resources, because only the people's congresses can claim to represent the ultimate will of the people. Moreover, the Communist Party wishes to strengthen the people's congresses in order to shore up the legitimacy of its own hold on power. The result is an elaborate set of procedures through which the party dominates (but not totally) the nomination and election processes at the people's congresses, all the while insisting that the party's role remains in the background. Even with these careful shows of respect, the party has found the people's congresses too potentially powerful to be safely managed at a distance. As a result, today most provincial-level party secretaries – 23 out of 31 as of March 2003 – also serve concurrently as chairmen of provincial people's congresses. This allows the party secretaries to legitimately get involved both in recommending appointees (as party leaders) and in approving the appointments in the legislatures (as legislative leaders).

In its relations with the people's congresses, then, the party displays increasing adherence to rules, or institutionalization, the second of Bo's two main themes. On the one hand, the party increases its interpenetration of non-party administrative systems; on the other hand, the party itself is increasingly bound by a set of rules of its own making. The rules are most important in shaping the way the cadre promotion system functions. Bo describes a series of key features that all tend to increase the institutionalization of the personnel system. These include the following:

- Rules for systematic promotion. No cadre should have more than 10 years in a job; cadres should retire at the age of 60 or 65 (depending on their final rank).
- Explicit evaluations of high-level cadre performance by the Organization Department and personnel bureaus.
- Requirement of credentials for higher office, including university education and minimum party tenure.
- Modest but significant external checks on individual performance and abuse of power. These include requirements for election by local and national people's congresses, consultation with various bodies, and audits by the Audit Office.[17]

These provisions have not been mere exhortations; they have been applied in practice with few exceptions. Put together, these features change quite fundamentally the expected nature of a successful career path. They ensure steady promotion paths and responsiveness to whatever promotion criteria the center chooses to emphasize. Politicians are much more likely to understand that success can only be achieved by visible, apparent compliance with central mandates.

---

[17] Note that these requirements are not significant enough to be considered "democratization," but they are significant enough to shape career incentives. Different constituencies must be consulted and at least minimally satisfied for a political career to develop smoothly.

Both Bo and Li point out that the measures that increase centralization were taken in response to other changes that had centrifugal effects on the cadre management system. For one thing, certain mechanisms designed to check individual performance tend to increase localism, because they give local organs – especially the local people's congresses – which are outside the immediate hierarchy, input into the selection of local leaders. In response to the increased articulation of local interests, the center again strengthens specific provisions needed to combat localism. Here the most important measure is the reinstatement of the rule of avoidance, which is discussed by both authors. For another, the trend toward reform and professionalization has continued. From early in the reform era, a process of administrative rebuilding had led to the strengthening of separate hierarchical systems, and an increasingly explicit set of administrative rules and professional standards to guide the operation of these systems. That process has continued throughout the 1990s and into the first years of the new century; Bo makes clear that the identity of the separate hierarchies has continued and been strengthened. In Chapter 4, Dali Yang shows just how far that process has progressed in the governmental administrative hierarchy, particularly in the sphere of economic governance.

This has given a new complexity to relations among hierarchies. In important respects, the Communist Party has bound itself to accept modest checks and balances on its decision-making authority, and especially its personnel decision making. Of course, we should not be deluded: These are extremely modest checks, and they take place within the framework of continued Communist Party dominance. However, the changes are important enough to affect the way power is maintained and transmitted through the system. Most important is the requirement at many levels of government hierarchy that Party candidates must win an election. To be sure, these are nothing like free elections. The selectorate is carefully delimited, and the Communist Party exercises enormous power over the membership of the selectorate, the process through which candidates are nominated, and the actual election.[18] Nevertheless, the process does bind the Party to consult with other members of the selectorate and obtain their

---

[18] The classic analysis of the selectorate and reciprocal accountability in China is Susan Shirk, *The Political Logic of Economic Reform in China* (Berkeley: University of California Press, 1993).

acquiescence. Though somewhat less prominent than in the late 1980s, the voting mechanism has also been retained in the choice of Central Committee members (Party Congress) and of provincial officials (People's Congress meetings). In the early 1990s, this mechanism resulted in poor showings for the "princelings" (children of veteran revolutionaries) and was thus a boon to Jiang Zemin, but more recently this institution has served to embarrass a number of candidates backed by Jiang. Bo argues that these steps are part of a process of steady institutionalization. [19] These changes provide a modest increase in the influence of local society on the selection of political leaders. Although certainly not democratizing the system in a formal way, they provide an additional access point for local interest groups. Thus, they can be seen as partial political reforms that reduce the degree of centralization of the system, reinforcing the argument in Chapter 1 about the greater institutionalized influence of local interests.

Whereas Li and Bo train their eyes on the national political system, Susan Whiting (Chapter 3) offers us a fascinating study of how local elites are monitored, evaluated, and rewarded. On the basis of careful fieldwork, she finds that county-level officials have adopted a cadre evaluation system – complete with detailed performance criteria and incentives – to motivate local cadres at township levels toward specific policy goals reflecting the main concerns of the central government. Although Whiting notes that the formal system of evaluations must interact with informal factors, she concludes that the formal cadre evaluation system with relatively high-powered incentives has been able to "elicit minimal acceptable levels of performance on the part of local officials." It has also helped "reinforce commitment to party goals, thereby contributing to the durability of CCP rule." Whiting shows how strengthening compliance incentives affects the lower levels of the hierarchy. In this case, by rewarding specific performance outcomes with substantial financial bonuses, local government and party officials are induced to renew their commitment to the Party-State structure. At the same time, the specific activities for which local cadres are rewarded are quite different from those cadres would have been expected to perform in the 1970s. In that sense, Whiting is describing a process not just of increasing compliance incentives, but also

---

[19] See also Andrew J. Nathan, "Authoritarian Resilience: China's Changing of the Guard," *Journal of Democracy*, 14, No. 1, (January 2003), pp. 6–17.

of shifting the nature of the activities in which officials are expected to engage. Whiting is observing the local manifestation of the ongoing re-definition of the state during the reform era. Indeed, since about 1994, we have witnessed a burst of activities to reconstruct the framework of the state to make it more responsive to emergent situations or as part of the effort to build a modern regulatory state.

Chapter 4, by Dali Yang, steps back and gives a broad national perspective on this process. Yang points to a variety of areas where the central government has stepped up its intervening role, including the collection of revenue, the regulation of banking and financial markets, and the enforcement of laws on quality, safety, environment, and intellectual property rights. In all these areas, the administrative hierarchy has been stream-lined and made more responsive to the center by adopting the practice of vertical administration. If left to the devices of the administrative hierarchy, some of these and other areas would have seen rampant localism fostering the tendencies of fragmentation. In the banking system, for example, had the banks been left at the mercy of local authorities, monetary chaos would have ensued and China would probably have truly fallen like a domino during the Asian financial crisis. Instead, since 1993, the Chinese leadership not only has worked hard to bring about monetary stability but also has undertaken arduous political negotiations to reform the fiscal and taxation system, the banking system, and other issues mentioned earlier.

In that sense, the reconfiguration of government has corresponded with a dramatic shift in the orientation of economic policy that occurred around 1994 as well. Policy since 1994 has been more authoritative – more able to override particularistic interest groups – and supplied a higher level of public goods. This shift has been widely noted and is often linked to the administration of Zhu Rongji.[20] For current purposes, what is important is that reconfiguration of the administrative hierarchy has given the government new capabilities that has allowed it to adopt new policies. New

---

[20] Barry Naughton, "Changing Horses in Midstream? The Challenge of Explaining Changing Political Economy Regimes in China," in Jaushieh Joseph Wu, ed., *China Rising: Implications of Economic and Military Growth in the PRC* (Taipei: Institute of International Relations, 2001), pp. 37–65; Yingyi Qian and Jinglian Wu, "When Will China Complete Its Transition to the Market?" in Nicholas Hope, Dennis Yang, eds., and Mu Yang Li, *How Far Across the River? Chinese Policy Reform at the Millennium* (Stanford, CA: Stanford University Press, 2003), Yongnian Zheng, *Zhu Rongji Xinzheng: Zhongguo Gaige de Xin Moshi [The New Policies of Zhu Rongji: A New Model of Chinese Reform]* (Singapore: Bafang wenhua qiye gongsi, 1999).

policies, in turn, have generated new economic resources that have been used, in part, to build new administrative capabilities. As Naughton argues in Chapter 8, the upturn in budgetary revenues after 1995 – traceable to the tax reforms in the previous year – was an essential prerequisite of the Western Development Program. New policies thus depend on the ongoing reconfiguration of the government.

These reconfigurations may seem like functional responses to system needs, but demand for institutions and state capacity is not always met with a ready supply. Instead, these reconfigurations of administrative hierarchy were the products of political negotiations and renegotiations. They reflect and embody a strong commitment to construct a functioning regulatory state, capable and effective in the enforcement of the relevant laws on the environment, safety, intellectual property rights, and other issues. What is equally important is that they demonstrate the Chinese leadership's ability to convert ideas, often incorporating lessons learned from abroad, into institutional reality. Thus, the Chinese state continues to surprise with its capacity to reformulate, reconfigure, and reorganize.

PART TWO. CASE STUDIES OF POLICY IMPLEMENTATION

The second part of the volume consists of four case studies. Each examines the reach of the Chinese state by studying policy implementation in an issue area that would test the capacity of any state. The picture that emerges is certainly not one of disintegration. In each case, the Chinese national government adopts and implements national policies of significant scope, but only after reformulating and adapting policy to the demands of local interests. Each author delves into unique features of the policy implementation process in their chosen field of study. All of the authors seek to explain the policy implementation process as a whole by referring to two underlying questions: What explains regional differences in policy implementation? Can we identify a process of interaction and policy reformulation as central government preferences and local interests negotiate policy outcomes? The answer to these questions with respect to specific policy arenas complements the generalizations about the overall capacity of the Chinese government in the first part of this book. If the center is able to implement difficult and sometimes unpopular policies, allow local input into the degree of implementation, and still gradually shift the focus of implementation toward a more professional mode, then the likelihood grows that this administrative and policy structure will be adequate to hold China together.

Dorothy Solinger, in Chapter 5, focuses on the implementation of labor market policies in three cities. Crucially, Solinger finds that, in initially promulgating its policies, the central government was already trying to balance competing, and to some extent conflicting, objectives. On the one hand, policy makers have welfare objectives: They want to provide as much income security as possible to workers being laid off from state-owned enterprises. On the other hand, policy makers want to foster more flexible and efficient labor markets. In particular, this has led them to look favorably on rural-to-urban migration and to subject laid-off workers to competitive pressures. These pressures force laid-off workers to look for new jobs that may pay considerably less than their former state-sector jobs. Because these objectives inevitably conflict, the central government gives local governments substantial leeway in determining the precise nature of the trade-offs in their locality.

Localities, in turn, react to the particular economic and political conditions in which they find themselves. Shenyang adopted the most welfare-oriented policies of the cities Solinger studied. Facing high levels of layoffs and slow growth of new jobs, officials in Shenyang were unwilling to subject local residents to the pressure of competition from rural migrants, and they maintained relatively generous unemployment compensation policies. Conversely, Guangzhou adopted policies most friendly to labor market development. With rapid employment growth and low unemployment, Guangzhou officials adopted relatively lenient policies toward immigrants, and they provided only short-term transitional assistance to laid-off state workers. Wuhan adopted policies that were generally between Shenyang and Guangzhou. Thus, what appeared initially to be divergent local policies turned out to be local adaptations of a complex central government mandate.

Yanzhong Huang and Dali Yang, in Chapter 6, look at the implementation of China's controversial population control policies. They note the historic irony that it is China's economic reformers who have been the most adamant about enforcing the coercive birth-planning policies in order to increase economic growth in per capita terms. As a result, while Chinese leaders have promoted freedom-enhancing socioeconomic reforms, they have also aggressively implemented population policies that impinge on fundamental human freedoms. To help sustain the unpopular birth-planning policies, the state has not only resorted to state socialist mobilization but has made major efforts to build administrative capacity. Through an examination of interprovincial variation, the authors find that raising the quality of the administrative staff helps moderate the intensity of state coercion. Provinces with better-educated birth-control workers use less coercive means to achieve birth targets, and in particular they resort to sterilization less often.

Nonetheless, administrative capabilities – or "infrastructural power" – are not sufficiently developed that the state is willing to abandon coercion. In fact, Huang and Yang find that the ability to coerce is explained by the existence of government agencies at local levels and by the remaining redistributive power of the rural collectives. Those capabilities are complements to coercion, making it cheaper and easier to carry out. Educated cadres are a substitute for coercion, making noncoercive means cheaper and making coercion a less attractive option. Ultimately, the authors conclude that fundamental changes to the current policies will most likely have to wait for significant transformations of population structure and dynamics.

In Chapter 7, Fubing Su examines the central government's efforts to restructure the coal industry as the central government attempted to stanch the flow of subsidies to coal mines. Su reports government data that suggest that the central government was ultimately able to restructure and stabilize the coal industry. Su confirms the analysis in the preceding chapter by finding that, alongside powerful incentive policies, the central government continued to use campaign policies with a coercive edge to enforce local-level compliance. However, he also finds that the central government made accommodations to local interests as it sought to bring coal output under control and specifically curb output by small local coal mines. Initial policy efforts failed because they did not take local interests sufficiently into consideration. Nevertheless, ultimately policy reformulations were able to strike a more or less successful balance between central and local interests and achieve the core objectives of policy makers.

Su combines a principal-agent framework with interesting direct evidence of the proliferation of corruption and rent-seeking opportunities that affect the incentives of local officials with authority over the coal industry. When the center tries to ignore and override this reality, its policies fail to be implemented at all. However, by providing stronger incentives within the hierarchy – in this case by devolving control over larger mines to provincial governments – the center realigns local interests with the central government and achieves an acceptable level of implementation. Su's narrative thus strongly reinforces the story told by Whiting in Chapter 3.

Finally, in Chapter 8, Barry Naughton looks at the much publicized Western Development Program. This program – rolled out with much fanfare beginning in 1999 – represents the Chinese government's most visible commitment to the goal of national unity. First and foremost an economic policy, it also has important symbolic and political uses. Moving from the institutional framework in Part One to a policy setting, the Western Development Policy answers this question: What is the Chinese government actually *doing* to foster national unity? By recognizing the yawning gap between economic and social conditions in Western versus coastal China, and by moving to address it, the Chinese government reaffirms that national unity is its top policy priority.

As already mentioned, the Western Development Program reflects the increased capabilities and resources of the Chinese central government, especially in the fiscal dimension. The center will take on additional obligations with respect to infrastructure investment, but also education, environment, and poverty alleviation. The Western Development Program also reflects increased capabilities in its design and relatively balanced approach to economic development. It avoids many of the mistakes of past Chinese policy, and it seeks to balance increased investment effort with greater respect for the environment, increased attention to education, and recognition of the importance of deregulation and market development. In this sense, the promotion of the Western Development Program points to increased administrative capabilities.

Yet the Western Development Program also shows some of the limitations of those capabilities. To succeed, the Program has to draw local government officials into its orbit, but local government incentives are not fully aligned with the grass roots development objectives of the Program. This creates a twin danger that, on the one hand, the program might degenerate into an overly large and dispersed patronage program for local cadres; or, on the other hand, fail to engage a broad enough section of the West's relatively poor and powerless people. The problems of implementation faced by the Western Development Program are similar to those discussed in the other policy areas. Indeed, the authors of these chapters all find interesting modifications of policy along the way, suggesting a capacity by state leaders to learn from previous policy implementations and adjust their implementation strategy accordingly.

In the final analysis, these studies of policy implementation underscore the ability of the Chinese state to bring its power to bear on issues. In areas of fundamental state interests, the state continues to be able to mobilize vast institutional and other resources to carry out its policy measures. Each issue area still carries the marks of government coercion and clumsy and indiscriminate policy dictates. However, alongside the coercive strand of implementation we also observe a slowly but steadily growing capacity to implement more sophisticated, differentiated, and successful policies. Charles Lindblom once famously characterized socialist systems as having "strong thumbs, no fingers," meaning they could achieve almost any objective based on mobilization and coercive power, but they had little capability for more subtle implementation of differentiated policies. The Chinese government today has grown fingers, but it is not ready to abandon its strong thumbs.[21]

FINAL THOUGHTS

In this volume, we analyze the hierarchical structure of the Chinese government as a dynamic, adaptive equilibrium. We observe the Chinese government continuously reformulating the rules and processes of its hierarchy in order to achieve a modicum of functioning in the face of constant change and newly emerging challenges. Some changes to the hierarchical structure are driven by changes on the "outside," toward a more diverse economy, for example, with more alternatives to bureaucratic compliance. Other changes to the structure are implemented from the top down. These changes are complex, and there are multiple trade-offs between options for structuring and motivating the hierarchy. Some top-down changes are best seen as reactive or adaptive, seeking to restore the effectiveness of the hierarchical structure eroded by external changes. In general, it is the breadth and depth of change that are most striking. Behind the façade of unchanging Communist Party power is a reality of

---

[21] Charles E. Lindblom, *Politics and Markets: The World's Political Economic Systems* (New York: Basic Books, 1977); see also Michael Mann, *The Sources of Social Power, Volume II: The Rise of Classes and Nation-States, 1760–1914* (New York: Cambridge University Press, 1993).

constant change and reformulation. Outside observers have been slow to grasp the magnitude of this change and the extent to which it has altered the political prospects of the Chinese government and Communist Party.

In seeking to maintain their dominance over the hierarchical structure of society, China's leaders have recourse to the full panoply of Weberian instruments, employing coercion, remuneration, and legitimacy. As the following chapters demonstrate, each of these is important, and crucial changes have occurred in the way that each instrument is used. Because the underlying administrative capabilities of the Chinese government are still weak, current adaptations still have an improvised character, and administration falls far short of international best practices. But such outcomes must be interpreted precisely as adaptations to the underlying scarcity of administrative resources. The Chinese government holds on to coercive and indiscriminate instruments, rather than take risks with weak administrative capabilities. Despotic power persists because infrastructural power grows slowly.

The Chinese national political hierarchy, controlled by the Communist Party, is thus currently the most important institution strengthening national unity. This institution reinforces other sources of Chinese unity, including perceived national identity and cultural community, as well as strong economic forces.[22] We have observed over the past decade that China's leaders display a capacity for selective adaptation of institutions and policies that has reinforced national unity and generally offset the impact of centrifugal forces. It is most likely that this selective adaptation will continue to be the stronger force in the future as well, and that disintegration will thus be avoided. However, the continuing reliance on hierarchical relations imposes handicaps as well as advantages on China's ability to adapt to a changing society. Ultimately, China is too vast and complex to be governed effectively by a small group of leaders at the top of all the important national hierarchies. Reformulation and adaptation

---

[22] These forces are, of course, well outside the scope of this book. It is worth noting, however, that the lure of the vast China market, so palpable to foreign businesses, also acts within China to induce ambitious, market-oriented individuals to support national economic integration. In fact, China's regions are already highly integrated with each other. See Barry Naughton, "How Much Can Regional Integration Do to Unify China's Markets?" in Nicholas Hope, Dennis Yang, and Mu Yang Li, eds., *How Far Across the River? Chinese Policy Reform at the Millennium* (Stanford, CA: Stanford University Press, 2003), pp. 204–32.

of that system must, in its next phases, inevitably involve a diminution of the overall degree of hierarchy. To be successful, the system must move beyond a flexible authoritarianism and institutionalize a genuinely open and responsive system of governance.

It is too early to say whether the changes described in this book will make a future evolution toward democratization in China easier or more difficult. Certainly, the model of democratization implied by 1980s reforms – progressive withdrawal of the Communist Party from direct management, combined with bottom-up democratization of government structures – has become more difficult. It remains to be seen whether other avenues to democracy will open up. As the following chapters make clear, institutional capacity has increased in China, making it more likely that public goals can be achieved without constantly resorting to the state's coercive power. Improved institutional capacity might make future steps toward democratization more feasible, but the system still relies on the ability of the administrative hierarchy to specify targets and goals, even when its coercive power is not directly invoked. China's handling of the SARS challenge in the spring of 2003 exemplifies the current situation. On the one hand, the initial response to the SARS epidemic was denial and deception, reflecting the still-closed character of the political system. On the other hand, once top leaders recognized the gravity of the situation, they were able to mobilize overwhelming administrative resources and implement an effective response in a remarkably short time. Nevertheless, that type of mobilization will not be adequate to handle the multiple challenges that face a future China. Leaders can achieve many key national objectives through the national hierarchy, but ultimately there are many more objectives than there are instruments to achieve them through the hierarchical process. Each time the hierarchy gives priority to one objective, it temporarily draws resources away from other legitimate objectives.[23]

---

[23] The case studies provide ample evidence of the designation by national leaders of certain objectives as key yardsticks for evaluating and rewarding local officials, including birth control (always) and closure of small-scale coal mines (in some times and places). A related, but peculiar, example comes from an episode in 1998, when municipal officials in Guangdong province were informed that (to save farmland lost to burial plots) the proportion of cadavers cremated would be designated a key performance indicator and tied to compensation. Guo Nei, "Guangdong: 'No Burial in Ground,'" *China Daily*, April 7, 1998. Given that local officials have many tasks they must perform, providing

At the same time, the Communist Party itself is changing, becoming less ideological and admitting members from a much broader range of social categories. The changes in the Communist Party are beyond the scope of this volume, but we note that such changes are consistent with the trends that we describe. The Party hierarchy is incorporated within a broader set of increasingly professional administrative hierarchies, which are defined more clearly, better rewarded, and more closely monitored than before. These hierarchies give the Chinese government more capacity, more authoritative policy making, and more resilience. But is this approach a dead end? Does it make the system as a whole more rigid, even as it makes the policy process more flexible and effective for any given policy? Is the system too impervious to fundamental change, even as it improves communication and consultation over specific policies? These questions can only be answered by China's future political evolution, and the authors represented in this book have a range of predictions.

A new generation of Chinese leaders – sometimes called the "Fourth Generation" – has taken over from the Jiang Zemin generation, and they will shape the Chinese system through the first decade of the 21st century. The new leaders are largely a product of the regularized personnel system described in Chapters 1–3. The top leader, Party Secretary Hu Jintao, exemplifies this system: He has an engineering degree from China's elite Tsinghua University. He had an important job in Beijing (head of the Communist Youth League), and then he was rotated through two important and difficult provincial jobs, in Guizhou and Tibet, before being brought back to Beijing for top leadership jobs. Hu and the rest of the new generation will have much invested in the institutionalized – but still hierarchical – system. That hierarchy has already been strengthened and begun to be professionalized: Their challenge will be to open it up and provide accountability and legitimacy.

high-powered incentives for one task inevitably diminishes the incentives to perform other tasks and reduces the effort committed to them.

The Institutions for Political and Economic Control: Adaptation of a Hierarchical System

1

Political Localism Versus Institutional Restraints: Elite Recruitment in the Jiang Era

Cheng Li

This chapter studies the formation of the new national and provincial elites during the era of Jiang Zemin.[1] The focus is on two trends that have been unfolding in parallel, but in tension, with each other. The first trend is growing political localism; the second is the strengthening of institutional control in an attempt to limit the abuses of power based on local interests and personal political networks. Political localism is stronger and more legitimate today than ever before in the history of the People's Republic of China.[2] Indeed, more generally, through the reform era – but especially since about 1997 – conflicts of interest between regions, factions, and social groups have come more out in the open than ever before. At the same time, new institutional mechanisms have been put in place to limit favoritism and abuse of power by particularistic (including localistic) interest groups. The central government has made continual efforts to coordinate the multifaceted political demands raised by various regions and by new socioeconomic forces in this fast-changing country.

[1] The author thanks the Woodrow Wilson International Center for Scholars, the United States Institute of Peace, the Chiang Ching-kuo Foundation, the Hong Kong Institute for the Humanities and Social Sciences at the University of Hong Kong and Hamilton College for their generous support. The author also thanks Sally Carman, Li Yinsheng, Qi Li, and Jennifer Schwartz for their research assistance, and Barry Naughton, Dali L. Yang, and three anonymous referees for suggesting ways to clarify the chapter. This study refers to the Jiang era during the period from June 1989 (when he was appointed secretary general of the CCP after the Tiananmen incident) to November 2002 (when he resigned from that post at the 16th Party Congress). This time period has been assigned for the sake of convenience and is, of course, subject to debate. One may argue that Jiang was largely under the shadow of Deng Xiaoping for the first five years of his tenure and may continue to wield power during the first years of the Hu Jintao administration.
[2] Political localism is defined as the inability of the central leadership to ensure that lower levels in the political system obey directives.

China's political and economic life during the Jiang era is filled with several seemingly contradictory trends. This is particularly evident in the recruitment of political leaders. On one hand, informal networks are ubiquitous in the formation of the new leadership.[3] These networks include regionally based groups (*tongxiang*, or fellow provincials), particularly the notorious Shanghai Gang, and those based on kinship with top leaders in Beijing (*taizi*, or princelings). Such favoritism and nepotism, however, have also caused a growing public demand, especially from backward inland regions, for a more representative leadership. Regional representation on the Central Committee of the Chinese Communist Party (CCP), for example, has become more institutionalized, with each provincial-level administration usually obtaining two full membership seats. As local officials demand greater regional autonomy in choosing their leaders, the central government has more frequently reshuffled top provincial leaders and limited the length of their terms within their own turfs. Jockeying for power among various factions was fervent and protracted at the recent 16th Party Congress and the 10th National People's Congress (NPC), but the power struggle did not lead to the systemic crises experienced during the reigns of Mao and Deng.

Not surprisingly, these paradoxical developments have often led students of Chinese politics to reach contrasting assessments of China's reality and its future, particularly in terms of regional fragmentation versus national integration.[4] It is premature to claim that one or more of these contradictory tendencies will prevail in the future: Both forces are shaping contemporary China. With respect to the trend toward localism, this

---

[3] For further discussion of various forms of informal networks, see Cheng Li, *China's Leaders: The New Generation* (Lanham, MD: Rowman & Littlefield, 2001); David M. Finkelstein and Maryanne Kivlehan, eds., *Chinese Leadership in the Twenty-First Century: The Rise of the Fourth Generation* (Armonk, NY: Sharpe, 2002); and Cheng Li, "The 'Shanghai Gang': Force for Stability or Cause for Conflict?" *China Leadership Monitor*, No. 1, Part II (Winter 2002), pp. 1–18.

[4] For example, see Michel Oksenberg, "China's Political Future," *JETRO China Newsletter* 120 (January–February 1996), pp. 4–5; Richard Baum, "China After Deng: Ten Scenarios in Search of Reality," *China Quarterly* 145 (March 1996), p. 154; and Xiaowei Zang, ed., *China in the Reform Era* (Commack, NY: Nova Science, 1999). For a more recent debate, see Andrew J. Nathan, "Authoritarian Resilience," *Journal of Democracy*, 14, No. 1 (January 2003), pp. 6–17; also see his remarks on the conference "The Sixteenth Party Congress and China's Future," January 8, 2003 (www.Chinesenewsnet.com); and Minxin Pei, "China's Governance Crisis," *Foreign Affairs*, 81 (September–October 2002), pp. 96–109.

chapter begins by describing the pivotal role of provincial leadership in today's China. It goes on to explore the uneven distribution of birthplace among current high-ranking leaders (provincial levels and above), the importance of the Shanghai Gang, and the prevalence of provincial leaders serving in their native areas. With regard to institutional coordination and control, this chapter discusses the consolidation of national personnel management, especially the central authority's new regulations, to restrain localism. Further, this chapter highlights the increasingly important role of elections in blocking appointments and nominations based on favoritism and nepotism in both the Party Congress and the People's Congress.

What does an analysis of the Chinese leadership reveal about some of the underpinnings of institutional developments in maintaining national unity during a period of rapid socioeconomic change? Was it misleading for some China watchers to place so much emphasis on "political institutionalization," the term used with growing frequency in the study of Chinese elite politics? Can this exploration of localism versus central domination in Chinese elite selection reconcile some contrasting perceptions about today's China, especially with respect to the relationship between central and local governments? Most importantly, how can a discussion of the patterns of Chinese elite recruitment and mobility shed light on our central concern about China's national integration and regional diversity in the Jiang era and beyond?

By addressing these questions, this chapter aims to create a better understanding of the changing nature of the Chinese political process, particularly the dynamic interaction between the need for national integration and the demand for regional autonomy. National and provincial leaders' biographical backgrounds, political socialization, and career patterns, the province in which they were born and the province in which they now serve as leaders, their length of tenure, and the rate and patterns of reshuffling are all crucial to an analysis of Chinese politics. In recent years, the rapid development of the Internet has made the access to Chinese official sources faster, more convenient, and more comprehensive.[5] In fact, the Organization Department of the CCP Central Committee encourages various levels of leadership to make their leaders'

---

[5]   For example, http://www.peopledaily.com.cn and http://www.xinhuanet.com.

biographical backgrounds available to the public. The increasing availability of official Chinese sources has been most helpful for the verification
of data from other sources.[6]

THE PIVOTAL ROLE OF THE PROVINCIAL LEADERSHIP
IN TODAY'S CHINA

Of all the personnel changes that occurred during the 16th Party Congress
in the fall of 2002, the predominant representation of leaders from
China's 31 provincial-level administrations was the most remarkable. All
62 provincial chiefs – party secretaries and governors or mayors – prior to
the congress secured full memberships on the 16th Central Committee. Of
the people serving on the new 24-member Politburo, 10 (42 percent) held
provincial leadership posts when they were selected, and 20 (83 percent)
have currently or previously served as top provincial leaders.[7]

Table 1.1 compares the fraction of current politburo members who have
been provincial leaders (deputy party secretaries and vice governors, or
above) with the two previous politburos. This provincial share started
high and rose sharply over the decade: 55 percent in 1992, 68 percent
in 1997, and 83 percent by 2002. The portion of politburo members who
were provincial chiefs increased from 50 percent in 1992 to 59 percent in
1997, and again to approximately 67 percent by 2002.

All four provincial party secretaries who served on the 15th Politburo
were promoted to serve on the nine-member 16th Politburo Standing
Committee, the highest decision-making body in the country. Jia Qinglin

---

[6] In addition to the online Chinese official data, the data used in this study are derived
    from the following main sources: Shen Xueming and Han Honghung, comp., *Zhong-
    gong di shiwujie zhongyang weiyuanhui zhongyang jilü jiancha weiyuanhui weiyuan
    minglu, [Who's Who Among the Members of the Fifteenth Central Committee of the Chi-
    nese Communist Party and the Fifteenth Central Commission for Discipline Inspection]*
    (Beijing: Zhonggong wenxian chubanshe, 1999); Liao Gailong and Fan Yuan (comp.)
    *Zhongguo renming da cidian xiandai dangzhengjun lingdaorenwujuan, [Who's Who in
    China, the Volume on Current Party, Government, and Military Leaders],* (Beijing: For-
    eign Languages Press, 1994); Ho Szu-yin, comp., *Zhonggong renmin lu [Who's Who
    in Communist China]* (Taipei: Institute of International Relations, National Chengchi
    University, 1999); and *China Directory* (Tokyo: Rapiopress, annually from 1985 to 2002).
[7] For a detailed discussion of the predominant representation of Politburo members with
    provincial backgrounds, see Cheng Li, "A Landslide Victory for Provincial Leaders,"
    China Leadership Monitor, No. 5 (Winter 2003), pp. 69–83. For an overview of the
    provincial leaders' representation on the Politburos during the past two decades, see Li
    Cheng and Lynn White, "The Sixteenth Central Committee of the Chinese Communist
    Party: Hu Gets What?" *Asian Survey*, 43 (July/August), pp. 572–573.

Table 1.1. *Provincial Leadership Experience of Full Members of the 1992, 1997, and 2002 Politburos*

Politburo	As High Provincial Leaders		As Top Provincial Chiefs	
	No.	%	No.	%
14th (20 members)	11	55.0	10	50.0
15th (22 members)	15	68.2	13	59.1
16th (24 members)	20	83.3	16	66.7

Note: High provincial-level leaders are deputy party secretaries, vice governors, or above; top provincial chiefs refer to party secretaries and governors only.

(former Party Chief of Beijing) now serves as Chairman of the Chinese People's Political Consultative Conference; Huang Ju (former Party Chief of Shanghai) serves as executive vice premier of the State Council; Wu Guanzheng (former Party Chief of Shandong) now holds the post of Secretary of the Central Commission for Discipline Inspection of the CCP; and Li Changchun (former Party Chief of Guangdong) has become the czar of CCP propaganda. All four of these leaders served as provincial chiefs for 16 or 17 years.

In addition, He Guoqiang (former Party Secretary of Chongqing), Liu Yunshan (former Deputy Party Secretary of Neimenggu), and Zhou Yongkang (former Party Secretary of Sichuan) not only obtained seats on the new politburo but also took charge of three important institutions: the CCP Organization Department, the CCP Publicity Department, and the Ministry of Public Security. All three individuals also serve on the new Secretariat, which handles the daily affairs of the entire politburo.

Never in the history of the People's Republic of China (PRC) have so many provincial leaders been so quickly promoted to posts in the top national leadership as at the 16th Party Congress. Top leadership positions in China's provinces and major cities have become the most important stepping stones to national political offices in the country. Potential candidates for the top leadership have often served extended tours of duty as provincial chiefs for more than one province. For example, Hui Liangyu, new politburo member and new vice premier, served as a provincial chief in four different provinces. Both Li Changchun, new politburo Standing Committee member and former Party Chief of Guangdong, and Zhang Dejiang, new politburo member and current Party Chief of Guangdong, headed three different provinces. To a certain extent, today's provincial chiefs may be in line for top national leadership positions, only a few steps behind President Hu Jintao, Vice President Zeng Qinghong, and Premier Wen Jiabao.

The meteoric rise of provincial leaders in the national leadership reveals several important trends in Chinese politics today. First, provincial party secretaries and governors have carried much more weight during the reform era of the past 25 years than during the first three decades of the PRC. Today, provincial leaders are far more concerned about advancing the regional economic interests of their own jurisdictions than ever before. At the same time, as part of the attempt to restrain growing economic localism, central authorities frequently reshuffle provincial chiefs from one province to another and promote some chiefs to the national leadership. As a result, this dynamic interaction knits together both local and national interests, which encourages ambitious provincial leaders to aspire to promotion to a national office rather than furthering provincial interests.

Second, the qualifications for provincial and national levels of leadership have shifted from revolutionary credentials, such as participation in the Long March and the Anti-Japanese War, to administrative skills, such as coalition building, both vertically and horizontally. Chinese provinces are large socioeconomic entities. It is often said that a province is to China what a country is to Europe. China's provincial chiefs, similar to top leaders in European nations, are constantly concerned with regional economic development and cope with daunting challenges such as unemployment, economic issues, political instability, and social welfare needs in their jurisdictions.[8] For China's future national leaders, provincial administration provides an ideal training ground.

Third, in addition to advancing their own careers through provincial leadership, top national leaders expand their power and influence at the national level through support from provincial-level administrations. Thus, appointments and promotions of provincial leaders are often a prelude to the jockeying for power that occurs among various factions at the center of power. For example, the promotions of Huang Ju, Jia Qinglin, and He Guoqiang to the central leadership, of Liu Qi and Chen Liangyu from mayors to party secretaries in Beijing and Shanghai, of Huang Huahua to Vice Governor of Guangdong, and of Wang Sanyun

---

[8] For a detailed discussion of the growing importance of provincial leaders, see Cheng Li, "After Hu, Who? Provincial Leaders Await Promotion," *China Leadership Monitor*, No. 1 (Winter 2002), pp. 1–20.

to Deputy Party Secretary of Fujian, all of which took place a few weeks prior to the 16th Party Congress, were examples of Jiang, Zeng, and Hu making sure that their own protégés would obtain seats on either the new politburo or Central Committee (CC). Within months after the 16th Party Congress, four of Hu's close allies were appointed as chiefs of four major provincial-level administrations. They were Sichuan Party Secretary Zhang Xuezhong, Henan Party Secretary Li Keqiang, Jiangsu Party Secretary Li Yuanchao, and Beijing Mayor Meng Xuenong. Although Meng Xuenong fell from power as a result of his mishandling of the SARS epidemic in Beijing, the other province heads are all leading contenders for politburo memberships at the next party congress.

Fourth, China's provincial leadership is a political force in its own right. During the past two decades, decentralization in both the political and economic arenas has reinforced the tension between the central and provincial governments. Many provincial leaders, especially those in the inland areas, have had reservations about the growing regional economic gap in the country and the overrepresentation in the central government of leaders born in the coastal regions. Deputies to the Party Congress from inland regions often use their votes to block the election of those nominees favored by top leaders, especially princelings or those officials who have advanced their careers from Shanghai.

All of these factors suggest that China is experiencing two contending trends: the trend of a growing demand for regional autonomy and the trend toward more institutional measures to curtail political localism and strengthen national integration. The unfolding of these paradoxical developments will not only test the effectiveness of new institutional mechanisms, but also determine how the most populous country in the world will be governed in coming years and decades.

TRENDS OF LOCALISM IN THE SELECTION OF PROVINCIAL LEADERS

Uneven Distribution of Birthplaces

One of the most interesting phenomena in the composition of political elites during the Jiang era is the predominance of leaders who come from eastern provinces, especially Jiangsu and Shandong.[9] Table 1.2 shows the

---

[9]   For a detailed discussion of this subject, see Li, *China's Leaders*, pp. 59–62.

Table 1.2. *Distribution of Birthplaces, by Province, of Full Members of the 1992, 1997, and 2002 CCs*

Native Province	14th CC (n = 187) No.	%	15th CC (n = 193) No.	%	16th CC (n = 198) No.	%	Population (2000) %	Gross Domestic Product (GDP)(1999) %
North								
Beijing	4	2.1	5	2.6	6	3.0	1.1	2.5
Tianjin	4	2.1	3	1.6	3	1.5	0.8	1.7
Hebei	22	11.6	10	5.2	8	4.0	5.3	5.2
Shanxi	7	3.7	7	3.6	3	1.5	2.6	1.7
Neimenggu	1	0.5	2	1.0	1	0.5	1.9	1.5
Subtotal	38	20.0	27	14.0	21	10.5	11.7	12.6
Northeast								
Liaoning	7	3.7	14	7.3	9	4.6	3.4	4.8
Jilin	8	4.2	10	5.2	7	3.5	2.2	1.9
Heilongjiang	2	1.1	2	1.0	5	2.5	2.9	3.3
Subtotal	17	9.0	26	13.5	21	10.6	8.5	10.0
East								
Shanghai	3	1.6	2	1.0	6	3.0	1.3	4.6
Jiangsu	25	13.2	33	17.1	29	14.7	5.9	8.8
Shandong	24	12.7	25	13.0	17	8.6	7.2	8.7
Zhejiang	14	7.4	11	5.7	13	6.6	3.7	6.1
Anhui	5	2.6	10	5.2	8	4.0	4.7	3.3
Fujian	2	1.1	4	2.1	2	1.0	2.7	4.1
Taiwan	1	0.5	1	0.5	0	0	—	—
Subtotal	74	39.1	86	44.6	75	37.9	25.5	35.6
Central								
Henan	5	2.6	5	2.6	8	4.0	7.3	5.2
Hubei	10	5.3	5	2.6	6	3.0	4.8	4.4
Hunan	8	4.2	12	6.2	10	5.1	5.1	3.8

Jiangxi	2	1.1	6	3.1	2	1.0	3.3	2.2
Subtotal	25	13.2	28	14.5	26	13.1	20.5	15.6
South								
Guangdong	4	2.1	6	3.1	4	2.0	6.8	9.7
Guangxi	1	0.5	1	0.5	1	0.5	3.6	2.2
Hainan	0	0	0	0	0	0	0.6	0.5
Subtotal	5	2.6	7	3.6	5	2.5	11.0	12.4
Southwest								
Sichuan (incl. Chongqing)	9	4.8	7	3.6	7	3.5	9.0	5.9
Guizhou	1	0.5	2	1.0	2	1.0	2.8	1.0
Yunnan	2	1.1	0	0	2	1.0	3.4	2.1
Xizang (Tibet)	1	0.5	2	1.0	2	1.0	0.2	0.1
Subtotal	13	6.9	11	5.6	13	6.5	15.4	9.1
Northwest								
Shaanxi	3	1.6	4	2.1	9	4.6	2.9	1.7
Gansu	1	0.5	1	0.5	2	1.0	2.0	1.1
Qinghai	0	0	0	0	1	0.5	0.4	0.3
Ningxia	0	0	0	0	1	0.5	0.4	0.3
Xinjiang	2	1.1	3	1.6	2	1.0	1.5	1.3
Subtotal	6	3.2	8	4.2	15	7.6	7.2	4.7
Unknown	8.7	5.8			22	11.1	0.2*	
Total	187	100.0	193	100.0	198	100.0	100.0	100.0

* This population is registered in the People's Liberation Army.

Sources: For the 14th CC, see China News Analysis, Nos. 1588–89 (July 1–15, 1997), pp. 15–20; Zang Xiaowei, "The Fourteenth Central Committee of the CCP, Technocracy or Political Technocracy," Asian Survey 33 (August 1993): p. 795. For the 15th CC, see Li Cheng and Lynn White, The Fifteenth Central Committee of the Chinese Communist Party," p. 246; some previously incomplete figures are updated. For populations, see National Bureau of Statistics of China, Diwuci quanguo renkou pucha gongbao [The Fifth National Census of the Population of the People's Republic of China], No. 2, May 15, 2001. For gross domestic product data, see http://www.stats.gov.cn/ndsj/zgnj/2000/C08c.htm

birthplaces by provinces of full members of the 16th CC, as compared with
the two previous CCs. In the 15th CC, 44.6 percent of the full members
were born in East China.[10] This declined somewhat to 38 percent in the
16th CC, still well above the 25 percent of national population accounted
for by the six provinces of East China. However, South China, especially
the wealthy province of Guangdong, is underrepresented. Guangdong,
with 7 percent of China's population and 10 percent of the gross national
product, has just 2 percent of the full seats. Southwest China, notably
the populous Sichuan, is also underrepresented. With 15 percent of the
national population, the Southwest accounts for only 7 percent of the full
memberships on the CC.

Today, natives of Jiangsu province comprise 15 percent of the 16th
CC. The portion of eastern natives, however, has declined by almost 7
percent compared with the previous CC. The Shandong delegation decreased from 13 percent in 1997 to only 8.6 percent today. Representation
of the Northwest on the CC has increased from 3 percent in 1992 to 8
percent now. (There are 11 percent of the full members of the 16th CC
whose birthplaces are still not identified.) However, it has yet to be determined whether the overrepresentation of eastern natives will change
on a significant level in the years to come. There is no sign of a decrease
in the number of politburo members from eastern provinces – 10 of 24
full members on the 16th politburo (42 percent) were born in East China.
No member of the current Politburo was born in the South or Southwest,
which accommodates over a quarter of China's population.

This regional imbalance is apparent not only in the Communist Party,
but also in the military, in which Shandong province is overrepresented.[11]
On the State Council formed during the Ninth NPC in 1998, 16 out of
29 ministers (55.2 percent) were natives of eastern provinces, including

---

[10] Cheng Li and Lynn White, "The Fifteenth Central Committee of the Chinese Communist Party: Full-Fledged Technocratic Leadership with Partial Control by Jiang Zemin,"
Asian Survey, 38 (March 1998), pp. 246–7. Some previously unknown figures are updated
based on recently released official biographical information.

[11] According to a study of military elites in the early 1990s, Shandong Province accounted
for well over one-quarter of China's senior military officers. See Cheng Li and Lynn
White, "The Army in the Succession to Deng Xiaoping: Familiar Fealties and Technocratic Trends," *Asian Survey*, 33 (August 1993), pp. 766–7. According to a report released
in the late 1990s, of the 42 highest ranking military officers whose birthplaces were identified, 13 were born in Shandong, and 6 were born in Jiangsu. A total of 22 top military leaders (52.4 percent) are from eastern China. *China News Analysis*, Nos. 1615–16
(August 1–15, 1998), pp. 15–19.

8 (27.6 percent) who were born in Jiangsu.[12] Among the 28 ministers selected at the Tenth NPC in March 2003, 8 were born in Jiangsu (28.6 percent) and 5 (17.9 percent) were Shanghaiese. In 2003, Jiangsu natives served as Party Chiefs of Beijing, Chongqing, Jilin, Jiangsu, Jiangxi, and Tibet, Mayor of Tianjin, or Governors of Hebei and Shandong. Shandong natives are Party Secretaries in five provinces: Neimonggu, Hainan, Shaanxi, Ningxia and Xinjiang.

Meanwhile, officials from the southern and southwestern provinces such as Guangdong (which produced a significant number of political and military elites during the Nationalist era) are underrepresented in China's high-level leadership. This is also in sharp contrast to the Mao era, when the majority of CCP leaders came from central China, especially from Hunan and Hubei provinces.[13] The Communist movement in the 1920s and 1930s attracted many peasants from central China. For example, approximately one-third of the members of the Eighth Politburo of the CCP formed in 1956 were born in Hunan, and about one-third of the members of the Ninth Politburo in 1969 were born in Hubei (most of these Hunan- or Hubei-born leaders had military backgrounds).[14] The leaders from provinces in central China occupied half the seats in the Politburo in these two Party Congresses.

The disproportionate overrepresentation of leaders from the East Coast may have multiple causes, and this phenomenon deserves further investigation, including studies of regional educational systems, subcultures, and the correlation between economic wealth and the formation of political elites. During the Jiang era, region-based favoritism resulted in higher representation of East China at the expense of South and Southwest China. The high percentage of Jiangsu natives in the civilian leadership may be partially due to the fact that Jiang Zemin, a Jiangsu native, liked to promote his fellow Jiangsuese. For example, Jiang's strong endorsement during the late 1990s of the promotion of Li Lanqing, a native

---

[12] "The New State Council," *China News Analysis*, April 1, 1998, pp. 4–6.

[13] For an earlier discussion of the origins of the CCP leaders, see Franklin W. Houn, "The Eighth Central Committee of the Chinese Communist Party: A Study of Elites," *American Political Science Review*, 51 (June 1957) pp. 392–404; Jurgen Domes, "The Ninth CCP Central Committee in Statistical Perspective," *Current Scene* (Hong Kong), 9, No. 2 (1969) pp. 1–9; Robert Scalapino, ed. *Elites in the People's Republic of China* (Seattle, WA. University of Washington Press, 1972); and Paul Wong, *China's Higher Leadership in the Socialist Transition* (New York: Free Press, 1976), pp. 190–203.

[14] Cheng Li and Lynn White, "The Thirteenth Central Committee of the Chinese Communist Party: From Mobilizers to Managers," *Asian Survey*, 28 (April 1988), p. 378.

of Zhenjiang city in Jiangsu province, to become a standing member of the politburo and executive vice premier confirms the practice of favoritism based on a shared birthplace.

The Formation of the Shanghai Gang

Indeed, Jiang Zemin's promotion of a powerful network of national leaders who originated from Shanghai – known as the Shanghai Gang by Western observers – may be said to exemplify region-based favoritism. The term "Shanghai Gang" refers to current leaders whose careers have advanced primarily as a result of their patron–client relations with Jiang Zemin in Shanghai. Membership in the Shanghai Gang is based on political association rather than regional origin, but a majority of the members were born in Shanghai and two nearby provinces, Jiangsu and Zhejiang. After Jiang was promoted by Deng from Party Secretary of Shanghai to General Secretary of the CCP in 1989, he promoted many of his friends from Shanghai to important national leadership positions. Jiang has apparently cultivated a web of personal ties based on Shanghai connections. Zeng Qinghong, Jiang's chief-of-staff in Shanghai when Jiang was party secretary of the city, moved with Jiang to Beijing in 1989. Zeng was promoted from deputy head of the General Office of the CCP, to its head, and then head of the Organization Department of the CCP. Now Zeng is Vice President of the PRC and a standing member of the politburo.

In the mid-1990s, two of Jiang's deputies in Shanghai, Wu Bangguo and Huang Ju, were also promoted to Politburo membership as part of Jiang's effort to consolidate his power in Beijing. In the late 1990s, Jiang also promoted Han Zhubin, former head of the Shanghai Railway Administration, to become both Procurator General of the Supreme People's Procuratorate and Executive Deputy Secretary of the Central Commission for Discipline Inspection, the important positions that oversee disciplinary problems among top officials. Chen Zhili, Jiang's other deputy on the Shanghai Party Committee, was later promoted to head the Ministry of Education, and she is now a state councilor.

Jiang has also promoted his Shanghai Gang to head the central government's main propaganda organs. Gong Xinhan and Zhou Ruijin were transferred from Shanghai to be deputy head of the Propaganda Department of the CCP and deputy editor-in-chief of the *People's Daily*, respectively. Xu Guangchun, former head of the Shanghai Branch of Xinhua News Agency, was promoted first to editor-in-chief of *Guangming Daily*.

He also served as a spokesperson for the 15th Party Congress and is now deputy head of the Propaganda Department of the CCP.[15]

In 2000, Jiang promoted Wang Huning, Cao Jianming, and Zhou Mingwei, three well-educated Shanghai leaders in their late 30s and early 40s, to the central government to serve as his personal "brain trust." Wang Huning, former dean of the law school at Fudan University, was promoted to Deputy Director of the CCP Policy Research Center. Wang often served as Jiang's personal assistant during Jiang's travels both at home and abroad. Cao Jianming, another professor of law and former President of the Institute of East China Political Science and Law, became Vice President of the Supreme People's Court. Zhou Mingwei received his Master's degree in Public Administration at the State University of New York, Albany and was a visiting scholar at Harvard University's Kennedy School of Government. Zhou served as director of the Office of Foreign Affairs in the Shanghai municipal government and was promoted to Vice Chair of the Association for Relations across the Taiwan Strait in 2001.

Not all leaders who originate from, or pass through, Shanghai belong to the Shanghai Gang. Some tensions may exist between officials who are primarily promoted by Jiang and those promoted by Zhu Rongji. As former Mayor of Shanghai, Zhu also promoted his associates in Shanghai to central government positions. For example, when Zhu took over as Governor of the People's Bank of China in 1993, he immediately appointed two close colleagues from Shanghai as vice governors of the bank. They were Dai Xianglong, former Governor of the Shanghai-based Bank of Communications, and Zhu Xiaohua, former Vice Governor of the Shanghai branch of the Bank of China. Lou Jiwei (former Vice Chair of Shanghai Economic Restructuring Commission and Zhu's personal secretary) was later promoted to Executive Vice Minister of Finance. Xu Kuangdi, former Mayor of Shanghai, was closer to Zhu than to Jiang. These protégés of Zhu were not members of the Shanghai Gang. In fact, their career advancement was often blocked by Jiang's people. Zhu Xiaohua was recently charged with corruption and is now in jail.

Table 1.3 lists the prominent members of Jiang's Shanghai Gang. They all serve on the 16th CC. Four brief observations can be made. First,

---

[15] For more discussion on Jiang's network in the propaganda circle in the central government, see Paul Cavey, "Building a Power Base: Jiang Zemin and the Post-Deng Succession," *Issues and Studies*, 33 (November 1997), p. 13.

Table 1.3. *Members of the Shanghai Gang on the 16th CC*

Name	Current Position	16th CC	Born	Native Province	Principal Experience in Shanghai
Zeng Qinghong (m)	Vice President of the PRC	Politburo SM	1939	Jiangxi	Head, Organization Department, 1985–1986; Chief-of-Staff, Deputy Party Secretary, 1986–1989
Wu Bangguo (m)	Chairman of the NPC	Politburo SM	1941	Anhui	Deputy Party Secretary, 1985–1991; Party Secretary, 1991–1995
Huang Ju (m)	Executive Vice Premier	Politburo SM	1938	Zhejiang	Chief of Staff, 1984–1985; Vice Mayor, 1986–1991; Mayor, 1991–1995; Party Secretary, 1994–present
Zeng Peiyan (m)	Vice Premier	Politburo member	1938	Zhejiang	Director of the Research Institute under No. 1 Machine Industry, 1978–1985
Chen Liangyu (m)	Party Secretary of Shanghai	Politburo member	1946	Zhejiang	Deputy Chief-of-Staff, 1992–1996; Deputy Secretary, 1997–present; Executive Vice Mayor, 1998–2001
Chen Zhili (f)	State Councilor	CC member	1942	Fujian	Head, Propaganda Department, 1988–1989; Deputy Party Secretary, 1989–1997
Hua Jianmin (m)	State Councilor	CC member	1940	Jiangsu	Vice Chair and Chair, Shanghai Planning Committee, 1994; Vice Mayor, 1994–1996

Name	Position	Membership	Year	Province	Career
Han Zheng (m)	Mayor of Shanghai	CC member	1954	Zhejiang	Deputy Chief-of-Staff, 1995–1996; Head, Shanghai Planning Commission, 1996–1998
Meng Jianzhu (m)	Party Secretary of Jiangxi	CC member	1947	Jiangsu	Deputy Chief-of-Staff, 1992–1993; Vice Mayor, 1993–1997; Deputy Party Secretary, 1996–2001
Zhao Qizheng (m)	Head, Information Office, State Council	CC member	1940	Beijing	Head, Organization Department, 1984–1991; Vice Mayor, 1991–1997; Head of Pudong District, 1992–1997
Zhang Wenkang (m)	Minister of Public Health	CC member	1940	Shanghai	Vice Commandant, No. 2 People's Liberation Army Medical University (based in Shanghai), 1984–1990
Wang Huning (m)	Deputy Director, General Policy Research Center	CC member	1955	Shanghai	Dean of Law School at Fudan University, 1993–1997
Xu Guangchun (m)	Head, State Administration of Radio, Film & TV	CC member	1944	Zhejiang	Director, Shanghai Bureau of Xinhua News Agency, 1985–1991
Li Yuanchao (m)	Party Secretary of Jiangsu	Alternate member	1950	Jiangsu	Secretary of Shanghai CCYL, 1983–1988

(continued)

Table 1.3 (*continued*)

Name	Current Position	16th CC	Born	Native Province	Principal Experience in Shanghai
Cao Jianming (m)	Vice President of Supreme People's Court	Alternate member	1955	Shanghai	President, Institute of East China Political Science & Law, 1998–present
Xie Qihua (f)	President of Baosteel Group Corp.	Alternate member	1943	Zhejiang	Director of Baosteel Group Corp. (located in Shanghai), 1990–1998
Yin Yicui (f)	Deputy Party Secretary of Shanghai	Alternate member	1955	Zhejiang	Deputy Chief-of-Staff, 1998–2001; Head, Shanghai Publicity Department, 2001–2002
Wu Qidi (f)	President of Tongji University	Alternate member	1947	Zhejiang	President of Tongji University, 1995–present
Liu Yungeng (m)	Deputy Party Secretary of Shanghai	Alternate member	1947	Zhejiang	Head, Public Security Bureau, Deputy Chief-of-Staff, 1990s
Xi Guohua (m)	President, China Commission	Alternate member	1951	Shanghai	Head, Telecommunication Bureau, 1980–1990

Note: f = female; m = male; SM = standing member.

Source: Shen Xueming and Han Honghong, comp., *Zhonggong di shiwujie zhongyang weiyuanhui zhongyang jilü jiancha weiyuanhui weiyuan minglu [Who's Who Among the Members of the Fifteenth Central Committee of the Chinese Communist Party and the Fifteenth Central Commission for Discipline Inspection]* (Beijing: Zhonggong wenxian chubanshe, 1999); Ho Szu-yin, comp., *Zhonggong renmin lu [Who's Who in Communist China]* (Taipei: Institute of International Relations, National Chengchi University, 1999); *China Directory* (Tokyo: Radio Press, published, annually); and http://www.chinesenews.com.

five members of the Shanghai Gang occupy seats in the 16th Politburo, including three seats on its Standing Committee, constituting a dominant faction in this most powerful decision-making body. Among the 10-member State Council (composed of the premier, 4 vice premiers, and 5 state councilors) selected at the 10th NPC, four persons are members of the Shanghai Gang.

Second, the number of the Shanghai Gang members on the 16th CC is insignificant. Members of the Shanghai Gang occupy only 20 seats (5.6 percent) of a total number of 358. This is largely because delegates at the Party Congress favored a more balanced geographic distribution and they likely blocked the election of additional nominees from Shanghai.

Third, 16 of these members of the Shanghai Gang (80 percent) were born in Shanghai or nearby Jiangsu and Zhejiang. Many worked in Shanghai for a long time. Most had leadership experience in the municipal government, especially as chiefs-of-staff (*mishuzhang*). During the past two decades, having served as a *mishu* (personal assistant) or a mishuzhang has often been seen as a stepping stone to further promotion.[16] Probably no patron–client tie is closer than the relationship between a mishuzhang and his or her boss.

Fourth, the Shanghai Gang's efforts to transfer Shanghai officials to other provinces and major cities thus far appear unsuccessful. Among the 60 current top provincial chiefs (party secretaries and governors) in other provinces, only two, Meng Jianzhu (Party Secretary of Jiangxi) and Li Yuanchao (Party Secretary of Jiangsu) are known as members of the Shanghai Gang. In fact, Li Yuanchao's political identity is even more dubious since he left Shanghai in the late 1980s and was also closely associated with the Chinese Communist Youth League (CCYL) when Hu Jintao was in charge of the CCYL secretariat. Meng is the only provincial chief elsewhere who has been transferred directly from Shanghai. Among several hundred deputy party secretaries and vice governors in the country, only one can be identified as having Shanghai connections. Huang Qifan, former chairman of the Shanghai government's Economic Commission, was recently appointed as Executive Vice Mayor of Chongqing. The fact that very few members of the Shanghai Gang currently serve in the leadership

---

[16] For a detailed analysis of mishu and mishuzhang, see Li Wei and Lucian Pye, "The Ubiquitous Role of the Mishu in Chinese Politics," *China Quarterly* 132 (December 1992), pp. 913–36; and Li, *China's Leaders*, pp. 127–174.

of other provinces suggests that Jiang and Zeng have faced strong local resistance in appointing Shanghai officials to serve on the others' turf.

Shanghai has a special privileged position. A study of fourth-generation leaders on the 15th CC of the CCP and the 15th Central Commission for Discipline Inspection shows that all of the Shanghai officials were born in Shanghai or nearby provinces (Jiangsu and Zhejiang). All have worked in Shanghai for a long time, most since their college graduation approximately two decades earlier.[17] Since Jiang became general secretary of the CCP in 1989, no high-ranking officers (deputy party secretaries and vice mayors) have been transferred from other regions to the Shanghai administration.[18] Table 1.4 lists 13 top officials in Shanghai in 2003. All of them were born in East China, especially in Shanghai or nearby provinces (Jiangsu and Zhejiang). Many attended colleges in Shanghai. Only Yang Xiaodu had work experience outside Shanghai.

The careers of these top Shanghai officials vary (many worked as factory directors and some served as county or district chiefs). Remarkably, nine of them (69 percent) have served as chiefs-of-staff either on the CCP Municipal Party Committee or the Municipal Government of Shanghai. The high percentage of top Shanghai leaders who have been chiefs-of-staff further illustrates the prevalence of personal relations in elite promotion.

The career advancement of many top Shanghai leaders can be directly attributed to assistance from patrons in higher positions. For example, Gong Xueping, new chairman of the Municipal People's Congress in Shanghai, is a confidant of Jiang Zemin. Gong does not have a good reputation in the city, and in 2002 he even failed to be elected as a standing member of the Shanghai Municipal Party Committee. Luo Shiqian, the newly appointed deputy party secretary, worked under Zeng Qinghong

---

[17] Li, *China's Leaders*, p. 67.

[18] The only exception is Yang Xiaodu, the newly appointed vice mayor of Shanghai. However, even Yang has had substantial previous experience in the city. Yang was born in Shanghai in 1953 and grew up during the Cultural Revolution. He was a "sent-down youth," sent to Anhui in 1970. Three years later, he returned to his birthplace where he attended the Shanghai Traditional Medical School. After graduation, he went to Tibet, where he advanced his political career from Party secretary of a hospital to prefecture Party secretary. He was a vice governor of Tibet before being transferred back to his natal city. For a discussion of the mobility patterns of Shanghai leaders in the lower-level administrative levels, see Shi Chen, "Leadership Change in Shanghai: Toward the Dominance of [Chinese Communist] Party Technocrats," *Asian Survey*, 38 (July 1998), pp. 671–87.

Table 1.4. *Top Officials in Shanghai (April 2003)*

Name	Current Position	Since	Born	Native Province	Education	Most Recent Post	Chief-of-Staff in Shanghai	Experience	
								Other Region	Main
Chen Liangyu (m)	Party Secretary	2002	1946	Zhejiang	PLA Institute of Engineering	Shanghai Executive Vice Mayor, 1998–2001	Deputy, CCP Committee, 1992–1996	None	Factory Director
Han Zheng (m)	Mayor	2003	1954	Zhejiang	East China Normal University (MA)	Head, Shanghai Planning Commission, 1996–1998	Deputy, Government, 1995–1996	None	Factory Director
Liu Yungeng (m)	Deputy Party Secretary	2000	1947	Zhejiang	Unknown	Head, Shanghai Public Security Bureau, 1997–1999	Deputy, Government, 1995–1997	None	Head, Public Security Bureau
Luo Shiqian (m)	Deputy Party Secretary	2001	1943	Anhui	Unknown	Head, CCP Shanghai Organization Department, 1991–2001		None	CCP Functionary
Yin Yicui (f)	Deputy Party Secretary	2002	1955	Zhejiang	East China Normal University (MA)	Head, Publicity Department	Office Director	None	CCP Functionary
Feng Guoqin (m)	Vice Mayor	1996	1948	Shanghai	CPS	Chief-of-Staff, Shanghai Government, 1995–1996	Government, 1995–1996	None	County Party Secretary

(continued)

Table 1.4 (continued)

Name	Current Position	Since	Born	Native Province	Education	Most Recent Post	Chief-of-Staff in Shanghai	Experience Other Region	Experience Main
Zhou Yupeng (m)	Vice Mayor	1998	1947	Jiangsu	Television University, New York University (V)	Chief-of-Staff, Shanghai Government, 1997–1998	CCP Committee, 1997–1998	None	District Director
Yang Xiaodu (m)	Vice Mayor	2001	1953	Shanghai	Shanghai Trad. Medical School	Vice Governor, Tibet, 1998–2001		Tibet	Provincial Government
Yan Junqi (m)	Vice Mayor	2001	1946	Jiangsu	Jiaotong University, Denmark (PhD)	Deputy Director, Shanghai IT Office		None	College President
Jiang Shixian (m)	Vice Mayor	2002	1954	Jiangsu	Shanghai Jiaotong University (MA)	Chief-of-Staff, Shanghai Government	Government, 2000–2002	None	CCP Functionary
Yang Xiong (m)	Vice Mayor	2003	1953	Zhejiang	CASS (MA)	Deputy Chief-of-Staff, Shanghai Government	Government, 2001–2003	None	Manager
Zhou Taitong (m)	Vice Mayor	2003	1952	Fujian	Shanghai Institute Of Finance (MA)	Deputy Chief-of-Staff, Shanghai Government	Government 1997–2003	None	Manager
Tang Dengjie (m)	Vice Mayor	2003	1964	Jiangsu	Tongji University (MA)	Director, Economic Planning, Shanghai Government		None	Manager

Note: m = male; f = female; CASS = Chinese Academy of Social Sciences; Trad. = Traditional; V = Visiting scholar.

48

for a long time. New party secretary of the city, Chen Liangyu, has worked under his predecessor, Huang Ju, since the early 1980s, when both worked in Shanghai's No. 1 Bureau of the Machinery Industry. Huang and Chen later promoted many of their associates in the bureau to municipal government leadership posts.

The presence of many leaders in the central government from Shanghai suggests that factional politics in the central and local governments has remained a determining factor in the career mobility of political leaders. A joke spread throughout China during the late 1990s illustrates this point: Whenever a line forms to board a train or bus, people are often teased, "Let the comrades from Shanghai go first."

Regional Leaders Serving in Their Native Areas

Another important trend in the formation of provincial and municipal leadership in China during the reform era is the selection of local officials for leadership positions in their native areas. This trend challenges the "law of avoidance" by which Mandarins were prohibited from serving in their native provinces and counties, a century-old policy characteristic of traditional China and a practice continued during the Mao era.

In his study of the city of Wuhan during the early decades of the PRC, Ying-mao Kau observed that 91 percent of municipal elites in the city were nonnative "outsiders."[19] Most of the major local leaders (especially at both the provincial and municipal levels) were not born in the area in which they served. However, this law of avoidance has changed during the reform era, as demonstrated by some recent studies of provincial and municipal leaders. Table 1.5 presents the general patterns of the correlation between birthplace and workplace of elites below the national level during the reform era. The very top jobs at the province level – party secretary and governor – display some important differences, which are discussed in the paragraphs that follow. However, when the entire group of provincial leaders is included, the trend toward increased localism is strong. The data on Chinese mayors in the mid-1980s show that, among 247 mayors, 144 (58.2 percent) were natives in the cities that they served and 31

---

[19] Ying-mao Kau, "The Urban Bureaucratic Elites in Communist China: A Case Study of Wuhan, 1949–1965," in A. Doak Barnett, ed. *Communist Chinese Politics in Action* (Seattle, WA: University of Washington Press, 1972), p. 227.

Table 1.5. *Distribution of Provincial and Municipal Leaders Who Work in the Same, Neighboring, or Distant Province or City*

Source	Province or City (%)			Unknown (%)
	Native	Neighboring	Distant	
1986 Survey of Mayors (*n* = 247)	58.3	12.6	23.9	5.3
1994 Survey of Provincial Leaders (*n* = 187)	47.1	13.4	39.6	
1999 Survey of Provincial Leaders (*n* = 124)	46.0	12.1	41.9	
2002 Deputy Provincial Leaders (*n* = 142)	48.6	17.6	33.8	
2002 Provincial Chiefs (*n* = 62)	17.7	17.7	64.5	

Note: Percentages do not add up to 100 because of rounding.

Sources: For the 1986 survey, Cheng Li and David Bachman, "Localism, Elitism and Immobilism: Elite Formation and Social Change in Post-Mao China," *World Politics* 42 (October 1989), pp. 64–94.

For the 1994 survey, Liao and Fan, *Zhongguo renming da* (the 1994 edition). The data were accumulated and tabulated by the author.

For the 1999 survey, Shen, *Zhonggong di shiwujie zhongyang weiyuanhui zhongyang zhongyang jilü jiancha weiyunahui weiyuan minglu*, (1999). The data were accumulated and tabulated by the author.

For the 2002 deputy leaders, Cheng Li, "Zhongguo shengji lingdao de xinggou: guojiazhenghe yu difangzizhu" ["Formation of China's provincial leaders: National integration and regional autonomy"], *Zhongguo shehui kexue pinglun [Chinese Social Sciences Review]*, 1 (Fall 2002), pp. 313–26.

For the 2002 chiefs, www.xinhuanet.com, November, 2002. The data were accumulated and tabulated by the author.

(12.5 percent) were from neighboring areas.[20] Two studies of provincial leaders show a similar trend of a large number of provincial leaders being selected from the same province.

In addition, many nonnative provincial leaders also have some sort of local connection; for example, they graduated from, or had many years of work experience in, the region in which they now serve as leaders. For example, Wang Yunkun, Party Secretary of Jilin, is a native of Jiangsu, but he has worked in Jilin for over 30 years since he graduated from college in 1966.

Table 1.5 also indicates that the lower levels of administration tend to have more leaders born in the same region, and deputy provincial leaders (deputy party secretaries and vice governors) are much more likely to

[20] Cheng Li and David Bachman, "Localism, Elitism and Immobilism: Elite Formation and Social Change in Post-Mao China," *World Politics* 42 (October 1989), pp. 64–94.

be promoted from the provinces in which they were born (48.6 percent) than provincial chiefs (party secretaries and governors; 17.7 percent). Although no provincial-level administrations are allowed to have all high-level leaders from the same province (except Shanghai), usually half of the 10–12 top leaders in a province are natives of that province. A norm exists that deputy provincial leaders who have worked in their native provinces for a long period of time are encouraged to have a sense of commitment to their jurisdictions, particularly to economic development. As a result, the performance of these provincial leaders will be better evaluated over a long period of time. Meanwhile, the practice that provincial chiefs are usually transferred from other provinces or the central government may help prevent political localism from spinning out of control.

These findings are closely connected with the ongoing reform of the Chinese nomenklatura system – the list of positions and the candidates who are qualified to fill them. The nomenklatura system has been the hallmark of personnel policy in Leninist countries (See Chapter 2 in this volume).[21] Since the 1980s, the system has changed: In general, Communist Party Committees make personnel appointments only for their immediate subordinates, that is, "one level down," instead of the more traditional policy of approving personnel appointments "two levels down."[22] In practice, this means that provincial party secretaries and governors are responsible for appointing the "second tier" provincial-level officials, including bureau chiefs in the provincial government and mayors and prefecture heads of medium-sized cities just below the province level.

Previously, the appointment of the second tier provincial-level officials was controlled by the Organization Department of the CC of the CCP. Now, only the first tier (provincial party secretaries and deputy party secretaries, governors, and vice governors) are still controlled by the CC. According to Cao Zhi, Vice Minister of the Organization Department of the CCP, the central authorities have given provincial leaders autonomy in appointing mayoral and prefecture heads since the mid-1980s. Consequently, the total number of cadres who are supposed to be

---

[21] John P. Burns, "China's Nomenklatura System," *Problems of Communism*, No. 33 (September–October 1987), pp. 36–51; and John P. Burns, "Strengthening Central CCP Control of Leadership Selection: The 1990 Nomenklatura," *China Quarterly* 138 (June 1994), pp. 458–91.

[22] Burns, "China's Nomenklatura System," pp. 37–8 and 40–1.

appointed by the CCP Organization Department decreased from 13,000 to 2,700.[23]

The lists of names for the provincial-level nomenklatura are now composed disproportionately of people from the province in question. In view of the degree to which Chinese officials defend their turf, it is hard to imagine that provincial leaders would search in other jurisdictions to find candidates for their posts.[24] The trend toward recruitment of more native-born elites is strengthened by local cadre elections and by the "election with more candidates than seats" (*cha'e xuanju*), which has been adopted in the party congress at various levels (from grass roots to the CC) since the 14th Party Congress in 1992. If all things are equal among candidates, deputies have a tendency to vote for candidates from their own region.

In local elections, people are highly likely to choose a native candidate to be their local leader if the other candidates' qualifications are roughly equal. In turn, these elected local elites may make "localist demands." In the 1990s, local People's Congresses sometimes refused to even approve candidates endorsed by the central authorities, producing what the Chinese official journal, *Liaowang*, called "unexpected results."[25] During the 1990s, the central authorities faced strong local resistance in appointing nonnative leaders to their provinces. Cantonese local officials, for example, were particularly resentful when the central authorities appointed Li Changchun, a native of Liaoning and a politburo member, to be Party Secretary of Guangdong, replacing Xie Fei, a native Cantonese who was a member of the politburo at that time.[26]

However, in most cases the central authorities are able to ensure that nominees from the central government are selected for provincial leadership positions. In fact, the interdependence of central and provincial leaders has been consolidated in recent years. As John Burns observes, "appointments are probably often the outcome of negotiation and bargaining

---

[23] Wu Guoguang, *Zhulu shiwuda: zhongguo quanli qiju [Toward the Fifteenth Party Congress: Power Game in China]* (Hong Kong: Taipingyang shiji chubanshe, 1997), p. 215.

[24] This discussion is based on Li and Bachman, "Localism, Elitism and Immobilism," p. 87.

[25] Quoted from Burns, "Strengthening Central CCP Control of Leadership Selection," p. 473.

[26] For a discussion of the conflict between the central authorities and Cantonese officials regarding the selection of Guangdong's top leaders, see *Shijie ribao [World Journal]*, September 17, 1997, p. 2; also see Gao Xin, *Xiangfu Guangdong bang [Taming the Guangdong Gang]* (Hong Kong: Mingjing chubanshe, 2000).

among faction leaders mindful of their needs to build and maintain personal relations networks and of the need for factional balance."[27] In the case of Guangdong, it took almost a year for local officials to accept Li Changchun, a non-Cantonese party boss.[28] This was largely the result of pressure from the central authorities as well as negotiation between the local and central governments. While serving as provincial leaders in Guangdong, Li Changchun and other non-Cantonese officials such as Wang Qishan (then Executive Vice Governor of Guangdong) repeatedly claimed that they would continue to rely on local officials and would not bring a large group of leaders from other regions to replace them.[29]

THE CENTER'S RESTRAINT OVER LOCALISM IN ELITE PROMOTION

The growing influence of localism during the reform era has alerted the central authorities. Since the late 1980s, the tension between the demand for regional representation and the restraint on the rise of localism has become a crucial issue in Chinese politics in general and elite recruitment in particular. Chinese authorities have adopted some institutional mechanisms, including both formal rules and informal norms, in order to curtail various forms of favoritism and localism in elite recruitment. Some regulations in particular are related to the selection of provincial leaders.

Term Limits

A term limit has been established for top posts in both the party and the government. An individual leader cannot hold the same position for more

---

[27] Burns, "Strengthening Central CCP Control of Leadership," p. 474.

[28] It was also reported that, in preliminary meetings before the Congress, central authorities intended to appoint a non-Cantonese Politburo member as the new Party secretary of Guangdong (now China's richest province) to replace Xie Fei, a Cantonese Party secretary and the most important politician in his region. Local officials in Guangdong rejected that proposal. They insisted that top officials in Guangdong should be Cantonese, even if they lost their representation in the Politburo. *Shijie ribao*, September 17, 1997, p. 2; and *South China Morning Post*, September 16, 1997, p. 1.

[29] Ding Wang, *Li Changchun yu Guangdong zhengtan – Guangdong jiebanqun, quyu jingji he zuqun wenhua [Li Changchun and Guangdong Political Scene: The Guangdong Successors, Regional Economics and the Culture of Ethnic Groups]*, 2nd ed. (Hong Kong: Celebrities Press, 1999).

Table 1.6. *Tenure of Top Provincial or Municipal Leaders (2003)*

Localities	Party Secretary	Tenure Since	Governor or Mayor	Tenure Since
Beijing	Liu Qi	2002	Meng Xuenong	2003
Tianjin	Zhang Lichang	1997	Dai Xianglong	2003
Hebei	Bai Keming	2002	Ji Yunshi	2002
Shanxi	Tian Chengping	1999	Li Zhenhua	2000
Inner Mongolia	Chu Bo	2001	Yang Jing (acting)	2003
Liaoning	Wen Shizhen	1997	Bo Xilai	2001
Jilin	Wang Yunkun	1998	Hong Hu	1999
Heilongjiang	Song Fatang	2003	Zhang Zuoji (expected)	2003
Shanghai	Chen Liangyu	2002	Han Zhen	2003
Jiangsu	Li Yuanchao	2002	Liang Baohua	2002
Zhejiang	Xi Jinping	2002	Lu Zushan	2003
Anhui	Wang Taihua	2000	Wang Jinshan	2002
Fujian	Song Defu	2000	Lu Zhangong	2002
Jiangxi	Meng Jianzhu	2001	Huang Zhiquan	2001
Shandong	Zhang Gaoli	2002	Han Yuqun	2003
Henan	Li Keqiang	2002	Li Chengyu	2003
Hebei	Yu Zhengsheng	2001	Luo Qingquan	2003
Hunan	Yang Zhengwu	1998	Zhou Bohua (acting)	2003
Guangdong	Zhang Dejiang	2002	Huang Huahua	2003
Guangxi	Cao Bochun	1997	Lu Bing (acting)	2003
Hainan	Wang Qishan	2002	Wang Xiaofeng	1998
Chongqing	Huang Zhendong	2002	Wang Hongju	2002
Sichuan	Zhang Xuezhong	2002	Zhang Zhongwei	1999
Guizhou	Qian Yunlu	2001	Shi Xiushi	2001
Yunnan	Bai Enpei	2001	Xu Rongkai	2001
Tibet	Guo Jinlong	2000	Legqot	1998
Shaanxi	Li Jianguo	1997	Jia Zhibang	2002
Ganxu	Song Zhaosu	2001	Lu Hao	2001
Qinghai	Su Rong	2001	Zhao Leji	1999
Ningxia	Chen Jianguo	2002	Ma Qizhi	1998
Xinjiang	Wang Lequan	1996	Simayi Tieliwaerdi	2003

Source: China Directory (Tokyo: Radio Press, 2002), and www.xinhuanet.com, April 2003.

than two five-year terms. Term limits are enforced for the provincial- or lower-level leaders. Top military officers of the military regions (commanders and political commissars) must also abide by this regulation.

Table 1.6 shows the appointment years of provincial party secretaries and governors in China's 31 provinces in 2003. All of them have been tenured in their current posts within the two term limits. The longest tenured provincial chief is Wang Lequan, a new politburo member

Table 1.7. *The Average Length of Tenure of Provincial Party Secretaries and Governors During the Reform Era*

	Average Tenure (years)	
Year	Provincial Party Secretaries	Governors
1985	4.5	2.5
1990	4.2	3.9
1995	4.8	3.5
2000	3.3	2.3

Note: The data were accumulated and tabulated by the author.
Source and *Note: China Directory* (Tokyo: Radio Press, 1985, 1990, 1995, and 2000).

who has served as Party Secretary of Xinjiang since 1996. Twenty-four provincial party secretaries (77 percent) and 28 governors (90 percent) were appointed to their current posts within the past five years and are thus serving their first terms. This evidence not only indicates that term limits have been strictly enforced for provincial chiefs, but also suggests the quick mobility (including frequent reshuffling) of top provincial leaders during the Jiang era. The new regulation that requires provincial leaders to be transferred more frequently to another province or the central government seems to be well implemented.

Table 1.7 compares the average year of tenure in the positions of provincial party secretaries and governors. The average number of years served in their positions by the two groups of leaders is shown for four sample years (1985, 1990, 1995, and 2000). They may serve longer terms than these years, but by examining the data over a twenty-year period, we can understand the change in tenure and mobility of China's top provincial leaders during the reform era. The data are exclusively from *China Directory*, which provides complete information about the appointment date of each leader. The table shows that the average year of tenure of China's top provincial leaders in 2000 was the shortest, demonstrating the quick reshuffling of local leaders during the late 1990s. From 1998 to 2001, the central government ordered three major reshufflings of top provincial leaders. A total of 43 provincial party secretaries and governors were transferred or replaced.[30] The table also shows that governors

---

[30]   *Shijie ribao*, March 2, 2001, p. A3.

Table 1.8. *Tenure of Current Positions of Provincial Leaders (September 2002)*

Tenure in Current Post	Provincial Chiefs		Provincial Deputy Leaders		Total	
	No.	%	No.	%	No.	%
1975			1	0.7	1	0.5
1988			1	0.7	1	0.5
1992			2	1.4	2	1.0
1993			11	7.7	11	5.4
1994	2	3.2	5	3.5	7	3.4
1995			7	4.9	7	3.4
1996	2	3.2	15	10.6	17	8.3
1997	6	9.7	9	6.3	15	7.4
1998	12	19.4	38	26.8	50	24.5
1999	9	14.5	12	8.5	21	10.3
2000	10	16.1	9	6.3	19	9.3
2001	14	22.6	26	18.3	40	19.6
2002	7	11.3	6	4.2	13	6.4
Total	62	100.0	142	99.9	204	100.0

Sources: Shen Xueming and Han Honghung, comp., *Zhonggong di shiwujie zhongyang weiyuanhui zhongyang zhongyang jilü jiancha weiyuanhui weiyuan minglu [Who's Who Among the Members of the Fifteenth Central Committee of the Chinese Communist Party and the Fifteenth Central Commission for Discipline Inspection]* (Beijing: Zhonggong wenxian chubanshe, 1999); *China Directory* (Tokyo: Radio Press, various years from 1985 to 2002); and news releases by Xinhua News Agency.

have shorter tenures than party secretaries in every year examined by the study (they are also generally younger).

Table 1.8 shows the length of tenure in 2002 of provincial chiefs and provincial deputy leaders for whom biographical information is available. Once again, none of the 62 provincial chiefs has held his or her current post for more than two terms. Among the 142 provincial deputy leaders under study, only two have served in their current posts for more than two terms.[31] They are Raidi (Deputy Party Secretary of Tibet) and Sang

---

[31] The biographical information of these 142 provincial deputy Party secretaries and vice governors is derived from websites of provincial party organizations or governments. In 2002, of 31 provincial level administrations, only 4 (Beijing, Shanghai, Hunan, and Guangxi) provided biographical information on all deputy Party secretaries and vice governors (or vice mayors); 9 (Tianjin, Liaoning, Jinlin, Heilongjia, Zhejiang, Guangdong, Hainan, Guizhou, and Xinjiang) released the biographical information of all vice governors (or vice mayors); and 2 (Hebei and Jiangxi) supplied the information about deputy Party secretaries).

Gye Gya (Deputy Party Secretary of Qinghai). The former has served in the post since 1975 and the latter since 1988. Both are Tibetans. Their long tenure in these provincial leadership posts is mainly due to the CCP Organization Department's special treatment of minority leaders.

In general, provincial deputy leaders have served in their current posts much longer than provincial chiefs. For instance, 35.8 percent of provincial deputy leaders have held their current posts for more than five years, but this value for provincial chiefs is only 16 percent. This is understandable because central authorities frequently reshuffle party secretaries and governors to prevent the formation of strong province-based factionalism and economic localism.

Age Limits for Retirement

On the basis of either CCP regulations or norms, leaders cannot exceed a certain age limit above a certain level of authority. According to the regulations issued by the politburo in 1997, provincial chiefs should be under the age of 65 and their deputies should not continue to serve after the age of 63.[32] Table 1.9 shows the age distribution of provincial leaders in 2002. None of the sixty-two provincial chiefs are older than 65; thus all have met the age requirement for provincial chiefs.

In 2001, the average age of party secretaries was 58.3 years and the average age of governors was 57.6 years. The average age of all sixty-two provincial chiefs was 58 years. In 2002, 73 percent of these provincial chiefs were in their fifties or younger. Three governors at the time, Li Keqiang (born 1955; Governor of Henan), Xi Jinping (born 1953; Governor of Fujian), and Zhao Leji (born 1957; Governor of Qinghai), were in their forties. Li now serves as Party Secretary of Henan, Xi is Party Secretary of Zhejiang, and Zhao is Party Secretary of Qinghai. In addition to these three individuals, several other provincial chiefs in their forties and early fifties are often seen as leading contenders for the politburo seats in the next Party Congress. They include Shanghai Mayor Han Zheng (born 1953), Jiangsu Party Secretary Li Yuanchao (born 1950), and Fujian Governor Lu Zhangong (born 1952).

---

[32] *Shijie ribao*, February 11, 2001, p. A1. The regulations on the age requirement of retirement for high-ranking military officers were made at the Beidaihe meeting in the summer of 2001. See www.chinesenewsnet.com, August 26, 2001.

Cheng Li

Table 1.9. *Age Distribution of Provincial Leaders (September 2002)*

Age (Birth Year)	Provincial Chiefs		Provincial Deputy Leaders		Total	
	No.	%	No.	%	No.	%
62–64 (1938–1940)	11	17.7	3	2.1	14	6.9
57–61 (1941–1945)	33	53.2	65	45.8	98	48.0
52–56 (1946–1950)	15	24.2	40	28.2	55	27.0
47–51 (1951–1955)	2	3.2	30	21.1	32	15.7
42–46 (1956–1960)	1	1.6	4	2.8	5	2.4
Total	62	99.9	142	100.0	204	100.0

Sources: Shen Xueming and Han Honghung, comp., *Zhonggong di shiwujie zhongyang weiyuanhui zhongyang zhongyang jilü jiancha weiyuanhui weiyuan minglu [Who's Who Among the Members of the Fifteenth Central Committee of the Chinese Communist Party and the Fifteenth Central Commission for Discipline Inspection]* (Beijing: Zhonggong wenxian chubanshe, 1999); *China Directory* (Tokyo: Radio Press, various years from 1985 to 2002); and news releases by Xinhua News Agency.

Not surprisingly, deputy party secretaries and vice governors are generally even younger. Table 1.9 shows that approximately a quarter of them were born in the 1950s. Some rising stars in the provincial leadership were born in the 1960s. They include Vice Mayor of Beijing Lu Hao (born 1968), Vice Mayor of Shanghai Tang Dengjie (born 1964), and Vice Governors of Jiangsu Zhang Taolin (born 1961), Huang Lixin (born 1961), and Huang Wei (born 1961).

Holding provincial leadership positions at a relatively young age is a great political advantage for a leader's future career. Several Standing Committee members on the 16th Politburo, such as Hu Jintao, Wu Bangguo, Wu Guanzheng, Li Changchun, and Luo Gan, were among the small number of "front-runners of the younger generation" who held provincial leadership posts in the 1980s. These promising young provincial leaders are more likely to be assigned to different provinces or bureaucratic sectors in order to gain more leadership experience. In a way, providing national leadership opportunities for young capable provincial officials is a measure adopted by the central authorities to consolidate the power and influence of the central government. Effective implementation of age limits for cadre retirement at the provincial-level leadership contributes to both the fluidity of elite circulation and the dynamic interaction between the national and provincial leaderships.

Regional Representation on the CC of the CCP

Since the mid-1990s, institutional measures and political norms have been established to curtail the growing overrepresentation of certain regions in the central leadership. Table 1.10 displays the distribution of provincial leaders holding full and alternate memberships on the latest two CCs. An institutional norm exists that each province holds two full seats, which was first implemented at the 15th CC in 1997 and was reinforced at the 16th CC in 2002. Although coastal regions are overrepresented on the politburo, full memberships on the CC are evenly distributed with practically absolute strictness across all provincial leaderships. These province-based CC members are usually governors or mayors and party secretaries.

This phenomenon further explains why Jiang transferred his close friend, Chen Zhili, to Beijing, where she took charge of China's educational system just a few days before the 15th Party Congress. Otherwise, she would probably not have been elected to full membership on the 15th CC. Jia Qinglin and Huang Ju were transferred to the central government a few weeks before the 16th Party Congress. With their departures, Executive Vice Mayor of Beijing Meng Xuenong (a protégé of Hu) and Executive Vice Mayor of Shanghai Han Zheng (a Shanghai Gang member) could obtain full CC seats. Otherwise, Meng and Han would probably not have been elected to full membership because of the "one province administration, two full seats" quota that has become a norm in CC elections.

Yunnan in 1997 and Xinjiang and Tibet in 2002 are the only exceptions to this standard. These aberrations may arise from affirmative action by the CCP Organization Department. It is unclear how nominees for alternates are chosen for Congress approval. Some provinces, notably Shandong and Guangdong, have more alternates than others.

The pattern of even distribution of the full memberships on the CC can also be found in China's seven greater military regions, each of which has two representatives in the CC. It is also reported that each province and ministry has one representative on the Commission for Discipline Inspection of the CCP.[33] Hu Angang, an outspoken scholar who studies regional economic development in China, proposed a "one province,

---

[33] Li, *China's Leaders*, pp. 167–8.

Table 1.10. *Provincial Leaders Holding Full or Alternate Memberships on the 15th and 16th CCs*

Province	15th CC (1997)			16th CC (2002)		
	FM	AM	Total	FM	AM	Total
Beijing	2	3	5	2	3	5
Tianjin	2	3	5	2	3	5
Hebei	2	3	5	2	2	4
Shanxi	2	3	5	2	3	5
Neimenggu	2	3	5	2	3	5
Liaoning	2	1	3	2	3	5
Jilin	2	3	5	2	2	4
Heilongjiang	2	3	5	2	3	5
Shanghai	2	2	4	2	2	4
Jiangsu	2	3	5	2	2	4
Shandong	2	4	6	2	5	7
Zhejiang	2	3	5	2	3	5
Anhui	2	2	4	2	3	5
Fujian	2	2	4	2	3	5
Henan	2	3	5	2	2	4
Hubei	2	2	4	2	2	4
Hunan	2	3	5	2	2	4
Jiangxi	2	2	4	2	3	5
Guangdong	2	5	7	2	6	8
Guangxi	2	3	5	2	4	6
Hainan	2	2	4	2	2	4
Sichuan	2	3	5	2	3	5
Chongqing	2	2	4	2	2	4
Guizhou	2	3	5	2	3	5
Yunnan	1	4	5	2	3	5
Xizang (Tibet)	2	2	4	3	2	5
Shaanxi	2	3	5	2	3	5
Gansu	2	2	4	2	3	5
Qinghai	2	2	4	2	2	4
Ningxia	2	2	4	2	2	4
Xinjiang	2	3	5	4	3	7
Total	61	84	145	65	87	152

Note: FM = full member; AM = alternate member.

Source: Cheng Li and Lynn White, "The Sixteenth Central Committee of the Chinese Communist Party: Hu Gets What?" *Asian Survey*, 43 (July/August), p. 576.

one seat" policy for the politburo. His plan would give every province a voice in party policy and reduce the disparity between coastal and inland provinces.[34] Hu is very close to several provincial chiefs in the inland region and is widely known for his disputes with officials in the coastal regions, such as the Party Secretary of Shenzhen. However, the governors in Guizhou and Yunnan have regarded Hu as a hero and publicly expressed their appreciation for his appeal for more balanced regional development in the country.[35]

The equal distribution among provincial governments of full CC seats does not remain static. Top provincial leaders are often reshuffled among regions or promoted to the central administration. Almost immediately after the November 2002 Congress, Wu Guanzheng (Shandong Party Secretary), Li Changchun (Guangdong Party Secretary), Zhang Dejiang (Zhejiang Party Secretary), Zhou Yongkang (Sichuan Party Secretary), Hui Liangyu (Jiangsu Party Secretary), Ji Yunshi (Jiangsu Governor), and Bai Keming (Hainan Party Secretary) were transferred to Beijing or other provinces. This allowed top leaders such as Hu Jintao and Zeng Qinghong to appoint their protégés to important provincial posts, apparently to prepare them for further promotions in the future. For example, Hu's confidant, Zhang Xuezhong, is now Sichuan Party Secretary; and Li Yuanchao, an alternate CC member who is close to both the Shanghai Gang and the CCYL faction, now serves as Jiangsu Party Secretary.

The even distribution of full membership among provincial administrations during the elections of the two most recent CCs is an institutional improvement. Although top national leaders can still attempt to manipulate outcomes before or after voting, they are constrained by rules. Leaders from wealthy coastal provinces dominate the politburo and especially the powerful standing committee, but representatives from inland provinces have a majority on the CC if it comes to a vote. Consequently, an institutional norm or mechanism is created. This Chinese style of checks and

---

[34] Quoted from Wu An-chia, "Leadership Changes at the Fourth Plenum," *Issues and Studies*, 30 (October 1994), p. 134. Hu Angang also argues that the Financial Committee of the National People's Congress, which is responsible for deciding budgetary matters, should consist of 30 members (each province has one representative on the committee). Hu Angang, *Zhongguo fazhan qianjin [Prospects for China's Development]* (Hangzhou: Zhejiang remin chubanshe, 1999), p. 312.

[35] Zhang Xiaoxia, *Zhongguo gaoceng zhinang [China's High-Level Think Tanks]* (Beijing: Jinghua chubanshe, 2000), Vol. 1, pp. 182–3.

balances within the CCP political system may serve to reduce political tensions across the regions, thus contributing to national integration.

The Law of Avoidance and the Regular Reshuffling of Provincial Heads

The Organization Department of the CCP has recently attempted to limit the number of provincial top leaders who work in their native areas. In June 1999, it issued "The Regulation of Cadre Exchange," which specifies the following three rules:

1. County and municipal top leaders should not be selected from the same region.
2. Someone who heads a county or city for more than 10 years should be transferred to another area.
3. Provincial leaders should be transferred more frequently to another province or to the central government.[36]

The implementation of this regulation has varied from region to region. The CCP Committee of Guangdong, for example, recently reinforced the rule that county chiefs in the province cannot be selected from the same county.[37]

With respect to the effort to better control county-level leaders, the central authorities have recently adopted a new training program through the Central Party School (CPS). During the past three years, all the party secretaries in China's over 2,500 counties were required to attend the CPS in Beijing, where everyone received six-month-long political and administrative training.[38] This is the first time in PRC history that comprehensive training at the CPS has been required of county-level leaders. In the past, the county-level leaders usually attended the provincial party schools. This new practice helps the central authorities more conveniently reshuffle and replace county-level leaders.

For provincial-level leadership, more pressure has been brought to bear to restrain the selection of provincial chiefs from the same province. In 2003, only three provincial party secretaries (those in Tianjin, Liaoning,

---

[36] *Liaowang [Outlook]*, June 7, 1999, pp. 15–16.
[37] *Shijie ribao*, November 8, 2001, p. A7.
[38] *Shijie ribao*, August 9, 2000, p. A1.

and Hunan) served in the province in which they were born (there were four in 2000, six in 1999, seven in 1998, and nine in 1997). There is only one province, Hunan, in which both the party secretaries and governors are natives.[39] In addition, a head of the public security bureau (*gonganju*) of a provincial government now must be transferred to another province after working in the province for a few years.[40]

Although a majority of deputy provincial party secretaries and vice governors often work in the provinces in which they were born (as discussed earlier), full provincial party secretaries and full governors are frequently transferred from other provinces. Many current provincial leaders, who often formerly served in their native provinces, move from the level of grass-roots leadership to posts of deputy party secretary or vice governor, and then they are transferred to another province to become party boss or governor (many first served in deputy posts for only a few months before assuming the full posts).

This pattern is observed among many members of the fourth-generation leadership. For example, Du Qinglin, a native of Jilin, and Wang Xiaofeng, a native of Hunan, recently (or currently) served as Party Secretary and Governor of Hainan, respectively. However, prior to their leadership posts in Hainan, Du served as Deputy Party Secretary in Jilin and Wang was the Deputy Party Secretary of Hunan. Both had worked in their native provinces for decades. Du was recently transferred to the central government, where he serves as Minister of Agriculture.

Another example is Qian Yunlu, the newly appointed Party Secretary of Guizhou. He was born in Hubei in 1944, and, after graduating from Hubei University in 1967, he worked in his native province as the party secretary of a people's commune, Deputy Party Secretary in Hanchun County, head of the CCYL in Hubei, Party Secretary of Wuhan city, and Deputy Party Secretary of Hubei before being appointed to his posts in Guizhou (first as deputy party secretary, then as governor, and now as party secretary).

Table 1.11 shows the promotion or transfer patterns of provincial leaders. Nineteen provincial chiefs (30.6 percent) were transferred from other provinces in their most recent career moves, including 8 (12.9 percent)

---

[39] *China News Analysis*, Nos. 1613–14 (July 1–15, 1998), p. 15; and http://www.peopledaily.com.cn, February 24, 2001.
[40] *Shijie ribao*, November 4, 1999, p. A9.

Cheng Li

Table 1.11. *Promotion or Transfer Patterns of Provincial Leaders (September 2002)*

	Provincial Chiefs ($n = 62$)		Provincial Deputy Leaders ($n = 142$)	
Pattern	No.	%	No.	%
Most Recent Post Prior to Current Post				
Transfer from other province				
From secretary to secretary	7	11.3		
From governor to governor	1	1.6		
From governor to secretary	3	4.8		
From deputy to full post	8	12.9		
Promotion from same province				
From governor to secretary	7	11.3		
From deputy to full post	23	37.1		
From lower administrative level	4	6.5		
Transfer from central government				
From minister to party secretary	4	6.5		
From CCP director to party secretary	2	3.2		
From minister to governor	2	3.2		
From deputy minister to governor	1	1.6		
Leadership Experience outside the Province				
In other province(s)	36	58.1	28	19.7
Two provinces	(10)	(16.1)	(4)	(2.8)
Three provinces	(2)	(3.2)		
In central government	21	33.9	11	7.7

Sources: Shen Xueming and Han Honghung, comp., *Zhonggong di shiwujie zhongyang weiyuanhui zhongyáng zhongyang jilü jiancha weiyuan minglu [Who's Who Among the Members of the Fifteenth Central Committee of the Chinese Communist Party and the Fifteenth Central Commission for Discipline Inspection]* (Beijing: Zhonggong wenxian chubanshe, 1999); *China Directory* (Tokyo: Radio Press, various years from 1985 to 2002); and news releases by Xinhua News Agency.

who were promoted from deputy posts to full posts. A large number of provincial chiefs (37.1 percent) were promoted within the same provinces. However, several provincial chiefs who were promoted from the same provinces had recently been transferred from other provinces. For example, in 2002 Song Fatang (Governor of Heilongjiang), Li Keqiang (Governor of Henan), and Shi Xiushi (Governor of Guizhou) were all promoted from the posts of deputy party secretary in the same province, but they were transferred to these deputy posts from other provinces, only a few months earlier. Song now serves as Party Secretary of Heilongjiang, and Li is Party Secretary of Henan.

There were 36 provincial chiefs (58.1 percent) who had any previous service in leadership posts in other provinces, including 12 (19.3 percent) who worked in more than two provinces; 21 provincial chiefs (33.9 percent) worked in the central government or the departments of the Central Committee of the CCP (most as deputy ministers or deputy directors).

Table 1.11 also shows that the percentage of work experiences in other provinces or the central government among provincial deputies is much lower. Only 19.7 percent of provincial deputy leaders previously worked in other provinces and 7.7 percent served leadership posts in the central government. Therefore, approximately three-fourths of provincial deputy leaders have worked exclusively in the same provinces. Although these provincial deputy leaders have worked for a long time in their native regions, they often rotated into different posts or were quickly promoted to higher offices within the province. As discussed earlier, only 2 out of 142 provincial deputy leaders stayed in their current posts beyond two terms.

In addition, the central authorities have also appointed provincial top leaders to the central government in order to restrain local power. For instance, Ye Xuanping, son of the late marshal, Ye Jianying, built a solid power base in Guangdong when he served as the party boss there in the 1980s. The growing economic and cultural autonomy of Guangdong made the central authorities nervous. To prevent the formation of a "Cantonese separatist movement," the central authorities "promoted" Ye to Senior Vice Chair of the Chinese People's Political Consultative Conference. Two non-Cantonese outsiders, Li Changchun and Zhang Dejiang, both serving as politburo members, have consecutively ruled the province since 1998.

Restraints on the Promotion of Princelings

As early as the mid-1980s, especially during Hu Yaobang's tenure as secretary general of the party, the Organization Department of the CC issued orders to limit the appointment of children of high-ranking officials (often called princelings), particularly those princelings whose revolutionary veteran fathers were still alive.[41] Generally, approval of the county, bureau, and prefecture leaders is made on the provincial and ministerial levels (previously, approval by the Organization Department of the CC was required), but the appointment of children of high-ranking officials to these levels of leadership or above must still be confirmed by the Organization Department of the CC.

Although several prominent national and provincial leaders are princelings, their overall representation is not large. Two current Politburo members (Zeng Qinghong and Yu Zhengsheng) have princeling backgrounds. The number of these CCP aristocrats on the previous Politburo was four (Jiang Zemin, Li Peng, Li Tieying, and Zeng Qinghong). The number of princelings on the 2002 CC is seventeen (5 percent), and the same number was on the 1997 CC.[42] As new leaders move into the highest level of authority, the princeling background that previously enabled them to succeed may become a liability. Delegates to the Congress, as the ballot tallies show, have increasingly prevented princelings and others very close to top leaders from receiving many votes.

At the 15th Party Congress, many princelings were among the 5 percent of candidates who were defeated. They included Chen Yuan, Wang Jun, and Bo Xilai. Among the ten elected alternate members receiving the lowest number of votes, five were princelings, including Deng Pufang (son of Deng Xiaoping), who received the next-to-last number of votes. At the 16th Party Congress, Jiang's bodyguard, You Xigui, received the lowest number of votes for election as an alternate on the CC. Jiang's former mishu and then Party Secretary in Shenzhen, Huang Liman, received the third-lowest number of votes. You and Huang obtained alternate seats on the CC, but their low votes were an embarrassment, not only for them but also for Jiang. Furthermore, Jiang Zemin's sister and son failed to obtain seats on the 16th CC. Jiang's close ally, former Shanghai Deputy Party Secretary and former Minister of Education, Chen Zhili, failed to obtain a seat on the Politburo. Chen was indeed promoted to become a

---

[41] Xiao Chong, *Zhonggong disidai mengren [The Fourth Generation of Leaders of the Chinese Communist Party]* (Hong Kong: Xiafeier Guoji Chubangongsi, 1998), p. 335.

[42] The princelings on the 16th CC are Zeng Qinghong, Yu Zhengsheng, Dai Bingguo, Liu Yandong, Liao Hui, Zhou Xiaochuan, Hong Hu, Bo Xilai, Xi Jinping, Li Yuanchao, Wang Qishan, Tian Chengping, Bai Keming, Deng Pufang, Chen Yuan, Wang Ruolin, and Li Tielin. For a list of the princelings on the 1997 CC, see Li and White, "The Fifteenth Central Committee of the Chinese Communist Party," p. 259.

state councilor, but she got the lowest number of votes in the state council election at the 10th NPC.

This does not necessarily mean that political nepotism is unimportant in Chinese elite recruitment today. Some princelings who failed to be elected to the 15th CC in 1997 obtained CC seats five years later at the 16th Party Congress. Examples include Bo Xilai (Governor of Liaoning) and Chen Yuan (President of China Development Bank). The total number of princelings and members of the Shanghai Gang in the central leadership may not be high, but numbers alone are not indicative of the true concentration of power. Some of the most important leadership posts are occupied by Jiang's confidants. The most recent example is the appointment of Zeng Qinghong as Vice President of the PRC.

However, Zeng's prominence in the Chinese leadership is only partially due to his princeling background, mishu experience, and Shanghai connections. Talent, competence, vision, and interpersonal skills have become increasingly important while institutional restraints on all sorts of nepotism have been implemented.[43] Jiang, Zeng, and their associates cultivated a web of personal ties based on Shanghai connections and various other forms of nepotism, and so have other factions in the Chinese leadership. Every new leader, regardless of background, must deal with elections, public opinion, coalition building and power sharing.

CONCLUSIONS AND IMPLICATIONS

What do the data and analyses tell us about the real nature of the new leadership? What are the implications for Chinese politics in the future? Elite recruitment and national personnel management in the reform era are fascinating, because of its diversity and the seemingly contradictory trends that exist. In terms of the geographical distribution of elites, the following six patterns are particularly noticeable.

- First, the top leadership positions in China's provinces and major cities have become the most important stepping stones to national political offices in the country. Provincial leaders' political advancement was partially due to favoritism and political networking, partially the result

[43] For a further discussion of Zeng Qinghong and his political "craftsmanship," see Li, *China's Leaders*, pp. 159–64.

of the growing importance of provincial-level administrations in Chinese politics, and partially the central government's effort to better rule the whole country with career incentives for capable and ambitious provincial leaders.

- The second pattern is the higher representation of the Eastern China provinces, such as Jiangsu and Shandong, at the expense of the South and Southwestern China provinces, such as Guangdong and Sichuan.
- The third trend is the higher percentage of overall provincial and municipal leaders who serve in their native areas. This reflects the rise of localism in elite recruitment, which is reinforced by the erosion of the Chinese nomenklatura system and the ongoing local elections.
- Fourth, partially offsetting the previous trend is the central authorities' frequent reshuffling of the *top* provincial leaders in order to consolidate the power of the central government or to serve the interests of factional politics. Moreover, in recent years, the central authorities have adopted more restrictive rules to limit the practice whereby provincial party secretaries and governors are selected from their native provinces. The central authorities have also required all county party secretaries to receive training at the CPS so that they can more conveniently control elite mobility and replacement at the county level.
- The fifth trend is that there are now more diversified channels through which new leaders can advance their political careers. Nepotism and favoritism in various forms, such as blood ties, mishu, and tongxiang (especially in the case of the Shanghai Gang), play a pivotal role in elite promotion. Nevertheless, new leaders are far more interested than their predecessors in seeking legitimacy through institutional channels.
- Last but not least, there is a strong effort, even among the political establishment, to restrict nepotism, favoritism, and localism in elite recruitment. Delegates in both the Party Congress and the NPC have increasingly used their votes to prevent both princelings and those favored by top leaders from being elected. In addition, full membership seats on the CC of the CCP, for example, are more evenly distributed among provinces.

These trends in the geographical distribution of elites are closely related to crucial political issues that China faced at the turn of this century, including the growing economic disparity between coastal and inland regions, the need for both regional autonomy and national unity, and the tension between the demand for regional representation and restraint on the rise of localism. What is presently most evident in Chinese elite politics is the broad shift from an all-powerful single leader such as Mao or Deng to the greater collective leadership characteristic of the Jiang era. It seems highly likely that post-Jiang leaders, because of both institutional restraints and their own limitations, will rely more on power sharing, negotiation, consultation, and consensus building than their predecessors did.

The trends in elite recruitment discussed in this chapter are divergent and sometimes seemingly contradictory. The current state of China's reform process is truly extraordinary, because problems in national and regional personnel management are often acknowledged, conflicts of interest in central–local relations and tensions between regions are recognized, and elite groups and the general public are constantly seeking the best possible equilibrium between national integration and local autonomy. This trend may very well signify one of the most promising aspects of China's unfolding transformation.

2

The Institutionalization of Elite Management in China

Zhiyue Bo

Since the late 1980s, the Chinese Communist Party (CCP) has weathered a series of crises but continues to dominate the Chinese political scene. Although the CCP has laid out rules and procedures over the past decade to govern its own activities and to clarify its relationship with other political institutions, this process of institutionalization remains partial and very much incomplete. Moreover, the party's willingness to submit itself to binding rules may ultimately conflict with its mission to guide and transform all of society. However, the CCP's ability to initiate a process of institutionalization has been a key source of its political resilience since the early 1990s. The strength of the CCP, in turn, has been an important factor contributing to national stability and unity.

Because Chinese politics has long been regarded as essentially informal,[1] much attention has been devoted to how extrainstitutional factors, such as a certain political figure or a network of politicians, exert decisive

---

[1] The University of California at Berkeley had a project on informal politics in East Asia in the 1990s, of which China was a major focus. The March 1996 issue of *Asian Survey* was a special issue on the subject. For the literature on informal politics in China in the 1990s, see, for instance, Lowell Dittmer and Lü Xiaobo, "Personal Politics in the Chinese *Danwei* under Reform," *Asian Survey*, 36 (March 1996), pp. 246–67; Lowell Dittmer, "Chinese Informal Politics," *The China Journal*, No. 34 (July 1995), pp. 1–34; Lowell Dittmer, "Chinese Informal Politics Reconsidered," *The China Journal*, No. 34 (July 1995), pp. 193–205; and Lowell Dittmer and Yu-shan Wu, "The Modernization of Factionalism in Chinese Politics," *World Politics*, 47 (July 1995), pp. 467–94. For an alternative (i.e., institutional) approach to Chinese politics, see Kenneth Lieberthal and Michel Oksenberg, *Policy Making in China: Leaders, Structures, and Processes* (Princeton, NJ: Princeton University Press, 1992); Susan L. Shirk, *Political Logic of Economic Reform in China* (Berkeley, CA: University of California Press, 1993); Yasheng Huang, *Inflation and Investment Controls in China* (New York: Cambridge University Press,

influence on Chinese politics. An analysis of formal institutions, with a few exceptions, has largely been neglected. Consequently, even though China's economic achievements in the past two and a half decades have been widely acknowledged, the development of political institutions during the same period has not been fully analyzed. Yet these political institutions are an integral part of Chinese politics, and the substantial changes undergone by Chinese political institutions are a reflection of the broader political shifts within China itself. In the history of the People's Republic of China, leaders have used institutions to achieve very different political objectives. Mao Zedong created and destroyed political institutions for the sake of ideology. Deng Xiaoping initiated institutionalization, but in a noninstitutional way, to further economic growth. Jiang Zemin has continued institutionalization through institutional channels to maintain growth and stability.

This chapter examines a major development in Chinese politics: In spite of its adaptations to accommodate the expansion of the power and autonomy of the people's congresses and the executive branch of the political system (i.e., the government), the Communist Party continues to dominate the processes of elite recruitment and management. Much of this chapter discusses how the party has institutionalized the procedures for elite recruitment and promotions for senior-level cadres and how the institutionalization has helped the party to retain its hold on power in China. In particular, systematic data are offered to discuss the transfer of officials and how such transfers have provided leverage to the central leadership.

CHINESE POLITICAL STRUCTURE

The Chinese political structure is composed of several partially independent, but interlocking, hierarchical systems. This chapter focuses on three of these hierarchies: the Communist Party, the government, and the people's congresses.[2] Of the three systems, the CCP system is the most

---

1996); and Zhiyue Bo, *Chinese Provincial Leaders: Economic Performance and Political Mobility Since 1949* (Armonk, NY: Sharpe, 2002).

[2] The other two important hierarchies, not dealt with in this chapter, are the military and the judicial systems. Although Chinese leaders have repeatedly emphasized that

hierarchically organized. Although, in theory, deputies to the local CCP congress elect members of the local party committee, in practice the party committee of the next higher level controls the personnel of the local party committee. The party committee of the next higher level may transfer or appoint the responsible person of the party committee of the next lower level, as it deems necessary.[3] For example, Zhang Quanjing, the Director of the Central Organization Department at the time, simply flew to Heilongjiang province in July of 1997 with a candidate from the central government and announced the appointment of this central leader as the party secretary of the province. Clearly, within the CCP system, superior organs can and do exercise direct authority over subordinate organs, and party members are required to observe "party discipline."

The government system is less hierarchically organized, though there is also a leader-led relationship between a higher level and a lower level. According to the Constitution of the People's Republic of China (1982), the executive organs of all provincial units are under the leadership of the State Council. Moreover, local governments lead the governments at lower levels (cf. Figure 6.2, page 202). A local government is answerable to both the executive organ of the next higher level and to the local people's congress in its own region (Article 110).

The congressional system is the least hierarchically organized. According to law, as Peng Zhen, then a standing committee of the National People's Congress vice chairman, explained, the people's congress standing committee at any level is accountable to its people's congress. A higher-level people's congress standing committee may step up its efforts to communicate with the standing committee of a lower level, but there is no leader-led relationship between them.[4] Provincial people's congresses, as the legislative branch of provincial authority, can make local laws within the framework of the constitution and national laws.

China would not adopt a system of checks and balances as in the West, there are in fact identifiably separate executive, legislative, and judicial branches in China.

[3]   Articles 13, 26 and 27, the Constitution of the CCP (1992), *Dangnei Faqui*, p. 15.

[4]   Peng Zhen, "Guanyu Difang Renda Changweihui de Gongzuo (April 18, 1980)" ["On the Work of the Standing Committee of the Local People's Congress"], in Quan-guo Renda Changweihui Bangongting Yanjushi, ed., *Zhonghuarenmingongheguo Ren-mindaibiaodahui Wenxianziliao Huibian, 1949–1990 [The Collection of Materials and Documents of the National People's Congress of the People's Republic of China, 1949–1990]* (hereafter *Renda Wenxian*) (Beijing: Zhongguo Minzhufazhi Chubanshe, 1990), p. 581.

On the surface, the reform era has witnessed much in the articulation and differentiation of formal political institutions. The CCP hierarchy has been more clearly separated from the government hierarchy, and the party secretary is no longer the concurrent head of the government. Moreover, government leaders are separate from congressional leaders.[5] In statutory terms, the local people's congress enjoys tremendous powers in the area of elite recruitment and management. According to the Organic Law of the Local People's Congresses and Local Governments, first enacted in 1979 and later amended thrice,[6] local congressional leaders, local government leaders, and local court and procuratorate leaders are all elected or ratified by the local People's Congress.

These formal powers notwithstanding, the reality is that the CCP continues to dominate the government and People's Congress hierarchies through its control of the personnel process. The CCP has done so by invoking the principle that the party controls the cadres (*dang guan ganbu*).[7] However, recent reassertions of this principle have been a response to the institutional changes of the past decades. They are also an indication that the CCP is adapting itself to the growing influence of people's congresses at various levels.[8] Indeed, conflicts between the CCP and the legislative institutions can be linked to the uneasy coexistence of party control with laws that have invested a great deal of appointive power in the people's congresses.

---

[5] According to Article 36 of the Organic Law of the Local People's Congresses and Local People's Governments of the People's Republic of China, members of the Standing Committee of the local People's Congress at the county level and above should not assume any positions in the local people's government or local judicial organ, unless they resign their positions in the standing committee. See *Renda Wenxian*, p. 296.

[6] The third revision was passed at the 12th Session of the Standing Committee of the National People's Congress on February 28, 1995 (for a complete text in Chinese, see http://www.peopledaily.com.cn/item/flfgk/rdlf/1995/111201199512.html).

[7] See Melanie Manion, "The Cadre Management System, Post-Mao: The Appointment, Promotion, Transfer and Removal of Party and State Leaders," *The China Quarterly*, No. 102 (June 1985), pp. 203–33; and Hong Yung Lee, *From Revolutionary Cadres to Party Technocrats in Socialist China* (Berkeley, CA: University of California Press, 1991), especially Chapter 14.

[8] The Organization Department of the CCP, for instance, was resistant to establishing a civil service system, because this was regarded as undermining the principle that the CCP controls cadres. See Yan Huai, "Establishing a Public Service System," in Carol Lee Hamrin and Suisheng Zhao, eds., *Decision-Making in Deng's China: Perspectives from Insiders* (Almonk, NY: Sharpe, 1995), pp. 169–75.

In the early 1980s, when the local people's congresses and their standing committees started to exercise their constitutional authority over cadre selection and appointment, local party leaders accused congressional leaders of challenging the leadership of the party committees. Some local party committees simply ignored local people's congresses and their standing committees and announced the appointments of congressional and government leaders in the name of the party committees. In response to this dispute, Peng Zhen, then a standing committee of the National People's Congress vice chairman, asserted that the law was more important than any party committee or party secretary. According to Peng, "No matter at what level the party committee is, no matter who is the responsible person, if his opinion is different from law, then it is his own personal opinion. Everyone should obey the law."[9] What makes people's congresses a potential challenger to the monopoly of the CCP is the fact that people's congresses possess unique structural resources[10]: They are legitimate organs of state power as guaranteed by the constitution.

MAINTAINING CONTROL WHILE FOLLOWING
LEGAL PROCEDURES

Within this structural context, the party's response has been to attempt to maintain its real authority by working within the framework of the new constitutionalist rules. On September 8, 1983, the party's Organization

[9] Peng Zhen, in *Renda Wenxian*, p. 581.

[10] According to Kevin O'Brien, deputies to people's congresses are agents and remonstrators: They represent the government and the party in terms of policies, and they make suggestions to the government and the CCP on behalf of the masses [see his article, "Agents and Remonstrators: Role Accumulation by Chinese People's Congress Deputies," *China Quarterly*, No. 138 (June 1994), pp. 359–80]. According to Ming Xia, provincial People's Congresses are trying to expand their power through network building [see his article, "Political Contestation and the Emergence of the Provincial People's Congresses as Power Players in Chinese Politics: A Network Explanation," *Journal of Contemporary China*, 9 (July 2000), pp. 185–214]. Their research has advanced our understanding of the role of the deputies and the provincial people's congresses in Chinese politics. Nevertheless, this author is more concerned with structural relationship between the CCP and People's Congresses. Although the CCP still has the monopoly of power and organizational resources, people's congresses possess greater structural advantages. For more detailed discussions of the structural relationship between the party and provincial people's congresses in other areas, see Zhiyue Bo, "Governing China in the early 21st Century: A Provincial Perspective," *Journal of Chinese Political Science*, 2, Nos. 1–2 (2002), pp. 125–170.

Department issued a circular that instructed local party committees to "follow legal procedures." It reminded local party leaders that, according to the CCP Constitution, the CCP should operate within the framework of the State Constitution and the law.[11] This message was reiterated in another circular issued in the name of the CCP Central Committee about half a year later. According to this circular, local government leaders were to be elected or appointed by the local People's Congress or its standing committee, not by the local party committee. Deputies of the local People's Congress or members of the standing committee had the legal right to disagree with the local party committee over candidates.[12]

Yet these documents were not designed for the party to abdicate its leading role. Instead they offered detailed guidelines on how party leaders could strictly follow legal procedures while retaining their influence in elite management. According to the Organization Department circular, local party committees should study organic laws, especially the Organic Law of Local People's Congresses and Local People's Governments, and follow relevant procedures. After a local party committee has reviewed and screened a candidate for a certain post, it should use the phrase "(the party committee) agreed to nominate some comrade for some post" and send the recommendation either to the local People's Congress for election or to the standing committee of the local People's Congress or the local people's government for decision. The party committee should not make the appointment in its own name, nor should it announce the appointment in the newspaper or on the radio. Instead, the party should operate behind the scenes through its various organizations. For example, the results of the party committee's review should be passed on to the party group of the relevant standing committee of the local People's

---

[11] "Zhonggong Zhongyang Zuzhibu Guanyu Renmian Guojia Jiguan he Qita Xingzheng Lingdao Zhiwu Bixu Anzhao Falü Chengxu he Youguan Guiding Banli de Tongzhi (September 8, 1983)," ["The Department of Organization's Circular on Strictly Following Legal Procedures and Relevant Regulations in Appointment and Removal of Government and Other Administrative Leaders"], in Zhongyang Bangongting Faguishi, Zhongyang Jiwei Faguishi, and Zhongyang Zuzhibu, eds., *Zhongguo Gongchandang Dangnei Fagui Xuanbian, 1978–1996 [Laws and Regulations of the Chinese Communist Party,1978–1996]* (hereafter *Dangnei Fagui*) (Beijing: Falü Chubanshe, 1996), pp. 334–6.

[12] "Zhonggong Zhongyang Guanyu Renmian Guojia Jiguan Lingdao Renyuan Bixu Yange Yizhao Falü Chengxu Banli de Tongzhi (April 26, 1984)," ["The Central Committee's Circular on Strictly Following Legal Procedures in Appointment and Removal of Government Leaders"], in *Dangnei Fagui*, pp. 332–3.

Table 2.1. *Party Secretaries as Chairmen of the CP PPC*
(1983–2003)

Secretaries	1983	1988	1993	2000	2003
No. as chairmen	2	1	10	11	22
Total No.	29	30	30	31	31
% as chairmen	6.90	3.33	33.33	35.48	70.97

Source: Author's database.

Congress or the party group of the relevant government. They should not be disseminated to lower levels in the form of internal CCP documents. Similar treatment should occur in the appointment of administrative leaders of enterprises and offices, whereby the party committee should consult with the administrative leader in charge of the enterprise or office, make a decision collectively, and announce the appointment or removal in the name of the administrative leader. Again, the party committee should not issue the announcement in its name.[13]

Besides the formal injunctions to operate behind the scenes in making key personnel appointments, the party leadership has also developed other mechanisms to check the power of people's congresses. One important development is for party secretaries to serve concurrently as chairmen of people's congresses and thus directly guide these legislative institutions (Table 2.1). In 1983, only two out of twenty-nine party secretaries were concurrently chairmen of their respective provincial people's congresses (Xu Jiatun of Jiangsu and Xiang Nan of Fujian), and this declined to only one out of thirty (Sun Weiben of Heilongjiang) in 1988. The trend reversed in the 1990s, however, and the number of party secretaries who had taken on the chairmanship of their respective provincial people's congresses reached ten out of thirty in 1993, and by January 2003, the number was twenty-two out of thirty-one (over 70 percent).[14] In this way,

---

[13] "Zhonggong Zhongyang Zuzhibu Guanyu Renmian Guojia Jiguan he Qita Xingzheng Lingdao Zhiwu Bixu Anzhao Falü Chengxu he Youguan Guiding Banli de Tongzhi (September 8, 1983)," ["The Department of Organization's Circular on Strictly Following Legal Procedures and Relevant Regulations in Appointment and Removal of Government and Other Administrative Leaders"], in *Dangnei Fagui*, pp. 334–6.

[14] On line (http://www.peopledaily.com.cn/GB/shizheng/252/9667/9684/20021126/874879.html), accessed on January 30, 2003. This web page is being updated constantly as a result of leadership changes at the provincial level. Noticeably, among the remaining nine party secretaries, six of them (Liu Qi, Zhang Lichang, Chen Liangyu, Yu Zhengsheng, Zhang Dejiang, and Wang Lequan) are currently politburo members.

provincial party committees have assumed direct control of provincial people's congresses. Thus, these party secretaries are empowered to make personnel recommendations and then steer the appointments through the legislatures. At the national level, the recommendations for appointments are usually hammered out in the party congresses that precede full sessions of the National People's Congress, a pattern that has held since the late 1970s.

THE INSTITUTIONALIZATION OF ELITE MANAGEMENT UNDER JIANG ZEMIN

The CCP's 14th Congress held in October 1992 represented the beginning of the post-Deng era. Paramount leader Deng Xiaoping had already officially retired from politics. The Central Advisory Commission, the so-called "Sitting Committee,"[15] filled with elderly veteran leaders, was formally abolished. The new regime under Jiang Zemin made efforts to restore the authority of the party center and to strengthen the local party committee's control over elite management. To regularize the party's involvement in elite management, the Party Central Committee in 1995 issued a document entitled "Interim Regulations on Selection and Appointment of Party and Government Leading Cadres."[16] These

---

[15] I thank Dorothy Solinger for alerting me to this usage. For the same usage in print, see Richard Baum, "The Road to Tiananmen: Chinese Politics in the 1980s," in Roderick MacFarquhar, ed., *The Politics of China: The Eras of Mao and Deng* (New York: Cambridge University Press, 1997), p. 343.

[16] *People's Daily*, May 17, 1995, pp. 1 and 3 (Hereafter *The 1995 Regulation*). It should be noted that this document had been issued to the party committees of Provinces, Autonomous Regions, and Centrally Administered Municipalities as well as those of similar ranks as an internal document only three months earlier (February 9, 1995) before it was published in the *People's Daily*. It is a document issued by the Central Committee of the Chinese Communist Party instead of its Organization Department (*Zhongfa* instead of *Zhongzufa*), although the Organization Department is responsible for its interpretation. For English translation of this document along with other relevant materials, see Zhiyue Bo, ed., "Selection and Appointment of Leading Cadres in Post-Deng China," *Chinese Law and Government*, 32 (January–February 1999). After trials of seven years, the document was updated and released as "Regulation on Selection and Appointment of Party and Government Leading Cadres" in July 2002. This chapter is based mainly on the 1995 version with references to significant changes in the 2002 edition. For the complete text of the 2002 edition in Chinese, see Xin Hua, ed., *"Dangzheng Lingdaoganbu Xuanbarenyong Gongzuotiaoli" Xuexicailiao [Study Materials of "Regulation on Selection and Appointment of Party and Government Leading Cadres"]* (Beijing: Xinhua chubanshe, 2002), pp. 5–33.

regulations included procedures with regard to appointment, transfer, and demotion of cadres ranked at the county level or above. Cadres covered include those of the CCP; the government; standing committees of people's congresses; political consultative conferences; commissions for discipline inspection; courts; and procuratorates.[17] In other words, the document covers more than 400,000 cadres in China who are ranked at the level of deputy county head (division chief) or above.[18]

The Nomination Process

According to the 1995 regulations, the selection of political elites consists of four basic steps, which the party dominates before the formal legal elections or appointment procedures begin. These steps are democratic recommendation, screening, deliberation, and discussion and decision. It still is the primary responsibility of the party committee of the same level or the organization department of a next higher level to recommend a candidate for a post. Only designated elites are allowed to participate in this democratic recommendation process. They include:

(1) standing members of the party committee;
(2) leaders or party group members of people's congresses, the government, and political consultative conferences;
(3) leading members of commissions for discipline inspection;
(4) leaders of people's courts, people's procuratorates, departments of the party committee, departments of the government, and people's organizations;
(5) leaders of the party and the government of a lower level; and
(6) others as necessary. When candidates are sought for positions in people's congresses, the government, and political consultative conferences, leading members of democratic parties and nonparty

---

[17] *The 1995 Regulation*, Article 4. For a list of names of the units and positions of their leaders, see John P. Burns, "Strengthening Central CCP Control of Leadership Selection: The 1990 Nomenklatura," *China Quarterly* 138 (June 1994), pp. 458–91; see especially Appendix 1, pp. 479–80. One significant difference between the 1995 and 2002 editions is that the regulation in the 1995 edition applies to leaders in the departments of all these institutions but serves as a reference for leaders of the internal organs of these departments, whereas the regulation in the 2002 edition applies to both directly.

[18] Jiang Zemin, "Nuli Jianshe Gaosuzhi de Ganbu Duiwu" ["Strive to Foster a Contingent of Highly Qualified Cadres "], *People's Daily*, June 21, 1996, p. 1. For English translation, see Bo, "Selection and Appointment of Leading Cadres in Post-Deng China," pp. 84–98.

representatives should be invited.[19] Clearly, the concept of "democracy" here is limited to political elites and their immediate subordinates, because the masses are excluded from this process.

In addition, the party committee can delimit the pool of potential candidates. If a governor's position was vacant, for instance, the party committee would advise potential nominators that a candidate should be selected from the pool of vice governors with at least two years of experience in their positions. The party committee would solicit recommendations in one of three ways: meetings, individual talks, and written recommendations. The party committee of the same level, or the organization department of a higher level, would sum up the recommendations and write a report to the party committee of a higher level. If a leading cadre makes recommendations as an individual, that cadre should present recommendation materials in his or her name. The nominee may be listed as a candidate if the nominee is supported by the masses of his or her work unit.[20]

The organization (personnel) department is responsible for screening candidates, normally by dispatching a screening team with at least two members for each post.[21] The team screens a candidate in terms of virtues, abilities, diligence, and achievements. To gather information, the screening team may have private meetings with relevant individuals, solicit evaluations or conduct public opinion polls, carry out special investigations, and interview the candidate. Private meetings are regarded as the most effective way of gathering information. Article 20 of the 1995 regulations is devoted entirely to the scope of private meetings.[22] This reflects an official recognition that, in public, people tend to play artificial roles according to what is required by their positions in society, but they can be quite honest in private.[23] The written materials of the screening,

---

[19] *The 1995 Regulation*, Article 10.
[20] Ibid., Articles 11 and 14.
[21] Ibid., Article 23.
[22] It is split into two articles, Articles 23 and 24, in the 2002 edition.
[23] For an excellent discussion of this issue, see Pior Sztompka, "The Intangibles and Imponderables of the Transition to Democracy," *Studies in Comparative Communism*, 24 (September 1991), pp. 295–311. At a January meeting of the Wuhan People's Congress, Party Secretary Chen Xunqiu suggested that TV reporters present not film the meeting. He believed that deputies to the meeting might not dare to tell the truth if filmed. The incident became controversial on *People's Daily*'s website. Some supported Chen's action, but others disagreed with him. For the debate, see http://www.peopledaily.com.cn/GB/guandian/30/20030116/908618.html; http://www.peopledaily.com.cn/GB/guandian/

including the candidate's achievements and shortcomings, along with the results of democratic recommendation or opinion polls, are kept in the candidate's dossier.[24]

Drawing on the information gathered, the screening team reports to the Organization (personnel) Department, which in turn reports to the party committee.[25] Before the names are presented to the higher-up party committee, however, the list of candidates for party and government leading cadre positions must be vetted through a process of deliberation. The participants of the deliberation include:

(1) leading members of the party committee of the same level;
(2) chief leading members of the People's Congress, government, and Political Consultative Conference of the same level; and
(3) chief leading members of democratic parties and nonparty representatives, if candidates are from outside the party.[26]

Finally, whether a candidate is chosen for the particular appointment or recommendation is decided through collective discussions by the party committee. If a position is under the jurisdiction of the party committee of the next higher level, the party committee of this level may make suggestions regarding the selection. In the 2002 edition of the regulations, a new article regarding the chief positions of the municipal (prefectural) and county (city) party committee and government was introduced. According to this new article (Article 33), candidates for these positions are to be nominated by the Standing Committee of the party committee of the next higher level. These candidates are then reviewed and decided on by the plenum of the party committee of this level through a secret ballot. When the party committee is not in session, the Standing Committee of the party committee of this level may review and decide who will fill said positions, but only with prior consultation among all members

---

183/2181/2977/20030116/908963.html; http://www.peopledaily.com.cn/GB/guandian/
183/2181/2977/20030116/908907.html; http://www.peopledaily.com.cn/GB/guandian/
183/2181/2977/20030116/909310.html.

[24] *The 1995 Regulation*, Articles 22, 27, and 30. Article 21 of the 1995 edition was deleted from the 2002 edition because it is about democratic evaluation, not directly related to screening.

[25] Ibid., Articles 16–23.

[26] Ibid., Article 24. In the 2002 edition, these specifications are replaced with a general statement that proper deliberation should be conducted according to posts and candidates.

of the party committee. This measure seems designed to enhance the power of the party committee, and thus promote intra-party democracy with respect to these positions. A candidate is chosen if he or she receives the endorsement of more than half of the quorum (two-thirds of party committee members).[27]

The CCP has to coordinate with the people's congresses for elite appointment and removal because people's congresses in China are legal channels through which leading cadres are elected (selected) and appointed, and on various occasions the congresses have shown that they are no longer simply a rubber stamp. The regulations stipulate that the party committee should explain why a candidate is being nominated for the designated position in a recommendation letter to the Presidium of the People's Congress. In addition, the party committee is instructed to consult with responsible people of democratic parties and nonparty representatives regarding candidates for party and government leading positions.[28]

Qualifications for Getting Ahead

The 1995 regulation also laid out seven specific qualifications for the candidates vying for a position at the county level and above.[29] First, for leading positions at the county (or division) level, candidates should have at least five years of work experience, including at least two years in grass-roots units. Second, for leading positions above the county level, candidates should have experience in at least two different lower level positions.

---

[27] The 2002 edition specified several ways of making a decision: oral, raising hands, and secret ballots.

[28] Ibid., Articles 32–37.

[29] The regulations also specified six general boilerplate "requirements" for elites: (1) A good understanding of Marxism, Leninism, and Mao Zedong thought; mastery of the theory of building socialism with Chinese characteristics, and an attempt to use Marxism to solve practical problems (the 2002 edition added "three represents" here). (2) Following the basic line of the Party and implementing its policies; working hard to make solid achievements in the socialist construction and reform and opening. (3) Seeking the truth from facts and applying the guidelines and policies of the party to the realities of one's locality or department. (4) Practical experience, education, and special knowledge. (5) Using the power entrusted by the people conscientiously, being upright and clean, and serving the people; following the mass line; and opposing bureaucratism and misuse of power. (6) Being good at uniting comrades, including those of different opinions. See *The 1995 Regulation*, Article 6.

Third, for promotions at the deputy county head level and above, candidates should have at least two years of experience in deputy positions before they can be promoted to chief positions; and they should have at least three years of experience in chief positions at a lower level before they can be promoted to deputy positions at the next higher level. Fourth, all candidates should have at least a technical college (*da zhuan*) education, and candidates for provincial (or ministerial)-level positions should have at least a college education.[30] Fifth, these candidates should receive at least three months of training at party schools, colleges of administration, or other training institutes.[31] Sixth, they should be healthy. Finally, candidates for party positions should also have a minimum tenure in the CCP (e.g., five years for a provincial party chief).[32] Moreover, promotions should be one grade at a time, though in exceptional circumstances outstanding young and middle-aged candidates may be promoted by more than one grade at a time, as are candidates whose unique skillset is demanded by the job description.[33]

Discipline and Monitoring

These requirements are based on the premise that the CCP possesses a monopoly over cadre appointment and promotion processes. It has a vision of the well-regulated hierarchical order from the perspective of the center. To ensure compliance with the institutionalized process of elite management, the 1995 regulations also included a set of ground rules in the form of "Ten No Permits."[34] According to these regulations, it is forbidden to:

> (1) substitute personal endorsement for the party committee's collective discussion and decision regarding appointments and removals;

[30] The 2002 edition revised it into district (or ting) or department (or bureau) level positions.
[31] The 2002 edition specified it to be cumulatively three months within five years. If for some reason this is not done before promotion, it should be done within a year after promotion.
[32] *The 1995 Regulation*, Article 7. See Article 26, "The Constitution of the Communist Party of China (1992)," in *Dangnei Fagui*, p. 15.
[33] *The 1995 Regulation*, Article 8.
[34] The Ministry of Personnel stipulated "Six No Permits" in its "Temporary Regulation for the Promotion and Demotion of Public Servants," which were very similar to "Ten No Permits" here. See *Wen Wei Po* (Hong Kong), March 2, 1996.

(2) put forward extemporaneous motions regarding appointments and removals;

(3) individually decide appointment or removal;

(4) refuse to carry out the decision of a higher authority on personnel matters;

(5) request the promotion of a relative, or of a secretary or other close associate;

(6) disclose information regarding personnel discussions;

(7) rush through promotions or intervene in hometown personnel decisions;

(8) violate party rules during elections;

(9) hide or distort facts during cadre screening; and

(10) barter or sell promotions, or retaliate against individuals by withholding promotions.[35]

To enforce these rules, the CCP Organization Department issued another document to specify how the violators would be penalized. In this document, "Measures on Violations of 'Temporary Regulation on Selection and Appointment of Party and Government Leading Cadres'" (July 15, 1997),[36] specific measures were introduced to deal with the violations of each of the "Ten No Permits" rules. The creation of these measures to enforce discipline illustrates how the CCP is further regularizing and institutionalizing the process of elite management.

PARTY CONTROL AND THE MANAGEMENT OF ELITE MOBILITY

The institutionalization of the procedures for elite management has not dented the party's dominance of elite management; it was, in fact, designed to reinforce the party's dominance over transfers, resignations, and demotions. Although the procedures appear to be designed to curb the arbitrariness of individual leaders, they also provide a set of systematic

---

[35] *The 1995 Regulation*, Article 47. The 2002 edition added one item that states, "It is not permitted to hire more leading cadres than posts, or upgrade ranks of the leading cadres against relevant regulations." The total number of no permits remains ten in the 2002 edition because it incorporates Item 6 into Item 9.

[36] The document was published in the *People's Daily*, July 15, 1997, p. 3. For an English translation, see Bo, "Selection and Appointment of Leading Cadres in Post-Deng China," pp. 66–70.

institutions for central leaders to elicit local compliance and govern this vast and complex society.

The Rule of Avoidance and Conflict of Interest

The rules about candidate qualifications are combined with the avoidance rule. Although avoidance was mentioned prior to 1995,[37] the 1995 regulations attempted to establish a system of avoidance (*huibi zhidu*) for leading party and government cadres. The most familiar kind of avoidance is that related to one's place of origin. The 1995 regulations specified the avoidance of hometowns in the selection and appointment of party secretaries of counties (or county-level cities) and city heads (or county-level mayors). If they are elected in their hometowns, then they must be transferred elsewhere after the first term of their office.[38] In the 2002 edition, however, the term "hometown" (*yuanji*) was replaced by the "place in which one grew up" (*chengzhangdi*).[39] My previous research has found that, from 1949 through 1998, about one-third of provincial leaders served in their home provinces. In any particular province, the party leaders were more likely to be outsiders, and government leaders were more likely to be natives.[40] The era of economic reforms initially produced more native leaders in provincial party committees and governments,[41] but the trend had reversed by the end of the 1990s (see Chapter 1, this volume).

A similar kind of avoidance is that related to the avoidance of personnel decisions involving family members and relatives. Family members, including in-laws and members of one's own family within three generations, should avoid working in the same work unit or taking positions

---

[37] Burns, "Strengthening Central CCP Control of Leadership Selection: The 1990 Nomenklatura," p. 469.

[38] *The 1995 Regulation*, Article 39.

[39] I have long argued against the use of hometowns as an indicator of localism because a native is not necessarily more identified with his or her hometown than an outsider is. A more accurate measure, in my view, is the duration of the service in the locality. It seems that the CCP has recognized the conceptual difference between a hometown and a town where a person grew up and put it into its policy. For my view on localism, see Zhiyue Bo, "Native Local Leaders and Political Mobility in China: Home Province Advantage?" *Provincial China*, No. 2 (October 1996), pp. 2–15.

[40] See Bo, *Chinese Provincial Leaders*, Chapter 3.

[41] The proportion of native leaders over the total provincial leaders from 1949 through 1998 was like a "V" shape, starting at a high level in the 1950s, declining in the 1960s and 1970s, and increasing in the 1980s and 1990s. See ibid., Figure 3.5, p. 46.

with superior–subordinate relationship.[42] Individuals should also avoid any official discussion of the appointment or removal of a relative.[43]

Transfer

China is a unitary system in which the center is the principal and local cadres are agents; the center can move cadres from one location to another. During the eras of Mao and Deng, central leaders transferred political elites from one place to another for numerous purposes, including resolving a conflict, balancing or weakening the power of their opponent, and carrying out a certain policy at local levels.

The 1995 regulations institutionalized the system of transfers.[44] Specifically, a leading member of a local party committee or government must be transferred, if he or she has worked in the same position for ten years. The party secretary and governor of the same province should not, in principle, be transferred at the same time.[45] The tenure of ten years in one position as a limit is interesting. According to the CCP Constitution, positions in party committees at the county level and above have a term of five years.[46] If, by the end of the second term, a cadre has not reached the retirement age, he or she has to be transferred (in fact, this provision seems to assume that political careers will normally involve a lifelong duration until retirement). Government cadres at the county level serve three-year terms, so the ten-year limit permits them more than three terms.[47]

---

[42] *The 1995 Regulation*, Article 39.

[43] Ibid., Article 39.

[44] The Chinese Communist Party formally introduced the practice in the "Decision by the Party Central Committee on Rotating Main Leading Party and Government Cadres at all Levels in a Planned and Step-by-Step Way," adopted by the Tenth Plenum of the Eighth Central Committee in 1962. See Melanie Manion, "Cadre Recruitment and Management in the People's Republic of China," *Chinese Law and Government* 18, No. 3, p. 94, (Fall 1984).

[45] *The 1995 Regulation*, Article 38 (Article 52 in the 2002 edition). In practice, this principle is often violated. Between December 2001 and December 2002, for instance, six provincial units (Hebei, Jiangsu, Shanghai, Zhejiang, Shandong, and Chongqing) saw the replacement of both their party secretary and governor (or mayor).

[46] See "Zhongguo Gongchandang Zhangcheng (1992)" ["The Constitution of the Chinese Communist Party"], in *Dangnei Fagui*, p. 15. The term of office for positions at the county level used to be three years. It was revised to five years to coincide with the term of office at the provincial and national levels.

[47] This is based on the Constitution of the People's Republic of China (1982).

Political elites may be transferred between different areas, departments, levels of government, party and government offices and enterprises, and other social organizations.[48] Since the early 1990s, transfers
among provinces have become frequent for members of the political elite.
From January 1990 through December 2002, sixty-nine cases of interprovincial transfers[49] can be identified (Table 2.2). Ten governors, thirteen party secretaries, thirty deputy secretaries, and sixteen vice governors were transferred out of all provincial units but two.[50] Beijing
and Chongqing were absent because political leaders from these two
cities were mainly transferred to the center, as noted later. Among
the supplying provincial units, several stand out. Jiangxi, Hunan, Inner Mongolia, Liaoning, Shanxi, Qinghai, and Jilin all provided four
leaders for other provinces. Liaoning, in particular, provided two governors (Li Changchun and Zhang Guoguang) and one party secretary
(Yue Qifeng). These provincial units are followed by six other provincial units (Hebei, Shandong, Henan, Hubei, Yunnan, and Gansu) that
each supplied three provincial leaders for other provinces. These outgo-
ing provincial leaders were transferred into all provincial units except
for Tianjin, Shanghai, and Fujian, because these provincial units did not
receive any leaders from other provincial units. As Cheng Li noted in
chapter 1 of this volume, Shanghai has been special; it has only been
a source for and recipient of leaders from the center, not from other
provincial units. The largest recipient is Hebei (five), followed by Shanxi,
Hubei, Guangxi, and Shaanxi (four each). These provinces are well known
for their conservatism in economic reforms.[51] It is likely that the center intended to induce some changes in these places by transferring in
new leaders. With two exceptions, all the transfers were either lateral
transfers or promotions. Of the original ten governors, seven assumed

---

[48] *The 1995 Regulation*, Article 38.
[49] Transfers here are defined more broadly than the definition in my earlier work. They
     include lateral transfers, interprovincial promotions, and interprovincial demotions,
     whereas my original definition refers only to lateral transfers. For my original definition
     of lateral transfers and a detailed description of the transfers, see Bo, *Chinese Provincial
     Leaders*, Chapter 4.
[50] Taiwan, Hong Kong, and Macao are not included in the research.
[51] According to Peter T. Y. Cheung, there are three types of provincial leaders in terms of
     economic reforms: pioneers, bandwagoners, and laggards. Shaanxi's leaders, according to
     Kevin Lane, are laggards. See Peter T. Y. Cheung, Jae Ho Chung, and Zhimin Lin, eds.,
     Provincial Strategies of Economic Reform in Post-Mao China (Armonk, NY: Sharpe,
     1998), especially Introduction and Chapter 4.

Table 2.2. *Transfers Between Provinces (1990–2002)*

Name	From Province	Title	To Province	Title	Date
Huang Huang	Jiangxi	Vice Governor	Ningxia	Secretary	Jan. 1990
Bai Qingcai	Shanxi	Vice Governor	Shaanxi	Governor	Mar. 1990
Hou Zongbin	Shaanxi	Governor	Henan	Secretary	Mar. 1990
Cheng Weigao	Henan	Governor	Hebei	Governor	June 1990
Li Changchun	Liaoning	Governor	Henan	Governor	June 1990
Yue Qifeng	Hebei	Governor	Liaoning	Governor	June 1990
Nie Ronggui	Yunnan	Deputy Secretary	Sichuan	Deputy Secretary	Aug. 1990
Liu Ronghui	Hebei	Vice Governor	Yunnan	Deputy Secretary	Oct. 1990
Gu Jinchi	Sichuan	Deputy Secretary	Gansu	Secretary	Oct. 1990
Zhao Fulin	Hubei	Deputy Secretary	Guangxi	Secretary	Oct. 1990
Yao Minxue	Henan	Deputy Secretary	Ningxia	Standing Member	Nov. 1990
Ding Tingmo	Guizhou	Deputy Secretary	Guangxi	Deputy Secretary	Dec. 1990
Zhang Xuezhong	Gansu	Vice Governor	Tibet	Deputy Secretary	May 1991
Wang Lequan	Shandong	Vice Governor	Xinjiang	Vice Governor	July 1991
Du Qinglin	Jilin	Deputy Secretary	Hainan	Deputy Secretary	Mar. 1992
Chen Kuiyuan	Inner Mongolia	Vice Governor	Tibet	Deputy Secretary	Mar. 1992
Cao Bochun	Hunan	Vice Governor	Liaoning	Deputy Secretary	July 1992
Liu Ronghui	Yunnan	Deputy Secretary	Shaanxi	Deputy Secretary	Dec. 1992
Wang Xiaofeng	Hunan	Deputy Secretary	Hainan	Deputy Secretary	Jan. 1993
Jia Zhijie	Gansu	Governor	Hubei	Governor	Feb. 1993
Liang Guoying	Ningxia	Deputy Secretary	Shanxi	Deputy Secretary	Mar. 1993
Meng Qingping	Hainan	Vice Governor	Hubei	Vice Governor	May 1993
Liu Fangren	Jiangxi	Deputy Secretary	Guizhou	Secretary	July 1993

(continued)

87

Table 2.2 (continued)

Name	From Province	Title	To Province	Title	Date
Sun Wensheng	Hunan	Deputy Secretary	Shanxi	Governor	Sept. 1993
Wang Maolin	Shanxi	Secretary	Hunan	Secretary	Sept. 1993
Gu Jinchi	Gansu	Secretary	Liaoning	Secretary	Oct. 1993
Yang Yongliang	Anhui	Deputy Secretary	Hubei	Deputy Secretary	Dec. 1993
Guo Jinlong	Sichuan	Deputy Secretary	Tibet	Deputy Secretary	Dec. 1993
Wang Guangxian	Yunnan	Vice Governor	Guizhou	Vice Governor	Dec. 1993
Yue Qifeng	Liaoning	Secretary	Heilongjiang	Secretary	Apr. 1994
Liu Mingzu	Guangxi	Deputy Secretary	Inner Mongolia	Secretary	Aug. 1994
Zhao Zhihong	Inner Mongolia	Vice Governor	Gansu	Deputy Secretary	Nov. 1994
Wang Jiangong	Shandong	Vice Governor	Heilongjiang	Deputy Secretary	Dec. 1994
Hui Liangyu	Hubei	Deputy Secretary	Anhui	Governor	Dec. 1994
Zhang Yunchuan	Jiangxi	Vice Governor	Xinjiang	Vice Governor	Apr. 1995
Gao Yan	Jilin	Governor	Yunnan	Secretary	June 1995
Cong Fukui	Heilongjiang	Vice Governor	Hebei	Vice Governor	June 1995
Cai Zhulin	Qinghai	Deputy Secretary	Shaanxi	Deputy Secretary	Oct. 1995
Zhang Fusen	Xinjiang	Deputy Secretary	Beijing	Deputy Secretary	Feb. 1996
Lu Zhangong	Zhejiang	Deputy Secretary	Hebei	Deputy Secretary	July 1996
Wang Yunlong	Shanxi	Deputy Secretary	Chongqing	Deputy Secretary	Sept. 1996
Jia Qinglin	Fujian	Secretary	Beijing	Governor	Oct. 1996
Chen Yujie	Hebei	Deputy Secretary	Jilin	Deputy Secretary	Oct. 1996
Bai Enpei	Inner Mongolia	Deputy Secretary	Qinghai	Governor	Apr. 1997
Wu Guanzheng	Jiangxi	Secretary	Shandong	Secretary	Apr. 1997
Cao Bochun	Liaoning	Deputy Secretary	Guangxi	Secretary	July 1997

Li Jianguo	Tianjin	Deputy Secretary	Shaanxi	Secretary	Aug. 1997
Li Changchun	Henan	Secretary	Guangdong	Secretary	Mar. 1998
Zhang Dejiang	Jilin	Secretary	Zhejiang	Secretary	Aug. 1998
Qian Yunlu	Hubei	Deputy Secretary	Guizhou	Governor	Dec. 1998
Tian Chengping	Qinghai	Secretary	Shanxi	Secretary	June 1990
Hui Liangyu	Anhui	Secretary	Jiangsu	Secretary	Jan. 2000
Wang Hanmin	Qinghai	Vice Governor	Guangxi	Vice Governor	Apr. 2000
Chen Kuiyuan	Tibet	Secretary	Henan	Secretary	Oct. 2000
Zhang Guoguang	Liaoning	Governor	Hubei	Governor	Jan. 2001
Meng Jianzhu	Shanghai	Deputy Secretary	Jiangxi	Secretary	Mar. 2001
Yun Gongmin	Inner Mongolia	Vice Governor	Shanxi	Vice Governor	July 2001
Chu Bo	Hunan	Governor	Inner Mongolia	Secretary	Aug. 2001
Zhang Yunchuan	Xinjiang	Deputy Secretary	Hunan	Governor	Aug. 2001
Bai Enpei	Qinghai	Secretary	Yunnan	Secretary	Oct. 2001
Su Rong	Jilin	Deputy Secretary	Qinghai	Secretary	Oct. 2001
Zhang Gaoli	Guangdong	Deputy Secretary	Shandong	Deputy Secretary	Nov. 2001
Yang Zonghui	Sichuan	Deputy Secretary	Yunnan	Deputy Secretary	Dec. 2001
Chen Jianguo	Shandong	Deputy Secretary	Ningxia	Secretary	Mar. 2002
Yang Zhiming	Shanxi	Vice Governor	Gansu	Vice Governor	Aug. 2002
Xi Jinping	Fujian	Governor	Zhejiang	Governor	Oct. 2002
Zhang Dejiang	Zhejiang	Secretary	Guangdong	Secretary	Nov. 2002
Bai Keming	Hainan	Secretary	Hebei	Secretary	Nov. 2002
Ji Yunshi	Jiangsu	Governor	Hebei	Governor	Dec. 2002

Notes: Governors include mayors of centrally administered municipalities and chairmen of autonomous regions. Vice governors include vice mayors of centrally administered municipalities and vice chairmen of autonomous regions.

Source: Updated from Zhiyue Bo, "Managing Political Elites in Post-Deng China," *Asian Profile* 28 (October 2000), pp. 349–70.

governorships in the receiving provinces and three were promoted to party secretaries. Of the thirteen party secretaries, twelve continued as party secretaries in the receiving provinces but one was appointed governor. Of the thirty deputy party secretaries transferred, five were appointed governors, nine were promoted to party secretaries, fifteen remained deputy secretaries, and only one was demoted to a standing member. Among the sixteen vice governors transferred, one was made governor, one was made party secretary, six were made deputy secretaries, and eight stayed vice governors.

Interprovincial transfers were most common in 1990 and 1993 (with twelve cases for each year). The transfers in 1990 seem to be related to reshuffling after the student movement in 1989, but it is hard to pin down the specific reasons for the changes on a case-by-case basis. The transfers in 1993 partly were measures to ensure central control after a number of elections with "unexpected results." Two leaders, for instance, were transferred to Guizhou in 1993, after an unexpected candidate, Chen Shineng, was elected governor. Liu Fangren was transferred from Jiangxi to replace the party secretary, and Wang Guangxian was transferred laterally from Yunnan to serve as a vice governor.

In addition to transfers at the provincial level, transfers at the sub-provincial level also seem to be increasing. In 1996, for instance, the CCP rotated more than 2,200 cadres at the prefectural level and more than 30,000 cadres at the county level. Heilongjiang province rotated 166 cadres among its different regions between 1995 and 1996. From 1996 to 1998, Hubei province rotated 28,092 cadres, of which 3,000 were at the county level and above.[52]

Transfers between provinces and the center also became frequent during this period. From March 1990 through January 2003, there were eighty-six cases of transfers from the provinces to the center (Table 2.3) and forty-two cases of transfers from the center to the provinces (Table 2.4). In the former category, there were nineteen governors, twenty-one secretaries, seventeen deputy secretaries, and twenty-nine vice governors. The city of Beijing stood out as a supplier of leaders to the center, providing seven leaders to various offices in the center. Shanghai and Hubei were also prominent, each sending five leaders to the center. Among Shanghai

---

[52] See Jiang Jiquan and Jiang Shan, "Woguo Ganbu Zhidu Gaige de Guiji" ["An Outline of the Cadre System Reform in China"], *Liaowang [Outlook Weekly]*, No. 45 (November 9, 1998), p. 4.

Table 2.3. *Transfers from the Provinces to the Center (1990–2003)*

Name	From Province	Title	To Ministry	Title	Date
Guo Zhenqian	Hubei	Governor	Central Bank	Vice Minister	Mar. 1990
Doje Cering	Tibet	Governor	Civil Affairs	Vice Minister	May 1990
Wang Zhaoguo	Fujian	Governor	Taiwan Office	Minister	Nov. 1990
Li Dezhu	Jilin	Vice Governor	United Front	Vice Minister	Nov. 1990
Ma Zhongchen	Shandong	Vice Governor	Agriculture	Vice Minister	Dec. 1990
Jiang Zhuping	Jiangxi	Vice Governor	Civil Aviation	Vice Minister	Jan. 1991
Hui Liangyu	Jilin	Vice Governor	Policy Research	Vice Minister	Feb. 1991
Zhu Rongji	Shanghai	Secretary	State Council	Vice Premier	Apr. 1991
Jin Renqing	Yunnan	Vice Governor	Finance	Vice Minister	Nov. 1991
Wang Zhongyu	Jilin	Governor	Economic Commission	Vice Minister	Mar. 1992
Xu Penghang	Hubei	Vice Governor	Office of Economic Affairs and Trade	Vice Minister	Aug. 1992
Hu Jintao	Tibet	Secretary	Politburo	Standing Member	Oct. 1992
Zhang Haoruo	Sichuan	Governor	Light Industry	Vice Minister	Nov. 1992
Hou Zongbin	Henan	Secretary	Discipline	Deputy Secretary	Dec. 1992
Chen Bingfan	Hunan	Vice Governor	Overseas Association	Vice Minister	Dec. 1992
Jin Jipeng	Qinghai	Governor	Auditing	Vice Minister	Dec. 1992
Deng Hongxun	Hainan	Secretary	State Dev. Office	Vice Minister	Jan. 1993
Liu Jianfeng	Hainan	Governor	Electronics	Vice Minister	Jan. 1993
Guo Shuyan	Hubei	Governor	Planning	Vice Minister	Feb. 1993
Wu Yixia	Jilin	Deputy Secretary	Agriculture	Vice Minister	May 1993
Ujie	Shanxi	Vice Governor	Economic Reform	Vice Minister	June 1993
Mao Rubai	Tibet	Deputy Secretary	Construction	Vice Minister	June 1993
Liu Zhengwei	Guizhou	Secretary	State Organs	Deputy Secretary	July 1993

(*continued*)

Table 2.3 (*continued*)

Name	From Province	Title	To Ministry	Title	Date
Zheng Silin	Shaanxi	Vice Governor	Foreign Trade	Vice Minister	Aug. 1993
Wang Xudong	Tianjin	Deputy Secretary	Organization	Vice Minister	Aug. 1993
Zhang Guoying	Guangdong	Deputy Secretary	Women Association	Vice Minister	Sept. 1993
Zhang Dinghua	Inner Mongolia	Deputy Secretary	Trade Union	Vice Minister	Oct. 1993
Ge Hongsheng	Zhejiang	Deputy Secretary	SEZs Office	Vice Minister	Oct. 1993
Wang Jialiu	Beijing	Deputy Secretary	Party School	Vice Minister	Dec. 1993
Chen Yunlin	Heilongjiang	Vice Governor	Taiwan Office	Vice Minister	Feb. 1994
Yao Zhongmin	Henan	Vice Governor	Development Bank	Vice Minister	Feb. 1994
Cheng Faguang	Ningxia	Vice Governor	Tax Bureau	Vice Minister	Apr. 1994
Shao Qihui	Heilongjiang	Governor	Machine	Vice Minister	May 1994
Sun Jiazheng	Jiangsu	Deputy Secretary	TV & Movie	Minister	May 1994
Jiang Chunyun	Shandong	Secretary	State Council	Vice Premier	Sept. 1994
Wu Bangguo	Shanghai	Secretary	State Council	Vice Premier	Sept. 1994
Zhang Weiqing	Shanxi	Vice Governor	Family Planning	Vice Minister	Sept. 1994
Li Haifeng	Hebei	Vice Governor	Overseas Association	Vice Minister	Nov. 1994
Liu Mingkang	Fujian	Vice Governor	Development Bank	Vice Minister	Dec. 1994
Bai Qingcai	Shaanxi	Governor	Supply	Vice Minister	Dec. 1994
Chen Bangzhu	Hunan	Governor	Domestic Trade	Minister	Jan. 1995
Lin Yongsan	Inner Mongolia	Vice Governor	Labor	Vice Minister	Apr. 1995
Li Huifen	Tianjin	Vice Governor	CUT Corp.	Manager	July 1995
Zhang Xuezhong	Tibet	Deputy Secretary	Personnel	Vice Minister	Aug. 1995

Name	Location	Position	Portfolio	Position	Date
Yang Zhihai	Heilongjiang	Vice Governor	Light Industry	Vice Minister	Apr. 1996
Chen Shineng	Guizhou	Governor	Chemistry	Vice Minister	July 1996
Zhang Wule	Gansu	Governor	Economic Commission	Vice Minister	July 1996
Li Qiyan	Beijing	Governor	Labor	Vice Minister	Nov. 1996
Liu Mingqi	Hainan	Vice Governor	Hong Kong & Macao Office	Vice Minister	Nov. 1996
Zhang Yuqin	Guizhou	Vice Governor	Family Planning	Vice Minister	Jan. 1997
Yin Kesheng	Qinghai	Secretary	CC Work Committee	Deputy Secretary	Apr. 1997
Zhao Baojiang	Hubei	Vice Governor	Construction	Vice Minister	Apr. 1997
Liu Hong	Guangxi	Vice Governor	Statistical Bureau	Director	May 1997
Kang Yi	Ningxia	Deputy Secretary	Nonferrous Metals Corporation	Vice Minister	July 1997
Chen Zhili	Shanghai	Deputy Secretary	Education	Vice Minister	Aug. 1997
Wei Jianxing	Beijing	Secretary	Discipline	Secretary	Aug. 1997
Bai Lichen	Ningxia	Governor	Supply	Minister	Dec. 1997
Gao Yan	Yunnan	Secretary	Electricity	Vice Minister	Sept. 1997
Xu Yongyue	Hebei	Deputy Secretary	National Security	Minister	Jan. 1998
Zhao Qizheng	Shanghai	Vice Governor	News Office	Vice Minister	Jan. 1998
Jin Renqing	Beijing	Vice Governor	Tax Bureau	Minister	Apr. 1998
Lou Jiwei	Guizhou	Vice Governor	Finance	Vice Minister	Apr. 1998
Qu Weizhi	Tianjin	Vice Governor	Information	Vice Minister	Apr. 1998
Liu Jing	Yunnan	Vice Governor	Customs	Vice Minister	Apr. 1998
Lu Zhangong	Hebei	Deputy Secretary	Trade Union	Vice Chairman	Oct. 1998
Sun Wensheng	Shanxi	Governor	Resources	Vice Minister	June 1999
Hu Fuguo	Shanxi	Secretary	State Council	Vice Minister	June 1999
Tian Fengshan	Heilongjiang	Governor	Resources	Minister	Dec. 1999

(continued)

93

Table 2.3 (*continued*)

Name	From Province	Title	To Ministry	Title	Date
Chen Yujie	Jilin	Deputy Secretary	Finance	Vice Minister	Feb. 2000
Zhang Fusen	Beijing	Deputy Secretary	Justice	Minister	Nov. 2000
Wang Qishan	Guangdong	Vice Governor	State Council	Minister	Nov. 2000
Wang Guangtao	Beijing	Vice Governor	Construction	Minister	Nov. 2001
Jiang Zhuping	Hubei	Secretary	NPC	Vice Minister	Dec. 2001
Li Chunting	Shandong	Governor	NPC	Vice Minister	Dec. 2001
Chai Songyue	Zhejiang	Governor	Power	Minister	Oct. 2002
Jia Qinglin	Beijing	Secretary	Politburo	Standing Member	Oct. 2002
Huang Ju	Shanghai	Secretary	Politburo	Standing Member	Oct. 2002
He Guoqiang	Chongqing	Secretary	Organization	Minister	Oct. 2002
Wu Guanzheng	Shandong	Secretary	Politburo	Standing Member	Nov. 2002
Hui Liangyu	Jiangsu	Secretary	Politburo	Member	Nov. 2002
Li Changchun	Guangdong	Secretary	Politburo	Standing Member	Nov. 2002
Wang Yunlong	Chongqing	Deputy Secretary	NPC	Minister	Dec. 2002
Zhou Yongkang	Sichuan	Secretary	Public Security	Minister	Dec. 2002
Wang Xudong	Hebei	Secretary	Information	Vice Minister	Jan. 2003
Zhang Baoqing	Shaanxi	Deputy Secretary	Education	Vice Minister	Jan. 2003
Chen Kuiyuan	Henan	Secretary	Academy of Social Sciences	Minister	Jan. 2003

Notes: Governors include mayors of centrally administered municipalities and chairmen of autonomous regions. Vice governors include vice mayors of centrally administered municipalities and vice chairmen of autonomous regions. Ministers and vice ministers refer to ranks instead of specific titles. PPC = provincial People's Congress, including municipal and regional People's Congress; SEZ's = Special Economic Zones; HK & Macao = Hong Kong & Macao Office; CC Work Committee = the Party Work Committee of Organs Directly Under the Central Committee; SS = Social Sciences; CUT Corp. = China United Telecommunication Corporation; NPC = National People's Congress.

Sources: Updated from Zhiyue Bo, "Managing Political Elites in Post-Deng China," *Asian Profile* 28 (October 2000), pp. 349–70.

Table 2.4. *Transfers from the Center to the Provinces (1990–2002)*

Name	From Ministry	Title	To Province	Title	Date
Zhang Dejiang	Civil Affairs	Vice Minister	Liaoning	Deputy Secretary	Nov. 1990
Lin Yongsan	CPPCC	Vice Minister	Inner Mongolia	Vice Governor	Oct. 1991
Chen Shineng	Light Industry	Vice Minister	Guizhou	Vice Governor	Jan. 1992
Hu Fuguo	Coal Mine Co.	Minister	Shanxi	Governor	Aug. 1992
Hui Liangyu	Policy Research	Vice Minister	Hubei	Deputy Secretary	Oct. 1992
Ma Zhongchen	Agriculture	Vice Minister	Henan	Governor	Dec. 1992
Ruan Chongwu	Labor	Minister	Hainan	Secretary	Jan. 1993
Gao Dezhan	Forestry	Minister	Tianjin	Secretary	Mar. 1993
Linghu An	Labor	Vice Minister	Yunnan	Deputy Secretary	Oct. 1993
Xu Yongyue	Advisory	Vice Minister	Hebei	Deputy Secretary	Mar. 1994
Zheng Silin	Foreign Trade	Vice Minister	Jiangsu	Governor	Sept. 1994
Jiang Zhuping	Civil Aviation	Vice Minister	Hubei	Governor	Feb. 1995
Wei Jianxing	Discipline	Secretary	Beijing	Secretary	Apr. 1995
Jin Renqing	Finance	Vice Minister	Beijing	Vice Governor	Nov. 1995
Qu Weizhi	Electronics	Vice Minister	Tianjin	Vice Governor	Jan. 1996
Wu Yixia	Agriculture	Vice Minister	Guizhou	Governor	July 1996
He Guoqiang	Chemical Ind.	Vice Minister	Fujian	Governor	Oct. 1996
Xu Youfang	Forestry	Minister	Heilongjiang	Secretary	July 1997
Mao Rubai	Construction	Vice Minister	Ningxia	Secretary	Aug. 1997
Wang Qishan	People's Bank	Vice Minister	Guangdong	Vice Governor	Jan. 1998
Liu Qi	Metallurgy	Minister	Beijing	Vice Governor	Mar. 1998
Li Keqiang	Youth League	Minister	Henan	Governor	June 1998
Hong Hu	State Council	Vice Minister	Jilin	Governor	Sept. 1998

(continued)

95

Table 2.4 (*continued*)

Name	From Ministry	Title	To Province	Title	Date
Niu Maosheng	Water	Minister	Hebei	Governor	Oct. 1998
Bao Xuding	Planning	Minister	Chongqing	Governor	Aug. 1999
Bu Zhengfai	Personnel	Vice Minister	Jiangxi	Deputy Secretary	Aug. 1999
Wang Jun	Coal Bureau	Vice Minister	Jiangxi	Vice Governor	Sept. 1999
Zhou Yongkang	Resources	Minister	Sichuan	Secretary	Jan. 2000
Wang Xudong	Organization	Vice Minister	Hebei	Secretary	June 2000
Wang Xianzheng	Coal Bureau	Vice Minister	Shanxi	Vice Governor	Sept. 2000
Li Yuanchao	Culture	Vice Minister	Jiangsu	Deputy Secretary	Oct. 2000
Shi Xiushi	State Council	Vice Minister	Guizhou	Deputy Secretary	Dec. 2000
Song Defu	Personnel	Minister	Fujian	Secretary	Dec. 2000
Lu Zhangong	Trade Union	Vice Chairman	Fujian	Deputy Secretary	Jan. 2001
Xu Rongkai	Flood Control	Vice Minister	Yunnan	Deputy Secretary	May 2001
Bai Keming	People's Daily	Minister	Hainan	Secretary	Aug. 2001
Zhang Baoshun	Xinhua News Agency	Vice Minister	Shanxi	Deputy Secretary	Sept. 2001
Yu Zhengsheng	Construction	Minister	Hubei	Secretary	Dec. 2001
Huang Zhendong	Transportation	Minister	Chongqing	Secretary	Oct. 2002
Wang Qishan	State Council	Minister	Hainan	Secretary	Nov. 2002
Zhang Xuezhong	Personnel	Minister	Sichuan	Secretary	Dec. 2002
Jiang Yikang	Central Office	Vice Minister	Chongqing	Deputy Secretary	Dec. 2002

Notes: Governors include mayors of centrally administered municipalities and chairmen of autonomous regions. Vice governors include vice mayors of centrally administered municipalities and vice chairmen of autonomous regions. Ministers and vice ministers refer to ranks instead of specific titles.

Sources: Updated from Zhiyue Bo, "The Provinces: Training Ground for National Leaders or a Power in Their Own Right," in David Finkelstein and Maryanne Kivlehan, eds., *China's Leadership in the Twenty-First Century: The Rise of the Fourth Generation* (Armonk, NY: Sharpe, 2003), Tables 4.2 and 4.3.

leaders who were transferred to the center during this period, there were two vice premiers (Zhu Rongji and Wu Bangguo) and one standing member of the politburo (Huang Ju). Transfers to the center obviously were promotions for Zhu Rongji, Hu Jintao, Wu Bangguo, Jiang Chunyun, and many others, whereas for others such as Li Qiyan, Liu Zhengwei, Liu Jianfeng, and Deng Hongxun, the transfers to the center were moves from powerful provincial positions to central jobs with less power and prestige and little hope for further promotion.

Transfers from the center to the provinces provide a direct way for central leaders to manage the provinces. Of the forty-two central cadres sent to twenty provincial units (1990–2003), there were ten governors, thirteen secretaries, eleven deputy secretaries, and eight vice governors. As almost all party secretaries and governors are members of the Party Central Committee, the provincial appointments are an important venue by which central leaders stack supporters. The provincial appointments also provide opportunities for the appointees to broaden their experiences and prove themselves before they are slated for new and more substantial central party or government duties. With rare exceptions (such as Premier Wen Jiabao), top party and central government officials, led by Hu Jintao, now all boast extensive provincial-level careers. For an essentially local leader, going to the center will help him or her to learn more about central operations and political processes. Wu Yixia, Ma Zhongchen, Zhang Dejiang, and many others all have such experiences. Their career paths share the common features of starting from provinces, going to the center, and coming back to the provinces for a more important position.

Sometimes an appointee from the center may be parachuted to a province or centrally administered city to cope with local tensions or clean up a local mess. When the Hainan Party Secretary could not get along with the Hainan Governor, Ruan Chongwu (born in June 1933 and a native of Huai'an, Hebei) was sent in to replace both officials. After corruption scandals sent Chen Xitong, the Beijing Party Secretary, into disgrace, Wei Jianxing (born in January 1931 and a native of Xinchang, Zhejiang) was moved in to control the situation.

A different type of transfer involves a movement from provincial leading positions to national institutions other than the CCP or the central government. This type of transfer was not included in the aforementioned province-to-center transfers, because it is often used to retire senior provincial leaders and make room for new appointees. For instance, Ye Xuanping, former Guangdong Governor and a political heavyweight, was made Chinese People's Political Consultative Conference (CPPCC) Vice Chairman in May of 1991 after he passed the retirement age for governors. Likewise, Xie Fei, former Guangdong Party Secretary, was made a Standing Committee of the National People's Congress (NPC) Vice Chairman in March 1998. One may also find many other former provincial leaders on the list of leading members of the CPPCC or NPC, such as Yang Rudai (Sichuan), Mao Zhiyong (Jiangxi), Uliji (Inner Mongolia), Yue Qifeng (Heilongjiang), Huang Huang (Ningxia), Fu Xishou (Anhui), and Quan Shuren (Liaoning), all in the Standing Committee of the Ninth CPPCC; and Buhe (Inner Mongolia), Cheng Kejie (Guangxi), Tomur Dawamat (Xinjiang), Wang Chaowen (Guizhou), Yin Kesheng (Qinghai), Gu Jinchi (Liaoning), and Gao Dezhan (Tianjin), along with many others, in the Standing Committee of the Ninth NPC.[53] The most recent examples of these "retirement transfers" include Liu Mingzu (Inner Mongolia), Wang Maolin (Hunan), Mao Rubai (Ningxia), and Liu Fangren (Guizhou). They were appointed vice chairmen of various committees in the NPC. In this manner, transfers are also used to make positions available to younger candidates by moving elder candidates to other positions.

Resignation and Demotion

The 1995 regulations also established a system of resignation for leading party or government cadres. Resignation may be for work-related reasons, by personal request, or when an official is ordered to do so (*zeling cizhi*). When ordered to resign for inappropriate behavior, a defiant official will be dismissed from office while a compliant official may be given an appropriate job.[54] In the 2002 edition, a new term, "removal" (*mianzhi*), was added to this category. It may occur when the official has reached the age limit specified for the post or his or her retirement age, or if the official does poorly (with more than one-third of negative votes) in evaluations. Finally, the 1995 regulations introduced the idea of demotion for leading party and government cadres. Cadres would be demoted

---

[53] This list is from the *People's Daily* (overseas edition) (March 17, 1998), p. 1. Many people are no longer on the list as of 2003. Cheng Kejie was executed for corruption.

[54] *The 1995 Regulation*, Articles 40–45. According to the 2002 edition, a leading cadre should also resign because of serious mistakes in work (Article 59).

mainly for performance reasons, though they could be demoted for other reasons as well. If they later have outstanding performances in their new positions, the demoted cadres will be eligible for promotion after a year of probation.[55] Although, in the past, officials were rarely demoted except in political purges, the use of demotions furnishes the central leadership with a powerful weapon for promoting discipline and compliance.

CONCLUDING REMARKS

Although the power and authority of the CCP center over localities were somewhat weakened by the decentralization measures in the 1980s, the CCP remains a powerful institution. With the decentralization of economic and administrative powers in the reform era, control over cadre management has become increasingly important for the authority of the CCP. The institutionalization of elite management discussed in this chapter has helped to reinforce the party's dominant role in cadre management.

The institutionalization of elite management has introduced a number of mechanisms designed to curb arbitrary personal decisions while enhancing the institutional dominance of the party. Most interestingly, a system of transfers has become institutionalized. In both the Mao and Deng eras, central leaders often used transfers to weaken political opponents, enforce central policies, or resolve a conflict. The new system of transfers may still be used for these purposes, but it also institutionalizes a broader range of relatively frequent elite rotations. Such rotations provide an enormous leverage for central leaders over local officials.

It should be noted, however, that these institutional adaptations of the party's involvement in cadre management have occurred as People's Congresses have become more assertive. In some instances, the party leadership has had trouble installing its candidates in the local government. In 1993, for instance, several provinces produced "unexpected" governors. The CCP's candidates in Guizhou and Zhejiang provinces were rejected by the provincial people's congresses, which elected their own candidates. In 1998, five candidates nominated by deputies were elected

---

[55] Ibid., Article 46. The 2002 edition gives them a year of probation. If the demoted cadres do well in their new jobs in a year or longer, they could be promoted back to the original position or other similar positions (Article 62).

vice governors in the absence of formal endorsement by the party leadership. In February 2000, the standing committee of the Guangdong Provincial People's Congress rejected two candidates nominated by the governor for department positions. The Standing Committee Chairman, Zhu Senlin, reportedly said calmly, "(They) were not passed because they did not get more than half of the votes. This is the result of the standing members exercising their democratic power. It could not be more normal."[56] In response to the assertiveness of legislative institutions, many provincial party secretaries have become concurrently chairmen of the standing committees of their respective provincial people's congresses. Although the CCP is still dominant in the Chinese political structure, it has had to redefine itself in order to stay on top of the game.

ACKNOWLEDGMENT

An earlier version of this chapter was presented to a conference on "National Integration and Regional Diversity in China" at The University of California Institute on Global Conflict and Cooperation (IGCC), San Diego, California, June 14–15, 2000. The author thanks the conference participants, especially Barry Naughton and Dali Yang, as well as four anonymous readers, for their comments and suggestions. He also thanks Stephine M. Corso for her assistance.

[56] *Zhongguo Qingnianbao [China Youth]*, February 23, 2000 (see http://www.peopledaily. com.cn/zgrdxw/news/200002/23/22311.html).

3

The Cadre Evaluation System at the Grass Roots: The Paradox of Party Rule

Susan H. Whiting

The Chinese party-state shares with other large, hierarchical organizations significant agency problems; local agents of the state tend to behave opportunistically, contrary to the interests of their principals.[1] Such agency problems stem from conflicts of interest between principals and agents and from information asymmetries that typically characterize principal–agent relations.[2] State officials in China employ a formal evaluation system (*kaohe zhidu*) to control the behavior of their subordinates. Drawing on principal–agent theory, this paper contends that the nature of the evaluation system helps to explain dysfunctional aspects of policy implementation at the grass roots and that problems with policy implementation, in turn, help to explain subsequent changes in the evaluation system itself. This characterization is consistent with adaptive learning on the part of principals. In the final section, the chapter argues that, paradoxically, even as the evaluation system has exacerbated problems in policy implementation, it has simultaneously contributed to the durability of rule by the Chinese Communist Party (CCP). Indeed, the relative stability of CCP rule, in contrast to the loss of power by communist parties in other former socialist states and contrary to claims of pervasive political decay in China,[3] demands explanation.

---

[1] Victor Nee and Peng Lian, "Sleeping with the Enemy: A Dynamic Model of Declining Political Commitment in State Socialism," *Theory and Society,* 23 (1994), pp. 253–296.

[2] Terry M. Moe, "The New Economics of Organization," *American Journal of Political Science*, 28 (1984), p. 757.

[3] In addition to those studies cited in the introduction to this volume, see also Minxin Pei, "China's Governance Crisis," *Foreign Affairs* (September 2002), pp. 96–109; Andrew G. Walder, ed., *The Waning of the Communist State: Economic Origins of Political Decline in China and Hungary* (Berkeley, CA: University of California Press, 1995).

The chapter begins by providing some background on the development of the cadre evaluation system since the initiation of reform in 1978, arguing that changes in cadre evaluation represent an early and important element of political reform in China – albeit not democratic political reform. The next section analyzes the characteristics of the system in terms of principal–agent theory. It demonstrates that the cadre evaluation system has used a combination of specific performance-based measures and high-powered incentives – a combination that is unusual among lower- and middle-level managers in large organizations. This combination has contributed to severe moral hazard problems in certain policy arenas. The concluding section argues that, at the same time, the system has provided substantial rewards for cadres who perform well, thereby enhancing their commitment to the party, and has elicited minimally acceptable levels of performance from other cadres, thereby contributing to the effectiveness of CCP rule.

BACKGROUND

Although Chinese leadership has become infamous for undertaking economic without political reform, important but often-overlooked changes in the formal system by which local state officials are evaluated were initiated contemporaneously with reforms in the economic system. The process of cadre evaluation began to receive significant attention shortly after the Third Plenum of the 11th Central Committee in December 1978, which signaled the beginning of the reform era. Hua Guofeng addressed the issue briefly in his "Work Report of the Government," delivered to the Second Session of the Fifth National People's Congress in July 1979, and, in November 1979, the Organization Department of the Central Committee of the CCP issued a document calling for the establishment of a new evaluation system.[4] This document instructed each jurisdiction to formulate clear and specific content and standards for assessing cadre performance. The system was to be developed on an experimental basis

---

[4] Organization Department document No. 52 (1979): "Zhonggong zhongyang zuzhibu guanyu shixing ganbu kaohe zhidu de yijian de tongzhi," in *Renshi gongzuo wenjian xuanbian – ganbu guanli bufen [Selected Documents on Personnel Work – Cadre Management Section]* (Beijing: Laodong renshi chubanshe, 1987), pp. 12–15.

initially, with the goal of instituting a formal system within two to three years. Experiments were to be conducted in counties, communes, party and government organs, and various other government institutions.[5]

The document specified that the methods and content of evaluation should be specific to cadres' positions. With respect to cadres in local leadership positions, the Organization Department directed that evaluations should cover political thought, organizational and leadership abilities, familiarity with substantive issues, and democratic work style, as well as actual achievements (*gongzuo de shiji chengxiao*). According to the document, the evaluation system should specify both material and non-material rewards; consistently poor performance should result in transfer; and the results of evaluations should be taken into account in promotions.

The 1983 National Organization Work Conference built on the foundation put in place in 1979. However, it moved in the direction of placing greater weight on the assessment of concrete achievements rather than political attitudes or work style, and it reiterated the importance of such criteria in determining material rewards and penalties as well as promotions.[6]

The commentary surrounding the process that the 1979 document set in motion is useful in putting the development of a cadre evaluation system in context. Commentators emphasized the importance of moving away from what were seen as subjective evaluations of political attitudes toward specific, measurable, and quantifiable indicators of performance[7]:

Using concrete achievements as the main standard to assess both cadre ability and political integrity will help to negate the phenomenon of cadres who do more

---

5   The following paragraphs draw on Susan H. Whiting, *Power and Wealth in Rural China: The Political Economy of Institutional Change* (New York: Cambridge University Press, 2001).

6   Organization Department document No. 7 (1988): "Zhonggong zhongyang zuzhibu guanyu shixing difang dangzheng lingdao ganbu niandu gongzuo kaohe zhidu de tongzhi," in *Zhongguo renshi nianjian, 1988–89 [Personnel Yearbook of China, 1988–89]* (Beijing: Zhongguo renshi chubanshe, 1991).

7   Jiang Zhaoyuan, "Xuanba kaocha ganbu yao zhuzhong gongzuo shiji," *Renmin ribao [People's Daily]*, July 9, 1985, reprinted in Han Qing and Yue Furong, eds., *Laodong renshi zhidu gaige wenxuan [Selected Essays on Reform of the Labor and Personnel System]* (Changsha: Hunan renmin chubanshe, 1987), pp. 503–5. See also Li Lei, "Shiji shi kaocha ganbu de weiyi biaozhun," *Gongren ribao [Workers' Daily]*, September 13, 1985, reprinted in ibid., pp. 506–8; and Yang Bohua, "Jianli yange de ganbu kaohe zhidu," *Beijing ribao [Beijing Daily]*, July 15, 1985, reprinted in ibid., pp. 509–13.

and less, who perform well and poorly, all eating from the same "big pot" and the phenomenon of cadres who simply try to make no mistakes but who achieve nothing passing their days in office in mediocrity sitting in an "iron armchair."[8]

Thus the cadre evaluation system was seen in part as a means to break the paralysis of many cadres following the Cultural Revolution and to actively mobilize cadres to pursue specific goals set by their superiors. Other commentators emphasized the degree to which the new system of cadre monitoring being put in place was a departure from past practice. For example, one commentator in the *Beijing Ribao* highlighted that, since the mid-1950s, evaluations in many locales had not taken place on an annual basis but rather only at the time of appointment or transfer.[9]

In 1988, the CCP Organization Department provided official guidelines for the annual evaluation of party secretaries and government executives at the county level, and it reiterated that the evaluation should provide the basis for rewards and penalties, promotions and demotions.[10] Moreover, the guidelines explicitly sought to encourage competition (*guli jingzheng*) among party secretaries and government executives at the same level of the administrative hierarchy. The guidelines included a format for evaluation by an inspection committee dispatched from the prefectural (municipal) level, a format for collegial evaluation by the leaders of major party and government organs at the county level, and a format for quantitative measures of performance on the main "social, economic, and cultural" targets. These measures ranged from the gross value of industrial output to tax remittances and procurement of agricultural and agricultural subsidiary products, and from realized investment in infrastructure to the population growth rate and the completion rate for nine-year compulsory education. (The complete list of measures is presented in Table 3.1.) These guidelines represented an attempt to standardize and systematize the evaluation of cadre performance on a range of government functions

---

[8] Jiang Zhaoyuan, "Xuanba kaocha ganbu yao zhuzhong gongzuo shiji," *Renmin ribao (People's Daily)*, July 9, 1985, reprinted in Han and Yue, *Selected Essays on Reform of the Labor and Personnel System*, pp. 503–5.

[9] Yang Bohua, "Jianli yange de ganbu kaohe zhidu," *Beijing ribao [Beijing Daily]*, July 15, 1985, reprinted in ibid., pp. 509–13.

[10] Organization Department document No. 7 (1988), *Personnel Yearbook of China, 1988–89*.

Table 3.1. *National Guidelines for Performance Criteria of Local Party and Government Leaders*

Category
Gross national product
Gross value of industrial output (not including any output below the village level)
Gross value of agricultural output (not including any output below the village level)
Gross value of output of township- and village-run enterprises
National income per capita
Rural income per capita
Taxes and profits remitted
Fiscal income
Labor productivity of state and collective enterprises
Procurement of agricultural and subsidiary products
Retail sales
Infrastructure investment realized
Natural population growth rate
Grain output
Local budgetary income
Local budgetary expenditures
Forested area
9-year compulsory education completion rate

Note: Each category was to be assessed by the relevant government organ, and data on both level and rate of increase were to be provided.

Source: Zhonggong zhongyang zuzhibu, "Guanyu shixing difang dangzheng lingdao ganbu niandu gongzuo kaohe zhidu de tongzhi" ("Notice Regarding Implementation of the Annual Job Evaluation System for Leading Cadres of Local Party and Government Organs"), *Zhongguo renshi nianjian* (Beijing: Zhongguo renshi chubanshe, 1991).

at the local level. Similar guidelines were established for township-level cadres.[11]

In June 2000, the State Council issued an "Outline on Deepening the Reform of the Cadre Personnel System."[12] This document reinforced earlier guidelines while placing greater emphasis on both professional competence and public opinion, albeit without introducing any meaningful democratization.

---

[11] See, for example, He Jizhi, Wei Shixiang, and Lin Luolun, eds., *Xiangzhen gongzuo renyuan gangwei guifan* [Norms for the Positions of Township Staff Members] (Beijing: Zhongguo renshi chubanshe, 1991), pp. 175–82.

[12] "Shenhua ganbu renshi zhidu gaige gangyao" ["Outline on Deepening the Reform of the Cadre Personnel System"], in *Guowuyuan gongbao [State Council Bulletin]*, No. 29 (2000), pp. 5–11.

THE FUNCTIONING OF THE CADRE EVALUATION SYSTEM AT THE LOCAL LEVEL

This section describes the characteristics of the cadre evaluation system at the local level in terms of the choice of performance measures and reward functions. It draws on data collected during field work in the two county-level units of Jiading and Songjiang in suburban Shanghai and in the county of Hezheng in Gansu during the 1990s.

Performance-Based Measures

Local versions of the cadre evaluation system reflected the central guidelines outlined herein but did not follow them precisely. The office of management and administration, the county-level organ responsible for setting performance criteria and overseeing implementation, used the evaluation system to convey local priorities to subordinate townships within the broader context of central guidelines. Nevertheless, local versions shared certain core characteristics of the central guidelines – namely, they used highly specific performance measures to evaluate a diverse array of governance tasks. The suburban counties of Shanghai began experimenting with the cadre evaluation system in the mid-1980s. Jiading County established a formal system for evaluating township cadres on a provisional basis in 1986, with the explicit goal of linking performance to remuneration.[13] Relatively complete data are available for Jiading for the year 1989; Table 3.2 reproduces the performance criteria for township party secretaries and township government executives.

The emphasis on township and village industry is reflected in the first set of indicators, which assigns highest priority to increases in the gross value of industrial output (GVIO) and industrial profits. The second set of indicators focuses on state procurement of agricultural and agricultural subsidiary products and the marketing of pork; it assigns highest priority to the sale of grain to the state. The third set of indicators covers party building; this refers to Communist Party functions, including

---

[13] Jiading Party document No. 8 (1989): Zhonggong jiadingxian wei jiadingxian renmin zhengfu, "Guanyu wanshan 1989 nian xiangzhen dang zheng jiguan ganbu kaohe jiangli banfa de tongzhi," [Notice Regarding Improvement of the Methods of Evaluation and Reward for Cadres in Township Party and Government Organs for 1989] *Jiading nianjian, 1988–1990 [Jiading Yearbook 1988–1990]*, pp. 44–5.

Table 3.2. *Performance Criteria for Township Government Executives and Party Secretaries, Jiading County, Shanghai, 1989*

Category	Points	County-level Unit Responsible for Evaluation of Target Fulfillment*
Township- and village-run industry	33	
Increase in gross value of industrial output	10	Rural Industry Bureau
Increase in industrial profits	10	Rural Industry Bureau
Increase in profit rate on gross value of output	5	Rural Industry Bureau
Township ranking by profit rate on total capital	4	Rural Industry Bureau
Increase in total value of exports	4	Rural Industry Bureau
Agriculture	30	
Sales to the state of grain and vegetables	15	Grain Bureau–Vegetable Office
Sales to the urban market of pigs	10	Animal Husbandry Bureau
Sales to the state of oil-bearing crops	3	Grain Bureau
Sales to the state of leather and cotton	2	Supply and Marketing Cooperative
Party building	21	
Building of party organizations	7	CCP Organization Section
Building of party spirit and discipline	7	Discipline Inspection Committee
Education of party members	7	CCP Propaganda Section
Education	9	
Completion rate for compulsory education	3	Education Committee
Participation rate for worker training	3	Education Committee
Scale of funds dedicated to education	3	Education Committee
Family planning	7	
Family planning compliance rate	7	Family Planning office
Public order	**	Politics and Law Leadership Small Group
Total	200	

* In most cases, this unit performs the actual evaluation. The county Statistical Bureau is also involved in the evaluation of fulfillment of all targets for industry and agriculture. The county party committee's Policy Research Office oversees the compilation of data at the end of the year.

** According to the document, "the performance of township party and government cadres with respect to their public order responsibilities is to be evaluated separately by the county's 'politics and law leadership small group.'"

Source: Jiading party document [Jiaweifa (1989), No. 8], promulgated on March 3, 1989.

the recruitment and education of party cadres, the maintenance of party discipline and exemplary behavior among party members, and the organization of activities for nonmembers that inculcate party values. The fourth set addresses education and includes both the completion rate for compulsory education and an indicator of investment in education. The fifth performance indicator is the family-planning compliance rate. The final indicator is public order, which was to be assessed separately by the Politics and Law Leadership Small Group.[14] With the exception of public order, performance on other indicators was to be determined by the relevant county-level bureau, as indicated by the table.

Similarly, Songjiang County used a core set of indicators to evaluate the performance of township party secretaries and township government executives. As of 1995, these indicators were:

(1) gross value of agricultural and industrial output (GVAIO),
(2) gross domestic product,
(3) industrial profits (of local public firms only),
(4) tax revenue (value-added and corporate income taxes only), and
(5) realized foreign and domestic investment in productive fixed assets.[15] Each item was evaluated on both the level and the rate of increase over the previous year.

Because performance criteria were tailored to reflect local interests and priorities, they varied somewhat across jurisdictions. Performance criteria for township officials in Hezheng County, a nationally designated poor county in Gansu, for example, reflected the particular developmental challenges of an agricultural county still striving to meet the basic needs of its residents. In 1996, township officials were evaluated according to the following criteria:

(1) local tax receipts (specifically those under the jurisdiction of the township Public Finance Bureau, such as the agriculture tax),

---

[14] The performance criteria for township officials in Yongqing County, Hebei, fall into similar categories, including economic performance (in both industry and agriculture), with specific indicators for township and village industry, party building, family planning, and public order.

[15] Author's interview, August 13, 1996. This research draws on interviews with a range of county, township, and village-level officials in the counties of Jiading and Songjiang in suburban Shanghai and Hezheng County in Ganbu. Interviewee's names are not provided in order to protect their identities.

(2) education surcharge receipts,

(3) area of land terraced or regraded,

(4) compliance rate for compulsory education,

(5) annual per capita income for rural residents,

(6) compliance rate for family planning, and

(7) upgrading of road surfaces within the township.[16] These indicators clearly reflect the particular development and governance challenges faced by local leaders.

High-Powered Incentives

In each locale, performance on these criteria was used to determine the bonuses of state cadres (*guojia ganbu*) and the total salaries of collective cadres (*jiti ganbu*).[17] In theoretical terms, the incentives contained in the cadre evaluation system were "high powered."[18] In other words, positive performances generated large payoffs for agents. Incentive pay accounted for a large portion of cadres' total incomes, and it created relatively large differentials among cadres in the same locale.

---

[16] Author's interview, September 18, 1997.

[17] State cadres (*guojia ganbu*) are those official state employees who are authorized to be on the state payroll (*guojia bianzhi*); their base salaries are set according to rank and are guaranteed by the formal state budget. Collective cadres (*jiti ganbu*) are official state employees whose salaries are not guaranteed by the formal state budget; their salaries are typically financed by "off-budget" (*yusuanwai*) revenues.

[18] "High-powered incentives" have been defined in a variety of ways in the literature. Oliver Williamson uses the term to refer specifically to residual claimant status, whereas others, such as George Baker et al., use it more broadly to refer to reward systems that structure compensation so that an agent's expected utility, typically expressed in monetary terms, increases with observed performance. This chapter employs the latter sense of the term. See Oliver E. Williamson, *The Economic Institutions of Capitalism* (New York: Free Press, 1985), p. 132; and George P. Baker, Michael C. Jensen, and Kevin J. Murphy, "Compensation and Incentives: Practice vs. Theory," *Journal of Finance*, 43 (July 1988), pp. 593–616, esp. p. 594. See also George P. Baker, "Incentive Contracts and Performance Measurement," *Journal of Political Economy*, 100, No. 3 (1992), pp. 598–614, esp. p. 609; Pascal Courty and Gerald R. Marschke, "Moral Hazard Under Incentive Systems: The Case of a Federal Bureaucracy," in Gary D. Libecap, ed., *Advances in the Study of Entrepreneurship, Innovation, and Economic Growth: Reinventing Government and the Problem of Bureaucracy* (Greenwich, CT: JAI Press, 1996), p. 157; Francine LaFontaine and Margaret E. Slade, "Retail Contracting: Theory and Practice," *Journal of Industrial Economics*, 45 (March 1997) pp. 1–25; and Bengt Homstrom and Paul Milgrom, "The Firm as an Incentive System," *American Economic Review*, 84 (September 1994), pp. 972–991.

For example, in Songjiang County in 1995, the leading cadres of the town with the strongest performance on the five core indicators enumerated earlier received the highest official salary of 17,500 yuan, whereas the leading cadres of the town with the weakest performance received the lowest salary of 6,000 yuan. A comparison of income differentials among township leaders in this single Chinese county and among managers of a single large manufacturing firm may help to put this difference in perspective. According to Baker et al., in a large manufacturing firm with several thousand managers, those "ranking lowest on the performance-rating scale are paid only 7.8 percent less than those ranking highest."[19] In contrast, among township leaders in Songjiang, the lowest-ranking township head was paid 66 percent less than the highest-ranking township executive. However, according to representatives of the county Office of Management and Administration, which oversaw the implementation of the evaluation system, the 6,000 yuan paid to the leaders of the lowest-performing town did not even fully reflect the penalties stipulated for poor performance. In this case, there appeared to be greater willingness on the part of county officials in Songjiang to employ positive as opposed to negative incentives. Even so, income differentials were relatively large, and strong performers received large payoffs.

Like its counterpart at the county level, the township Office of Management and Administration set the criteria used to evaluate both village leaders and collective enterprise managers, and, in this way, incentives created at the county level were ramified down through the administrative hierarchy.[20] Village leaders were usually collective cadres, who received no base salary from the state. For them, the performance criteria determined their entire incomes. In the seven villages for which data are available (from 1991, in this case), GVIO and industrial profits were the key targets in determining the incomes of village leaders. The case of a village party secretary in Jiading County illustrates how contract incentives were structured. According to his contract for 1991, his starting salary was linked to the level of industrial output achieved in the village that year; because the village's total output value exceeded a 2-million-yuan threshold,

---

[19] Baker et al., "Compensation and Incentives," p. 595.
[20] This section draws on Susan H. Whiting, "Contract Incentives and Market Discipline in China's Rural Industrial Sector," in John McMillan and Barry Naughton, eds., *Reforming Asian Socialism: The Growth of Market Institutions* (Ann Arbor, MI: University of Michigan Press), pp. 63–110.

he received a starting salary of 5,100 yuan. (Less successful village leaders received lower starting salaries; the minimum possible starting salary was 2,800 yuan.) In addition, this party secretary received 50 yuan for every 10,000 yuan of profit over and above the village's target level of 1.85 million yuan. Village enterprises produced total profits of 2.5 million yuan; therefore, he received a profit bonus of 3,250 yuan. Like township leaders, village leaders in Jiading were evaluated on a range of performance indicators, but their incomes were most closely linked to industrial output and profits. Performance on other, nonindustrial measures was typically linked only to small increments added to or subtracted from the bonus derived from industrial performance. In this case, the bonus for industrial output and profits accounted for the lion's share (about 85 percent) of the leader's income, which totaled 9,960 yuan.[21] In contrast, Baker et al. report that, in the typical large corporation in the United States, "explicit financial rewards in the form of transitory, performance-based bonuses" seldom account for a large percentage of the compensation packages of lower- and middle-level managers.[22]

Although cadres benefited from strong economic performances, they also paid a high price for weak economic showings. Moreover, a leader's remuneration was contingent upon the performance of other township or village leaders, thus pitting local cadres in competition with one another. Strong performance in one township or village tended to drive up target levels for the others. This characteristic of the evaluation system encouraged cadres to adopt policies intended to improve their performance relative to others. In two of the seven villages for which detailed data are available, village leaders' remuneration declined in light of declining relative performance and failure to meet rapidly increasing targets. A village in suburban Shanghai offers an example of the importance of this link. The village had been ranked third in the township in terms of output in 1989, but by 1991 it had fallen to ninth. The income of the village party secretary, who failed to meet his industrial targets, fell by several thousand yuan to 2,950 yuan, while higher-ranked village party secretaries earned more than 6,000 yuan each in 1991. Similarly, the leader of a village

---

[21]   Other case study evidence produces similar findings. Yan Yunxiang reports that bonuses constituted 80 percent of village leaders' incomes in Xiajia Village, Heilongjiang. Yan Yunxiang, "Everyday Power Relations: Changes in a North China Village," in Walder, ed., *The Waning of the Communist State*, p. 227.

[22]   Baker et al., "Compensation and Incentives," p. 595.

in another township presided over a period of declining economic performance relative to other villages in the township. As a result, his 1991 income of 4,046 yuan was 20 percent less than his 1988 income of 5,040 yuan, achieved three years earlier. Clearly, there were very real costs to failure to achieve the norms set by the cadre evaluation system.

Not only were the incomes of township and village leaders determined by their performance in rural industry, but their tenure in office and opportunities for advancement were to some extent as well. According to an official of the Shanghai Suburban Industry Management Bureau, which governed township- and village-run industry, during the 1990s, county leaders appointed township executives and party secretaries with the intention that they would participate directly in decision making with respect to this sector of the economy. As this official put it, they "rise or fall on the basis of economic success."[23] Similarly, published accounts of earlier evaluations by officials in Jiading County indicate that, on the basis of the results of cadre evaluations for 1989, 70 out of 327 township party secretaries, township executives, and leaders of county-level party and government organs were transferred out of their positions in 1990.[24]

The Impact of the Cadre Evaluation System on Policy Implementation: Dysfunctional Outcomes

As the preceding section has demonstrated, local versions of the cadre evaluation system combined specific performance-based measures with high-powered incentives. Formal principal–agent models predict that this combination will cause severe moral hazard problems[25] or what Baker et al. (1988) refer to as "gaming the system":

---

[23] Author's interview, February 10, 1992. Susan Shirk identifies a similar phenomenon at the provincial level: "Under the post-1980 incentive structure, the political ambitions of individual local officials became closely identified with the economic accomplishments of their domains.... Whether officials aimed to climb the ladder of success to Beijing or to become leading figures on the local scene, their reputation was enhanced by industrial growth and local building projects." Susan L. Shirk, *The Political Logic of Economic Reform in China* (Berkeley, CA: University of California Press, 1993), pp. 189–90.

[24] Wang Weifang, "Ganbu kaohe he tiaozheng lingdao banzi," in *Jiading Yearbook, 1988–1990*, p. 62.

[25] According to Thrainn Eggertsson, "Moral hazard arises in the enforcement of contracts when the performance of an agent is too costly to be observed as a whole and is measured at only one or a few margins. This may induce an agent to neglect various aspects of his or her assignments and concentrate on performing well [only] in the measured

Large monetary incentives generate unintended and sometimes counterproductive results because it is difficult to adequately specify exactly what people should do and therefore how their performance should be measured.... Mis-specifying the performance measure in an objective system results in resourceful employees "gaming the system" by optimizing with respect to actual instead of intended measures.[26]

Drawing on the insights of formal principal–agent models, I argue that the nature of the cadre evaluation system in China led to certain dysfunctional aspects of policy implementation at the grass roots. At the same time, however, superiors in the party-state hierarchy have shown sensitivity to this moral hazard problem by adjusting certain performance criteria and by avoiding others.

In the economic realm, moral hazard problems contributed to the development of overcapacity in many Chinese industries and led to the wasteful production of large quantities of useless products. With the introduction in the mid-1980s of specific performance indicators linked to personal income, GVIO took center stage as the indicator of industrial performance that received the most weight. Indeed, output value was prominently featured in the central guidelines issued in 1988 (Table 3.1), as it was in the cadre evaluation systems that initially emerged in both Songjiang and Jiading counties.[27] During the middle to late 1980s, township officials oversaw the rapid expansion of new and existing factories, even as existing factories accumulated large inventories of unmarketable products. This duplication of capacity resulted in heavy financial losses and the inability to repay the bank loans that had financed both fixed and working capital for the factories involved.[28] Local officials explicitly identified the use of output value as the key performance indicator as the culprit in eliciting such undesirable behavior – expansion without attention to the efficiency of the production process or to market demand for

dimensions." Thrainn Eggertsson, *Economic Behavior and Institutions* (New York: Cambridge University Press, 1990), pp. 44–45.

[26] Baker et al., "Compensation and Incentives," p. 597.

[27] It was also the case in other locales. See, for example, He Baoshan et al., on Jiangsu Province. He Baoshan, Gu Jirui, Yan Yinglong, Bao Zongshun, eds., *Jiangsu nongcun feinonghua fazhan yanjiu [Research on the Non-agricultural Development of Rural Jiangsu]* (Shanghai: Shanghai renmin chubanshe, 1991), p. 121.

[28] *Shanghai gongye jingji bao [Shanghai Industrial Economy]*, June 15, 1989, p. 1. See also Wang Xiaolu, "Capital Formation and Utilization," in William Byrd and Lin Qingsong, eds., *China's Rural Industry* (New York: Oxford University Press, 1990), p. 241.

or saleability of the products. This problem prompted officials in Jiading to modify the performance indicators. They incorporated profit into the indicators of industrial performance for the first time beginning in 1989, supplementing "increase in GVIO" with "increase in industrial profits," "increase in profit rate on gross value of output," and "township ranking by profit rate on total capital" (Table 3.2).[29] Similar problems were identified in Songjiang as well. As a representative of a township government in Songjiang noted, "Up to now, leaders have only worried about output value, but that's not what counts. What counts is profit."[30] In response to this problem, officials in Songjiang, like those in Jiading, added a measure for industrial profits to the existing measure of output value, as reflected in the 1995 performance indicators discussed herein.

Sensitivity to a potential moral hazard problem led some county-level supervisors to *avoid* using tax collection as an explicit performance indicator for the township officials they supervised, despite its inclusion in national guidelines. From the mid-1980s through the mid-1990s, local fiscal revenues were governed by a fiscal contracting system (*caizheng baoganzhi*) in which all tax revenues were shared with higher levels. Because of the sharing requirement, county officials sought to avoid revealing greater fiscal capacity to higher levels, which might result in an increase in the amount of revenue owed to higher levels. Rather, they preferred to tap the same revenue base locally through nontax levies, which were not subject to sharing.[31] Thus, the sensitivity to potential gaming behavior in the case of tax collection at the local level reflected strategic considerations in interactions between higher and lower levels. For these reasons, Songjiang County did not use tax receipts as an explicit performance indicator for township officials.[32] County-level supervisors did not wish to create incentives for township officials to concentrate their efforts on maximizing or gaming this particular dimension of their professional responsibilities.

---

[29] Jiading Party document No. 8 (1989): "Zhonggong jiadingxian wei jiadingxian renmin zhengfu, 'Guanyu wanshan 1989 nian xiangzhen dang zheng jiguan ganbu kaohe jiangli banfa de tongzhi,'" in *Jiading nianjian, 1988–1990 [Jiading Yearbook 1988–1990]*, pp. 44–5.

[30] Author's interview, April 17, 1992.

[31] Susan H. Whiting, *Power and Wealth in Rural China: The Political Economy of Institutional Change* (New York: Cambridge University Press, 2001).

[32] Author's interview, April 22, 1992.

It was only beginning in 1995 that tax revenue was used as an important performance measure in Songjiang County. The inclusion of tax revenue thus represents an important change from past practice. This change was motivated by the major fiscal reform instituted in 1994, which replaced the old fiscal contracting system with the new tax assignment system (*fenshuizhi*). Under the new system, taxes are designated as central or local tax types, with the revenues assigned to the level of government indicated. Only the value-added tax is shared, with 75 percent of the revenue going to the center and 25 percent going to the locality. Following this change, township officials in Songjiang began to be evaluated for the first time on the basis of collection of local tax types.

Expanding the Array of Performance-Based Measures: The Problem of Multitasking

Although middle-level supervisors manipulated performance criteria in the context of strategic interactions between higher and lower levels, the central party-state continued to use performance criteria to try to control local official behavior. As local officials increased their reliance on non-tax revenues and allowed nontax levies to proliferate, citizens began to protest against excessive financial burdens placed on them by the local state. The central state responded by adding new elements to the performance criteria for local officials. According to Central Party Document no. 13, which deals with the proliferation of nontax levies in rural areas,

Leadership must be strengthened, and top party and government executives must bear responsibility for reducing burdens [on farm households and TVEs]. They must attend to this personally and take overall responsibility – level by level. Reducing burdens will be used as an important criterion in the appointment and evaluation (*renyong he kaohe*) of leaders at each level, especially at the county and township levels. County and township leaders must ensure that within their jurisdictions (a) total burdens on farm households do not exceed five percent of household income on average in any village, (b) there are no levies violating central regulations or increasing burdens, and (c) no serious incidents or cases [of unrest] occur as a result of farmers' burdens. Agencies at every level, especially central agencies, must take the lead in implementing relevant regulations on reducing burdens, ensure uniform implementation of central directives, and strictly enforce all orders and prohibitions. Leaders of relevant agencies must take responsibility and manage their administrative hierarchies effectively. From this date, the core leader of any locality or agency that increases burdens will be held strictly responsible. Any cadre who is subject to disciplinary action for increasing burdens will not be eligible for promotion or appointment to an important position for the period specified.[33]

Thus, new measures continued to be added to the array of performance-based measures on which local officials were evaluated.

The sheer number and variety of tasks evaluated through performance-based measures posed additional problems. Specifically, multiple indicators were not necessarily mutually compatible. For example, performance on industrial profits and public order were at times in conflict. Whereas increasing industrial profits at times required laying off redundant workers, the maintenance of public order necessitated retaining redundant workers in their jobs. Higher-level officials addressed this problem by further classifying performance criteria into primary and secondary sets of indicators. In some locales the primary performance criteria were termed *fouding zhibiao* (loosely translated as critical targets) or *ying zhibiao* (translated as hard targets). These targets had to be met for overall performance to be considered adequate. Targets considered to be critical during the latter 1990s typically included tax receipts, public order, and family-planning compliance.[34]

CADRE EVALUATION AND THE DURABILITY OF CCP RULE

The continued reliance on performance-based measures and high-powered incentives is puzzling in light of the severe moral hazard problems and multitask coordination problems encountered during the implementation of the cadre evaluation system at the local level in China. It is also puzzling in light of findings from empirical studies of large organizations in other settings, which suggest that the "problems associated with determining and modifying objective performance measures and the dysfunctional behavior induced by resourceful employees faced with

---

[33] Central Party and State Council document No. 13 (1996): "Guanyu qieshi zuohao jianqing nongmin fudan gongzuo de jueding," in *Guowuyuan gongbao [State Council Bulletin]*, No. 12 (1997), p. 563–8.

[34] Author's interviews, August 13, 1996 and September 18, 1997. Kevin O'Brien and Lianjiang Li report similar findings. Kevin O'Brien and Lianjiang Li, "Selective Policy Implementation in Rural China," *Comparative Politics*, 31 (January 1999), pp. 167–186; See also Maria Eden, "State Capacity and Local Agent Control in China: CCP Cadre Management from a Township Perspective," *China Quarterly* 173 (March 2003), pp. 35–52, esp. p. 39.

such measures lead organizations to *avoid* pay-for-performance systems based on objective performance evaluation."[35] Paradoxically, however, continued reliance on the cadre evaluation system may have contributed to the durability of CCP rule. Indeed, recent documents on refining the cadre management system explicitly identify it as an important means for ensuring competence and checking corruption.[36] In developing this argument, I draw on Victor Nee and Peng Lian's model of "declining political commitment in state socialism" to suggest why high-powered incentives and performance-based measures may be useful in securing political commitment. As they suggest, "analysts need to pay attention to the organizational health of the communist party."[37]

According to Nee and Lian, "the penetration of market institutions – both informal and formal, domestic and international – increases the incentive for opportunism [on the part of cadres] at the same time that accompanying institutional change weakens the monitoring and enforcement capacity of the party." They attempt to show how the resulting increase in opportunism and concomitant decline in commitment to the party can lead to its collapse as an effective political organization; they do so by modeling cadres as agents in a multiagent repeated game, in which agents must choose whether to commit to or defect from the party. Agents defect if

$$bh + (1 - b)l > m,$$

where b is the probability that opportunism goes undetected (as a result of inadequate monitoring), h is the payoff for opportunism, l is the punishment for unsuccessful opportunism, and m is the payoff for commitment.[38] The significance of high-powered incentives in this context is

---

[35] Baker et al., "Compensation and Incentives," p. 599.

[36] "Shenhua ganbu renshi zhidu gaige gangyao" ["Outline on Deepening the Reform of the Cadre Personnel System"], in *Guowuyuan gongbao [State Council Bulletin]* No. 29 (2000), pp. 5–11.

[37] Nee and Lian, "Sleeping with the Enemy," p. 255. The authors define opportunism as "market-oriented entrepreneurship and rent-seeking" (p. 268). This line of argument is similar to that of Andrew Walder, who has also argued that the party-state has experienced significant decay. He attributes it to the economic reforms. See Andrew G. Walder, "The Quiet Revolution from Within: Economic Reform as a Source of Political Decline," in Walder, ed., *The Waning of the Communist State,* pp. 1–24.

[38] Nee and Lian conceptualize payoffs primarily in terms of personal, material gain. However, they recognize three types of party cadres: true believers, middle-of-the-roaders, and pure opportunists. Their model is most relevant to the latter two types of cadres,

that they can result in relatively high material payoffs for commitment (m) for an important core of cadres who are performing well on the most heavily weighted performance measures. Nee and Lian's model fails to account for this aspect of m. Rather, they assume m to be the same for all cadres who are committed to the party.[39] In contrast, the empirical findings presented in this chapter suggest that successful, committed cadres can obtain relatively high payoffs by working within the system, thereby decreasing the likelihood that they will defect, even when faced with "market temptations."

Nee and Lian also indicate that the monitoring capacity of the party is critically important to the durability of party rule. The cadre evaluation system, in which local officials are systematically supervised and evaluated on an ongoing basis, may contribute to the stability of the CCP regime through its contribution to more active monitoring. In terms of the model, the cadre evaluation system reduces b, the probability that opportunism goes undetected. As just demonstrated in the aforementioned empirical discussion, the cadre evaluation system holds local officials responsible for providing a specified level of public goods in addition to promoting economic growth within their communities. In Jiading County, for example, township leaders were explicitly evaluated on the scale of funds dedicated to education and the completion rate for compulsory education. In Hezheng County, township leaders were evaluated on the upgrading of road surfaces as well as on the completion rate for compulsory education. These measures most likely did not preclude corruption (such as the diversion of public funds away from public goods provision), but they increased the likelihood that those officials who failed to provide a minimum acceptable level of key public goods were discovered and faced real consequences, whether in terms of income, tenure, or promotion. In this way, the cadre evaluation system provided a check on public spending in certain key policy areas, such as education and infrastructure development. Furthermore, spending in these areas likely contributed to productivity growth in the formal economy. Finally, although false reporting may occur, the competitive framework in which cadres are evaluated may help to expose false reports to superiors over time.

who are susceptible, to a greater or lesser degree, to the lure of personal, material gain. Nee and Lian, "Sleeping with the Enemy," pp. 274–5.

[39] It "equals the total payoff minus the payoff to opportunists divided by the number of committors." Nee and Lian, "Sleeping with the Enemy," p. 269.

CONCLUSION

The evidence presented in this chapter suggests that, in the post-Mao period, specific performance criteria have been developed to mobilize local cadres around specific policy goals. Although these goals reflect the main concerns of the central government, they also reflect the interests and priorities of officials at the lower levels of the administrative hierarchy. County-level officials appear to adjust performance criteria for township officials in response to several factors, including changes in the broader policy environment and strategic interactions with higher levels, changes in the economic environment, and problems of contractual design such as those involving coordination among multiple tasks and moral hazard problems.

Further research is required to assess the relative importance of the cadre evaluation system in local governance. Local cadres are embedded in formal administrative structures and in informal networks, both of which likely affect their opportunities for reward and advancement and therefore their behavior. This chapter suggests that performance criteria (*kaohe zhibiao*) elicit minimal acceptable levels of performance on the part of local officials through annual evaluations in the context of competition with other officials at the same administrative level in the same region. However, the formal system also operates in tandem with informal relationships that introduce alternative criteria into the calculus of local cadres. Nevertheless, the relatively high-powered incentives contained in the cadre evaluation system, as applied to local party and government executives, help to reinforce commitment to party goals, thereby contributing to the durability of CCP rule.

4

Economic Transformation and State Rebuilding in China

Dali L. Yang

Historically,[1] the development of modern market economies in different countries has pushed states to "develop rules about property rights, governance structures, rules of exchange, and conceptions of control in order to stabilize markets" (Fligstein, 2001, p. 36). In the United States, the historian Robert H. Wiebe famously noted, the march of nationalization, industrialization, mechanization, and urbanization exerted enormous strains on the ethos and institutions of small-town America and prompted a search for order (Wiebe, 1967). The state that was forged in the Civil War became inadequate to the push and pull of industrialism, and "a qualitatively different kind of state" was built in the late 19th and early 20th centuries during what is now known as the Progressive Era (Skowronek, 1982, p. 4). Civil service reforms were introduced to curb the corrupt localism and particularism of patronage politics; a managerial and regulatory state arose to tackle problems ranging from poor public health to monopolies. Echoes of the Progressive Era's political struggles and negotiations over the shape of this regulatory state continue to be heard in today's United States, often magnified in episodes such as the collapse of Enron and Worldcom.[2]

As the postcommunist economies have dismantled their command economies, they have also faced the daunting challenges of refurbishing

[1] Earlier versions of this chapter were presented at the international conference on "Centre – Periphery Relations in China: Integration, Disintegration or Reshaping of an Empire?" March 24–25, 2000, The Chinese University of Hong Kong and at the American Political Science Association Annual Meeting, August 31–September 2, 2000, Washington, D.C. I thank John Burns and Alfred Stepan for their helpful comments.
[2] See, e.g., Carpenter, 2001.

the state for the era of markets. In the 1980s and through the early 1990s, the Chinese reforms parceled out resources and power to local interests. Most studies of China suggested that the decentralization and the flattening out of the organization of the Chinese state contributed to the rapid growth of the Chinese economy (Oi, 1992; Qian and Xu, 1993). Yet, although the decentralization provided incentives for local development, it also gave local authorities the wherewithal to engage in all manners of local protectionism. Such protectionism in turn served to undermine the formation of a national market as well as the fair administration of justice. More broadly, the institutional designs that stimulated local protectionism contributed to the legitimacy crisis of the party-state.

When Jiang Zemin was catapulted to Beijing to become the general secretary of the Chinese Communist Party in 1989, he was widely seen as a transitional figure much like Mao's immediate successor Hua Guofeng. In the aftermath of the Tiananmen tragedy of 1989 and the collapse of the Soviet Union as well as amid macroeconomic difficulties, Jiang, Premier Li Peng, and other central leaders were afraid of losing their grip over the ponderous organizational setup. In response, they have struggled to reconstitute the sinews of governance, especially the levers of central control.

Unlike Russian leadership, the Chinese leadership has retained and strengthened control over the Communist Party and the instruments of state violence. As the chapters by Cheng Li and Zhiyue Bo have discussed the party's oversight over personal management, in this chapter I focus on the restructuring of the fiscal, financial, and various administrative systems to reveal the extent to which central–local relations have been put on a different footing.

In contrast to commentators who have suggested that the recentralization of the 1990s would have had the approval of Mao and could go as far as to choke off growth (Chang, 1999), I suggest that China's leaders appear to have found a middle ground for reorganizing the framework for state action. Although some of the reforms, including taxation and the fiscal system, are aimed at shoring up the fiscal foundations of the central state, most of the reforms have a public goods aspect in that the center has to step in where the local authorities are likely to shirk. This is clearly the case in the reforms of the central banking system (macroeconomic policy), but it is equally important in the enforcement of laws for environmental protection, quality, safety, and intellectual property. In other words, I argue that much progress has been made toward the construction of a regulatory state.

REBUILDING THE TAX AND FISCAL INSTITUTIONS

Besides strengthening control over areas that the Communist Party had traditionally emphasized, including the military and armed police, personnel appointments, and the propaganda apparatus, the crisis in the economy at the turn of the 1990s, characterized by rising inflation, prompted the central leadership to seek to reassert economic control. As China's leaders grappled with the economic turmoil, they quickly realized that the Chinese financial system was not conducive to the sort of fine-tuning they had in mind. Frustrated by the difficulties of maneuvering a makeshift economic system and afraid that they might not be able to get the house in order before Deng died (Deng turned 89 in August 1993), the Chinese leadership began to push for sweeping rationalizing reforms of the economic system.

I have discussed the economic stabilization measures elsewhere (Yang, 1999). Simply put, concerns about political succession, macroeconomic difficulties, and the central government's take of government revenue were the leading factors behind the Chinese leadership drive to restructure the fiscal and tax systems. In 1993, the central government's share of the budgetary revenue was only 22 percent of the total, with the rest going to the provinces. The fiscal deficit reached 29.9 billion yuan. The fiscal enervation of the central government relative to the localities made central leaders feel that they were piloting an aircraft carrier by using the controls for a small boat. In the words of Finance Minister Liu Zhongli, "when the government does not have money, its words no longer count." Thus the central leadership, particularly Jiang Zemin and Zhu Rongji, decided to take the political risk and push for a revamping of the taxation and fiscal systems in 1993. They invoked alarmist visions and the authority of Deng to gain leverage over provincial authorities.[3] In driving the bargain, they promised that the provinces would not see a reduction in their current level of fiscal income. Afraid that provincial leaders

---

[3] For a succinct overview of problems with the prereform fiscal system, see Bahl, 1999, pp. 24–8.

would present a united front in collective bargaining, the central leadership marshaled its organizational and other resources and adopted a divide-and-rule strategy vis-à-vis local officials (Yang, 1994, pp. 85–7). A special working group, made up of over 60 people, including Vice Premier Zhu Rongji and officials from the Ministry of Finance and other government departments, traveled to 17 provinces one by one to hammer out the base revenue figures for each province and readjust the fiscal relations between the central government and the provinces.

By the end of 1993, a sweeping reform of the taxation and fiscal systems had been put together for implementation starting in 1994. In contrast to the fiscal contracting system that had given the central government only a set amount of revenue, the newly introduced tax assignment system designated different categories of taxes to the central and local governments, respectively, similar to the federalist system used in many Western countries.[4] The reforms standardized the taxation system, simplified tax categories and tax rates, and, by promoting fair taxation, were conducive to fair market competition (Xiang Huaicheng, 1997). The reforms were clearly designed to help the central government benefit from the marginal growth in the economy and in revenue generation (Chung, 1995; Yang, 1994).

The fiscal reforms were introduced without much difficulty and had an immediate impact on the division of revenue between the center and provinces.[5] In 1994, the central government's share of budgetary revenue rose to 56 percent, an increase of 33.7 percentage points from a year earlier. It has remained at more than 50 percent since then. Although most of the increased central revenue was returned to the provinces as rebates, the central government's effective control over the revenue stream has

---

[4]   According to the plenum decision (Article 18) and the Ministry of Finance, the major taxes and responsibilities shall be allocated as follows: The central government is responsible for funding national defense, diplomacy, armed police, key state projects, the national deficit, and governmental administrative departments, whereas other expenditures shall be the responsibility of local governments. Central revenue will come from tariffs, a consumption tax collected by customs, value-added taxes and (nationally based) business taxes. Taxes collected by local governments include business tax, income tax of local enterprises, and a personal income tax. Taxes shared by both central and local governments include the value-added tax, securities trading tax, and natural resources tax. In other words, the center will rely on indirect taxes, leaving the politically hazardous and administratively cumbersome personal income tax to local authorities.

[5]   For a discussion of the problems of implementation, see Sun and Wang, 1994.

been augmented. In the meantime, local authorities have less incentive to hide taxes and wealth from the central government as they collect their own taxes. In consequence, local tax revenue has also grown far more rapidly than before the fiscal reforms.

In connection with the tax reforms, major initiatives were undertaken to strengthen the institutional underpinnings of tax administration for the central government.[6] Prior to the 1994 reforms, the central government relied on locals to collect taxes for remission. Local governments used their discretionary power to negotiate tax payments with enterprises and offered tax exemptions to overseas investors to attract investments. There were multiple tax arrangements for different enterprises, enterprises of different ownership, and different industries. The delegation of tax authority to the local level was therefore not conducive to the creation of a level playing field. In contrast, the change from contracting to tax sharing calls for greater transparency and equity. It also dramatically increases the central government's desire to monitor the tax administration effort when it previously could simply wait for the delivery of the negotiated contractual amount from the local authorities. What better way to strengthen its monitoring than to set up its own tax-collection apparatus! Thus a key element of the tax reforms was a fundamental reform in tax administration and the establishment of separate central (national) and provincial (local) tax administrations. In short, the 1994 reforms not only demarcated the taxation powers between the central government and the provinces but also provided the establishment of separate state and local taxation bureaus at the provincial, prefectural, city, and county levels.[7]

In terms of organizational hierarchy, the State Administration of Taxation (SAT) directly oversees the provincial state taxation bureaus (*guoshuiju*) in what is known as *chuizhi guanli*, or vertical administration. Within this vertical administration structure, each level supervises the next level in matters of organization, staffing, budgets, and leader

---

[6]   All taxes collected from Customs go to the central government treasury. As the state tax bureaus are built up, the Customs Administration was upgraded to ministerial status and reconstituted. The reconstitution placed 41 Customs Offices directly under the supervision of the central administration (*Zhishu haiguan*) whereas previously they were under the dual leadership of center and localities with the balance favoring local authorities (*RMRB*, October 25, 1999).

[7]   In Heilongjiang, for example, the existing taxation personnel were transferred to state and local taxation bureaus according to the ratio of 6 to 4 (*Heilongjiang ribao [Heilongjiang Daily]*, September 19, 1994; FBIS-CHI-94-192).

duties.[8] This organizational strategy signaled a retreat from the emphasis on decentralization that had prevailed for more than a decade and was evidently a key element of the new focus on strengthening central control. The establishment of the state tax (*guoshui*) administration means that the central government is no longer dependent on the goodwill of the local authorities.

Because the state taxation bureaus are mainly staffed by locals, the Ministry of Finance is concerned about local influences on the behavior of these bureaus. Interviews suggest that local government officials, including deputy governors, sometimes ask the state tax bureaus to be more lenient in collecting taxes for the central government. In order to ensure compliance with central government policies, the Ministry of Finance has also set up special representative officials in provincial units as well as large cities with independent planning status (*jihua danlie shi*) in conjunction with the tax and fiscal reforms. The representative office in Shandong, for example, has a staff of more than forty (compared with over 30,000 employees in the state taxation bureau). The representative office has two major functions: the supervision of centrally disbursed expenditures to ensure compliance with central government spending targets and the supervision of the state taxation bureau to ensure the collection of taxes owed to the central government.[9]

Supervision of the provincial local taxation bureaus is shared between the SAT and provincial governments under dual leadership, but the provincial governments supply the funds and personnel and are the dominant partner. In various provinces, the director of the provincial finance department doubles as director of the provincial local taxation bureau.[10] Although the state and local tax bureaus collect different taxes, they also coordinate and collaborate with each other. This is most obvious in tax registration. The state taxation bureau is responsible for registering taxpayers liable for the value-added tax whereas the local taxation bureau registers those who pay the business tax and other local taxes. The two

---

[8] "Separation of State, Local Tax Systems Nearly Complete," Xinhua, August 15, 1994, FBIS-CHI-94-160.

[9] Shandong interview, June 26, 2000.

[10] "Guizhou Leaders Inaugurate State, Local Taxation Bureaus," Guizhou People's Radio Network, August 13, 1994, FBIS-CHI-94-157; "Sichuan Sets Up State, Local Taxation Bureaus," Chengdu Sichuan People's Radio Network, August 11, 1994, FBIS-CHI-94-158.

bureaus are to share their registration lists for reference and to conduct verification of the list jointly.[11]

In spite of the adoption of vertical administration and the establishment of the supervisory representative offices, the diversification of ownership made it more difficult for the central government to collect taxes that were proportionate to its share of ownership in various enterprises. When bureaus of industry and commerce register firms by capital structure, they do not differentiate between central and local ownership (both are referred to as state ownership), thus making it difficult for state taxation personnel to keep track of central-government-owned shares. Partly in response to these concerns but also to further boost the central government's fiscal strength, in 2002 the central government began to take a share of corporate and personal income taxes, both of which had been assigned to local governments in 1994. Over time the 2002 reforms, building on the basis of the 1994 reforms, are expected to dramatically expand the central government's fiscal prowess vis-à-vis the localities, just as the expansion of the personal income tax in the United States greatly facilitated the expansion of the Federal Government in the United States.

REVAMPING THE SYSTEMS FOR FINANCIAL SUPERVISION

Until the late 1990s, branches of the People's Bank of China (PBOC), officially the central bank only since 1984, were not only based in provincial capitals and larger cities but were also subject to the dual leadership of provincial and local governments.[12] Provincial party officials were key players in choosing heads of the PBOC's provincial branches; they also had much influence on the choice of branch officers of the major state banks. Consequently, as Lardy noted, until 1993 "the provincial branches of the central bank responded primarily to provincial level political leaders rather than central bank headquarters in Beijing" (Lardy, 1998, pp. 90–1).

Whereas fiscal decentralization increased the need for macroeconomic coordination and control, the decentralization of the banking system, by making central bank branches (as well as branches of the major state

---

[11] Jin Man, "Tax Bureaux Roles Defined," *CDBW*, September 18, 1994.
[12] The People's Bank was formally designated as the central bank by a State Council resolution on September 17, 1983.

banks) susceptible to local government influence, compounded that need. Local government officials seeking high growth rates – on which they tend to be evaluated – eagerly exerted pressures on state banks to make loans to local enterprises. For them, macroeconomic stability is a public good best left to others. Partly because of the intermarriage between political and financial power, the Chinese state banks through the first half of the 1990s became overextended in capital investment and real estate development, often through bank-affiliated investment and trust companies. Some of the bank funds were also funneled into speculative investments, including the nascent stock market. During the financial turmoil of 1993–1994, state bank branches often had little cash to pay farmers or lend to factories for operating funds and wage payments. According to veteran banking analyst Yang Peixin (1990), banks usually set aside as much as six yuan in cash reserves for each 100 yuan in deposits, but in May 1993, the average was reduced to only about 1 yuan. (*AWSJW*, May 31, 1993; *DJN*, June 30, 1993. Definitions of abbreviations used in this chapter are given at the end of the text.) China was on the brink of financial chaos in 1993.

Much of the lending from Chinese banks was made to state enterprises; a high percentage of the loans are nonperforming loans that plague the financial system (Lardy, 1998). Until bankruptcy of state enterprises became a real possibility in the late 1990s, it was rational for bank officials to follow the instructions of government officials and lend to state enterprises. Moreover, because domestic real interest rates were until recently consistently negative, credit demand far outstripped supply and bank lending was generally based on bureaucratic rationing through lending quotas rather than careful assessment of credit worthiness. The intermarriage of politics and finance thus provided patronage opportunities to officials in both local governments and banks.

Clearly, improvement in the regulation of the banking sector was sorely needed in China. The problem was not that the PBOC, the central bank, was not independent, though central bank independence is increasingly believed to contribute to stable macroeconomic performance (Alesina and Summers, 1993). Rather, the PBOC was until recently so beholden to local interests that it was often hardly acting like a central bank at all. By 1988, the PBOC had twenty-nine provincial branches, 529 city branches, and 1,760 county branches, and it had more than 130,000 employees (Holz, 1992, p. 31; World Bank, 1990b, p. 3). The more branches the bank boasted, the more access points it opened up for political influence by political elite in the localities. Local officials not only had much influence on lending decisions but also interfered in efforts by the central government to deal with financial irregularities.

To be fair, Chinese leaders in the reform era have constantly tinkered with the central banking system, beginning with the formal establishment of the PBOC as the central bank. There was also early recognition of the harmful effect of local influence over central bank branches. In 1988, the head office of the PBOC was empowered to appoint managers of local branch offices (World Bank, 1990b, p. 5). However, this order had a limited impact on local interference. Leaders of central bank branches continued to succumb to pressure from powerful local officials because the bankers needed the local governments' assistance in their work. The personal interests for bankers, including welfare for family members and postbanking jobs for themselves, also benefited from their rapport with local officials (*CD*, Dec. 22, 1998). Moreover, the large number of local bank offices also diluted the ability of the central bank headquarters to micromanage appointments.

As the central government worked hard to tame inflation and shore up the fiscal sinews of the state in 1993, it was again proposed that the central banking system should be revamped to make it more independent of local government interests.[13] The need for reform is clear from a comparison of the Chinese and American central bank systems. At the end of 1996, the PBOC employed some 180,000 people at more than 2,400 different offices around China.[14] In contrast, the U.S. Federal Reserve – the central banking system for the largest economy of the world – consists of its Washington headquarters, twelve regional reserve banks, and a staff of 23,000 (Epstein, 1999).[15] Such a comparison implies that any restructuring of the Chinese central bank should not only entail structural reorganization that reduces the influence enjoyed by local governments but would also involve staff reductions.

To reform the central banking system, the Third Plenum of the 14th CCP Central Committee held in November 1993 decided that a unified monetary policy demanded that the branches of the central bank be offices

---

[13] For information about the evolution of the PBOC up to 1992, see Holz, 1992.
[14] Karby Leggett, "China Central Bank Details Reorganization To Bolster Oversight," *DJN*, November 16, 1998.
[15] It should be noted that there have also been calls for reforming and downsizing the Federal Reserve.

representing the central headquarters. The plenum called for actively creating the conditions for setting up central bank branches that span provincial boundaries in order to insulate banks from heavy meddling by local and especially provincial leaders.[16] The Banking Laws, promulgated in 1995, also stipulate that the PBOC conducts an independent monetary policy under the leadership of the State Council and its operations shall be free from interference from local governments, government departments, social organizations, and individuals.[17]

In spite of these pronouncements, the banking reform plan did not get off the ground immediately. This was partly because central leaders focused their attention on negotiating with provincial leaders over taxation and fiscal reforms. These negotiations over central–provincial relations required the expenditure of significant political resources by central leaders. Not wanting to fight political battles on all fronts, the central leadership put aside the central bank restructuring, which also faced strong local opposition for the reduction of local influence as well as jobs. Instead, the central government combined monetary policy with political discipline, highlighted by the appointment of Vice Premier Zhu Rongji as PBOC governor in order to control credit and tame inflation. These measures were enough to bring about a soft landing for the Chinese economy (Yang, 1999). By late 1997, the Chinese economy, squeezed by domestic monetary tightening and the Asian economic crisis, had finally left inflation behind and entered into a period of deflation. In short, China's ability to fall back on extraeconomic measures to stabilize the economy actually served to dull the urgency to reform the central banking system.

The onset of the Asian financial crisis in the summer of 1997, however, sent a jolt to Chinese leaders. To be sure, compared with Thailand and other countries, China fared quite well during the crisis; this was partly because China had accumulated a large foreign-exchange reserve in the aftermath of the 1993–1994 macroeconomic crisis, and partly because the Chinese currency was not freely convertible for the capital account. Nevertheless, like most other Asian countries, China was also afflicted with the problems of an underdeveloped legal system, corruption, a banking

---

[16] This was further reiterated in the State Council's decision on the reform of the financial system issued in December 1993. The idea of superregional branches was also mooted in the Bank by 1990 (World Bank, 1990b, p. 5).

[17] For background on the drafting of the banking laws, see *RMRBO*, December 8, 1993.

system that would be insolvent by western standards, weak financial supervision, cozy relations between government and business, and other symptoms that were found to have contributed to the financial meltdown in Thailand, South Korea, and Indonesia. Moreover, China's status as one of the world's major traders and leading destinations for foreign direct investment also implied vulnerability to external shocks. The political fallout from the Asian crisis, as evidenced in elite turnovers in several countries and the dramatic fall of the Suharto regime in Indonesia, highlighted the potentially enormous political costs of financial failure for Chinese leaders. There was sufficient concern within China that a massive bank failure in China would not only bring the Chinese economy to its knees but could bring to an end the Communist Party's rule.[18] As a member of the Bank for International Settlements, the PBOC participated in the drafting and revision of the 25 core principles on effective banking supervision that were issued by the Basel Committee on Banking Regulations and Supervisory Practices in September 1997.

To cope with the effect of the Asian financial crisis and prevent the occurrence of a financial meltdown, the Chinese Communist Party Central Committee and the State Council convened a national financial work meeting in November of 1997. By now, the death of patriarch Deng Xiaoping had passed uneventfully. Once they had weathered Deng's departure, it was clear that Jiang Zemin and his colleagues were in control. It was decided at the meeting that a comprehensive restructuring of China's financial system, especially the central bank, would be undertaken over a three-year period in order to establish a sound regulatory and supervisory framework and to reduce financial risk.

This call for action in financial reform resurrected the plan for revamping the central banking system. First, the PBOC had to participate in the overall government reform. Some had expected that the PBOC head office would be spared from staff cuts, as had happened in past administrative reforms, so that it could focus its attention on strengthening key functions, including research and policy formulation, bank supervision, and financial regulation.[19] This was not the case; instead the headquarters

---

[18] A number of Chinese scholars in Beijing suggested such a possibility in interviews I conducted over 1996–1998.

[19] Kathy Chen, "People's Bank of China Plans To Slash Staff by Up to 50%," *WSJ*, April 30, 1998.

were expected to drastically reduce staff and improve efficiency. In a demonstration of commitment to reform, in August 1998, staff size for the PBOC was reduced from over 2,000 to 500 through early retirement, retraining, and transfers. As the head count at headquarters was cut as part of the State Council reorganization, there was also some effort to streamline the local branches. In September, 167 county and municipal branches were abolished and some others merged to boost supervision and cut costs (Reuters, July 22, 1998).

The need for financial reform was underscored by the failure of Guangdong International Trust & Investment Corporation (GITIC) in October 1998, when GITIC was unable to pay debts of more than $2 billion (U.S. billion). The failure of GITIC and other local government investment and trust vehicles, known as Itics, drove home the message that local authorities cannot be relied on to enforce the financial discipline that prudence demanded. This prompted the central leadership to accelerate financial reforms, including preparing the ground for overhauling the spatial structure of the PBOC. In particular, Dai Xianglong, PBOC Governor lamented the webs of local connections that enmeshed the local branches of the PBOC and seriously undermined the quality and efficiency of financial supervision. For Dai, intervention from local government officials was a major source of risky loans and major financial irregularities. According to Dai, countries including the United States, Great Britain, Japan, Mexico, India, and many others all have central bank branches covering whole regions rather than single states or provinces.[20] The abolition of provincial branches of the PBOC in favor of superprovincial branches should help guarantee the independence of the central bank in exercising its supervisory role (see Table 4.1).

In late 1998, the central government implemented a PBOC restructuring plan to abolish the thirty-two provincial-level branches and set up nine regional branches.[21] In addition to the regional branches, the Beijing head office oversees the Beijing and Chongqing branches of the PBOC. What is most important is that the PBOC directly appoints the directors of the regional offices. Indeed, in appointing directors of the regional branches,

---

[20] Interview with Dai Xianglong, Governor of the People's Bank of China, in *ZGB*, November 18, 1998.

[21] The designation of regions is based on the amount of supervisory work (or financial activities) rather than on geographical size. The regional branches have representative offices in provinces in which the regional branch offices are not present.

Table 4.1. *PBOC Regional Branches*

Branch	Coverage Area
Tianjin	Tianjin, Hebei, Inner Mongolia, and Shanxi
Shenyang	Liaoning, Jilin, and Heilongjiang
Shanghai	Shanghai, Zhejiang, and Fujian
Nanjing	Jiangsu
Jinan	Shandong, and Henan
Wuhan	Hubei, Hunan, and Jiangxi
Guangzhou	Guangdong, Guangxi, and Hainan
Chengdu	Sichuan, Guizhou, Tibet, and Yunnan
Xian	Shaanxi, Gansu, Ningxia, Qinghai, and Xinjiang

the central government took care not to place appointees in their native provinces. These managerial strategies have helped the PBOC to finally break the curse of local interference that plagued the Chinese banking system for decades (though it has also become more difficult to get local leaders to be involved in financial supervision). Moreover, the central leadership has rotated top officials of the central bank and the major commercial banks, as well as the China Securities Regulatory Commission, in order to reduce corruption and strengthen management of the Chinese financial system.[22]

By consolidating authority into regional branches not beholden to provincial authorities, this reorganization has strengthened the implementation of monetary policy. In general, the PBOC has increasingly behaved like a central bank in a market economy rather than performing the many administrative roles it used to play. Most prominently, it resumed open market operations in 1998 after an initial trial in 1996 was suspended, making it a major tool of monetary policy (Reuters, Jan. 5, 2000).

Equally significant has been the PBOC's role in supervising the financial sector. Following the dramatic collapse of GITIC, the PBOC has

---

[22] Most prominently, in March 2000, there were the following rotations: the president of the China Construction Bank was appointed chairman of the China Securities Regulatory Commission; the president of the China Bank of Industry and Commerce became vice president of the Bank of China; the director of the Shanghai Branch of the PBOC was promoted to deputy governor of the PBOC; the chairman of the Everbright Group became president of the Bank of China; a vice president of the Bank of the China was appointed president of the China Agricultural Bank; and the president of the Bank of China was transferred to the post of president of the China Construction Bank.

become more aggressive in dealing with potential risks to the financial system. A host of provincial and municipal trust and investment companies has been closed. The PBOC has also ordered the four largest state commercial banks to tighten internal monitoring and risk management while improving incentives for performance. These stipulations, coupled with the detention and arrest of many banking officers, including Wang Xuebing, former Bank of China President, have driven home the message that fundamental changes are needed, particularly because China's World Trade Organization membership will in time let in formidable foreign competitors. Caught between tougher regulatory demands and growing competition, the big commercial banks have each closed a large number of underperforming branches, tightened internal control and risk management, and developed new products (principally consumer loans for houses and automobiles). By 2001–2002, the reforms of the commercial banks finally began to produce dividends in reducing the ratios of nonperforming loans (NPL). During 2002, when each of the big four state-owned commercial banks had adopted the more stringent five-category loan classification scheme, the China Construction Bank reduced its NPL ratio by 3.99 percentage points to 15.4 percent. The Bank of China whittled down its NPL ratio by 5.1 percentage points to 22.4 percent. The NPL ratio for the Industrial and Commercial Bank of China dropped by 4.3 percent to reach 25.5 percent, whereas that of the Agricultural Bank of China, which has been loath to disclose its nauseating NPL ratio, decreased by 4.7 percentage points.[23] These ratios remain extraordinarily high by international standards, but, in light of the progress made so far, they offer the hope of working out China's banking mess through further NPL reductions by the banks themselves, government recapitalization, and share sales.

Whereas regulation of the banking sector has required the refitting of an old structure, the newly emerging markets for securities and insurance have necessitated the establishment of brand-new regulatory frameworks. For the sake of space, these are not discussed here. Suffice it to say that the regulation of these industries has also been centralized and strengthened.

---

[23] The NPL ratio for the China Construction Bank would be 15.2 percent if data from offshore branches are included. These bank data are from *Guoji jinrong bao [International Financial News]*, January 24, 2002; *Jingji cankao bao [Economic Reference Daily]*, January 24, 2003; and DJN, January 22, 2003.

In the case of the securities industry, the central government took control of the regulatory apparatus from local governments in 1998. With the formal implementation of the Securities Law on July 1, 1999, the branches of the China Securities Regulatory Commission became operational nationwide, thus forming a centralized and unified network of securities supervisors.[24] At the same time, a move was also made to establish a unified share registration, transaction, and settlement system for the two securities markets (Shanghai and Shenzhen) to enhance efficiency and reduce transaction costs for investors (*CD*, July 26, 2000). By the early 2000s, China's securities regulatory authority had acquired teeth that bite: chronic loss makers have been delisted from the stock exchanges; corporations and officers found to have engaged in massive accounting fraud have been subject to various forms of punishment, including legal proceedings.

STRENGTHENING THE REGULATORY INSTITUTIONS FOR MAINTAINING MARKET ORDER

The Chinese leadership has also restructured various regulatory and enforcement agencies that play vital roles in ensuring market order and fair competition and in promoting sustained economic development. These agencies were mostly established in the reform era and include the State Environmental Protection Agency, the State Administration of Industry and Commerce, the State Intellectual Property Office (formerly the State Patent Bureau), the State Copyright Office, the State Administration of Quality Supervision, the State Food and Drug Administration, and the reconstituted Ministry of Land and Resources.[25] Complemented by nongovernmental organizations such as the Chinese Consumers' Association, these agencies are charged with the enforcement of state laws on patents, copyrights, trademarks and brand names, the environment, and quality and technical standards, as well as with the protection of consumer rights.[26] All these agencies possess regulatory power and enforcement

---

[24] "Vice Premier Wen Jiabao Discusses Securities Market," Xinhua, June 27, 1999; FBIS-CHI-1999-0627.

[25] Although ministries and commissions are constituent departments of the State Council, all the agencies listed here are directly attached to (*zhishu*) the State Council.

[26] The State Administration of Industry and Commerce added a new bureau of consumer rights protection in 1998.

authority and are designated to protect the rights of owners and consumers. The State Administration of Industry and Commerce, for example, not only registers companies and oversees the regulation of various markets but also devotes much of its manpower to cracking down on trademark infringements, illegal advertising, and other practices that impair fair trade and harm consumers (particularly in the wholesale and retail areas; see Zhang Shengzu et al., 1999, pp. 76–7).

Although the growing prominence of these regulatory and enforcement agencies is evidence of the Chinese leadership's commitment to protect and sustain markets and an environment for fair competition in the market, these agencies have also been plagued by problems of local protectionism similar to those that affected the legal system. First, rather than emphasizing compliance with government product standards, some local officials tolerated local manufacturers who produced and sold substandard or counterfeit products because these businesses yielded profits for the producers and generated employment and government revenue that improved the career prospects of local officials. According to an investigation in Henan Province, 63 percent of products sold on the market were without a certificate of inspection (*CD*, Nov. 27, 1999). It is not unusual for local enforcement personnel and government officials to take bribes from producers of fake and substandard products and get directly involved in protecting the producers. After all, as one commentator wryly noted, crackdown on fakes does not generate revenue (*JJRB*, Aug. 11, 1999).[27]

Second, the incentives for local authorities to crack down on local producers of fake and shoddy products are reduced because the products tended to be sold beyond the local confines. Indeed, there is a tendency for local enforcement offices to focus their enforcement efforts on goods from the outside. By the same token, there is little reason for local enforcement authorities to cooperate on interregional cases.[28] The enforcement of national and industry standards is thus a public good that has tended to be undersupplied by local enforcement authorities. However, without adequate enforcement, shoddy and counterfeit products served only to

---

[27] For a good example of how battery producers sought to forge an alliance to combat counterfeiting and how the alliance floundered in the face of local protectionism, see *CET*, September 3, 1999.

[28] Commentary: "Dealing Blows to Fake Products, We Must First Deal Blows to Local Protectionism," *Shanxi ribao [Shanxi Daily]*, December 1, 1995; FBIS-CHI-96-002.

undermine the reputation of Chinese products and hurt lawful producers. In a written instruction to the National Conference on Quality Work,
then-Premier Zhu Rongji noted that China would have no hope if fake
and shoddy products were tolerated.[29]

For years, the Chinese press has aired complaints about products, ranging from exploding beer bottles to water heaters that leak poisonous
carbon monoxide. Chinese critics have argued that efforts to supervise
and enforce quality and technology standards have suffered because local quality supervision departments are departments within local governments. The national administration could only guide the local offices.
According to Vice Premier Wu Bangguo, "The current local administration system is hard to ensure independent, unified, strict, and impartial
law enforcement, which is inevitably subject to the interference of regional protectionism; it is difficult to deal with cases or impose a fine, and
law-enforcement personnel are even subjected to persecution and retali-
ation" (Wu Bangguo, 1999). Thus, the local departments must first please
local government officials. In this way, institutional incentive induces local
protectionism. By fragmenting and undermining enforcement authority,
manufacturers of fake and shoddy products thus had little fear of punishment. The proliferation of fake and shoddy products harms consumers,
hurts the reputation of quality producers, and detracts from China's efforts to build world-class manufacturing, a goal that the Chinese leadership has been keen to pursue. The Development Research Center of
the State Council estimates that, in 1998, the proliferation of counterfeit
products caused the government to lose 24.6 billion yuan in taxes.[30] In the
words of Wu Bangguo, problems with Chinese product, engineering, and
service quality had become a major factor restraining China's economic
development.

There is thus a need for a unified and effective quality and technology
supervision system to alleviate the problems of poor quality, low grade,
fake, and shoddy products. In a sense, exploding beer bottles and dangerous water heaters caught the attention of consumers and government
leaders alike in China, just as Upton Sinclair and the muckraking jour-
nalists were able to capture the imagination of consumers and lawmakers
in the United States decades earlier.

[29] *RMRBO*, November 6, 1999.
[30] *QB*, July 3, 2000.

The promotion of unified, effective law-enforcement departments that help protect economic integration and fair competition was an important theme of the government rationalization introduced in 1998. Rather than being downsized, the State Administration of Quality and Technical Supervision (hereafter referred to as the Quality Administration), previously subordinate to the State Economic and Trade Commission, was upgraded to the status of government bureau directly under the State Council. Moreover, its staff size in the Beijing headquarters remained at 180. In addition, staff at affiliated centers and organizations in Beijing numbered around 4,000. Altogether the quality and technical supervision "system" had about 100,000 employees, generating two billion yuan in fees per year. Its 200-plus technical centers make it one of the most technical government services (Interview with Quality Administration official, June 22, 1999). In 1999, the Quality Administration conducted random tests of 8,905 products belonging to 218 categories (*ZXS*, Jan. 18, 2000). The government reorganization also allowed the Quality Administration to expand its functions. Previously the industrial ministries and departments and the Ministry of Labor were primarily responsible for issuing quality licenses for products such as boilers and elevators, leaving enforcement to the Quality Administration. In the fall 1998, the Guangdong Provincial Bureau of Quality and Technical Supervision took over the issuance and management of product licenses (*RMRBO*, Aug. 30, 1998; *RMRB*, Sept. 22, 1999). With its power to oversee quality management systems certification such as ISO 9000 and product certification and the authority to publish the results of such certification, the Quality Administration has become one of the main arms of the regulatory state.

Since 1998, a system of vertical administration has been introduced in these various administrations. In December of 1998, lower-level industry and commerce offices beneath the provincial level were placed under the direct management of their superior organs instead of local governments (*CD*, Dec. 2, 1998). In the spring of 1999, the party Central Committee and the State Council decided to adopt vertical administration of the quality and technical supervision system under the provincial level. As Vice Premier Wu Bangguo noted at a National Working Conference in March 1999, whereas local quality and technical supervision bureaus, primarily those at the county level, were previously administered by local governments, vertical administration empowered the provincial department to directly supervise the offices ranked immediately below it in prefectures and counties. Moreover, quality and technical supervision bureaus are also empowered to directly oversee technical units affiliated with them. The State Environmental Protection Agency and the State Food and Drug Administration also undertook similar organizational changes.

By the year 2000, vertical administration had become a model of institutional design and spread to various other areas, including the Ministry of Land and Resources, the administrations of coal mine safety inspection, maritime safety, and aquatic safety, as well as to the management of central government grain reserves (Xinhua, April 13, 2000; May 10, 2000). In virtually all these areas, vertical control was imposed following disasters or reports of gross mismanagement in certain areas. In response to a major maritime disaster in Shandong, the Ministry of Communications decided that local officials had been ineffective and chose to set up twenty maritime safety administrations in eleven coastal provinces. These administrations are directly answerable to the ministry so that central government regulations governing shipping safety are implemented (Xinhua, Dec. 28, 1999). In the case of coal mines, although ownership of mines was devolved to local authorities in recent years, the State Administration of Coal Industry centralized the supervision of safety in a newly created Bureau for Supervising Coal Mine Safety. Previously, local coal industrial administrations supervised coal mine safety in the localities but did not always make safety a top priority. The State Administration of Coal Industry, which became responsible for industrial safety, emphasized that the new supervisory authority in the central government would "operate as an independent entity...and will not be easily affected by local interests" so as to better regulate China's accident-prone coal mines (Xinhua, Jan. 10, 2000; March 8, 2000).

The intention of the reformers is evidently to enable the state regulatory agencies to enhance the hierarchical administration of the functions such as quality supervision and more effectively enforce the relevant laws with relative autonomy from the influence of local authorities. In the case of the Quality Administration, the Beijing headquarters previously only guided local developments. The reorganization under the rubric of vertical administration empowered Beijing to direct the provincial bureaus. Because Beijing can now veto appointments of the provincial bureaus, this system of vertical administration can thus strengthen the chain of command radiating from Beijing to the localities; it is no longer a system of administration pulled in different directions by local interests (*CD*, March 29, 1999). With this institutional reorganization, the headquarters have gained more control over cadre management, organizational structure, staff size, funding, and international exchanges. A particularly significant development is the consolidation of budgets. The Planning, Finance and Technology Bureau of the Quality Administration coordinates with the Ministry of Finance on a unified budgeting for the system and allocates funds for technical labs, thereby giving it much leverage. Budgets for local quality and technical supervision offices are consolidated in provincial-level budgets. Moreover, bureaus of quality and technical supervision at various levels and their subordinate technical units are required to promptly deliver all fines, proceeds from confiscated property and goods, and administrative fees to the central or provincial-level finance departments in full. There was also hope that the reform would improve staff quality by making it more difficult for local authorities to transfer personnel into quality and technical supervision departments (Wu Bangguo, 1999). By gaining more organizational control, the central government should be able to improve the consistent and fair implementation of laws and regulations and thus promote market order.

It should be pointed out that the system of vertical administration adopted in 1998–1999 was not complete but resulted from a compromise. The State Environmental Protection Agency is a good example. Originally there was a push for putting local agencies under the direct command of the central administration rather than making them dependent on local governments whose leaders tended to put growth above the environment. Indeed, some of the most vocal advocates for vertical control over the past decade were local environmental officials who were caught between the task of protecting the environment and the interference of local governments that had much leverage over their agencies. However, in the final push for vertical administration, some of these local advocates changed their positions.

One central official I interviewed indicated that the personal interests of local officials might explain this change of heart. When these local officials first advocated placement of local agencies under the direct command of the central agency, they were middle-aged bureaucrats with professional ambitions and would presumably benefit from a streamlined ladder of bureaucratic promotions. By 1998–1999, however, these advocates were getting closer to retirement age. If vertical command were adopted, they faced the prospect of retirement within a few years. In contrast, if they stayed within the local political establishment and placed their appointments under the authority of the local leaders, they could expect to transfer to the local people's congresses or political consultative conferences upon their retirement from government administration. They would thus retain not only perks and benefits associated with their ranks but also participation in monitoring the government and thus some political influence. As a result of local resistance, when the reform was finalized for the environmental agency, it was agreed that local environmental officials would not be under the sole direction of the central agency but would be subject to the dual leadership of both the agency and the local government.[31] Interviews with local offices of the State Administration of Industry and Commerce confirmed that officials of the field offices are still subject to the supervision of local party committees. Officials in these administrations comment that theirs is only half *chuizhi guanli*.

To be sure, the adoption of vertical administration within provincial units falls short of a nationwide unified administration and also reinforces existing boundaries among the provinces.[32] Nevertheless, given the size of each of China's provinces, it appears that provincial units should possess strong incentives to protect the reputation of their products. Provinces such as Shanxi and Zhejiang have seen their reputation ravaged by widely reported fatal incidents arising from the production of fake and shoddy products such as liquor. In response, officials from these provinces recognized that tolerating fake and inferior products is the same as drinking poison to quench thirst and cannot bring about sustained development.[33] Indeed, officials in Liaoning's Anshan found that their tough stand on the quality of food products not only helped save legitimate businesses but helped the local government garner popular support (*XDT*, May 26, 1999). In some localities such as Zhejiang's Wenzhou, officials have recognized the reputational value of high quality and have undertaken various initiatives, such as publicly burning counterfeit products, to burnish the reputation of locally produced products (Ye Chunjiang, 1999). Likewise,

---

[31] Interview with State Environmental Protection Agency official, June 18, 1999.

[32] Since 1996, the central government has been conducting a survey of provincial boundaries to reduce conflicts over resources. *CD*, February 1, 1999.

[33] Commentary: "Dealing Blows to Fake Products, We Must First Deal Blows to Local Protectionism," *Shanxi ribao [Shanxi Daily]*, December 1, 1995; FBIS-CHI-96-002.

liquor poisoning in Shanxi prompted the province to enact regulations on liquor making and especially to introduce licensing on liquor production, transport, and sales (*FZRB*, Sept. 10, 1999). Thus, despite the political incompleteness of the reorganization, the adoption of vertical administration at the provincial level still represented a major advance for organizational control. Following the adoption of vertical administration, the Quality Administration has been able to strengthen its work in several provinces, including Zhejiang, Fujian, and Guangdong, which are areas known for the widespread incidence of counterfeiting (Interview, June 16, 1999).

The effort to strengthen the Quality Administration and other regulatory agencies has been spurred on by the national legislature.[34] Take the case of the Product Quality Law. In 1999, the Standing Committee of the National People's Congress (NPC) made inspection of the enforcement of product quality laws a key item on its agenda. The NPC's inspection group went to Zhejiang, Chongqing, Shandong, Guangdong, and Henan in June and concluded that the situation in product quality remained grim. The inspection group concluded that the Product Quality Law was flawed, because it stipulated inadequate punishment for violators and did not sufficiently empower law-enforcement agencies. In response, the NPC took up the amendment and improvement of the Product Quality Law and formally approved the proposed amendments in July 2000. The amended Product Quality Law went into effect on September 1, 2000, giving law enforcers more power to inspect and providing for stiffer penalties against violators. The amended law includes articles targeted at the government itself. Article 25 forbids the Quality Administration and other government agencies from recommending products so that the administration or others would not compromise its administrative integrity. Article 65 provides penalties for government employees involved in protecting and abetting counterfeiters.[35]

Armed with more administrative muscle and strong legislative mandates, the regulatory agencies have become more forceful in enforcing

---

[34] Ironically, as a consequence of the adoption of vertical administration, local administrators in the administrations are more attentive to directives from their bureaucratic superiors in the provincial administration but have become less receptive to supervision by local people's congresses (*RMRB*, August 2, 2000).

[35] *RYD*, July 10, 2000; see *NFZM*, July 20, 2000, for criticisms of the amended law by Wang Hai, China's well-known and controversial consumer advocate.

laws, conducting more searches, and giving out stiffer penalties to violators. In the spring of 2001, the central leadership pooled the initiatives of
the individual regulatory agencies together into a national drive to rectify
market economic order. Authorities shut down half a million workshops
producing fake products, and they confiscated 158 million illegal publications and 4.2 million copies of pirated software in 2001.[36] Much remains
to be done, and China's rapidly evolving economic structure has also
brought to the fore new problems (e.g., complaints about automobile,
computer, and housing purchases). As Vice Premier Li Lanqing, head of
the Leading Group in Charge of National Rectification and Standard-
ization of Market Economic Order, noted, the quest for orderly market
competition will be "protracted, difficult, and complex."[37] Nevertheless,
measured in terms of consumer complaints, the national drive for an orderly market environment, coupled with the effect of market competition
and growing consumer savvy, has helped address long-standing concerns
about quality. According to data from the China Consumer's Association,
the association received 309,231 consumer complaints in the first half of
2002, down 8.9 percent from the period one year earlier.[38]

CONCLUSIONS

Writing about the origins of the liberal economy, Karl Polanyi (1957)
emphasized that "[t]here was nothing natural about *laissez-faire*; free
markets could never have come into being merely by allowing things to
take their course . . . *laissez-faire* itself was enforced by the state" (p. 139).
China's leaders also do not have illusions about the market. Indeed, the
expansion of market competition in China has been accompanied by myriad types of criminal activities ranging from financial fraud to the counterfeiting of goods that threaten to undermine popular support. In response,
the Chinese government has devised a variety of institutional mechanisms
to promote market order. These institutional initiatives have been complemented by a flurry of legislative activities to produce laws governing
economic activities. The institutional renovations discussed in this chapter

---

[36] "China To Continue To Improve Market, Economic Order," Xinhua, January 24, 2002.
[37] "Li Lanqing Addresses Meeting on Rectifying Market Economic Order," Xinhua, June
24, 2002.
[38] Xinhua, August 13, 2002.

certainly help the ruling elite stay in power, but what is equally important is that they help pay for the upkeep of the central government, promote stability of the financial system, and are generally conducive to the further development of market forces. Thus, contrary to the fears of some commentators, although China's post-Tiananmen leadership has sought to alleviate the decompository fissures through a reconfiguration of the system of political and especially economic governance, the institutional changes have *not* meant a return to the status quo ante of the Maoist era and the stifling of local initiatives. Instead, it does appear that the current leadership in China has found a middle road for organizing China that would provide the means for implementing the will of the central government while leaving room for local initiatives.

The reconstitution of the sinews of central control promises not only to furnish the fiscal prowess for the central state but also to provide the foundations for the pursuit of the American Progressive's ideal of the regulatory state. With strong administrative muscle that is no longer beholden to local authorities, central state power can potentially be used to offer fair administration such as uniform registration for companies, protection for consumers, safety on the seas (through central control of maritime patrol), and more evenhanded justice. In this sense, the ruling regime is not simply doing something that is only for its own good but also for the good of the public. The reconstitution of the central state is therefore not just a rebuilding of the old state that had an iron fist but short and weak fingers. Instead, with the reconstitution, the central state may finally possess elaborately constructed arms, hands, and fingers that could play in coordination to produce good music.

ABBREVIATIONS

AWSJW	*Asian Wall Street Journal Weekly*
BYD	*Beijing qingnian bao [Beijing Youth Daily]*
CD	*China Daily*
CDBW	*China Daily Business Weekly*
CET	*Zhongguo jingji shibao [China Economic Times]*
DJN	Dow Jones Newswire
FBIS	Foreign Broadcast Information Service
FZRB	*Fazhi ribao [Legal Daily]*
JJRB	*Jingji ribao [Economic Daily]*

NFZM   *Nanfang zoumo [Southern Weekend]*
QB   *Qiaobao [China Press]*
RMRB   *Renmin ribao [People's Daily]*
RMRBO   *Renmin ribao [People's Daily]*, overseas edition
WSJ   *Wall Street Journal*
XDT   *Xinhua meiri danxun [Xinhua Daily Telegraph]*
Xinhua Xinhua she (Xinhua News Agency)
ZGB   *Zhongguo gaige bao [China reform news]*
ZXS   Zhongguo xinwen she (China News Agency)

REFERENCES

Alesina, Alberto and Lawrence H. Summers, "Central Bank Independence and Macroeconomic Performance: Some Comparative Evidence," *Journal of Money, Credit, and Banking*, 25 (May 1993), pp. 151–62.

Bahl, Roy, *Fiscal Policy in China: Taxation and Intergovernmental Fiscal Relations* (San Francisco: The 1990 Institute, 1999).

Carpenter, Daniel, *The Forging of Bureaucratic Autonomy: Reputations, Networks, and Policy Innovation in Executive Agencies 1862–1928* (Princeton, NJ: Princeton University Press, 2001).

Chang, Gordon, "China Rediscovers Mao," *Far Eastern Economic Review*, October 7, 1999.

Chung, Jae Ho, "Beijing Confronting the Provinces: The 1994 Tax-Sharing Reform and Its Implications for Central-Provincial Relations in China," *China Information*, 9 (Winter 1995), pp. 1–23.

Epstein, Gene, "No Place Like Home," *Barron's*, August 2, 1999.

Fligstein, Neil, *The Architecture of Markets* (Princeton, NJ: Princeton University Press, 2001).

Holz, Carsten, *The Role of Central Banking in China's Economic Reforms* (Ithaca, NY: Cornell University East Asia Program, 1992).

Oi, Jean, "Fiscal Reform and the Economic Foundations of Local State Corporatism in China," *World Politics*, 45 (1992), pp. 99–126.

Polanyi, Karl, *The Great Transformation: The Political and Economic Origins of Our Time* (Boston: Beacon Press, 1957) (originally published 1944).

Qian, Yingyi and Chenggang Xu, "The M-Form Hierarchy and China's Economic Reform," *European Economic Review*, 37 (1993), pp. 541–8.

Skowronek, Stephen, *Building a New American State: The Expansion of National Administrative Capacities* (Cambridge, England: Cambridge University Press, 1982).

Sun Wenxue and Wang Yuwu, "A Discussion on Obstacles to All-Around Implementation of the Tax-Assignment System and Their Solutions," *Caijing wenti yanjiu [Research on Financial and Economic Problems]*, No. 10 (October 5, 1994), pp. 43–6; FBIS-CHI-95-002.

Wiebe, Robert, *The Search for Order 1877–1920* (New York: Hill and Wang, 1967).

World Bank, *China: Between Plan and Market* (Washington, D.C.: The World Bank, 1990a).

    China: Financial Sector Policies and Institutional Development (Washington, D.C.: The World Bank, 1990b).

    Entering the 21st Century: World Development Report 1999/2000 (New York: Oxford University Press, 2000).

Wu, Bangguo, "Wu on Quality, Technical Supervision," Xinhua Domestic Service, March 26, 1999; FBIS-CHI-1999-0405.

Xiang Huaicheng, "Socialist Market Economy and Building the Taxation System," *RMRB*, July 10, 1997; FBIS-CHI-97-212.

Xie Ping, "Bank Restructuring in China," in *Bank Restructuring in Practice* (Basel, Switzerland: Bank for International Settlements, 1999), Policy Paper No. 6 (August).

Yang, Dali L., "Reform and the Restructuring of Central-Local Relations," in David Goodman and Gerald Segal, eds., *China Deconstructs: Politics, Trade and Regionalism* (London, Routledge, 1994), pp. 59–98.

    Calamity and Reform in China: State, Rural Society, and Institutional Change Since the Great Leap Famine (Stanford, CA: Stanford University Press, 1996a).

    "The Dynamics and Progress of Competitive Liberalization in China," *Issues & Studies*, (1996b).

    "Governing China's Transition to the Market," *World Politics*, 48 (April 1996c), pp. 424–52.

    Beyond Beijing: Liberalization and the Regions in China (London/New York: Routledge, 1997).

    "Economic Crisis and Market Transition in the 1990s," in Edwin Winckler, ed., *Transition from Communism in China* (Boulder, CO: Rienner, 1999), pp. 151–77.

Yang Peixin, *Chengbao zhi: qiye fada biyou zhilu [The Contracting System: The Only Road to Enterprise Prosperity]* (Beijing: Zhongguo jingji chubanshe, 1990).

Ye Chunjiang, "'Wenzhou moshi' zai tupo" ["The Wenzhou model is Being Remade"], *ZGB*, June 2, 1999.

Yuan Yanghe, Bao Yonghui, and Tang Jian, "Sunan xiangzhen qiye zai kuner zhong yunniang xin de xiwang" ["TVEs in Southern Jiangsu Brew New Hope Amid Difficulty"], *Liaowang [Outlook]*, No. 17 (1998), pp. 4–6.

Zhang Shengzu, Li Jian, and Wang Yan, eds., *Zhengfu jigou gaige yu renyuan fenliu zhengce fal"u zhishi shouce [Handbook of Policies and Legal Knowledge on Government Administrative Reform and Personnel Diversion]* (Beijing: Fal"u chubanshe, 1999).

PART TWO

Case Studies of Policy Implementation

5

Policy Consistency in the Midst of the Asian Crisis: Managing the Furloughed and the Farmers in Three Cities

Dorothy J. Solinger

As marketization of the economy and a concomitant decentralization of economic decision making became increasingly entrenched after 1980, new factors appeared, both political and economic, that determined a place's possibilities for growth, instead of – as in the past – its position in the state plan alone had.[1] Thus, the provinces became much more diverse economically than they had ever been in the previous three decades, with growth in those along the coast markedly more successful than that in the provinces in the interior.

In accord with this drive to marketize, at the 1997 15th Congress of the Chinese Communist Party, the leadership at last announced a mammoth project of worker cutbacks in a sudden push for enhanced enterprise efficiency.[2] A few quotations from the following year embrace this spirit. On the domestic economy, a book on Liaoning makes this allegation:

To meet market economic demand, industrial enterprises must continue to reduce staff and increase efficiency to raise their productivity. Taking a long view, this will promote economic development, and eventually provide more employment

---

[1] See Peter T. Y. Cheung, "Introduction: Provincial Leadership and Economic Reform in Post-Mao China," in Peter T. Y. Cheung, Jae Ho Chung, and Zhimin Lin, eds., *Provincial Strategies of Economic Reform in Post-Mao China: Leadership, Politics, and Implementation*, (Armonk, NY: Sharpe, 1998), pp. 3–46; Jae Ho Chung, "Recipes for Development in Post-Mao Chinese Cities: Themes and Variations," in Jae Ho Chung, ed., *Cities in China: Recipes for Economic Development in the Reform Era* (London: Routledge, 1999), pp. 1–17; and Dorothy J. Solinger, "Despite Decentralization: Disadvantages, Dependence and Ongoing Central Power in the Inland–The Case of Wuhan," *The China Quarterly*, No. 145 (1996), pp. 1–34.

[2] Dorothy J. Solinger, "Demolishing Partitions: Back to Beginnings in the Cities?" *The China Quarterly*, No. 159 (September 1999), pp. 629–39.

opportunities, but in the short term we can't absorb new labor but instead the demand for labor will decline.[3]

On the international economy, a major labor journal gives this caution:

We must optimize the investment environment ... raise the ability to absorb foreign capital. [For this] lowering labor costs is decisive.[4]

Indeed, the switch from plans to markets did not just mean relinquishing planning domestically. The splendid performance of the country – especially the coast – in attracting foreign capital and in parlaying cheap labor into world-market success rendered development progressively more reliant on exports and foreign investment as the 1990s wore on.[5] Throughout the 1980s and into the early 1990s, the center's supremacy at home and the nation's integration internally became ever more uncertain, as China grew steadily more enmeshed in the global economy and thus potentially subject to its vagaries.

Subsequently, the financial crisis that spread across East and Southeast Asia in 1997 and 1998 was clearly a threat to China. As its neighbors in seriatim devalued their currencies and as foreign investors pulled out from the region, China's export growth came to a halt in 1998, and 1999 even saw a startling 11 percent *drop* in actual foreign direct investment. By the late 1990s, China's regional economies had been reshaped by multiple cross-cutting currents. How seriously had these several forces – market approaches to operating the economy, increased local autonomy, growing subnational diversity, and uneven degrees of international involvement across the nation – diminished the control of the center and the cohesion of the whole?

---

3   Xu Jinshun, Cao Xiaofeng, and Zhang Zhuomin, *1997–1998 nian Liaoning sheng jingji shehui xingshi fenxi yu yuce [1997–1998 Liaoning Province Economic Social Situation Analysis and Prediction]* (Shenyang: Liaoning renmin chubanshe, 1998), p. 276.
4   Yan Youguo, "Wanshan laodongli shichang shixian" ["Realize the perfection of the labor market"], *Zhongguo laodong [Chinese Labor]* (hereafter *ZGLD*), 1 (1998), p. 17.
5   Barry Naughton, "China's Emergence and Prospects as a Trading Nation," *Brookings Papers on Economic Activity*, 2 (1996), pp. 273, 280. He notes that, between 1984 and 1995, China's real gross domestic product grew by 10.2 percent annually, according to official statistics, as the nominal value of manufactured exports increased by 22 percent per year. By 1994, the ratio of foreign trade to gross domestic product had jumped up to 44 percent, from just 10 percent 16 years before.

In this chapter I examine these issues as they were operating in employment policy in three quite disparate cities. I do this by relating a telling episode in which local compliance with central-level programs trumped local recalcitrance during this period of stress, primarily the years 1997 and 1998. I also show that, despite their divergences, both with regard to a set of variables and in style of implementation, all three local governments remained quite responsive to central-level objectives, even if they did so each in their own way.

One could hypothesize that, once decentralizing forces had become significant, a period of economic difficulty might be particularly apt to reveal emergent centrifugal forces. At such a juncture, relatively autonomous localities, facing economic stress more or less on their own, and already trained in contending on the global market, might be likely to scramble to retain any leverage they had in foreign trade. A situation of economic strain could entice them to ignore central injunctions that might cut into their profits (especially if the center had really lost control). Furthermore, they might attempt to pursue any path that could help them to slash their costs in order to promote their own local products more profitably on the world market.

Thus, given the unequal ability among localities to succeed in the global economy – an inequality that had been nurtured by reform policies – one might expect that a time of economic squeeze would expose regional differences quite starkly, even more so than would normal times. At the same time, one might conjecture, a central government under external pressure would be less able than usual to direct or support the localities, and it might even encourage those areas that could survive on their own accord to do so by any means, or at least it might turn a blind eye toward their behavior. In terms of employment, this ought to have meant that enterprise managers (along with their local authorities) would have been even more prone than they would at other times to hire low-wage migrant farmers and to release at an ever faster rate their higher-priced urban employees, while neglecting in the process the concerns of those dismissed.

However, I argue that, to the contrary, central relations with the localities were in fact in no danger in this policy domain in those years. On the basis of policy pronouncements and programs of implementation pertaining to newly unemployed people and immigrating peasants, I demonstrate that, in three very dissimilar areas, policy consistency (and even a certain unification in the modes of implementation) was present across the country and up and down the hierarchy, even during this time of tension and trial.

In my explanation, in contrast to some of the other studies reported in this volume, I find that the reasons for this relative uniformity and acquiescence were not so simple as just that obedience was ordered and then obtained. Nor were these outcomes necessarily the result of new mechanisms of control in the capital, novel instruments of management, changed incentives, or reshaped institutions (save for the institution of the market itself). Rather, I show that, by end of century, two decades of market influences on a once-planned system had inclined Chinese leaders at all levels within the administrative system – whether central, provincial, or urban – to entertain shared, if unfortunately mutually opposed, objectives.

It is safe to state that the political elite as a whole by then was agreed on the goal of enhancing productivity and profits by means of competitiveness and efficiency (a post-1980 project), which, by the late 1990s, was understood to entail cutting back workforces. However, at the same time, as inheritors of a long legacy from socialist days, politicians at all levels *also* aimed to provide sustenance and, if possible, employment for local urban labor (an ideal reflecting pre-1980 socialist pro-proletariat values as well as current elites' abhorrence of instability). Consequently, these contradictory aims thrust all of officialdom onto the prongs of an identical predicament.

True, the emergence of an incipient national labor market enabled localities with lively markets to attract dirt-cheap farmer workers (and was thereby functional in elevating national coordination and cohesion). Nevertheless, the long-accustomed proclivity of municipal bureaucrats of favoring and hiring their own native city-bred people over "outsiders" (meaning peasants) simultaneously worked against this market. Because the expanded scope for policy making at the local level would appear to have offered leaders at lower administrative echelons the ability to handle such trade-offs between conflicting objectives by their own dictates, we might expect some real variation among provincial and urban leaders whose economies were more or less marketized and globalized and that were therefore performing differently when the Asian crisis unfolded.

However, data from three very differentially placed cities – all provincial capitals (Guangzhou in Guangdong, Shenyang in Liaoning, and Wuhan in Hubei) – reveal that common ends and familiar means instead forged a generous measure of homogeneity between the designs of Beijing leaders and the actions of their appointees below. This homogeneity obtained even as the specific procedures utilized amounted to variations on a theme, located as they were at differing points along a continuum stretching from plan to market in the late 1990s, and even in a time of enhanced market pressure.

Each of the cities I review is a major metropolis, and each is the node of one of the country's principal regions. One is a city on the coast (Guangzhou), one is in the rust-belt debt-ridden Northeast (Shenyang), and one is in the interior (Wuhan). Each is the site of a different type of political economy, the product of its geographical location, its resource endowment and industrial structure, and, last but by no means least, its treatment over time by the central government.

Each place was accordingly more or less marketized and thus more or less affected, first by the Asian crisis (Guangzhou was the most marketized and the most entangled in the global economy and thus the most affected), and also by the 1997 plan to discharge labor from indebted firms (Shenyang, a long-standing heavy industrial base, where there were more failing firms than elsewhere and which was therefore suffering the most unemployment). As we will see in the paragraphs that follow, Guangzhou's leaders adopted a more Thatcherite approach and Shenyang's a more Keynesian one, with Wuhan in between. However, despite their cities' differing fates and these varying styles, leaders in all of them behaved in accord with central policy, broadly understood.

I begin by outlining the ambivalent central government policy toward urban employment in the late 1990s, and then I sketch the pertinent features of the three cities' political economies. The body of the paper tells how each city grappled with the issues of urban unemployment versus low-cost peasant migrant labor as uncertainties from markets abroad closed in. I use documentary material and interviews with scholars and urban bureaucrats from these cities to examine how they were coping with the center's essentially opposed imperatives as of autumn of 1998. My data come from interviews with local officials and scholars in the three cities and in Beijing in 1998, from newspaper reports, and from information in statistical yearbooks. I also have some later material from official documents and interviews in Wuhan.

Two caveats: First, ultimately, my judgments about each city were subjectively reached, the result of perusing the local newspapers in each city and talking to its respective natives, rather than relying just on the official (or any other published) numbers. Second, my access was by far the best in Wuhan, which may have influenced my findings and comparisons, though it is difficult to discern in what way.

AMBIGUITIES IN CENTRAL POLICY TOWARD LABOR MARKETS

With China's opening to the global economy around 1980, a mentality enshrining profits and high productivity quickly began to dominate over other values. This mentality lay at the heart of the move to restructure state enterprises and restrict their previous unlimited access to state credit, which, beginning in the early 1990s, led to mounting firm losses and, especially after 1994, growing numbers of worker layoffs. Another crucial prong in the effort to achieve more efficiency was a move beginning in 1995, but taking on new and intensified stress in 1997 and 1998, to restrict the entry into cities of, and when possible, send home, rural migrants aiming to make a livelihood in town.[6] The stated objective was to clear out ruralites and turn over their posts to the (then) recently unemployed or *xiagang* ("laid-off")[7] workers among urbanites.[8]

Nevertheless, ambiguities attended this initiative, because there are two distinct faces to peasant migrants at work in Chinese urban areas: In one perspective, rural workers offer competition and stimulation to the economy, and, because of their willingness to work at undesirable posts and at very low wages, they also cut production costs and thus mean higher profits and cheaper exports, which are valuable in capturing international markets in a time of new difficulties.[9] From another viewpoint, peasants'

---

[6] Quoting the sociologist Feng Lanrui in *South China Morning Post* (hereafter *SCMP*), August 8, 1998, p. 15.

[7] "Laid-off" or *xiagang* workers are those who have left their production and work post and are not doing any other work in their own unit owing to the enterprise's production and work situation, but who retain their labor relationship with the unit. See No author, "Woguo di shiye renyuan he xiagang zhigong tongji diaocha" ["A statistical investigation of our country's unemployed personnel and layoffs"], *ZGLD*, 5 (1998), pp. 15–16. There is also a definition in *Wuhan wanbao [Wuhan Evening News]* (hereafter *WHWB*), May 30, 1998, p. 1.

[8] Liu Zhonghua, "Guanyu zaijiuye gongcheng yu laodongli shichang jianshe di sikao" ["Thoughts on the Reemployment Project and Labor Market Construction"], *Laodong neican [Labor Internal Reference]*, 2 (1998), p. 42.

[9] Peasant migrants' wages can be anywhere from 20 to 30 percent to 40 to 50 percent less than those of urban workers. See Chen Huilin, "Guanyu nongmingong qingkuang di diaocha yu sikao" ["Thoughts and Research on Peasant Labor's Situation"], *Zhongguo*

presence in cities threatens the jobs of "native" urban workers. In this way there developed a direct conflict between making profits and developing a locals-only job market to absorb the furloughed workforce. The rejected city laborers' plight was the product of the switch to a market economy and the resultant need to reduce costs to meet external competition, which was an imperative growing out of China's mesh with markets, both domestic and global.

Thus, simultaneously with advocating succor for shedded labor, central policy makers also paradoxically admitted that a genuine solution to the predicament of urban employment would be to strengthen a national labor market. As announced in a State Council decision in early June 1998, this should entail the following:

Establish[ing] and perfect[ing] the market mechanism, and under state policy direction carry[ing] out a combination of workers' autonomous job selection, labor market adjustment of employment, and government promotion of employment.[10]

City administrations were thus handed the daunting and probably impossible task of facilitating the formation of a national, unified labor market that could at once manage outside, peasant labor and yet also guarantee locals' employment.[11]

As one mode of coping with the task, cities dutifully created their own local versions of a national "Reemployment Project,"[12] a monumental effort that, after trials in 1994 in a few places, was extended nationwide in April 1995, with the ambiguous aim of somehow arranging the settlement of the laid-off workers and yet also feeding them into an incipient labor market that could function on its own.

Although the goals of promoting enterprise reform – with its call for efficiency and layoffs – and of establishing a genuine labor market, one that would serve a national (i.e., both urban and rural) population, were mutually reinforcing, they were at odds with leaders' third labor-related aim, which was their persisting concern about placing (termed

gongren [Chinese Worker], 5 (1998), p. 17; in addition, they are often denied the welfare benefits that at least in principle (though less and less in practice) are to be accorded city laborers and the social security payments firms are obliged to make for urbanites.

[10] *Guangming ribao [Bright Daily]* (hereafter *GMRB*), June 23, 1998, p. 4.

[11] Yan Youguo, "Wanshan Laodongli," p. 17.

[12] Ru Xin, Lu Xueyi, and Dan Tianlun, eds., *1998 nian: zhongguo shehui xingshi fenxi yu yuce [1998: Analysis and Prediction of China's Social Situation]* (Beijing: shehui kexue wenxian chubanshe, 1998), p. 86.

"reemploying") locals. The imperatives presented by the Asian crisis and the 15th Party Congress – more threatening unemployment to assuage, but also a heightened urgency to producing cheap exports and high profits – only muddied notions about the appropriate strategies that could be used to achieve reemployment.

At the outset, the Reemployment Project (REP) was to rest on four pillars: unemployment insurance, professional introduction services, retraining, and labor service enterprises.[13] After Shanghai set up the model of the "reemployment service center" – which was to provide a caretaker role for an industry's workers by helping with the disbursal of their basic livelihood allowances, medical insurance, and pensions; retraining them; and finding them new employment – this system became one more key component of the project. However, the project was also touted as one that, in forcing at least some workers out of the factory and providing them with preferential treatment (such as tax exemptions and reductions; cancellation of licensing, management, sanitation, and other fees; and provision of market sites and stalls) if they were to start up new businesses, could be billed as symbiotic with the development of a market economy. The actual mode of implementation of these locally selected measures reflected the ambiguity of the center's approach, as well as the varying capabilities and concerns of local leaders.

In sum, one could characterize the REP as potentially having either a Keynesian or a Thatcherite thrust, or a bit of both. Whereas the former emphasis, entailing more activist state guidance and direction, rested on distrust of a market in labor to guarantee the employment of discarded urban workers (or on doubts about their ability to compete in one), the latter was grounded in a faith that reasonably fair and, more importantly, cost-effective outcomes could come from reliance on the unadulterated workings of the forces of supply and demand.

THREE CITIES: DISPARITIES

I posit that three geoeconomic independent variables had a crucial bearing on the manner in which these different cities approached – and, indeed,

---

[13] Wang Tianxing, "Kunjing yu chulou" ["Difficult Straits and the Way Out"], *Shehuixue yanjiu [Sociology Research]*, 6 (1997), in *Xinhua wengao [New China Documents]*, 3 (1998), p. 25.

Table 5.1. *Population of Municipality and Urban Districts: UHR of Guangzhou, Shenyang, and Wuhan in 1997*

City	Municipality	Urban Districts	UHR
Guangzhou	6.56	3.90	3.22
Shenyang	6.71	4.77	3.84
Wuhan	7.16	5.17	3.82

Note: Numbers are shown in the millions. UHR = urban household registration.

were capable of approaching – three interconnected issues, or dependent variables: retrenching their workforces (as seen in the amount of unemployment there); forming a functioning labor market (and, consequently, reemploying those who had been laid off); and receiving outsiders (as measured in the number of peasant migrants resident in a city).

The three independent variables are these: (1) the health and wealth of a city's economy (principally a function of the nature of its industrial structure, including factors such as how much of its industry was at the time in question composed of heavy industry, how large was its gross domestic product, or GDP, and gross value of industrial output, or GVIO, and how fast was its growth in the relevant years); (2) the vitality of its domestic markets (as measured by such factors as its level of retail sales, the number of its market sites, the proportion occupied by its tertiary sector – meaning chiefly its service (and thus, informal sector – and the vigor of its nonstate industry as of the late 1990s); and (3) its international involvement, as seen in levels of both foreign investment and exports. All of these variables in turn derived from a place's geographical location and resource base, and from central governmental policy toward it.

The populations of the three cities I researched – Guangzhou, Shenyang, and Wuhan – were roughly comparable at the time of this story, as the table reveals (see Table 5.1).[14] In terms of other variables listed in Table 5.2, however, the cities were quite disparate: Guangzhou (and its surrounding area) had, since 1980, been the part of the country

---

[14]   The population holding urban household residence permits is literally termed *"feinong,"* or "nonrural." In practice it refers to people with urban registration. *Source*: Zhongguo tongjiju chengshi shehui jingji diaocha zongdui bian [Chinese Statistical Urban Social and Economic Research General Team, ed.], *Zhongguo chengshi jingji nian jian 1997 [1997 Chinese Urban Statistical Yearbook]* (Beijing: Zhongguo tongji chubanshe, 1998), pp. 53, 63, 64.

most involved in the external economy, both as the recipient of foreign investment and as exporter. Shenyang was an old industrial base, where the central government decades ago invested much capital in creating heavy industrial infrastructure, equipment, and output, and the level of industrial losses was especially high there in the 1990s. Wuhan, though like Shenyang also the home of many aging and failing industrial, state-owned plants, is notable as well as one of the chief hubs of the national transport network and as a national-level market, for it lies at the intersection of the Guangzhou–Beijing trunk rail line going north–south and the Yangtze River, along the east–west axis. Overall, Guangzhou had the healthiest local economy, the most active domestic markets, and the most international involvement, and it was the most marketist in its strategy; Shenyang was generally at the other extreme.

Geography, combined with past central-level policies, quite vividly set the context for major variations among the three cities as of 1997–1998. Guangzhou had had the benefit since 1980 of the central government's preferential policies toward the Southeast, and also of proximity to Hong Kong with its links to the world beyond. Its industrial development, thwarted in Maoist times because of its perceived locational vulnerability, never saw the intensive investment in huge and heavy industrial plants that occurred inland and to the north.

As of 1997, on the eve of the regional financial crisis and the convening of the 15th Party Congress, the city's GDP was increasing at 13.5 percent, a rate above the national average. Its industrial growth rate that year was even higher, at 16 percent, and its GVIO grew 17.6 percent over 1996. Quite favorably for workers' jobs, only 31 percent of the city's firms were suffering loss. Probably contributing to the health of the urban economy – for light industrial output was easier to export and its equipment in general more apt to have been renovated or imported than that of the heavy sectors – the city's light industrial output represented a full 61.3 percent of the GVIO in 1997.

The state-owned sector accounted that year for just 33.5 percent of ownership, the collectively owned for 18.3 percent, and "other" categories (private and foreign invested) for as much as 48.2 percent. The city also ranked number 1 nationally in number of market sites, with four sites for every 100 persons, and the tertiary sector's output value increased in 1997 by 13.8 percent, with its output accounting for 48.4 percent of the GDP.[15] One scholar just back from field work in the Pearl River Delta commented in late summer of 1998 that "[the problem of] *xiagang* [workers] in Guangzhou is not serious... there are more and more jobs in the informal sector." However, he also noted that peasant workers were being made to pay fees both in the countryside (on leaving their rural homes) and in the city of Guangzhou as well, indicating that even marketized Guangzhou was making life difficult for peasant migrants during the financial crisis.[16]

In northeastern Shenyang, first Japanese investment in the 1930s and 1940s and later Soviet aid in the 1950s led to early development of large-scale, capital-intense, heavy industry. Later, because new parts were expensive and production always took priority over technical transformation, aging and outdated equipment came to mark the city's industrial stock. Another detrimental factor was that its location in the far Northeast meant that the city had at best been a regional center, but it had not attracted national-scale commercial traffic as of the late 1990s.

In many ways, Shenyang stood at the other extreme from Guangzhou. Not only were there substantially more laid-off workers but there were fewer peasants as well. The city was producing mainly for the internal market, with vastly less foreign investment than Guangzhou was attracting.[17] By 1997, our starting point, 51.7 percent of state-owned firms were suffering losses (as compared with 31 percent in Guangzhou).[18] Other comparisons with Guangzhou and its province are equally arresting: In the first 8 months of 1997, Liaoning's financial income was 11.77 billion yuan, an increase of 8 percent over the same period the year before, whereas Guangdong's was 32.92 billion, having increased 21.2 percent.[19]

---

[15] Guangzhou shi jihua weihyuanhui [Guangzhou City Planning Committee] (hereafter Guangzhou shi), ed., *Jingji shehui bai pishu [Economic-Social White Paper]* (Donghuang: Guangdong jingji chubanshe, 1998), pp. 79–81, 156, for Guangzhou; and, for Guangdong, Zheng Zizhen, "Dui Guangdong sheng renkou qianyi liuru wenti di zhanlue sikao" ["Strategic Considerations About the Issue of Guangdong's Population Migration and Inflow"], *Zhongguo renkou kexue [Chinese Population Science]* (hereafter *ZRK*), 3 (1997), p. 43; and Li Zhao and Li Hong, eds., *Guangdong jingji lanpishu: jingji xingshi yu yuce [An Analysis and Forecast of the Guangdong Economy]* (Chaoqing: Guangdong renmin chubanshe, 1998), pp. 237, 242.

[16] Huang Ping interview, September 3, 1998.

[17] Interview with Jin Weigang of the Division of Strategy in Ministry of Labor and Social Security's Institute for Labor Studies, August 27, 1998.

[18] Xu et al., *1997–1998 Liaoning*, p. 28.

[19] *Ibid.*, 142.

Table 5.2. *Size of Municipal Economies, 1997*

Parameter	Guangzhou	Shenyang	Wuhan
GDP	164.6	85.1	91.2
GVIO	237.5	115.0	115.4
Profit and taxes (billion yuan)	156.9	63.8	70.7
Fixed investment (billion yuan)	65.7	16.6	40.8
Local budgetary revenues (billion yuan)	8.4	4.2	3.9

Note: Profits and taxes are for all independent accounting industrial firms in urban districts. *Source:* Zhongguo tongjiju chengshi shehui jingji diaocha zongdui bian [Chinese Statistical Urban Social and Economic Research General Team, ed.], *Zhongguo chengshi jingji nian jian 1998 [1998 Chinese Urban Statistical Yearbook]* (Beijing: Zhongguo tongji chubanshe, 1998); (hereafter *Urban Yearbook*), pp. 121, 132–14, 188, 191–2, 212, 215–16, 250, 253–4. Unless otherwise specified, figures are for the entire municipality (*diqu*).

In the first 10 months of the year, Liaoning's GVIO grew at the rate of 9.4 percent, whereas Guangdong's GVIO grew at a rate nearly double that (18.2 percent).[20]

The Liaoning Provincial Planning Commission's bureaucrats alleged in 1998 that one-third of the province's workers were employed in the tertiary sector.[21] In Shenyang, a major effort had been made in that area in the late 1990s: Before 1996, workers in this sector had represented only one fourth of the total staff and workers of the city. However, over the next two years, these laborers increased to half the total, in response to much governmental investment and a set of official preferential policies, with a leap from about 300,000 workers up to over 500,000 in just a year or so.[22] Nevertheless, Liaoning Planning Commission officials maintained, a mere 5 percent of the province's workers were employed in foreign-invested firms as of 1998. As one example of the impact of the two shocks of 1997–1998 (the Asian crisis and the 15th Congress), the textile trade in particular saw a sharp drop in its exports, especially among the state-owned firms.[23]

---

[20] Li Zhao and Li Hong, eds., *Guangdong jingji lanpishu*, p. 404.

[21] Interview, August 14, 1998, with a bureaucrat in the provincial Planning Commission.

[22] Interview with city labor bureau official, August 18, 1998.

[23] Interview at provincial Planning Commission, August 14, 1998. In 1997 there was a decline of 20 percent, and in the first half of 1998 the fall was as much as another 31 percent, compared with the same period the year before, according to this interview.

Table 5.3. *Market Development, 1997*

Parameter	Guangzhou	Shenyang	Wuhan
Proportion of urban district employment in tertiary (service) sector (%), 1997			
	53.8	44.5	46.5

Source: Urban Yearbook, pp. 133, 143–4, 412, 423–4.

Wuhan shared with Shenyang the very mixed blessing of having been an early recipient of investment in heavy industrial plants. Given the central government's selection of the city as a foundational site for its program of heavy industrialization in the First Five Year Plan, its proportion of state-owned firms within the economy was from the start – and still remains – overwhelming.[24] As late as 1996, the state and collective sectors still accounted for over 80 percent of employment (80.6 percent, with each of these sectors representing about half the total); the private sector accounted for only 6.2 percent and other sectors 3.3 percent.[25] However, Wuhan's situation at a national crossroads allowed its leaders to rapidly reinvent the city as a major thoroughfare and commercial capital, once policies of market reform became the vogue after 1980. So, partially because of this re-creation, Wuhan's economy grew quickly in the mid-1990s in spite of the drag of this strong state-owned presence. In addition, although the state sector was decidedly dominant, the city's nonstate sector also boasted some vitality: More than 1 million people were employed in it as of the middle of 1998 (see Tables 5.2, 5.3, 5.4, and 5.5).[26]

Official data (for many reasons,[27] surely inaccurate in absolute numbers, but perhaps roughly comparable among the cities) demonstrate the policy effects of these geographical and political factors. First of all,

[24] Wang Baoyu, "Zaijiuye gongcheng renzhong dao yun" ["Reemployment Project: The Burden is Heavy and the Road is Long"]. Unpublished manuscript prepared for the Wuhan City People's Congress (Wuhan, 1997), p. 6.

[25] These are the figures provided by officials from the city's Planning Commission's tertiary sector planning coordination office, September 9, 1998. Possibly I misrecorded their information, as the total is just 89 percent. Perhaps they really said that 16 percent was private.

[26] Wuhan labor interview.

[27] In "Why We Cannot Count the Unemployed," *The China Quarterly*, No. 167 (2001), pp. 671–88, I detail the causes for inaccuracy, including that official numbers exclude vast numbers of people who have lost their jobs, but who are not labeled "*xiagang*" because they do not meet the official definition for this term.

Table 5.4. *Employment in Private Enterprises: Total Number of*
Self-Employed Persons in Provincial Urban Areas

	Private Firms		Self-Employed	
Province	Firms	Workers	Firms	Workers
Guangdong	89	1,058	717	1,380
Liaoning	40	548	638	1,004
Hubei	24	335	682	1,418

Notes: Numbers are in thousands, as of the end of 1997. Private firms more than
7 employees; self-employed refers to household firms.
Source: Zhongguo tongji ju bian [Chinese Statistical Bureau, ed], *Zhongguo tongji*
nian jian 1998 [Chinese Statistical Yearbook 1998] (Beijing: Zhongguo tongji
chubanshe, 1998), pp. 153, 154.

registered unemployment was by far the most serious in Shenyang as of
1996 and 1997 (though Wuhan had caught up by 1998; see Table 5.6). Each
of the provinces in which the cities are located had about 6 million workers
in State Firms in 1996. The percentage of laid-off state workers in Liaoning
among the total state workers there was also considerably higher than that
in the other two provinces (15 percent vs. 10.5 and 6.9 percent) in 1997,
but it shot up in all three cities by 1998 (see Table 5.7). By 1998, almost half
of Liaoning's SOE workers had been laid off. Another difference is that
the average amount of per capita arable land in the district around each
city and in the provinces in which these cities are situated was also quite
discrepant. There was by far the most per capita acreage in Liaoning–
Shenyang. Because land scarcity is a major factor in peasant outmigration, this may explain the much lower level of geographical mobility
of peasants in Liaoning and around Shenyang (see Tables 5.8 and 5.9).

Table 5.5. *International Economies, 1997*

Parameter	Guangzhou	Shenyang	Wuhan
Utilized foreign direct investment ($U.S. million)			
	2,480	538	453
Total imports and exports ($U.S. thousands)			
	753.8	95.3	94.1

Sources: For utilized investment, see *Urban Yearbook*, 431 ff. For total
imports and exports, see Wuhan nianjian bianzuan weiyuanhui zhubian
[Wuhan Yearbook Compilation Committee, ed.], *Wuhan nianjian 1997*
[Wuhan 1997 Statistical Yearbook] (Wuhan: Wuhan nianjian she, 1997),
pp. 359–61.

Table 5.6. *Registered Unemployed (Thousand Persons Year-End)*

	Guangzhou	Shenyang	Wuhan
1996	48.2	72.0	57.0
1997	52.6	76.6	73.1
1998	45.6	66.6	86.5

Sources: Guojia tongjiju renkou yu jiuye tongjisi, Laodongbu zongje jihua yu gongzesi, bian [State Statistical Bureau, Population and Employment Statistics Department, Department of Overall Planning and Wages, Ministry of Labour, ed.], *Zhongguo laodong tongji nianjian 1997 [China Labour Statistical Yearbook]* (Beijing: Zhongguo tongji chubanshe, 1997) (hereafter *Labor Yearbook*), pp. 100, 105, 106; 1998: 105, 110–1; 1999: 95, 102–3.

Table 5.7. *Laid-Off SOE Workers by Province (% of Total SOE Workers)*

	Guangdong	Liaoning	Hubei
1996	4.6	9.5	6.7
1997	6.9	15.0	10.5
1998	15.8	46.7	26.7

Source: Labor Yearbook 1997, pp. 213, 227; 1998, pp. 230, 243; 1999, pp. 205, 223.

Table 5.8. *Average Arable per Capita Acreage (District), Urban Areas, 1996 (mou)*

Province	Numbers
National	1.10
Shenyang	1.27
Wuhan	0.47
Guangzhou	0.29

Source: Urban Yearbook, 91ff.

Table 5.9. *Average Arable per Capita Acreage, Provincial, 1996 (mou)*

Province	Numbers
National	2.30
Liaoning	2.96
Hubei	1.60
Guangdong	0.88

Source: Guojia tongjiju bian [State Statistical Bureau, ed.], *Zhongguo tongji nianjian 1997 [1997 Chinese Statistical Yearbook]* (Beijing: Zhongguo tongji chubanshe, 1997), p. 379.

Table 5.10. *Migrants*

Year Province	Guangdong	Liaoning	Hubei
A-1. Rural labor employed outside their homes, 1995–1998			
1995	1,572,800	300,460	1,700,000
1996	1,799,600	380,900	1,804,700
1997	1,507,500	443,100	1,520,400
1998	1,451,600	450,800	1,772,200
A-2. Of which, employed in other counties in own province			
1995	1,493,300	250,500	600,000
1996	1,720,500	295,600	523,600
1997	1,398,800	340,800	412,100
1998	1,315,600	368,600	516,100
B. Employment of rural labor from other provinces			
End of 1995	3,940,300	464,600	850,000
End of 1996	4,672,100	308,200	853,500
End of 1997	4,824,600	297,200	398,100
End of 1998	5,193,000	301,000	405,500

Source: Labor Yearbook 1997, pp. 126–127; 1998, pp. 135–137; 1999, pp. 128–130.

In fact, in Liaoning there was barely any geographical mobility relative to the other two places, and what little there was remained mostly within the province.

In contrast, in Hubei there was a great deal of movement, much of it entailing leaving the province. In Guangdong there was even more mobility, but a lot of it was being accommodated locally (a measure of the very active markets there and also of the high level of foreign investment; see Table 5.10). In the spring of 1999, economist Hu Angang reported that foreign-invested enterprises had created nearly 18 million new jobs, around 10 million of which were located in Guangdong province alone.[28] Other official data show that only Liaoning was able to reduce the numbers of outsiders (mainly peasants) coming in after 1995. In Hubei, the numbers dropped substantially after 1996 but began to rise again in 1998, and in Guangdong they continued to increase steadily (see Table 5.10).

I proceed to examine how these three cities coped with the contradictions in central labor policy during this period of economic challenge,

---

[28] In *Gangao jingji [Hong Kong and Macao Economy]*, March 1, 1999, in Summary of World Broadcasts (hereafter SWB) FE/3514, April 21, 1999, G7.

policy confusion, and heightened competition. Clearly the conditions just reviewed made for disparate thrusts and emphases. Still, and what is most significant for the arguments in this volume, all three cities were clearly heeding central policy (if in their own ways and in accord with their own conditions, endowments, and interpretations), and they were – if variably – all quite obviously politically integrated into the national polity.

HOW THREE CITIES HANDLED ECONOMIC CHALLENGE AND CENTRAL POLICIES

The 15th Party Congress and the Southeast Asian Crisis

As of late 1997, given its felicitous economic conditions and the strength of its nonstate economy, Guangdong chose, in Thatcherite fashion, to focus on just one particular aspect of the 15th Party Congress's message: Its leadership noted that the congress had called for "actively readjusting the ownership structure" while making the private economy into a new growth point. According to a quite sanguine quotation from a responsible person from the provincial bureau of labor, "the 15th Party Congress's assessment of the nonstate economy's position will enable the share system, foreign-invested [*sanzi*] firms, private [*minying*] and the individual economies to supply even more employment opportunities in the next several years."[29]

However, it wasn't long before a less optimistic outlook began to appear in provincial and urban statements. Indeed, even before the Asian crisis broke, a national economic slowdown began to have adverse effects in the area. An analysis of the provincial economy prepared late in 1997 or early in 1998 noted the following:

Because the market element is very active in Guangdong, when supply surpasses demand nationally, restraints on production created by low demand are most obvious here; Guangdong is more affected by the market than is the rest of the country, so the drop in the growth speed will be greater here than the national average drop.[30]

---

[29] Li Zhao and Li Hong, eds., *Guangdong jingji lanpishu*, p. 237; and *Yangcheng wanbao [Sheep City Evening News]* (hereafter *YCWB*), November 26, 1997.
[30] Li Zhao and Li Hong, eds., *Guangdong jingji lanpishu*, p. 236.

As for Guangzhou itself, although the city had "emphasized competitive employment in the past," by early 1998, a city paper announced – in a manner quite consonant with what would soon be officially promulgated as national policy – that, "this year we will turn the keypoint to guaranteeing employment."[31] However, at the same time, as the effects of the Asian crisis began to be felt, Guangzhou leaders realized that for the sake of the city's economy they needed to consider seriously a problem they had not really had to worry about up until then: international competition. By the end of 1997, as neighboring nations devalued their currencies, competition pushed Guangzhou's export growth down, so that the rate was even slower there than the national average.[32]

Despite its lesser involvement in foreign trade and investment (see Table 5.5), the ongoing problems in Shenyang's industry also became more severe with the onset of the Southeast Asian crisis. In the machinery trade, the Southeast Asian crisis had a big impact, because one-fourth of the province's exports had gone to that region before the crisis began; by mid-1998 that amount had been cut in half. Furthermore, although the trade's export growth rate in Liaoning had been in the range of 10 to 20 percent in the earlier half of the 1990s, in 1997 it grew at a mere 2.5 percent.[33] Investment from Asian countries in 1998 also fell by 32.6 percent, with that from Japan alone declining by 55 percent. This was particularly serious because over half of the investment in the province in recent years had come from Japan, South Korea, and Thailand,[34] all at that point in varying degrees subject to the crisis. According to an official from Shenyang's Labor Bureau, the Southeast Asian crisis was indeed one contributing factor in the city's problems with mounting unemployment.[35]

---

[31] *YCWB*, January 3, 1998. Although as of summer 1998 a State Council decision still reaffirmed the Party Congress pronouncement on state enterprise reform (*GMRB*, June 23, 1998, p. 1), it seemed that the "spirit" of the original message had been altered: At a special meeting on unemployment and layoffs held in May, a call was sounded stating that this "spirit" entailed "realiz[ing] the Fifteenth Party Congress and the Ninth People's Congress's objectives of arranging the work of state enterprise layoffs": *Jingji ribao [Economic Daily]* (hereafter *JJRB*), May 18, 1998.

[32] Guangzhou shi, p. 126, states that Guangzhou's rate went down to 15.7, whereas the national average was 20.9 percent.

[33] Interview, provincial Machinery Bureau, August 19, 1998.

[34] *China Daily Business Weekly*, August 23, 1998, p. 7.

[35] Interview with Song Naiyi, August 18, 1998.

However, unlike Guangdong, Liaoning's more Keynesian reaction to the 15th Party Congress emphasized the state sector, selecting for emphasis the meeting's call to "readjust the ownership structure" in the state sector and to intensify state enterprise reform.[36] Still, the congress's credo of efficiency and competition did have an impact on the province as well. For instance, even as a senior engineer at the provincial Machinery Bureau bragged that no other Chinese city's products could possibly compete with those turned out in Liaoning, he (almost mindlessly, it seemed) professed that "we have to increase our competitiveness; to increase our efficiency, we must cut off some workers."[37]

A somewhat different third story unfolded in Hubei's capital city. In the past, Wuhan's labor-intensive products had found a ready market in Southeast Asia. However, with the drop in receptivity to Chinese imports in that region after 1997, a large number of goods that were once exported there had to be sold domestically, where heightened competitiveness then increased the pressure on local employment in Wuhan.[38] Some products that had once been exported not only could not be at that time but instead had to be imported, because their Southeast Asian versions had become so cheap. City Economic Commission administrators related in late summer of 1998 that the regional financial crisis had also had an effect on steel exports – a serious concern in a city where the Wuhan Iron and Steel Corporation was the most crucial company – because Korean and Russian output had become so much less costly.[39]

Along with the Asian crisis, the 15th Party Congress's stress on competitiveness also found its echo in Wuhan, with both influences intensifying unemployment, as they did elsewhere. As then-Mayor Wang Shouhai proclaimed just after the March 1998 Ninth National People's Congress, "To strengthen the vitality and competitiveness of the large and medium enterprises, an important route is to cut back and divert personnel."[40] Nevertheless, as we will see, discharged workers remained a serious concern for city policy makers.

In all three cities, then, given sudden new attacks from the global economy, plus pressures from the Party Congress, one might expect that local

---

[36] Xu et al., *1997–1998 Liaoning*, p. 274.
[37] Interview with Ma Daming, August 19, 1998.
[38] Labor Bureau interview.
[39] Interview with officials from the City Economic Commission, September 8, 1998.
[40] *Changjiang ribao [Yangzi Daily]* (hereafter *CJRB*) (Wuhan), April 9, 1998, p. 1.

administrators would – if in their own ways – turn their attention to trying to compete. One might also surmise that they would be likely to ignore any central mandates that might undercut their competitiveness, especially if the country had become more decentralized and less integrated politically than before.

The Reemployment Project

Yet, surprisingly enough, despite their differences and regardless of new challenges, all of these localities to varying degrees remained obedient to central pronouncements about caring for those cut off from their jobs and about becoming more unfriendly to incoming farmers.[41] Guangzhou, whose economy had been thriving, was the latest of the three to take up these missions, a sudden shift evidently driven by the twin shocks of 1997. A Guangdong provincial economic study remarked that, "in 1996, urban unemployed staff and workers' reemployment *suddenly* [emphasis added] became a hot point of social concern, and it did so even more in 1997," when the numbers of layoffs saw an increase of 13.3 percent over the year before.[42]

By the end of 1997, slow growth, along with state enterprise reform, was perceived to be making "employment and reemployment increasingly serious" in the view of local analysts.[43] Although Guangzhou had the lowest number of *xiagang* personnel among the nation's ten largest cities and also the lowest proportion of its workforce laid off at that juncture,[44] abrupt unemployment was still disturbing in an area that had had nothing but good news for well over a decade.

---

[41] This is by no means to deny the severe financial and administrative inadequacies that kept millions of laid-off workers from being served, especially in Shenyang and Wuhan.

[42] Li Zhao and Li Hong, *Guangdong jingji lanpishu*, p. 241.

[43] *Ibid.*, p. 234.

[44] *Shijie ribao [World Daily]*, April 25, 1998, p. A9, claimed that 53,400 or 2.67 percent of all staff and workers were furloughed in Guangzhou, in comparison with a national official average rate of 8.18 percent. However, according to *Ming Pao [Bright Daily]* (hereafter *MP*), January 13, 1998, the city's mayor claimed that only about 40,000 were *xiagang*'d but that more than an additional 60,000 were officially unemployed as of the end of 1997. However, SWB FE/3369 (October 28, 1998), G/5 (from *XH*, October 26, 1998) stated, quite discrepantly, that 55,600 workers who had been laid off by state firms had found new jobs in 1997(!). There is no good explanation for the divergent figures.

Its various abrupt difficulties led Guangzhou to embark in earnest on a program of reemployment finally as late as 1998, with the city really only then for the first time taking this as "important work."[45] Guangzhou leaders adopted a distinctive approach to the campaign, relying on a strategy much in line with the city's prior promarket and non-state-sector-based growth. Of the three cities, it was the one closest to having what I have called a Thatcherite, marketist strategy. Even as the city's economy began to falter in early 1998, official statements continued to emphasize that "the precondition for solving reemployment is to guarantee a certain growth speed."[46] Forcefully developing the tertiary sector and promoting the nonpublic economy were held to be the winning tactics through 1998.[47]

Guangzhou's leaders did join the rest of urban China in worrying about the reemployment of the laid-off workers, and their solutions included – as other places were doing – the development of a series of supportive active labor market policies, such as preferential rents, loans, provision of sites, reduction of fees, and free licensing.[48] However, they fashioned a version of the Reemployment Project that explicitly aimed at "pushing labor toward the market, using the labor market to arrange labor resources."[49] Thus, in promoting reemployment, unlike the administrators of the other two cities, Guangzhou's administrators used the program as a means of entrenching a nonstate market employment mechanism.[50] In contrast to authorities from the other two cities, Guangzhou's authorities believed they could control the rate of flow and the scale of the numbers of layoffs so that they matched the city's absorptive capacity.[51]

This strategy appeared to be working fairly well by the summer of 1998. In the first half of the year, the announced rate of registered unemployed people had dropped 0.19 percent compared with the same period a year earlier, whereas the nonpublic sector had allegedly "arranged" nearly

---

[45] Article from July or August 1998 in *Guangzhou ribao [Guangzhou Daily]* (hereafter *GZRB*). Unfortunately there is no citation because I received this article from a Beida student who did not note the article's date. However, photos of the summer floods on the same page as the cut-out article place it in either July or August.

[46] *Caijing zhoukan [Asian–Pacific Economic Times]* (the paper has these two names on its masthead), April 2, 1998, p. 1.

[47] *Ibid.* and *GZRB*.

[48] *MP*, May 17, 1998, and *JJRB*, March 24, 1998.

[49] *Caijing zhoukan*, April 2, 1998, p. 1.

[50] *JJRB*, March 24, 1998.

[51] *YCWB*, February 26, 1998.

30 percent of the city's unemployed.[52] A few months later, Xinhua reported on a survey conducted by the city's statistics bureau that had found that 73.28 percent of 10,000 respondents had become reemployed by their own efforts, and a full 46.58 percent of those reemployed had found work in the private sector.[53]

In contrast, as early as mid-1996, when the problem of layoffs was only just beginning to be noticed in Guangzhou, the city of Shenyang, where unemployment had become severe, had announced that there were over 300,000 *xiagang* people, at a time when the total number of staff and workers in the city was said to be 2.3 million.[54] According to one account, by the end of that year, when the average combined total of registered unemployed[55] and laid-off personnel was 10.3 percent nationally, in Liaoning it was 16.7 percent.[56]

By early 1998, Shenyang's officially admitted *xiagang* figure had shot up to 378,000 persons, of whom 249,000 remained without any new placement. Even of those who had been settled into new work situations, approximately 30 percent were engaged in only temporary or seasonal work and so would soon need a new arrangement.[57] Late that summer, interview informants put the likely figure at 400,000 or more, with one scholar estimating that some 40 percent of Shenyang's staff and workers were either laid off or unemployed.[58]

The causes behind Shenyang's labor troubles were both structural and cyclical. Structurally, Shenyang, like all of the Northeast, had been the heartland of the planned economy, dependent on generous state

---

[52] *GZRB*.

[53] *XH*, October 26, 1998, in SWB, FE/3369, G/5.

[54] *Liaoning ribao [Liaoning Daily]* (hereafter *LNRB*), October 17, 1996. *LNRB*, September 4, 1996, gives the number of staff and workers as of early September; if the laid-off people were being counted as members of the staff and workers, this would mean that 13.04 percent of the total had already been laid off.

[55] This term refers to those whose firms had been merged, had gone bankrupt, or were otherwise shut down, so that these former workers no longer had any linkage with their previous enterprises.

[56] No author, "Woguo dengji shiyelu gediqu bupingheng" [The Imbalance Among Various Districts in Our Country's Registered Unemployment Rate], *ZGLD*, 1 (1998), p. 44.

[57] Wang Chengying, ed., *Zhongguo zaijiuye* [Reemployment in China] (Chengdu: Sichuan daxue chubanshe, 1998), p. 201.

[58] Interviews with the city Industrial and Commercial Administration, August 19, 1998, and with Zhou Qiren of Beijing University's Chinese Economy Research Center on September 1, 1998, in Beijing.

investment (especially in heavy industry and energy), reliant on guaranteed state purchases whatever the quality of the output, and free from paying back any debts incurred. This ensured support thus provided no incentive to turn out marketable products, so that even the city's name-brand goods got stocked in warehouses and generated continuously increasing storage costs. The problems caused by excessive and unbalanced investment in heavy industry became all too apparent once the national economy shifted to operating according to the market mechanism. With that vital switch, heavy losses began to emerge, and the demand for labor plummeted along with the drop in demand for local products, particularly the output of such "sunset industries" as steel, coal, chemicals, and energy, which were the chief components of the area's economy.

The cyclical dimension – the second type of cause behind the employment problems in Shenyang – was one that the city shared with the rest of the nation, when the total demand for labor fell after 1994. This drop in demand occurred as national policy decreed a slowdown in the speed of growth, entailing mandated cutbacks in investment and a tightening of credit; indeed, the economy even entered a recession at that point.[59] At the same time, following the Third Plenum of the 14th Party Congress in late 1994, the proportion of output taken by state purchases declined sharply.[60] Against this background, the 15th Congress's call for speeding up reform, restructuring assets, and putting increased emphasis on competitiveness and efficiency hit the city with a severe blow. The only way its leaders could imagine raising productivity and meeting the demands of the new market economy was to implement drastic cuts in staff.[61]

Of the three cities, Shenyang's layoff policy was implemented first but in the most Keynesian fashion, because, on balance, city leaders relied rather more on state initiatives than on leaving people to the market. Liaoning instituted its REP as early as 1994, initially placing the focus on readjusting the province's industrial structure and deepening enterprise reform. Although official statements recognized that the project was to be concerned with finding work for displaced labor, they referred at first

[59] Interview, Liaoning Academy of Social Sciences (hereafter LASS), August 18, 1998, and Xu et al., *1997–1998 Liaoning*, pp. 143, 274–6, and 280–1.
[60] LASS interview.
[61] Xu et al., *1997–1998 Liaoning*, p. 276, and interview with an official from the Shenyang Labor Market Management Committee's Office and the city's Employment Work Leadership Small Group Office, August 18, 1998.

mainly to "grasping the large[r enterprises]" and carrying out mergers to strengthen and reorganize assets and thereby to redeploy personnel. Under this program, Shenyang created 17 large enterprise groups in electronics, automobiles, and clothing, among other industries, which was a plan that was said to solve the arrangement of surplus labor. Thus provincial and urban leaders in Liaoning grabbed the REP as a chance to take advantage of their comparative superiority in being the site of many very large plants, in typical local opportunistic fashion.[62]

However, in Liaoning's cities, the project had another dimension: this was to create a "new iron rice bowl" for idle urban workers, as one booster article in Shenyang's press described the effort in that city's hardest hit district, Tiexi.[63] Shenyang was one of three cities the province selected as an experimental point for the REP, where the mission of the program was to organize neighborhoods and enterprises and to develop preferential policies, both for laid-off workers to encourage them to set up businesses and for firms to spur them to employ sizable numbers of these workers, while spreading propaganda about self-reliance.[64]

The tactics to be emphasized in the campaign smacked eerily of the planned economy in Shenyang. They involved developing a unified hierarchy of leadership, each member of which was to have assigned work targets and responsibility certificates. Their goal was to arrange new placements for the laid-off workers, whether under the auspices of the original firm or in the burgeoning, subsidized, and, supposedly, fee-free marketplaces of the city.

By the autumn of 1996, the city already boasted 13 reemployment "bases" providing free training. At the start of 1998, the local government there was actively sponsoring private industry and the tertiary sector and offering basic livelihood fees to those whose firms could no longer

---

[62] No author, "Yi bashou gongcheng zai Liaoning" ["Number One Project in Liaoning"], *Zhongguo jiuye [Chinese Employment]*, 3 (1998), pp. 13–14.

[63] *LNRB*, June 1, 1995.

[64] The preferential policies were essentially the same as those offered in Guangzhou or in any other city to deal with the local laid-off workers, including free business licenses for the first year, no management fees, sites for carrying out their new businesses, tax exemption for the first year, and reduction in commercial and other types of management fees for the first year. Firms in which over 60 percent of the workers had previously been unemployed or laid off could escape income tax for three years. However, the government of Shenyang seemed more energetic in pursuing these policies than Guangzhou's did.

disburse wages sufficient to sustain them. In addition, its publications claimed that it had already set up over 250 basic-level job introduction stations and six specialized labor markets, and it had allocated funds to open some 128 new commercial markets, build new factory sites, and offer training.[65]

But despite a multitude of measures aimed at providing new opportunities for employment to those who had lost their former posts, Shenyang, like the Northeast in general, was plagued by two stubborn obstacles: a serious shortage of funds and a gross insufficiency of jobs. As one writer lamented,

the financial situation of the state-owned enterprises all over the Northeast is below the average level in the other regions. And because the financial situation is inferior, there are so many *xiagang*'d staff and workers; it is also the cause of the low level of compensation [that can be offered to those without jobs].[66]

Given these impediments, the city had an incentive to attempt to invigorate the individual and private economies. Allegedly, by the end of 1997, 44 percent of the laid-off workers who were "diverted" or arranged for (*fenliu anzhi*) were able to find work, either in these economies or in the local government's district and neighborhood enterprises. These workers tended to be allocated to the commercial, catering, housework, and community service trades, which demanded relatively little municipal investment. Given the difficulties in the Northeast, however, it is not surprising that, whereas the rate of overall reemployment of the laid-off workers nationwide ranged between 40 and 50 percent at this time, with

---

[65] For instance, Wang Chengying, ed., *Zhongguo zaijiuye*, pp. 201–4; No author, "Shishi 'zaijiuye gongcheng' jingyen jieshao" ["Enforce the Introduction of Experience on the Reemployment Project"] *Gongyun cankao ziliao [Workers' Movement Reference Materials]* (hereafter *GYCKZL*), 1 (1996), pp. 12–15; *LNRB*, September 5, 1996; interviews with city's labor official, August 18, 1998, and with officials at the city's Industrial and Commercial Administration, August 19, 1998. See also Shenyang renmin zhengfu [Shenyang People's Government], "Pizhuan shi laodongju guanyu shishi zaijiuye gongcheng anshan fenliu anzhi qiye fuyu zhigong yijian di tongzhi" ["Circular Transmitting the City Labor Bureau's Opinion on Implementing the Reemployment Project, Properly Diverting and Arranging Enterprise Surplus Staff and Workers"], Shenyang, No. 31, 1996. This document was obtained for me by a student at Beida and there is no further documentation.

[66] Niu Renliang, "Xiagang zhigong chulu sikao" ["Thoughts on the Way Out for the Laid-Off Staff and Workers"], *Lingdao canyue [Leadership Consultations]*, 1 (1998), p. 10. Similarly, Xu et al., *1997–1998 Liaoning*, p. 283; and No author, "Yi baoshou," p. 14.

the city of Shanghai reportedly able to reemploy as many as 70 percent or more, in Liaoning the total rate did not even reach 40 percent.[67]

Wuhan's troubles and approaches resembled those of Shenyang. However, like Guangzhou, it also boasted a thriving market, so its options were greater than Shenyang's. By the end of 1996, according to the finding of a locally commissioned study, Wuhan's laid-off workers totalled 289,000, or 13.7 percent of the total of staff and workers in enterprises.[68] A year later, one estimate was 340,000, or 16.5 percent of what was said to be 2.08 million staff and workers.[69]

These high numbers had several sources. Most prominently, many commentators agreed, as in Shenyang, they were the offshoot of the prior economic system, including the relative (but less unbalanced) dominance in Wuhan of heavy industrial state-owned firms[70] and the previous regimen of state planning and purchases. As market consciousness became more prominent, many firms and construction projects that duplicated each other were forced to cut back or even cease production. Besides, the city was turning out few name-brand products of the sort whose producers could form large-scale enterprise groups that might absorb personnel.[71] Moreover, under the press of the market competition, Wuhan's GDP between 1991 and 1997 fell among what are called deputy-provincial-level (*fu-sheng*) cities from eighth to eleventh place.[72] Alongside the decline of the city's older industry, new growth points did emerge, as in the city's development zones, but these required relatively few workers and demanded highly skilled ones at that.[73]

Matching its middling position between Guangzhou and Shenyang economically and geographically, Wuhan's approach to reemployment

[67] Niu Renliang, "Xiagang," p. 9.
[68] Jianghan daxue ketizu [Jianghan University Project Group], "Wuhan shi shishi zaijiuye gongcheng duice yanjiu" ["Policy Research on Wuhan City's Implementation of the Reemployment Project] (Wuhan, 1998), p. 2.
[69] This report was from, I believe, *GMRB*, December 21, 1997 (the article was clipped for me without the source having been noted).
[70] As of 1989, in Shenyang heavy industry accounted for 65 percent of the gross value of industrial output and only 55 percent in Wuhan (Solinger, "Despite Decentralization," p. 11).
[71] *Ibid.*, p. 11.
[72] Si Yuan and Zeng Xiangmin, "Wuhan 1998 hongguan zhengce shou xuan mubiao–zaijiuye" ["Reemployment–Wuhan's 1998 Macro Policy's First Objective"], *Wuhan jingji yanjiu [Wuhan Economic Research]*, 3 (1998), p. 56. Also see Solinger, "Despite Decentralization."
[73] Wang Baoyu interview, September 9, 1998.

partook of both a Keynesian emphasis and a Thatcherite or marketist one. It appears that many of the city's solutions remained within the state sector, as in Shenyang, with government departments pressured to arrange the laid-off workers[74] and both government offices and enterprises told to strive to create more jobs for those without work.[75] The city expended much effort in directly guiding the process, as by arranging labor exchange meets and forming reemployment bases, such as evening markets that offered preferential policies just for the *xiagang* workers (but not for outside peasants). City offices also mandated that firms and trades set up reemployment service centers to which their laid-off workers could be entrusted.[76] The Wuhan government also invested in infrastructure and the private sector.

Sharing certain legacies and liabilities with Shenyang, Wuhan also got started early in its efforts to address unemployment: There the program took off in the second half of 1994. In 1995, the city set up a leadership small group at the urban level, composed of officials from twelve units.[77] The city determined that its primary targets for placing workers would be the tertiary sector and the district and street-level economy, both official and both of which were showing the most vitality and ability to absorb laid-off personnel.[78] This strategy contrasts with that of Guangzhou, where the private sector was to be the chief recipient of laid-off workers, and also with Shenyang, where the city seemed most concerned with officially granted preferential policies for laid-off people and with merging giant plants. Wuhan, again like Shenyang, was woefully deficient in funding for the REP. In 1995, a special fund was created of just 10 million yuan, with another 10 million added in 1996 and again in 1997. Thus, by 1997 the city had 30 million in the till, at a time when Shanghai had over 200 million just for its two reemployment service centers and 626 million in all.[79]

Nonetheless, to judge from the press, city leaders in Wuhan seemed to take the project very seriously. Leadership small groups were drawn up at

---

[74] Interview with Planning Commission officials.
[75] Instructions from the mayor, in *CJRB*, April 9, 1998, p. 1.
[76] Labor interview. I read a lot about these centers, but I do not explore that topic in this chapter.
[77] *JJRB*, May 2, 1998; labor interview, September 6, 1998.
[78] *GMRB* (probably), December 21, 1997, and planning interview.
[79] On Wuhan, no author, "Wuhan shi zhuazhu," p. 16, *JJRB*, May 2, 1998, and Jianghan daxue ketizu, "Wuhan," p. 61, on Shanghai, Yang Yiyong et al., *Shiye chongji bo [The Shock Wave of Unemployment]* (Beijing: Jinri zhongguo chubanshe, n.d. [probably 1997]), p. 230. On both, see Si Yuan and Zeng Xiangmin, "Wuhan 1998," p. 56.

every administrative level, in the various trades, and, supposedly, in each enterprise and department. In addition, the Mayor of Wuhan instituted a monthly reporting meeting on the progress of the campaign in June 1997. Also in 1997, the party and government leaders here named this work the number 1 topic for research that year and issued over ten separate policy documents concerning it.[80]

Yet this was not the whole picture. In a manner similar to that of Guangzhou, if to a lesser degree, there was a nod to Thatcherism. For instance, in 1995, Wuhan eliminated the management fee for people working in the private sector, something only done in Shenyang two years later.[81] Moreover, the key to everything, according to an optimistic local press in the spring of 1998, was to maintain a level of 15 percent economic growth.[82] Official reports boasted that 70 percent of those arranged had gone into the tertiary sector in the two years between 1995 and 1997.[83] More specific data, however, came from a local mid-1997 survey of laid-off and reemployed people. Its researchers found that, of the 300 reemployed persons questioned, just 26 percent were working in state firms, and 21 percent were working in collectives. The remainder were all in the nonstate sectors: 14 percent in joint ventures, another 31 percent in private firms, and the last 7 percent in individual operations.

The Issue of Peasant Migrants

Simultaneously with the press to place the laid-off workers, peasants suddenly became less welcome in cities across China around 1997. Among the tactics specified to cut back on rural workers were regulations dividing jobs into three categories – those for which peasants were not permitted to be hired, those for which they could be hired only if there were an insufficient urban labor supply, and those for which they could be hired. These

---

[80] *CJRB*, November 5, 1997, and another article from the same paper sometime just after the Ninth National People's Congress (article clipped for me but without the date).

[81] For Wuhan, interview with Industrial and Commercial Administration officials, September 10, 1998; for Shenyang, interview with the same office there on August 19, 1998.

[82] *CJRB*, April 9, 1998, p. 1, and May 30, 1998; and No author, "Wuhan shi zhuazhu," p. 17.

[83] No author, "Guanyu Wuhanshi Zaijiuye went di diaocha bao" [An investigation report on Wuhan City's reemployment question], probably written around mid-1997–8 and Planning Commission interview.

rules were first promulgated in 1995 in Shanghai and elsewhere at the urban level, but they were repeated more vigorously in 1997 and 1998.[84]

Despite the marketist bias in Guangzhou's REP, the city clearly absorbed some of the center's policy orientation about peasants, as time went on, just as it had about caring for the furloughed. By early 1998 concerns about layoffs had led local officials to decide that it would no longer do just to allow the unguided market to supply the city's needs for manual and mass-production manufacturing workers. Because native laid-off ex-employees were often not as suited [and not as cheap] as peasants, ran one commentary, "we can't entirely let the market economy govern whom enterprises hire;" "Guangzhou must restrict the proportion of outsiders in certain trades to solve the reemployment of local labor," it read.[85]

Perhaps such injunctions to dispose of peasants was merely rhetoric. After all, one scholar opined that the priority in Guangdong remained cheap labor for boosting exports into 1998 and that the city therefore was willing to ignore the *xiagang* workers.[86] However, there are indications to the contrary. Another scholar maintained that nearly one-third of foreign firms had closed down or temporarily suspended production in nearby Dongguan, and that peasant workers from these firms had simply given up hope of an urban position for the time being and had returned to their villages. The U.S. Consul General in Guangzhou related in the summer of 1998 that not just foreign enterprises but Chinese companies in the city as well were sending outside labor home because business had fallen off, with both foreign investment and exports down.[87] In addition, the Program Officer at the Ford Foundation (which was sponsoring several projects on peasant migration at the time) concurred, reporting that Guangzhou had indeed tightened up against incoming peasants in the throes of the Southeast Asian crisis.[88] Adding to this evidence, a woman managing a small neighborhood reemployment service center observed that there

---

[84] For instance, see *Foreign Broadcast Information Service* (hereafter *FBIS*), February 23, 1995, p. 68, March 16, 1995, p. 33, April 10, 1995, p. 46, and June 28, 1995, p. 81 for some of the earlier rulings; see Xiao Lichun, "Shanghai shiye, xiagang renyuan xianzhuang ji fazhan qushi" ["Shanghai Unemployment, Laid-Off Personnel's Situation and Development Trend], *ZRK*, 3 (1998), pp. 26–37.

[85] *MP* (Hong Kong), January 13, 1998.

[86] Interview with Zhou Qiren, September 1, 1998.

[87] Interview with Edward McKeon, August 11, 1998.

[88] Interview with Stephen McGurk, August 28, 1998.

were fewer "outside workers" in the city in the summer of 1998 than there had been earlier.[89]

Guangdong province issued orders in 1997 proclaiming that hiring out-of-province labor should be "controlled," in the interest of guaranteeing the province's own labor employment.[90] However, just as with the city's relatively tardy recognition of the problems of the unemployed, it was not until 1998 that the city became inclined to enforce this rule, at least to some extent.[91] Professor Zhou Daming of Zhongshan University's Anthropology Department commented that 1998 was the first year in which Guangzhou promulgated a policy forbidding migrants from taking certain jobs.[92] According to a city paper, "from this year Guangzhou will formally implement various policy measures announced last year to restrict the numbers of outsiders...to create more jobs for its own labor."[93] Even harsher regulations appeared in early 1999.[94]

Also evincing a growing concern with stemming the tide of immigrants, the province reported in 1997 that – relying on a nine-province inter-regional program organized years before – it had undertaken stronger macrocontrol measures toward the labor market, and toward rural sur-plus labor moving across regions in particular. As a result, according to the authors of the report, numbers fell for the first time in 1996 and continued to drop in 1997. New entrants from other provinces coming for

---

89 Informal interview at the center, Haizhu district, Guangzhou, August 11, 1998.
90 *Nanfang ribao* [Southern Daily], March 31, 1997, p. 1. This was not the first such effort. In 1994, the authorities in Guangdong proclaimed an end to the hiring of labor from outside the province, although at that time the ban was merely to last through the New Year period (*SCMP*, December 14, 1994, p. 9, in *FBIS*, December 14, 1994, pp. 10–11). According to *XH*, January 5, 1999, in SWB FE/3426, G/5, Guangdong had laid out its first set of regulations governing the control of transients in 1995.
91 The official data in Table 5.10 do at least indicate a much slower increase in Guangzhou of rural labor arriving from other localities at the end of 1997 and 1998 than at the end of 1996, as compared with the year before in each case (18.5 percent in 1996, 3 percent in 1997, and 7.6 percent in 1998).
92 Interview, August 7, 1998.
93 *YCWB*, February 26, 1998.
94 The rules, drawn up to retard the inflow of migrants looking for jobs, were devised to make it easier for what were said to be 100,000 local unemployed workers to find jobs. Though allowing certain transients to apply for permanent residence status, these were just those who had resided in the same locations for seven consecutive years and had permanent housing. This was reported in *China News Digest*, January 6, 1999, in *Global News*, No. GL99–004, January 8, 1999, and in SWB FE/3426, G/5, from *XH*, January 5, 1999.

work declined by 9 percent, they reported.[95] Probably as part of this same policy thrust to limit incoming workers, a new public security regulation appeared on the city's walls in the summer of 1998. The notice decreed that one's identification card should be merged with one's household registration card and that the items used to identify an individual would be increased to include his or her blood type and height, along with a photograph.[96]

Again following the spirit of central orders, the province also promulgated a new hiring policy, demanding that employers recruit urbanites before ruralites, locals before outsiders, and provincials before those from other provinces, giving priority to the unemployed and the laid off. This would make outsiders face more severe employment competition than they had before, regulators acknowledged. They even went so far as to grant that the new step would mean a "serious attack on peasant workers' wish for equal competition in employment and to stay in the city."[97] Thus, "even in rich Guangdong," commented the usually frank and informative *Ming Pao*, "dealing with local workers' livelihood would have to entail extending a hand toward the labor market [i.e., manipulating it in urbanites' favor]."[98]

In sum, of the three cities, Guangzhou was surely the one best situated – because of its location, favorable central policies, and its industrial structure, and the stimulus these factors provided to both its domestic market and to foreign trade and investment – to generate jobs and absorb labor

---

[95] Li Zhao and Li Hong, *Guangdong jingji lanpishu*, p. 243. Note that their figures disagree with the national labor yearbook data in Table 5.10, but there is no explanation given. The program, or "agreement plan" (*xieyi jihua*), that the nine provinces devised involved setting up labor coordination centers in each province that were responsible for channeling and modulating the outflow of workers [interview, Zhongshan University, May 12, 1992; see also *FBIS*, December 24, 1991, p. 38, from *XH*, December 17, 1991; and *FBIS*, April 7, 1992, p. 30, from *Liaowang* (Overseas Edition), 12 (1992), pp. 5–6]. By the spring of 1995, a Center for Information Exchange on the Labor Needs of South China, created to provide estimates of demand and to integrate information on regional supply and demand conditions, was at work, with the support of ministries and commissions under the State Council, as well as with the cooperation of the provinces involved in the network (*FBIS*, March 16, 1995, p. 34, from *JJRB*, December 20, 1994, p. 1).

[96] Document observed on the street, August 7, 1998.

[97] "Guangdong sheng zhigong, duiwu di zhuangkuang ji zhuyao tezheng" ["The Situation and Important Special Characteristics of Guangdong's Staff and Worker Ranks"]. No documentation. This article was given to me by a Beida student who acquired it from "a friend."

[98] *MP*, May 17, 1998.

of all kinds, whether peasant or unemployed local worker. Initially its leaders shrugged off the concerns besetting other places, not really paying attention to the problem of reemployment until 1996, 1997, or even later.

Furthermore, the city's elite was able to give a very marketist interpretation to the decisions of the 15th Party Congress. Nonetheless, there were signs that, even in this wealthy and open metropolis, the fallout of those decisions, when combined with the financial crisis affecting China's neighboring countries, plus domestic factors slowing down the entire national economy, caused city officials – in line with central policy – to constrain their earlier receptivity toward migrants. There are also some indications that their policies may have had some results.

In Shenyang, as in Guangzhou, by late summer of 1998 there was a perception among residents that the numbers of outside peasants in town had decreased.[99] Certainly there had been far fewer to begin with, both because the person-to-land ratio was very favorable in the area under the city's jurisdiction (see Tables 5.8 and 5.9) and also because the city was not the kind of commercial magnet that either Guangzhou or Wuhan was. Still, in the years when urban construction had flourished, numbers of rural laborers had migrated toward the city, enough so that as of early 1998 their presence was said to be rendering the solution of urban unemployment more difficult.[100] One source, depicting the situation three years earlier (as of 1995), claimed that at that time as many as 900,000 rural surplus laborers were moving into the cities of the province every year.[101]

A change must have occurred over the ensuing few years, for an early 1998 book on Liaoning records that, by then, only 400,000 outsiders in total were coming into all of Liaoning per year, in response to the province's efforts to guide the peasants to flow in an "orderly" manner.[102] In part, the stagnation of the local economy after 1994 caused the number of peasants working in the Shenyang economy to diminish. However, this drop in number was apparently also an intentional outcome. One administrator from the provincial textile system made this remark:

Before 1993 the economic situation here was good and the textile sector was prosperous. At that time there were about 20,000 *mingong* [term popularly used

[99] Random street interviews, summer 1998.
[100] Xu et al., *1997–1998 Liaoning*, p. 305.
[101] No author, "Shishi," p. 13.
[102] Xu et al., *1997–1998 Liaoning*, p. 277.

for peasant workers in the cities; emphasis added] in the textile mills throughout the province. We used them to cut costs. But now there are none. *We can't deal with the xiagang workers, how could we hire peasants?* [emphasis added] Those who have finished their contracts have already left, and the enterprises suffering losses are reducing personnel, not adding anyone.[103]

A scholar at the Liaoning Academy of Social Science (LASS) agreed with this characterization, stating, for example, that "the state-owned firms are reducing people, so they won't be hiring peasants."[104] A labor bureaucrat concurred, remarking that the state firms were employing fewer peasants than they once had.[105] In late summer of 1998 in an open, outdoor produce market, salespeople confirmed that, at one time, before urban industrial workers had been laid off in great numbers, the market's business had mainly been conducted by peasants, many of whom of late had left.[106]

As early as 1995, the Liaoning provincial government formulated a directive entitled "Methods to Strengthen the Management of Outside Labor," requesting various levels of government to restrain the speed and scale of the movement of rural surplus labor into the cities. It also ordered giving priority to unemployed and surplus city workers as posts were cleared of their current peasant staff.[107] By 1997, managers in over 100 work categories in the machinery, chemical, electronics, and building materials trades were told explicitly to reduce their use of outside labor. Firms were instructed first to hire their own surplus workers; they were made to wait until there were not enough of these before they could recruit other workers from Shenyang's own ranks, a recruitment that had to be done publicly. Only if there were no way to meet its needs could any unit use outsiders, and, even then, the unit was to recruit these through the official labor department and just to engage those who (at a cost) had acquired work permits (*wugong xukezheng*). Firms behaving otherwise were to be fined.[108]

---

[103] Interview with Dong Chengli, August 17, 1998.
[104] Interview, August 18, 1998.
[105] Interview with Song Naiyi, August 18, 1998.
[106] Talks with marketers, August 20, 1998.
[107] No author, "Shishi," p. 14.
[108] Li Zhonglu, "Zai jiuye gongcheng di diaocha yu jishi" ["An Investigation and On The Spot Report of the Reemployment Project"], *GYCKCL*, 11 (1997), p. 19; Xu et al., *1997–1998 Liaoning*, p. 277; Wang Chengying, ed., *Zhongguo zaijiuye*, p. 203; and August 18, 1998, interview with Labor Bureau official. In an interview at the Liaoning Academy of

In my interviews I was able to find only a little evidence suggesting a less harsh attitude toward migrant labor in the city. One sign of leniency was that the city's Industrial and Commercial Administration was, as is typical of that unit nationally,[109] more sympathetic to inmigrating peasant workers than the labor department was. Its officials pointed out that some 20 percent of the private firms in the city were still being run by peasants as of August 1998, and that if a market were a very large one, these bureaucrats were permitting ruralites to work there with the locals.

As a general statement, Shenyang's government appeared to have focused its energies on the overwhelming issue of its laid-off workers as early as 1995. Because of its location, its shortage of capital, its decayed plants, and its dearth of new employment posts, there was more laying off in the first place and more difficulties catering to those dismissed there than in most of the rest of the nation. Peasants were surely restricted to some degree in Shenyang, but probably the work of officialdom was spent more on job creation for the locals than on active expulsion of outsiders.

Once again we find that Wuhan was middling in its hospitality to labor coming in from elsewhere, as compared with Shenyang and Guangzhou. Even though there is evidence that Guangzhou tightened up against outsiders somewhat in 1997 and allegedly more so in 1998, Table 5.7 shows that, at least in the period running up to 1996, Guangdong province was attracting ever more immigrants, as was Hubei province. The difference was that those coming into Guangdong amounted to a far larger annual increase from 1995 to 1996 (+18.57 percent into Guangdong as against +0.41 percent for Hubei).

From the start of the reform period, Wuhan had extended a special welcome to outsiders. This accommodation occurred under the auspices of a slogan coined by Wuhan University Professor Li Chonghuai, who made Wuhan famous as the home of the "two tongs" (*jiaotong* and *liutong*, or communications and circulation), and under the push of then-Mayor Wu Guanzheng to make Wuhan into a regional central city.

Social Science, August 18, 1998, one scholar affirmed that peasants were perceived as competitors for jobs with locals and so were being made to pay money and get certificates to enter town, whereas no such controls had existed previously.

[109] See Dorothy J. Solinger, *Contesting Citizenship in Urban China* (Berkeley, CA: University of California Press, 1999), Chapter Three. In Wuhan, representatives of this system said the same thing in an interview on September 10, 1998.

There continued to be evidence of flexibility toward outsiders in Wuhan, even into 1998. An anecdotal comparison with Beijing may be instructive. A maid in my hotel in the latter city in midsummer 1998 told me that the staff there were half local peasants and half Beijing city laid-off workers. Another told me that there had been people working in that hotel from other provinces more than two years before, but not now, because of "regulations" (*guiding*).[110] However, the staff in my Wuhan hotel that same season included Wuhan *xiagang* workers, Hubei peasants, and also people from other provinces (presumably peasants), all mixed in together.[111] In addition, among pedicab drivers, despite the occupation's ability to absorb and thus mollify displaced workers, it was not reserved for locals at that point: operators included peasants and other outside workers.[112]

Perhaps these signs of receptivity reflected the attitude of city leaders. Unlike what I heard about other cities, one local informant, a member of the Wuhan People's Congress, declared, "The enterprises *and* the city government [in Wuhan] don't want to limit incoming peasant workers."[113] Moreover, peasant labor entering Wuhan mostly came from nearby counties and provinces. Rather than organizing an interregional macrocontrol program such as the one attempted in Guangdong, the city allowed these workers to move in spontaneously. Densely populated countryside around the city (see Table 5.9), plus Wuhan's central location – which means it attracts people in transit – combined to raise the numbers of outsiders.[114]

How many peasants were there in Wuhan in the late 1990s? As is the case for Shenyang, estimates vary, but most researchers placed the number of those at work in the city in 1998 at approximately 700,000.[115] One source

---

[110] Interviews, August 25 and 28, 1998.
[111] September 5, 1998 interview.
[112] Street interview, September 6, 1998.
[113] Interview with Yang Yunyan of Central China Finance and Trade University, Wuhan, September 6, 1998.
[114] Also see Si Yuan and Zeng Xiangmin, "Wuhan 1998," p. 56.
[115] Although the Labor Bureau officials claimed a figure of 800,000, many other sources said 700,000, and one (an undated newspaper clipping from 1997 or 1998) said 600,000. The Planning Commission officials and *CJRB*, December 1, 1997, p. 11, both said 700,000, and Si Yuan and Zeng Xiangmin, "Wuhan 1998," p. 56, noted that in 1995 there was a floating population of 1.5 million in the city but that only about 700,000 of them were working.

noted that, for every four urban staff and workers in the city as of 1997, there was one peasant contract worker[116]; if this is correct, that would mean that approximately 500,000 were working on contracts. This source, however, did not include the large numbers of outsiders doing industrial and commercial work on their own in the nonpublic economy, nor did it add in those multitudes engaged in various sorts of noncontractual casual labor. The source also noted that a total of 470,000 outsiders were using formal channels to obtain temporary work permits from the city's public security.[117]

Peasants were clearly numerous in particular occupations in Wuhan. One paper claimed that, in the more than 2,000 clothing enterprises in the city, over 90 percent of the staff and workers were peasants from the outside[118]; one informant judged that 50 to 60 percent of those laboring in construction were also peasants.[119] In addition, though there are mixed reports on the textile trade, unlike in Shenyang, in Wuhan everyone interviewed on this topic agreed that peasants remained at work in that trade despite efforts to reemploy the natives.[120]

Officials at Wuhan's Labor Bureau maintained that there were actually plenty of jobs in the city, but that the employers offering these posts plainly preferred to hire peasants.[121] The main reason for this was, obviously, peasant workers' cheapness, which, researchers noted, presented a sharp challenge to the reemployment of the city's own jobless persons.[122] The city's labor officials reported that an enterprise needed to invest 30,000 yuan to hire one urban worker, but just 10,000 for a peasant one. The result of this was that "though the city controls peasant workers, their [i.e., peasants'] seizure of employment posts is still serious."[123]

---

[116] Jianghan daxue ketizu, "Wuhan," p. 58.
[117] No author, "Guanyu wuhanshi zaijiuye wenti di diaocha bao" ["An Investigation Report on Wuhan City's Reemployment Question"], probably written around mid-1997, p. 3.
[118] *Ibid.*, p. 4.
[119] Wang Baoyu interview. Mr. Wang was formerly the head of the city's Social Science Academy.
[120] "Among those still working in textiles, some are peasants," according to the Planning Commission informants; and Yang Yunyan claimed that "Textiles uses peasants on a large scale." However, Wang Baoyu said that "the factories are shrinking, so peasants are leaving."
[121] Labor interview, September 7, 1998.
[122] Jianghan daxue ketizu, "Wuhan," p. 60.
[123] *Ibid.*, p. 3. Wang Baoyu said much the same thing in his interview.

Nonetheless, as in a number of other places (but as distinct from Guangzhou, which only did this much later), the city government began as early as July 1995 to issue rulings dividing job categories into those that could and could not hire peasant workers.[124] However, given the laxity in the city leaders' stance and the difficulties of supervising every firm, these rulings did not stick.[125] Many outsiders entered the city without going through any procedures, and they went on to do business without reporting their presence.[126] One obstacle to tightening up control was that, even as late as the autumn of 1998, the city still had not begun to assess a planned "adjustment fee" (*tiaojiefei*) on firms that employed outsiders. The reason for this was that Hubei's leaders, concerned about the whole province, where there was much surplus rural labor, hoped to have these laborors absorbed into the Wuhan labor market, and so they had refused to authorize the fee.[127]

Also in Wuhan, despite much publicity about "clearing out" peasants from their employment posts to make way for unemployed and laid-off locals[128] – with the city's party, governmental, people's congress, and political consultative conference taking the lead – even when this was done, results failed to meet expectations. For instance, when city offices pushed as many as 13,500 peasants out of posts in 1996, only 8,123 laid-off personnel got jobs, either because the jobs were too unattractive to the workers or because the employers found the applicants unsuitable for the work.[129] Moreover, the commitment to perform this task was apparently weak; this became apparent when the city paper on one occasion announced that the local people's congress had received a letter asking why the regulation on clearing out outside labor had not been implemented well.[130] Furthermore, when, at the end of May 1998, a local listing was printed in

---

[124] Wuhan city labor officials told me about these rulings. For other cities, see "Shanghai xianzhi mingong zeye" ["Shanghai Limits Peasant Workers' Choice of Jobs"], *Singdao ribao [Singdao Daily]*, March 4, 1995; and Beijingshi laodongju tongzhi [Beijing City Bureau of Labor Circular] (Beijing, 1998), pp. 23–37.

[125] Labor interview, Sept. 7.

[126] No author, "Guangyu Wuhan shi," p. 4. In *Contesting Citizenship* I note that this has tended to be more the case in cities farther from Beijing and where the market is more active.

[127] Labor interview.

[128] *WHWB*, December 1, 1997, p. 1 and Wang Baoyu, "Zai jiuye," p. 11.

[129] *CJRB*, November 5, 1997, p. 1.

[130] *CJRB*, April 23, 1998, p. 4.

the press of five channels to use in finding solutions for unemployment, the issue of outside labor was not even mentioned at all.[131]

Interviewees from Wuhan's Economic Commission declared that there were not that many peasant workers left in the state firms, and surely less than before the rise in urban layoffs.[132] Similarly, Wuhan Planning Commission bureaucrats believed that, in the past, peasants had served as the salespeople at some night markets that were later restyled as reemployment bases providing work just for the *xiagang* workers. However, in general, most informants agreed that Wuhan's recent economic development had opened up new jobs over time, so that overall there were not fewer peasants there than in the past.[133]

So we see that, in these three disparate municipalities, a common rhetoric echoed central policy in urging a reduction in the numbers of ruralites employed in the cities. Surely some efforts were made in this direction in each case, but the failures to respond fully to the call for cuts had different causes in each spot. Still, one could not really classify these failures as "disobedience" to the center; they were, instead, varying local manifestations of attempts to balance competitiveness with compassion toward native workers, aims shared by top leaders in Beijing as well.

Building a Labor Market

As opposed to Guangzhou, where city authorities seemed content to trust the spontaneous emergence of a labor market, around the country many other local leaders worried about the inadequacies of placement opportunities for their furloughed workers. In such cases, sometimes energetic administrators assayed to fashion a labor market bureaucratically. However, with the numbers of laid-off and unemployed workers constantly rising in the city of Shenyang, with funding scarce, and with even the numerous programs of the city incapable of redeploying well over half the dismissed urban workforce, the official efforts at constructing a labor market to absorb the jobless were similarly deficient.

Although the city did develop its own formal labor market in October 1995 with Labor Ministry endorsement, expressly to expedite the

---

[131] *CJRB*, May 30, 1998, p. 1.
[132] Interview with Xia Xiping, September 8, 1998.
[133] Interview, Wuhan Economic Commission, September 8, 1998.

solution of the problems of the *xiagang* workers, its grasp was woefully short of its reach.[134] The hope was to connect the city – along with all of its subordinate counties, districts, neighborhood and resident-committee levels, townships, and towns – with other cities throughout the province and to shift laborers in need of work to places where they could be employed.

Reportedly, all the way from the metropolitan level right down to the residents' committees, professional introduction networks, labor adjustment exchange meets, specialized talk hot lines, and newspapers were created to serve the laid-off workers. However, as of the end of 1997, information channels were hardly in existence: Only the labor department had by then been able to install some minimally effective networks of communication, whereas job placement organs run by the trade unions, women's federation, and other social groups had not yet even managed to begin to do this.

For the most part, though a Northeast labor market was established in 1996 that was centered in Shenyang, the labor exchange that occupied officialdom remained quite localized. The city labor department claimed to have formed five information networks, interlinked by means of a microcomputer network, but of these, four operated just within the city itself and only the fifth was supposedly connected with eight nearby Liaoning cities. Yet as of early 1998, when the number of Shenyang's laid-off workers approached at least 400,000, a mere 10,000 workers had been moved around among trades and firms.[135] According to one source, fewer than 5,000 workers had gone to other regions for jobs throughout the whole year of 1997.[136] Overall, what labor market construction occurred in and around Shenyang remained constricted within very localized limits and was also apparently taking place chiefly under the aegis of severely capital-strapped state organs.

---

[134] The following discussion draws on Li Zhonglu, "Zai jiuye," 18; *LNRB*, September 5, 1996; No author, "Yi bashou," p. 15; and interview with official from the city labor bureaucracy, August 18, 1998. The one big labor market that developed, the Wu-ai (five love) market, was nevertheless a boon to many a furloughed worker.

[135] Wang Chengying, ed., *Zhongguo zaijiuye*, p. 203.

[136] Xu et al., *1997–1998 Liaoning*, p. 282. No author, "Yi bashou," p. 15, which saw publication at just the same time, claims that the province had organized nearly 20,000 unemployed and *xiagang*'d to go to other provinces and other countries to work. Even so, this is still not very many, given that just one city in the province contained 20 times that many in the category of *xiagang*, not to mention those fully "unemployed."

Wuhan, surprisingly enough in light of its geographical and commercial centrality, was unable through late 1998 to realize the formation of a labor market even within the confines of the city itself, much less beyond it. There were plans to make Wuhan into the core of a regional labor market, ideally built from professional introduction organs and an active information network, but these continued to run into snags.[137] Though there were arrangements in the works for a nationwide labor market based on seven regional centers, Wuhan had not even begun to establish its own portion of this plan as of September 1998.[138]

One sticking point appears to have been conflicts among the cities involved. A Yangtze liaison committee (*lianxihui*), preparing to organize an employment service for the mid and lower Yangtze, designed by the Ministry of Labor to run from Wuhan to Shanghai, struggled over pleas from Chongqing to join.[139] The problem must surely have been that the huge numbers of surplus rural laborers in the Chongqing area were perceived as a threat to the trade in workers between Wuhan and Shanghai.

In the meantime, Wuhan concentrated on developing a computer network for jobs just within the city, sponsoring periodic labor exchange–reallocation meets at the urban level and establishing one large building where the jobless could come to try to locate positions.[140] The city decreed that each of its seven districts was to install a localized labor market of its own, each of which would share job information with the city's central labor market computer network, and to organize training and reemployment meets.[141]

But even these smaller scale projects fell short. As of the end of 1997 the city's labor market mechanism was said to be "only initially formed," because "utilizing the market mechanism to deploy labor resources must still undergo a difficult transformation process."[142] A few months later, the urban-level market had not yet connected up even with the city's own districts and the neighborhoods within them, much less with other sites

---

[137] No author, "Wuhan shi zhuazhu sanxiang gongzuo da da zaijiuye gong jianzhan" ["Wuhan City Grasps Three Items of Work, Boldly Storms the Strongholds of the Battle of Reemployment"], *Zhongguo jiuye [Chinese Employment]*, 2 (1998), pp. 16–17.

[138] Planning Commission interview, September 9, 1998.

[139] Wuhan labor interview, September 7, 1998.

[140] No author, "Wuhan shi zhuazhu," p. 17; labor interview; Planning Commission interview; *CJRB*, December 18, 1997.

[141] *WHWB*, February 24, 1998.

[142] *CJRB*, December 1, 1997, p. 11.

within the central China region. This made it hard for the city to claim its superiority as a "central city," insofar as employment went.[143]

CONCLUSION

In 1997 and 1998, a financial crisis sweeping across China's neighbors, combined with a quite market-oriented Party Congress, intensified pressures of competitiveness that the central political leadership had been stirring up already. In response, localities were charged from above with simultaneously deepening the process of enterprise reform – which meant rising layoffs and unemployment, plus enhanced cost and profit consciousness – and finding work for those displaced. I studied this moment in time as an episode through which I could try to determine the extent to which major, large municipalities attempted to break free of central directives as economic stresses mounted.

Indeed, the conflicting tasks and attendant tensions, one might surmise, could easily have caused municipalities to ignore injunctions from the central government and seek out their own most suitable strategies for survival. This would seem to have been especially likely given that cities had become by that point steadily more and more on their own over a period of some twenty years. Had localities indeed disregarded Beijing's appeals, this would have constituted evidence that, when push came to shove, the country had become less integrated politically than previously, and that the central government's ability to command its subordinate echelons had indeed waned, as some have suggested.[144]

I used data from 1995 to 1998 from three cities, Guangzhou, Shenyang, and Wuhan, which differ in location, research endowment, and central treatment, and, in turn, in industrial health, extent of domestic marketization, and involvement with the world economy, to examine how various places weathered the stresses in their own efforts to shore up their economies. In particular, I reviewed the way these three urban administrations were affected by the economic crisis and by somewhat altered

---

[143] *CJRB*, April 2, 1998, p. 14; also *CJRB shichang zhoukan [Market Weekly]*, April 30, 1998, p. 14.

[144] See, for instance, Shaoguang Wang, "The Rise of the Regions: Fiscal Reform and the Decline of Central State Capacity in China," in Andrew G. Walder, ed., *The Waning of the Communist State: Economic Origins of Political Decline in China and Hungary* (Berkeley, CA: University of California Press, 1995), pp. 87–113.

central policy, and what they did about these new influences. I investigated the somewhat differing impact of these new influences upon each, and their leaders' choices in regard to reemployment, receptivity toward peasant migrants, and the formation of a labor market.

My data demonstrated that, although each jurisdiction was either constrained or privileged by its own endowments – endowments that, not surprisingly, were often outside their leadership's control and that surely shaped the nature of their responses – in the main the outlines of central policy were quite visible in the behavior of each. The three cities interpreted the state's REP in different ways, emphasizing either a more Keynesian approach – in which government assistance almost substitutes for the market in creating jobs – or a more Thatcherite one, which favors forcing people onto the market, and, for China, thereby leads to the creation of a labor market de novo with the termination of the planned economy. The cities also differed in the timing of their reactions, as well as in the extent to which they viewed the peasant laborer as a stimulus to the economy or as a competitor for their own people's posts. Further, each had somewhat different roots for its unemployment and differing attractions and degrees of attraction for migrant workers.

Guangzhou's leaders at first hoped to compete internationally, as before, just by generating the growth requisite to meeting the need for jobs, and by encouraging the entry of cheap farm labor. However, in time, it too fell subject to national concerns for protecting jobs, even if its officials and managers were probably less energetic in pursuing this path than those elsewhere. Still, in its ongoing openness to peasants (while trying at least somewhat to thin out the numbers or the rate of them coming in), Guangzhou's labor market appears to have been the one most akin to a Thatcherite style, the one most driven by economic forces. These forces served to integrate the city into the nation economically, without much intervention by politicians.

In Shenyang, in contrast, the more Keynesian local leadership was much involved, first of all in trying to ensure that a state-led strategy was in place to sustain somewhat the shattered state workforce. In this vein the city was faithful to the prong of central policy that was directed at the dismissed. Thus, its behavior exemplified that there was ongoing policy integration in at least parts of the country. Moreover, it seems that the central government may have rewarded the area for this acquiescence (or responded to its emergency calls): in both April and August of 1999 there are reports of Beijing's having sent financial assistance there.[145] There is less evidence that markets – a weaker factor in this area – were the integrating force here.

In Wuhan, both a political and an economic mode of integration were in evidence: not only did urban bureaucrats bow to central policy in promoting reemployment to a certain degree; they also left their gates at least partly ajar to the farmers from nearby regions. Overall, then, although no city failed to take note of central perspectives and prescriptions, some emphasized one aspect and some another. The outcome was the persistence of integration in managing labor and labor deployment, whether by the market or in reaction to rulings emanating from the capital.

But more was involved in this coordination than simply "compliance" with central governmental orders. The state's program of marketization and opening had crafted a political economy at that point embodying opposed objectives. Compliance and integration or their lack in the late 1990s entailed much more than a matter of local obedience or willfulness. Instead, they ought to be viewed as the result of a shared value placed on urban order, as well as newer urges at every level of the state to thrive in the market to the extent that that jurisdiction's resources, location, and policy permit.

With time and the passing of the immediate economic strains, pressures arising from opposed policy targets appear to have diminished overall. In late 2001 in Wuhan, for instance, laid-off informants driving pedicabs for a living complained that the local police were "not managing as well as they did last year, so peasants can come into the city, which influences our business and means our income goes down."[146] Within just over another year, the central government itself, no doubt at least in part as a result of an interactive dynamic with the localities, made further moves in the market direction as far as migrant labor was concerned. In mid-January, 2003, the

---

[145] When Vice Premier Wu Bangguo inspected Liaoning in April, he stated that "We should, through extending direct loans and reassessing debts, actively help state enterprises address their financial problems thorugh restructuring" [SWB, FE/3512 (April 19, 1999, G/9], from *XH*, April 12, 1999; and when President Jiang Zemin visited industrial plants in the province four months later, he promised that "The state will give these regions more support for asset realignment and restructuring, and in terms of the money they need for the resettlement of laid-off state enterprise workers" [SWB FE/3616 (August 18, 1999)], G/2).

[146] October 28, 2001, Wuhan street interview.

State Council issued a regulation on eliminating the "irrational obstacles" that it perceived as interfering with peasants entering the cities to work, and calling out for all manner of services and welfare to be accorded the migrants, as well as demanding that respect be paid to their rights and interests.[147] Whether this orientation is set for good, or whether later shocks in the international market might further or arrest it, is impossible to predict. However, if the lesson given by the case story herein continues to hold, the nation and its many parts seems set even yet to experience economic episodes in tandem.

ACKNOWLEDGMENT

Material in this chapter was collected with the aid of a grant from the Smith-Richardson Foundation. An earlier version, drawing on some of the same data, was published in Chien-min Chao and Bruce J. Dickson, eds., *Remaking the Chinese State: Structure, Society, and Strategy* (New York: Routledge, 2001). Routledge has granted permission to publish this revised, updated, and reorganized version in this volume.

---

[147] "Guowuyuan bangongting fachu tongzhi, 'Guoban: zuo hao nongmin jincheng wu-gong jiuye guanli he fuwu gongzuo'" ["State Council Office Issues Circular, Do a Good Job of Management and Service for Peasants Entering the Cities to Work"], www.people.com.cn/GB/shizheng/3586/20030116/908641.html, January 16, 2003. An English-language version appeared in the *China Daily*, January 23, 2003. The original notice was dated January 5, 2003, and was printed in the *Renmin ribao [People's Daily]* (Beijing), January 16, 2003.

6

Population Control and State Coercion in China

Yanzhong Huang and Dali L. Yang

To observers of contemporary China, few Chinese policies are as controversial as its population control policy. Critics term the policy practice "Orwellian" and "Gestapo-like" and focus on its toll on human rights (Mosher, 1983; Aird, 1990; and Carter, 1998).[1] In contrast, those impressed by China's success in taming its fertility trends – mostly academic researchers – stress the need to make allowances for China's overwhelming demographic challenges in evaluating the population control policy. However, even sympathetic observers view the policy as a necessary evil and would distance themselves from some of the practices that have occurred under the rubric of population control. Indeed, in a cruel historical twist, whereas the post-Mao economic reforms have expanded the freedom of production in China, the implementation of a stringent birth control policy has severely limited the freedom of reproduction that the Chinese people had enjoyed for centuries. Thus, greater economic freedom has gone hand in hand with less personal freedom to control one's own body.

In this paper we use both qualitative and quantitative data to examine how the post-Mao Chinese state has maintained the draconian birth control policy in an era of economic liberalization. First, we provide a narrative of the birth control policy's evolution. Then we discuss the issue of state capacity in implementing birth control, with emphasis on the government's efforts at institutional building and mobilization. Next we offer an analysis of the patterns of state coercion in population control.

---

[1] According to John Aird, although China's birth control program is "the most successful state-sponsored family planning effort in a developing country," it is also "the most draconian since King Herod's slaughter of the innocents" (Aird, 1990, pp. 1, 3).

Drawing on the analyses presented, we conclude with some reflections on state–society relations in post-Mao China and their implications for China's governance.

THE EVOLUTION OF POPULATION POLICY

China was a late convert to the belief that population growth has to be controlled. In the early 1950s, China was heavily influenced by the Soviet Union's "Heroic Mother" policy and adopted a pronatalist approach.[2] Sterilization and abortion were strictly limited. In January 1953, the Ministry of Health (MoH) even directed the China Customs Service to prohibit the import of contraceptive devices and medicine (Chang Congxuan, 1992, p. 64).

When the Chinese Communist Party's (CCP's) promotion of women's rights led to strong demands for birth control, the Chinese government's stance on population control eased somewhat. Nevertheless, family planning was then motivated not by fears of a large population but by a concern about the health and welfare of women and children (Tang Yan, 1994, pp. 144–145). It was based on voluntarism rather than coercion. Instead of dictating behavior in the bedroom, the Chinese government emphasized the spread of contraceptive knowledge and services.

It was not until after the Great Leap Famine that the Chinese government began to take the negative consequences of a large population seriously.[3] As the economy and population began to recover from the worst famine in human history, a government directive was issued in late 1962 to affirm the need for "emphasizing and strengthening leadership" in birth planning work (CCP Central Committee Document Research Office, 1994, p. 763). In 1964, the State Council or cabinet set up a National Family Planning Commission (NFPC) to direct and coordinate propaganda work and the supply of contraceptives. Still, the family planning program of the early 1960s was confined to urban areas and mainly based

---

[2]   In a rebuff to U.S. Secretary of State Dean Acheson's pessimism on China's ability to feed its increasing population, Mao made this statement: "It is extremely good for China to have a large population; a solution can be found no matter how many times the population increases [in the future], and this solution is production.... Under the communist leadership, as long as we have people, any human miracle can be created" (Mao, 1964, pp. 1400–1).

[3]   On the famine, see Yang, 1996.

on persuasion and limited propaganda.[4] State health facilities were directed to conduct abortion or sterilization surgeries only to help prevent "illness, injuries, and death caused by 'unscientific' or private abortion" (CCP Central Committee Document Research Office, 1994, pp. 764–5).

In August of 1965, Mao directed the MoH to extend family planning to rural areas, but this effort was soon interrupted by Mao's own Cultural Revolution, which paralyzed the bureaucratic apparatus, including the recently established NFPC. It was not until domestic order was restored in 1969 that a campaign was launched to control population growth. This time the policy rationale was no longer women's health but concern about the negative economic consequences of a rapidly expanding population. In the words of Premier Zhou Enlai (1970), "family planning belongs to national planning; it is not a health issue, but a planning issue" (Chang Congxuan, 1992, pp. 19–20). In June 1973, China became the first country to formally incorporate population targets into the national plan on economic development (Yang Zihui, 1996, p. 1730).

As planners took on population policy, the state began to loom large in decisions about childbearing. According to Zhou, "the implementation of birth control work should be based on the dual principle of state guidance and mass volunteerism" (Chang Congxuan, 1992, p. 19). In December 1973, the central leadership formally enunciated the "later, longer, fewer" policy (later marriage, longer spacing between births, and fewer births) to guide marriage and childbearing. Shortly thereafter, each couple was directed to have only two children, and to space the two births over four to five years. Nevertheless, the economically oriented policy goal led localities to rely on material means to encourage planned parenthood and discourage early marriage and childbearing.[5] Following Mao's death, there was some softening in the official stance. In early 1978, the State Council Family Planning Leading Small Group and the MoH announced that the "masses" would be allowed to choose the appropriate contraceptive methods so as to reduce the number of sterilization and abortion cases (*ZGRKNJ*, 1985, p. 18).

---

[4] The party center made it clear in December of 1962 that national-level newspapers not participate in family planning propaganda, and that oral and small-sized propaganda be the major form (Yang Zihui, 1996, p. 1727).

[5] Disincentives include measures such as refusing to admit married youth to colleges and not providing subsidies to multiple-child families (Chang Congxuan, 1992, pp. 68–9).

By the late 1970s, the national fertility rate had started to fall (Xu Dixin, 1988, p. 422). However, it was precisely at this time, as Deng Xiaoping took power and turned to economic reforms, that the Chinese state began to up the ante in birth control. From December 1978 on, per capita income became the yardstick for measuring economic development, making population size the "denominator" of economic indicators. If family planning had been a social adjunct to economic planning in the early 1970s, then it had, in the late 1970s, become an essential part of economic development. This policy orientation fed on the alarmist views on population growth that were being churned out by statisticians and demographers from 1979 on. The negative and sometimes exaggerated scenarios on the dire consequences of rapid population growth convinced the top leadership that radical measures were needed to avert a demographic crisis (see Xiao Zhenyu, 1990, pp. 80–2). Although government leaders might disagree over the pace and direction of economic reform, the perceived demographic crisis helped forge a consensus among political elites for more stringent population control. As then Premier Zhao Ziyang stated in 1980, if the government did not take "resolute measures," China's socioeconomic development would be harmed by the forthcoming "extremely large peak in population increase" (Xiao Zhenyu, 1990, p. 82; *ZGRKNJ*, 1985, p. 26).

The strong esprit de corps among key elites unleashed a torrent of state action. Unable to map out a formal birth control regulation in a short period of time, the CCP Central Committee in September 1980 took an unprecedented step in its history by issuing an "open letter" to all party and youth league members, urging them to "take the lead" in having only one child. Three months later, the central government formalized the letter into a "one child per couple" policy for all but some ethnic minorities and some Han couples in certain rare situations. In September 1982, Party General Secretary Hu Yaobang announced that birth control was a "fundamental state policy," which would be enshrined in the 1982 Constitution. The main policy target in the early 1980s was to hold China's population size to 1.2 billion by year 2000, with annual targets calculated backward from that. Economic liberalization would thus be accompanied by a more coercive population policy.

In short, by the turn of the 1980s, China's population policy had shifted from an anti-Malthusian extreme to systematic birth control. State autonomy in policy making reached its climax in the early 1980s, when a perceived demographic crisis prompted top leaders to mobilize the state's organizational resources to strengthen its grip on reproductive behavior. Within a short time period, mandatory birth control (in particular, one child per couple) was made official policy in urban China.

THE IMPLEMENTATION OF THE BIRTH CONTROL POLICY

In addressing the issue of state capacity, Michael Mann differentiates two types of power: despotic power and infrastructural power. Whereas the former denotes the range of actions that state elites can undertake without routine, institutionalized negotiation with civil society, the latter is defined as "the institutional capacity of a central state, despotic or not, to penetrate its territories and logistically implement decision" (Mann, 1993, p. 59). The state's ability to promote certain types of social change is proportionate to its infrastructural power. Therefore, state autonomy in policy making, by itself, should not be equated with the capacity to implement the policies. As a matter of fact, in despotically strong states such as China, the reach of the central authorities is not unlimited.[6] This is all the more so in enforcing birth control policies in post-Mao China. First, the reforms have profoundly altered the context in which the state birth control program must be carried out. In rural areas, decollectivization has not only diminished state control over people's lives but also increased the demand for more children, especially males (Greenhalgh, Zhu, and Li 1994; Tian Xueyuan 1997). Second, the push for draconian population control is hardly legitimate among the people. The issue of reproductive behavior and family size was one of the few matters over which the people retained control during the Mao era. Repeated surveys have found that, given a choice, most Chinese couples prefer to have two children, ideally of the opposite gender.[7] Thus the emphasis on one child

---

[6] This is captured in an old Chinese saying: "Just as heaven is high, the emperor is far away" (*tian gao huangdi yuan*). When Nixon flattered Mao in his 1972 visit to China that Mao's books had moved a nation and changed the world, Mao replied, "I haven't been able to change it. I've only been able to change a few places in the vicinity of Peking" (quoted in Nixon, 1978, p. 561). For a theoretical treatment of this issue, see Shue, 1988. Yang (1996) uses space as a dimension in examining the patterns of policy and institutional change.

[7] A survey of 826 women who already had one child in the countryside of Hubei province in 1989 found that 74.7 percent of the respondents wanted to have at least two children (Cheng Du, 1991, p. 194).

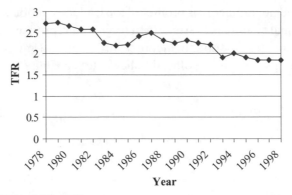

Figure 6.1. TFR, 1978–1998.

Note: TFRs for 1991 and 1997 are calculated by using the formula TFR = number of births/base number of births; base number of births is estimated by averaging the base number of births in the previous year and the year after. See Jiang Zhenghua (ed.) (1996, p. 108) for this method.

Source: Xu Dixin (1988), pp. 11–12, 28; *ZGRKTJNJ* (1993), p. 283; 1998, pp. 360, 444; *ZGJSNJ* (various years); and http:www.sfpc.gov.cn for more recent data.

per family runs counter to the needs and desires of the people, especially rural folk who lack access to government retirement and welfare benefits. As state-sponsored birth control generates intense negative feelings toward the government, it could cause a challenge to established authority relations.

Yet in practice the central policy objectives have largely been translated into reproductive reality. As Figure 6.1 shows, when the state intensified birth control in 1983, the total fertility rate (TFR) dropped from 2.6 to 2.25, the single largest annual drop since 1978.[8] In contrast, when the state relaxed its one-child rule in 1984 to allow couples with "practical difficulties" to have a second birth, an increase in TFR followed during the 1985–1987 period. Thereafter, despite some relaxation in population targets, state birth planning has been largely maintained, with an emphasis on annual targets and by holding local officials responsible for such targets. Partly as a result of the government commitment to population control, China's TFR dropped below the replacement level of 2.1 for the first time in 1993, far earlier than would have been the case had a country of China's income

[8] The TFR is defined as the average number of lifetime births per woman.

level not adopted strict population control policies.[9] Whereas it took 100 years or so for fertility in industrialized countries to decline to the replacement level, it took less than thirty years in China.[10] The fertility decline helped keep China's natural population growth rate in the late 1990s to less than 1 percent per year – very low by developing country standards.[11]

Using provincial-level data, we can further examine the impact of the birth control policy on fertility level. Even though the Chinese Constitution as well as the Law on Marriage established the legal basis for birth planning, the policy of one child per couple was never formally written into national law. Until December 2001, when the Law on Population and Family Planning was enacted, the government relied mainly on local regulations and exhortations to promote birth planning. Not surprisingly, birth control policy has varied from province to province. In the early 1990s, four groups of provinces could be identified according to their level of policy strictness (Table 6.1). By this measure, Beijing, Tianjin, Shanghai, Jiangsu, and Sichuan, with their emphasis on one child per couple, practiced demographic radicalism whereas ethnic Tibet and Xinjiang were on the other end of the spectrum by allowing third- or higher-parity births.

For a better understanding of the policy impact on fertility level, Table 6.1 also provides the percentage of second- or higher-parity births for the years 1980 and 1992. The 1980 data point to large variations among the four groups of provincial units before birth control policy implementation became more draconian in the fall of 1981. A similar pattern of variations

---

[9] As has been true in many other developing countries, factors such as rising levels of education and increased incomes have resulted in a reduction both in the number of children desired and in the number of children born. Chinese government officials have acknowledged that the reduction in fertility could not be solely attributed to the population policy (Johnson, 1999, pp. 10–11). Nevertheless, the government claimed that, between 1971 and 1998, implementation of the population control policy accounted for 338 million fewer births whereas other factors accounted for 296 million avoided births (*RMRB*, October 12, 1999). A statistical analysis by Zhang (1994) found that the family planning policy introduced in the early 1970s appears to have led to a declining importance of socioeconomic variables in affecting cumulative fertility. It concluded that the policy effect was responsible for one-third or two-thirds of the reduction in fertility between the 35–39 age group and the 45–49 age group.

[10] *Sanlian shenghuo zhoukan*, June 12, 2000 (at http://edu.sina.com.cn). Accessed on June 18, 2000.

[11] The natural growth rate is the difference between the birth rate and the mortality rate (for the most recent data on China's natural growth rate, see http://www.sfpc.qov.cn).

Table 6.1. *Provincial Policy Variation in Population Control*

| Type | Policy | Provincial Unit (No.) | Second- and Higher-Order Births (%) | | Percent Change |
			1980	1992	1980–1992
1	One child per couple; exceptions allowed only for 10 percent of the couples	Beijing, Tianjin, Shanghai, Jiangsu, Sichuan (5)	41.92	19.20	22.72
2	Two children allowed for couples whose first child is a girl	Hebei, Inner Mongolia, Shanxi, Liaoning, Jilin, Heilongjiang, Zhejiang, Anhui, Fujian, Jiangxi, Shandong, Henan, Hubei, Hunan, Guangxi, Guizhou, Shaanxi, Gansu (18)	57.89	40.95	16.94
3	One child per couple encouraged but two children allowed	Ningxia, Yunnan, Qinghai, Guangdong, Hainan (5)	65.14	54.07	11.07
4	Limits applied to fourth or fifth birth in minority childbearing	Tibet, Xinjiang (2)	74.32	63.00	11.32

Source: For provincial policy variation, see Jiang Zhenghua (1996), p. 219 and *ZGJSNJ* (1989), pp. 237, 302. The fertility data for 1992 are compiled from *ZGRKTJNJ* (1993), pp. 24–5. The fertility data for 1980 are compiled from *ZGRKNJ* (1985), pp. 809, 848; (1991), pp. 528–9.

still existed in 1992. Although each group of provincial units went through significant declines in its proportion of second- or higher-order births from 1980 to 1992, the gap among the different groups of provinces in the proportion of second- or higher-order births had actually expanded by 1992.

The persistence of spatial variations in fertility suggests the existence of spatial variations in population policy implementation. Nonetheless, all of the provinces experienced significant declines in the percentage of second- or higher-order births. This is consistent with the results from other population surveys and studies. A survey carried out in Jilin province in 1985, for instance, revealed that more than 66 percent of rural married women with one surviving child practiced contraception in response to the government programs (Choe and Tsuya, 1991, p. 42). Using data from surveys conducted in four counties of northern China in 1991 and 1994, Merli and Smith (2002) found that fertility behavior between the surveys was largely a function of family planning policy. As Greenhalgh and others observed, even in an era of market reform and political loosening, "the demographic reach of the Chinese state can be formidable indeed" (Greenhalgh, Zhu, and Li, 1994, p. 389). The question is this: With all the complexities in policy enforcement, how did the central state project its will into the bedrooms of a vast society?

Dynamics of Policy Implementation: Institutionalization and Mobilization

In implementing the population control policy, the first problem the central government faces is how to ensure that birth control enforcers carry out the central directives in a coherent and competent way. In the terminology of institutional economics, this is an agency problem because it involves two actors interacting in a hierarchical structure (Eggertsson, 1990, pp. 41–5). To obtain local compliance, the central Chinese state has used multiple delegation to make both mandate and monitoring relatively clear (Winckler, 1999). Under this institutional arrangement, enforcement is delegated to birth planning professionals, other bureaucratic organs, subnational governments, and quasi-governmental organizations (Figure 6.2).

Great efforts have been made to build an organizational structure for routine administration. Once the State Family Planning Commission

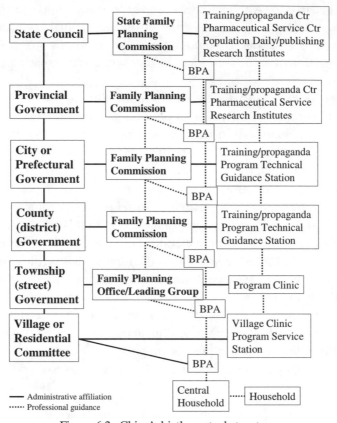

Figure 6.2. China's birth control structure.

(SFPC) replaced the Family Planning Leading Small Group and achieved ministerial rank in 1981, it began to construct its stand-alone administrative capabilities. These capabilities include the following: formulating overall targets and policy direction; training family planning cadres; financing birth control projects; conducting surveys and publishing newspapers; and building its own sterilization clinics and research institutes (see *ZGJSNJ*, various years). In the mid-1980s, the provincial family planning leading small groups were also replaced by regular state organs. This trend of professionalization continues as demographers, sociologists, and other social scientists become involved in the policy making and implementation processes and as full-time family planning workers are trained and placed at and above township level. Over time, and more recently aided by new technologies such as computers, the family planning bureaucracy

Table 6.2. *Institutional Building for Program Structure, 1987, 1991, and 1995*

Year	Administrative Expenditure	No. of Birth Planning Professionals	Membership of Birth Planning Associations
1987	850	140	4,270
1991	1,560	292	40,000
1995	3,190	406	83,000

Notes: Birth planning professionals are "enforcers" only and do not include medical personnel; numbers are given in the thousands. Membership of Birth Planning Associations is also shown in thousands; administrative expenditure is in millions of yuan.
Source: ZGJSNJ (various years).

and delivery network have been strengthened. Funding and personnel have increased, routine procedures have been developed to administer the work and coordinate with other relevant departments (e.g., departments of public health and civil affairs), and supplemental regulations have been drafted to clarify policy. By the late 1980s, the SFPC had established a relatively complete network that supplied and sold contraceptive devices and medicines and provided instruction in their use. By 1997 the number of full-time family planning workers had reached 400,000, and the emphasis of this ponderous organization was on the provision of family planning services through clinics at the prefecture, county, and township levels (*ZGJSNJ*, 1998, p. 39. Also see Table 6.2).[12]

However, in strengthening its gynecological capacity, the Chinese government faces a critical information problem, which is how to penetrate couples' privacy to monitor reproductive behavior continuously and exhaustively (Winckler, 1999, p. 198). The state can resort to persuasion, propaganda, penalization, persecution, and provision of services to enforce the one-child limit, but by itself it cannot acquire the capacity for such social surveillance. This finitude of the state's power to act is explained by Foucault as an immediate consequence of the limitation of its "power to know" (Burchell, Gordon, and Miller, 1991, p. 16). To deal with this problem of inadequate information, the state has also promoted the Birth Planning Association (BPA) since the early 1980s. In December 1992, BPAs were established in 98 percent of the prefectures (cities), 95 percent of the counties (districts and cities), 92 percent of the townships

---

[12] In 1997, there were 210 prefecture-level program clinics, 2,083 county-level program clinics, and 29,169 township-level program clinics (data provided by the SFPC).

(urban neighborhoods), and 89 percent of the villages (residential committees; see *JKB*, December 6, 1992). Led by party veterans Wang
Shoudao and Song Ping, these quasi-governmental "mass organizations"
were deliberately designed to bypass the local cadres, taking over some
of the work they had been unable – or unwilling – to do. BPA members are each assigned a few households to make sure women in those
households report for periodic medical checkups, to ascertain that they
are still using contraception, and to identify pregnancy when that hap-
pens. By 1997 there were over 1 million BPAs at various levels, with more
than 83 million members (see Table 6.2; also see *ZGJSNJ*, 1998, p. 15).
Directors of local family planning commissions usually act as executive
vice presidents of BPAs at the same level, thereby making these mass
organizations the handmaidens of the state in monitoring and regulating
individual activities.

Despite these efforts, China's population control program, like most
other state institutions, has suffered from underfunding and a lack of
qualified personnel. As former SFPC head Peng Peiyun noted, in the first
half of the 1990s the state failed to provide contraceptive services for
more than 6 million people as a result of inadequate funding; between
1991 and 1995, birth planning departments incurred a deficit of 2 billion
yuan for performing birth control surgeries (*ZGJSNJ*, 1996, p. 18). The
program staffers are generally poorly remunerated and face relatively
poor career prospects, thus making it difficult for family planning departments to attract qualified personnel. Speaking at a national birth planning
conference, SFPC head Zhang Weiqing admitted that among the 400,000
family planning cadres, nearly 20 percent had only a junior high school
education, and only 14 percent received more than two years of college
education (*ZGJSNJ*, 1998, p. 39). The problem is even worse below the
county level. Unlike the county-level bureaucratic apparatus, township
governments do not have the human resources and the skills to carry out
birth control work effectively and consistently. At the village level, family planning enforcers are not full-time employees of the state, making it
even more challenging for the full implementation of central policies that
run counter to villager interests (see Zhang, 1999).

To fulfill its ambitious policy goals with limited organizational and financial resources, the specialized birth planning bureaucracy is heavily
dependent on support from local authorities and the cooperation of other
bureaucratic actors. The involvement of local leaders helps ensure that

budgeted resources are allocated and used for program purposes, and it mobilizes resources from other systems, including free manpower transferred to program tasks. However, this process builds a bias against routine administration into the implementation structure. As Barnett pointed out long ago, in such a party-dominated policy context, actors tend to view a vast range of decision making as at least potentially political, regardless of the intrinsic nature of the task addressed (Barnett, 1967, p. 36). This explains why periodic crash campaigns are still used in the population policy arena, even though the Chinese leadership has discontinued large-scale campaigns in most other policy areas (e.g., financial inspections) and replaced them with routine monitoring and inspections.[13] In fact, until the early 1990s, the Chinese leaders were still calling for intensified efforts in birth control implementation, especially in rural areas, through "mobilization of the entire Party and the entire society" (FBIS, June 12, 1991). In autonomous regions heavily influenced by Islam, such as Gansu and Ningxia, local religious leaders were asked to "mobilize" couples to accept birth control surgeries. The regional Islamic association in Ningxia organized senior imams to collect texts favorable to birth control from Islamic classics, and it distributed them to imams in 2,200 mosques in the region with the expectation that the latter would use their authority to propagate the government's population policy (*JKB*, October 24, 1989). Such societal mobilization remains in favor in some of China's most prosperous provinces such as Guangdong (*NFRB*, April 29, 1999; *NYT*, July 23, 2002). Coupled with pressure on local cadres to fulfill population targets, the mobilization drives highlight the authorities' determination and help override fiscal constraints and bureaucratic inertia (White, 1990).

Through the combination of institutionalization and mobilization, the post-Mao Chinese state obtains high infrastructural power to implement its ambitious birth control program on a recalcitrant society. Over time, a growing number of people have come to accept the arguments put forward by the state about the relationship between economic development and population growth.[14] In some rural areas, people have acquiesced to the

---

[13] In 1980, the post-Mao leadership formally rejected the use of political campaigns as tools of policy implementation (Deng Xiaoping, 1983, p. 296). Here we differ from the seminal work of White (1990) and note that Chinese leaders have tended to use new institutional mechanisms to replace campaigns during the reform era.

[14] Zhang, 1999. However, the validity of the argument is cast into doubt by some prominent economists, such as Johnson, 1999.

wishes of the state and developed community norms bearing the firm imprint of state desires for limiting fertility (Greenhalgh, 1994). Thus many people have come to accept, internalize, and reproduce the hegemonic view of the state in their daily lives.

PATTERNS OF STATE COERCION IN POPULATION POLICY IMPLEMENTATION

According to Putnam (1993), societies can evolve into two different equilibria as they solve collective action problems. One, the civic equilibrium, is built on a "virtuous circle" that nurtures healthy norms of reciprocity, cooperation, and mutual trust. The other, the Hobbesian equilibrium, features vertical dependence, exploitation, and coercion. If we view population control as a collective action problem in China, the policy goal, the institutional building mode, and the use of mobilization all seem to point to the latter type of equilibrium. Simply put, the post-1980 population policy has been order oriented. Generally speaking, order goals are most readily achieved through the application of coercive means (Etzioni, 1961, pp. 72–4). They are essentially negative in that organizations with such goals attempt to prevent the occurrence of deviance.

With its results-oriented implementation structure in which all other considerations are secondary to the attainment of birth quotas, there is little doubt that the enforcement of population control policy has been highly coercive. During campaigns, population targets tend to be specified into easily monitored surgery quotas with emphasis on producing practical results by taking immediate "technical measures" (a euphemism for required sterilization, abortion, and IUD insertion). In the early 1980s, for example, as political elites quickly jumped onto the bandwagon of population control, the state launched a nationwide mass campaign of forced sterilization, abortion, and IUD use. The campaign peaked in 1983–1984 and resulted in a surge in the number of women at reproductive age who received at least one of the three "birth control operations,"[15] a figure almost 2.5 times the total for 1981 (Figure 6.3). It was targeted at couples with two children, especially two girls, who were often sterilized on the

---

[15] Whereas in the United States the insertion of an IUD is not considered a surgery, the "Regulation on Family Planning Technical Management" promulgated by the Ministry of Health in 1983 treats as operations (*shoushu*) the insertion and removal of IUDs; tubectomy; vasectomy; and induced abortion (*ZGWSNJ*, 1984, p. 444). We thank Professor D. Gale Johnson for pointing out this difference.

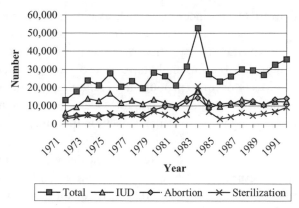

Figure 6.3. Number of birth control surgeries (in thousands), 1971–1991.
Source: ZGWSNJ (various years).

spot as soon as either member of the couple was "convinced" to submit to sterilization after intensive indoctrination. Once performed, the sterilization operation was assumed to be irreversible. As Figure 6.3 shows, in 1983 alone there were more than 20 million cases of sterilization, a ninefold increase over 1981. From then on, around 40 percent of women and 12 percent of men, or approximately half of all couples, have had one partner sterilized (*ZGJSNJ*, 1993, p. 335).

Meanwhile, there has been a major shift in the government policy toward IUD insertion and abortion. In the late 1970s, IUD use began to spread. In late 1982, the SFPC ordered all women of childbearing age with one child to be fitted with IUDs, thus making IUD use a crucial ingredient of national policy. Unlike in the 1970s, the new policy made it clear that once the IUD was in place, couples could not have it removed without official approval. The government authorized severe penalties for those who illegally removed IUDs, and in some localities women with an IUD in place were subject to periodic physical examinations to ensure that their IUDs had not fallen out or been removed. In some other localities, strings were deliberately not attached to IUDs, making removal more difficult and potentially dangerous. As far as abortion is concerned, the official policy was that women with unauthorized pregnancies must adopt "remedial measures" (a euphemism for induced abortion) as soon as possible. Local cadres were asked to "mobilize" (i.e., coerce) these women to have an abortion. For such women, the continual official harassment throughout their pregnancies was both physically and emotionally draining.

Symbolic and material incentives, such as glorification meetings and cash rewards, have also been used to encourage compliance. Nevertheless, once the party-state intervention was translated into specific quotas and disseminated, local cadres might have to resort to unusual, sometimes extreme measures in order to produce immediate results and fulfill their targets. In some localities the surgery quotas were set so high in the early days of birth planning that women approaching their menopause age received surgeries so that the quotas could be fulfilled (Jiang Zhenghua, 1996, p. 6). Those who resisted state mobilization were subject to punishment that sometimes went beyond economic sanctions to obligatory sterilization and abortion (Aird, 1990). To add insult to injury, China has had problems with the low quality of such operations, especially in rural areas (see Kaufman et al., 1992; Kaufman, 1993). Under this policy structure, those individuals hearty enough to pursue the freedom of births have to migrate to desolate and remote places where government control is significantly weak or nonexistent (Tang Yan, 1994, pp. 88–90).

The results-oriented implementation structure has been sustained by a set of institutional arrangements designed to overcome the enforcement problem. Since the early 1980s, the national government has popularized the "family planning responsibility system," which docks wages and blocks promotions for those failing to meet assigned birth planning targets.[16] Some localities have gone even further. In response to the rapidly growing population, Henan province in 1989 pioneered a "one vote veto" system under which a unit would not be elevated to "advanced status" (and thus its head would not be entitled to rewards and promotions) if it had failed to fulfill assigned birth planning goals (*JKB*, May 4, 1989). Since the early 1990s this approach has been extended nationwide, and provincial party secretaries and governors are made personally responsible for overall program performance in their respective localities (*ZGJSNJ*, 1992, pp. 6–9).

Because rewards and penalties depend on the fulfillment of the assigned population targets, especially the surgery quota, and because IUD insertion and sterilization involve only a one-time motivation on the part of the user, local birth control enforcers have few incentives to promote the use or adoption of safer, more easily reversible, and client-controlled means

---

[16] A survey of eight provinces in China revealed that by 1993 more than 90 percent of the urban neighborhoods and rural villages had adopted such a system (CHNS, 1993).

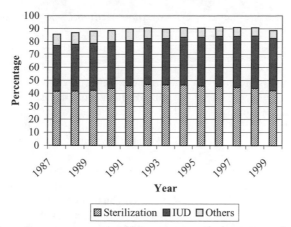

Figure 6.4. Composition of the contraception rate, by method, 1987–1999.

Source: ZGRKTJNJ (various years); *ZGJSNJ* (various years). Data for 1998 and 1999 are from http://www.sfpc.gov.cn (date of access was June 7, 2000).

such as diaphragms, cervical caps, and condoms. Instead, they prefer low-cost, long-term, and provider-controlled contraceptive means such as IUDs and sterilization. Couples, especially those in the countryside, are subject to the strong influence of local enforcers in family planning and are often not allowed to choose their contraceptive method.[17] A survey in five counties in Hubei province in 1989, for example, found that, on average, a married woman at the childbearing age had knowledge of 3.86 contraceptive methods, compared with 7.3 in Beijing and 6.7 in Shanghai. Among the nine information channels, village cadres ranked first (78.8 percent), followed by local state-sponsored meetings (75.1 percent; see Cheng Du, 1991, pp. 204–6). Figure 6.4 shows the contraception rate by method from 1987 to 1999. It is clear that sterilization and IUD insertion remain the primary methods of contraception in China.[18] Although the contraception rate (percentage of married women at the childbearing age who take contraceptive measures) rose to around 90 percent in 1990s, the

---

[17] According to the SFPC, until 1997 only 39 percent of women who underwent tubal ligation had counseling before surgery (*NYT*, November 1, 1998). In other countries such as the United States, sterilization conducted immediately after a person has been persuaded to be sterilized is by its very nature a coercive procedure, because the person does not have enough time to reflect upon that decision (Banister, 1987, p. 211).

[18] In fact, among the 221 million users of modern methods of contraception in 1999, 92.9 percent were either sterilized or fitted with an IUD (for more information, see http://www.stpc.gov.cn). Accessed on June 7, 2000.

Table 6.3. *Patterns of Contraceptive Method Use, by Province*

Pattern	Provinces
Stability	
IUD consistently preferred	8 provinces: Beijing, Tianjin, Shanghai, Liaoning, Jilin, Heilongjiang, Jiangsu, and Yunnan
Sterilization consistently preferred	13 provinces: Hebei, Anhui, Fujian, Jiangxi, Shandong, Henan, Hubei, Hunan, Guangdong, Hainan, Guizhou, Gansu, and Ningxia
Change	
Shift to IUD	4 provinces: Inner Mongolia (1996), Zhejiang (1995), Sichuan (1989), and Xinjiang (1989)
Shift to sterilization	4 provinces: Shanxi (1991), Guangxi (1992), Shaanxi (1990), and Qinghai (1991)

Note: Number in parentheses is the year that preference was shifted.
Source: ZGRKTJNJ (various years); *ZGJSNJ* (various years).

percentage of women at the childbearing age using the pill, diaphragm, cervical cap, and condom (categorized as "others" in Figure 6.4) dropped from 8.8 percent in 1987 to 6.6 percent in 1999.

Table 6.3 presents data on the patterns of IUD and sterilization use at the provincial level between 1987 and 1997. It shows that although eight provincial units consistently preferred IUD use to sterilization, thirteen others had more sterilization than IUD insertion. Although since 1989 IUD use has become more popular in four provincial units (Inner Mongolia, Zhejiang, Sichuan, and Xinjiang), the rate of sterilization has gained in four others (Shanxi, Guangxi, Shaanxi, and Qinghai).[19]

Explaining State Coerciveness: Bureaucratic Competence and Policy Outcomes
The provincial data cited here thus point to significant variations in the degree of state coercion. In 1997, for example, the rate of sterilization in Shanghai was only 4.75 percent, compared with a whopping 63.25 percent in Gansu province (*ZGRKTJNJ*, 1998, p. 414). What factors lie behind these variations? To explain, we begin with a discussion of several hypotheses and the relevant variables.

---

[19] We have highlighted the most prominent pattern but we are aware that other factors such as population structure may play an important role in contraceptive choices as well.

BUREAUCRATIC COMPETENCE. Bureaucratic competence matters because those within key government agencies have expertise and command significant institutional resources in the policy process. As a World Bank report noted, "whether making policy, delivering services, or administering contracts, a capable, motivated staff is the lifeblood of an effective state" (World Bank, 1997, p. 9). Equally important, rationalization of the bureaucratic structure may reduce the use of state coercion. Our examination of the enforcement of population policy reveals two types of social control: one is triggered and sustained by party-dominated mass mobilization, and the other gains momentum from intensive administrative capacity building. This typology of social control corresponds to the two notions of power that Michel Foucault proposed: sovereign power and disciplinary power (Foucault, 1979; Burchell, Gordon, and Miller, 1991). Whereas sovereign power tends to force people to accept authority of the state by violence or the threat of violence in a discontinuous manner, disciplinary power partitions the social space into surveillable units that can be consistently regulated and administered. Because authority under disciplinary power is enforced internally and aimed at "self-improvement," coercion tends to be more subtle, private, and informal. By helping nip in the bud the possible challenges to state power, for example, BPAs function to enhance state control without resorting to overt coercion. We therefore hypothesize that the more competent a provincial family planning bureaucracy, the more institutionalized and routinized the family planning program will be and the less likely for a province to favor ineluctably coercive measures, such as sterilization. Conversely, in provinces lacking competent family planning bureaucracies, the family planning program will be less institutionalized, forcing the bureaucrats to rely heavily on mobilization and crash campaigns.

BASIC EDUCATION OF WOMEN. Women with basic education – as a measure of cognitive abilities – will likely have more knowledge about contraception and thus will be less influenced by family planning enforcers in choosing contraceptive methods than their less-educated peers. In the meantime, educated women tend to be more self-conscious in exercising birth control, which also reduces the necessity for coercive measures such as sterilization. We therefore introduce the basic education level of women as a control variable.

MINORITY POPULATION. Under current government population policies, minority nationalities have been treated more leniently than the majority Han nationality. In Tibet, for example, Han couples are generally not allowed to have a third child, whereas there are few constraints on child-bearing for minority couples (*ZGJSNJ*, 1989, p. 303). It is thus expected that in areas with a concentration of minority population, there is less need for radical birth control measures. The minority population will also be used as a control variable.

The dependent variable here is state coerciveness. Given that systematic data on overt state coercion are not available, for measurement purposes we choose two indicators that differ in their level of coerciveness: the prevalence rate of IUD insertion and the prevalence rate of sterilization. Although high IUD prevalence rates and heavy reliance on sterilization both reflect strong state intervention, sterilization is obviously more coercive, not only because it is generally irreversible in China but also because it is a riskier procedure.[20]

In operationalizing and testing the hypotheses, we already have provincial data on the prevalence rates of sterilization and IUD use for 1997. Because bureaucratization in a narrow, limited sense means professionalization, we measure bureaucratic competence by using the percentage of family planning professionals that are college educated (we have data for 1995). For women's educational level, we use the 1990 census data on the percentage of the female population that is illiterate in each provincial unit. To test the impact of minority population on the use of coercion, we create a dummy variable according to whether the provincial unit is a minority autonomous region (coded as "1" if yes and "0" if no). Ordinary least-squares regression produces the results shown in Table 6.4.

The regression results show that our proxy measure for bureaucratic competence has a statistically significant relationship to the degree of state coercion. Other things being equal, one percentage increase in the number of family planning professionals who are college educated will lead to a

---

[20] Women prefer an IUD to sterilization. A survey of women in five counties of Hubei province in 1989 demonstrated that, when women with one child were asked about their contraceptive preference, only 24.6 percent chose sterilization, compared with 45.2 percent who preferred IUD (Cheng Du, 1991, p. 210). A recent survey conducted by the SFPC in ten cities found that, after couples were allowed to choose an informed and voluntary way, the rate of sterilization dropped whereas IUD usage remained large (http://www.sfpc.gov.cn).

Table 6.4. *Determinants of the Rate of Sterilization and IUD, 1997*

Explanatory Variables	Percentage	
	Sterilization	IUD
Bureaucratic competency	−1.96**	0.93**
	(0.320)	(0.284)
Basic education for women	0.0001	−0.47**
	(0.156)	(0.139)
Minority population	−13.15*	1.91
	(5.728)	(5.094)
Constant	75.23**	39.28**
	(8.659)	(7.700)
Adjusted R^2	0.59	0.49
SE of regression	11.37	10.11
No. of observations	30	30

* $p < .05$.
** $p < .01$.
Notes: SE = standard error. Numbers in parentheses are SEs.
Source: ZGRKTJNJ (various years).

2 percentage point decline in the prevalence rate of sterilization and a 1 percentage point increase in IUD use. Although a high proportion of illiterate women reduces the prevalence rate of IUD use, its impact on the use of the more coercive sterilization method is neither statistically significant nor strong. The table also shows that women in a minority autonomous region are less likely to be sterilized. The adjusted R^2 figures (0.59 and 0.49) indicate that the three independent variables explain approximately 59 percent of the variation in the sterilization rate and 49 percent of the variation in the IUD use rate.

The relationship between bureaucratic competencies and coercion can be explored further with the aid of Figure 6.5. On the horizontal axis is the percentage of family planning professionals with a college diploma as of 1995; on the vertical axis is the rate of sterilization in 1997. Clearly, there is an inverse relationship between bureaucratic competence and state coerciveness in population control. All four provincial units (Hebei, Fujian, Guangxi, and Guizhou) with less than 10 percent of college-trained professionals had a sterilization rate of more than 50 percent, compared with less than 30 percent for five provinces or municipalities (Beijing, Tianjin, Shanghai, Liaoning, and Jilin) that boast more than 25 percent of college-trained professionals.

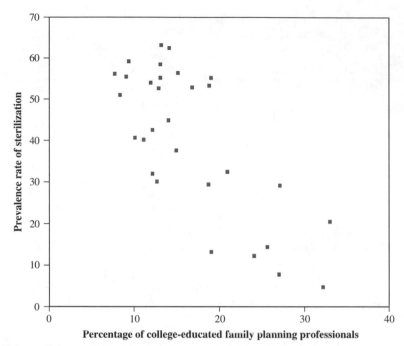

Figure 6.5. Bureaucratic capacities and prevalence rate of sterilization, 1997.

Explaining Variations of State Coerciveness: Grass-Roots Organizations and Policy Outcomes

Although bureaucratic competence is a crucial factor in accounting for the variations in program coerciveness at the provincial level, it does not tell much about how policy is implemented at the grass-roots level. Because cases of coercion often happen in the countryside, we also employ statistical analysis to explore the factors leading to the variations of policy implementation or coercion at the village level. To do this, we rely on data, with permission, from three rounds of community-level surveys conducted by the population center of the University of North Carolina.[21]

---

[21] The China Health and Nutrition Survey (CHNS) is a collaborative project of the Institute of Nutrition and Food Hygiene, Chinese Academy of Preventive Medicine, and the University of North Carolina at Chapel Hill. The survey covers eight provinces that vary substantially in geography, economic development, public resources, and health indicators – Guangxi, Guizhou, Henan, Hubei, Hunan, Jiangsu, Liaoning, and Shandong. A multistage, random cluster process was used to draw the sample surveyed in each of the provinces (see http://www.spc.unc.edu/china for further information). On the quality of the data, see Short and Zhai, 1998.

Again, here the dependent variable is state coerciveness. In this case, we use the amount of the fine imposed on couples having an extra child as a proxy measure of coercion. The fines are not simply an economic penalty but also involve a threat (usually credible) to use force against violators and their other properties.[22] Indeed, the U.N. Population Fund criticized China's policy of taxing families who have too many children as coercive (*NYT*, July 23, 2002).

STATE GRASS-ROOTS ORGANIZATIONAL PRESENCE. As to the independent variables, two political–institutional variables are of special interest. The first one is the presence of state organizations at the grass roots. As members of local society, village leaders are usually predisposed by cultural values and social obligations to soften state policies to accommodate the demands of local residents (Shue, 1988). Research shows, however, that the extent to which these local leaders actually do so varies according to the amount of pressure exerted on them from above (Unger, 1989). When the presence of the state is weak at the grass-roots level, local cadres are more likely to choose collusion, rather than coercion, in implementing birth control policies. When birth control is actively promoted by their superiors, however, village leaders may feel that they have little choice but to do their best to reach the targets, which usually means the adoption of more coercive means (Greenhalgh, 1994, p. 13). It is thus expected that the level of state organizational presence at the local level is positively associated with the level of coercion in birth control. A higher level of state organizational presence will lead to higher level of coercion in birth control. We measure this presence by the monthly frequency of the community leaders going to the town or county seat for meetings in normal times.

LOCAL COLLECTIVE POWER. The second independent variable of interest is local collective power, indexed by the percentage of land under collective irrigation. Before the reform era, rural collective organizations such as communes and production brigades possessed the organizational and economic resources to dictate the lives of farmers. Decollectivization

---

[22] In one Anhui township, peasants who refused to pay fines for exceeding birth limits were held for "reeducation" for more than 40 days in a crowded room with no toilet (*SCMP*, January 27, 1999).

Table 6.5. *Determinants of the Fine for One Extra Child (in logged form), 1991*

Explanatory Variables	Coefficient and SE
State grass roots organizational presence	0.088*
	(0.042)
Local collective power	0.006*
	(0.003)
Minority (1 for minority village; 0 otherwise)	0.073
	(0.273)
Income level (in logged form)	0.841**
	(0.261)
Intercept	1.450
	(1.658)
Adjusted R^2	0.279
SE of regression	0.891
No. of observations	63

* $p < .05$.
** $p < .01$.
Notes: SE = standard error. Numbers in parentheses are SEs.
Source: China Health and Nutrition Surveys, Community Survey 1989, 1991, 1993, provided by the Population Center, University of North Carolina.

in the early 1980s undermined this enforcement mechanism and expanded the scope for resistance to the birth control policy by shifting the balance of power toward the farmers (Greenhalgh, 1994, especially pp. 13–14; Yang, 1996). However, the incidence of "local corporatism" or "new collectivism" as an institutional form implies that village leaders in some communities still retain substantial organizational and economic resources (Oi, 1992; Wang, 1996). Such resources may in turn be mobilized to facilitate the enforcement of birth planning. We thus hypothesize that the higher the level of local collective power, the higher the level of coercion in birth planning.

As for the control variables, conventional wisdom suggests that the amount of fines for one extra child is likely to be higher in areas with a higher income level. In addition, a dummy variable is created to differentiate minority and nonminority villages, as the birth control policy is known to be more lenient toward ethnic minorities.[23] Ordinary least-squares regression produces the results shown in Table 6.5.

---

[23] Here the analytical focus is on rural areas.

Table 6.5 shows a statistically significant relationship between income level and the amount of the fine for one extra child. What is interesting is that the coefficients for the variables of state organizational presence and local collective power are also statistically significant and point to the expected direction. Thus, the more vigorous the local government, the higher the level of coercion. In fact, if we set the values of other independent variables at their mean values and let the variable of state grass roots organizational presence take different values,[24] a village whose leaders visit the town or county seat for meetings nine times a month will impose 1,500 yuan more in fines than a village whose leaders never go to the town or county seat for meetings in normal times. Moreover, the degree of local collectivism is positively related to the level of coercion. If we set the values of other independent variables at their mean values and let the variable of local collective power take different values, a village with all its land irrigated collectively will impose 1,148 yuan more in fines than one with all its land privately irrigated. In sum, the statistical analysis substantiates the view that the enforcement of birth control policy in rural areas is highly dependent on existing political institutions, rather than program institution alone.

CHANGE AND STABILITY IN PROGRAM IMPLEMENTATION

China's ability to use demographic engineering in an era of growing economic liberties points to the enduring power and reach of the Chinese state. In fact, the population control program got a boost in connection to the aftermath of the Tiananmen crackdown in 1989. Amid the diplomatic freeze that greeted China, General Secretary Jiang Zemin argued that China's economic independence rested on controlling population growth and called for doing "a good job in family planning by all means" (*JKB*, October 17, 1989). As a result of the central leadership's push, implementation of birth planning policies was more vigorous in the early 1990s. In 1991, for example, the number of surgeries again rose sharply, with more than 35 million surgeries conducted (Figure 6.3).

---

[24] The mean values for "state grass roots organizational presence" and "local collective power" and "income" are 3.46, 38.53, and 666.35, respectively. For the constant, the mean value is 1. For the dummy variable, the mode is 0, so I set its mean value to 0. The product of these mean values and their coefficients is a constant.

Yet as Rousseau put it in *The Social Contract*, "The strongest is never strong enough to be always the master unless he transforms strength into right and obedience into duty." Although overall the Chinese government has achieved a high level of compliance in implementing its population control policies, many families have developed a myriad of strategies to evade state control so as to get the number and sex of children they deem desirable (see Wasserstrom, 1984; Lavely, 1998; White, 2000). They hide pregnant women, feign compliance, surreptitiously remove IUDs, conspire with community leaders to conceal "excess" births from higher authorities, and even physically attack birth planning officials.[25]

The pressure to achieve population control targets has thus induced various distortions in population figures. On one hand, the attempts to conceal "excess" children have led to the significant underreporting of births, particularly of girls. The underreporting rate in some rural areas, according to the SFPC, may be as high as 30 percent (*ZGJSNJ*, 1996, p. 18). Between 1991 and 1998, the underreported population in Sichuan province alone was estimated at over 400,000, approximately the population of a midsized county (*Sichuan ribao*, July 13, 2000). This has created serious problems for policy and planning and forced government agencies such as the National Statistical Bureau to work hard on strategies to adjust for such statistical "errors" annually. On the other hand, and more distressingly from a human rights perspective, the limits on the number of births per couple have prompted some couples to choose drastic measures, including selective abortion (aided by the availability of the ultrasound machine and other advances in science), female abandonment, and even infanticide. Strict population control coupled with the desire for at least one male child have thus resulted in millions of missing girls and contributed to a remarkable rise in the reported sex ratio at birth (Weisskopf, 1985; Johnson, 1993; Tuljapurkar, Li, and Feldman, 1995). Clearly, although the state birth control policy requires otherwise, many Chinese people have not fundamentally changed their childbearing preferences.

Needless to say, the draconian birth planning policies have exacerbated the tensions between state and society. According to the Communist Party's "mass line," leaders in the formulation or modification of policies

---

[25] In one prominent case, one woman who had been forced to undergo an abortion vented her anger by poisoning her fellow villagers, resulting in six deaths and more than 200 injuries (Lianhe Zaobao, on-line, April 13, 2000).

are expected to ascertain the perceived interests of the masses, obtain feedback from them, and systematize these interests before taking the results back to the masses (Lewis, 1963; Tsou, 2000). Although the Chinese leadership has pursued the birth planning policies as a necessary evil and by invoking the commonweal, the leadership's awareness of the popular resistance to the policies has over time led to some soul searching within the professional elite and efforts to smooth the rough edges of existing policies without abandoning them. Drawing on experiences from Jilin province, central leaders have since the early 1990s encouraged the implementation of "three combinations" in rural areas – combining birth control with economic development; combining birth control with helping peasants get rich; and combining birth control with building civilized and happy families (*ZGJSNJ*, 1998, pp. 71–6, and 220–6).

The 1990s also saw a program reorientation toward better reproductive services and more choice in contraception. Compared with the early 1990s, the cases of abortion decreased by nearly two-thirds in the late 1990s; by 2000, the abortion rate for married women in their childbearing years dropped to less than 2 percent.[26] In October 1999, Beijing eliminated the onerous system of permits for pregnancy, giving women choice in deciding when to have a child. Invoking a long-standing exception, most provincial units, including metropolitan cities such as Beijing, now permit parents who are only children themselves to have two kids. In most rural areas, couples whose first child is a girl are also permitted to try a second time after a suitable interval (four to six years). By the end of the 1990s, many localities had largely put an end to the coercive techniques of the past, like bulldozing the homes of disobeying couples or physically dragging women from their houses for mandatory sterilization (*NYT*, April 14, 2000; author's interview). Instead, the state has developed new and somewhat more humane techniques to exercise birth control. The recent Population and Family Planning Law, for example, virtually legalized unauthorized births by instituting a new "baby tax" on couples violating state family planning policy.[27]

Although they are introducing modifications, the Chinese leadership is convinced that China's low birth rate is not stable in that without the heavy state intervention in family childbearing decisions a substantial hike

---

[26] See http://www.sfpc.gov.cn/cn/news20010720-3.htm; accessed on July 5, 2002.

[27] For more information, see http://www.sfpc.gov.cn/cn/news20020107-1.htm.

in the total fertility rate would follow. Thus, on various occasions, Chinese leaders have stressed that the population control policy cannot be jettisoned. In 1997, Jiang Zemin explicated "three no changes" in birth planning: no change in the existing birth planning policy; no change in the previous population control targets; and no change in the leaders' responsibility system for birth control (*ZGJSNJ*, 1998, p. 1). The new law on family planning also makes it clear that the basic orientation of existing population policy would not be cast aside. This may help explain why, even in many coastal regions where the surgery quota has been abandoned in policy implementation, population targets remain an important indicator for measuring performance of birth control cadres. Ultimately, the number of children a couple can have is still at the behest of the state. In most places, the system of permits for pregnancy is still maintained, under which a quota on childbirth must be obtained before pregnancy and used in the same year. Needless to say, the ponderous birth planning apparatus has a vested interest in perpetuating the status quo.

CONCLUSIONS

There is no denying that political and economic reforms since the late 1970s have ushered in fundamental changes in the state–society relationship in China. Some scholars have suggested that, as a result of these changes, the regime is facing imminent institutional decay (Walder, 1995; He, 2002). Others have suggested that the regime cannot but democratize (Friedman, 1995; Chen, 1999). If so, the pattern of state–society relations in post-Mao China would simply follow that of the other formerly socialist countries: the state weakened, society strengthened. If and when the economy began to perform poorly, regime transformation resulted (see Bunce, 1999).

The Chinese case, however, points to the coexistence of a liberalizing economy with the continuing presence of a hard party-state as far as population policy is concerned. Indeed, this coexistence is encouraged by the Chinese leadership's shift to using per capita gross domestic product and other economic indicators of development as a major source of their performance legitimacy. As a result, for the past two decades or so, while China's leaders have promoted socioeconomic reforms that have greatly enhanced personal freedom, they have also aggressively implemented population policies that impinge on fundamental human freedoms. Hence the reduction of the state's role in the economy has not meant a simple or similar pattern of state withdrawal in all policy sectors. The population policy implementation, for example, features significant efforts in building administrative capacity, which has helped sustain an unpopular policy for more than two decades.

Our analyses also reveal significant ethnic, spatial, and temporal variations in the implementation of population policies. Whereas the provincial-level analysis indicates that strong administrative competence moderates the intensity of coercion, the community-level analysis suggests that the level of state coerciveness is higher in localities where grass-roots political institutions are more robust or the legacy of collective institutions is more enduring. We therefore anticipate that China's efforts at administrative reforms, including raising the education level of civil service staff, should help make implementation of the unpopular population policies kinder and gentler through an emphasis on service rather than coercion. Nonetheless, without dramatic changes in the population picture, we do not expect fundamental changes to current population policies within the existing political framework.

Finally, the case of China's population control highlights the need to reconceptualize state power in the study of Chinese politics and society. For a long time, the analysis of state–society relations in China has tended to focus on the Foucaultian sovereign power. Because this notion of power creates a dichotomous world in which there are the oppressors and the oppressed, analysis along this line often leads to conclusions or predictions that emphasize either continuous state repression or inevitable state withdrawal. Instead, we need to examine the emergence of new governance mechanisms alongside old patterns of coercion. We should also pay attention to how the increasing sophistication of techniques of surveillance and discipline are adapting to and reshaping the evolving patterns of state–society relations.

ACKNOWLEDGMENT

We thank the Smith Richardson Foundation for financial assistance. Thomas Bernstein, Yu Xuejun, and participants of the University of Chicago Workshop on East Asia offered helpful comments and suggestions. We are grateful to the China Health and Nutrition Survey and the China Population Information and Research Center for allowing us to use their data sets. We take sole responsibility for the views, opinions, and content herein.

REFERENCES

Aird, John S., *Slaughter of the Innocents: Coercive Birth Control in China* (Washington, DC: AEI Press, 1990).

Banister, Judith, *China's Changing Population* (Stanford, CA: Stanford University Press, 1987).

Barnett, A. Doak, *Cadres, Bureaucracy, and Political Power in Communist China* (New York: Columbia University Press, 1967).

Bunce, Valerie, *Subversive Institutions: The Design and Destruction of Socialism and the State* (Cambridge, England: Cambridge University Press, 1999).

Burchell, Graham, Colin Gordon, and Peter Miller, *The Foucault Effect, Studies in Governmentality with Two Lectures by and an Interview with Michel Foucault* (Chicago: University of Chicago Press, 1991).

Carter, Tom, "Chinese official tells tales of state-enforced abortion," *Insight on the News*, July 20, 1998, pp. 14, 26.

CCP Central Committee Document Research Office, ed., *Jianguo yilai zhongyao wenxian xuanbian [Selections of Important Documents Since the Founding of PRC]* (Beijing: Zhongyang wenxian chubanshe, 1994), Vol. 15.

Chang Congxuan, ed., *Dangdai zhongguo de jihuashengyu shiye [China Today: Family Planning]* (Beijing: Dangdai zhongguo chubanshe, 1992).

Chen, An, *Restructuring Political Power in China: Alliances and Opposition, 1978–1998* (Boulder, CO: Lynne Rienner, 1999).

Cheng Du, *Disanchi quanguo shengyu gaofeng de tezheng ji duiche* [Features and Countermeasures for the Third National Reproductive Peak] (Wuhan: Wuhan daxue chubanshe, 1991).

CHNS, China Health and Nutrition Survey (Chapel Hill, NC: University of North Carolina, Carolina Population Center, 1989, 1991, 1993).

Choe, Minja Kim, and Noriko O. Tsuya, "Why do Chinese women practice contraception? The case of rural Jilin Province," *Studies in Family Planning*, 22 (1991), pp. 39–51.

Deng Xiaoping, *Deng Xiaoping wenxuan, 1978–1982 [Selected Works of Deng Xiaoping, 1978–1982]* (Beijing: Renmin chubanshe, 1983), Vol. II.

Eggertsson, Thrainn, *Economic Behavior and Institutions* (New York: Cambridge University Press, 1990).

Elster, Jon, *Ulysses and The Sirens: Studies of Rationality and Irrationality* (Cambridge, MA: Cambridge University Press, 1979).

Etzioni, Amitai, *A Comparative Analysis of Complex Organizations* (New York: Free Press, 1961).

FBIS (Foreign Broadcast Information Service), Daily Report: China. Washington, DC.

Foucault, Michel, *Discipline and Punish* (New York: Vintage Books, 1979).

Friedman, Edward, *National Identity and Democratic Prospects in Socialist China* (Armonk, NY: M. E. Sharpe, 1995).

Greenhalgh, Susan, "Controlling Births and Bodies in Village China," *American Ethnologist*, 21 (1994), pp. 3–30.

Greenhalgh, Susan, Zhu Chuzhu, and Li Nan, "Restraining Population Growth in Three Chinese Villages, 1988–1993," *Population and Development Review*, 20 (1994), pp. 365–95.

He, Qinglian, "A Volcanic Stability," *Journal of Democracy*, 14 (January 2002), pp. 66–72.

Jiang Zhenghua, ed., *Yijiu jiuer nian zhongguo shengyulu chouyang diaocha lunwen ji [The Collection of Research Papers of the 1992 fertility Sampling Survey in China]* (Beijing: Zhongguo renkou chubanshe, 1996).

JKB, Jiankangbao [Health News]. Beijing.

Johnson, D. Gale, "Population and Economic Development," *China Economic Review*, 10 (1999), pp. 1–16.

Johnson, Kay, "Chinese Orphanages: Saving China's Abandoned Girls," *Australian Journal of Chinese Affairs*, 30 (1993), pp. 61–87.

Kaufman, Joan, "The Cost of IUD Failure in China," *Studies in Family Planning*, 24 (1993), pp. 194–6.

Kaufman, Joan, Zhang Zhirong, Qiao Xinjian, and Zhang Yang, "The Quality of Family Planning Services in Rural China," *Studies in Family Planning*, 23 (1992), pp. 73–84.

Lavely, William, "Managing Birth Planning at the Local Level," paper presented at the Workshop on Cadre Monitoring, San Diego, CA, June 5–7, 1998.

Lewis, John Wilson, *Leadership in Communist China* (Ithaca, NY: Cornell University Press, 1963).

Mann, Michael, *The Sources of Social Power, Volume II: The Rise of Classes and Nation-States, 1760–1914* (New York: Cambridge University Press, 1993).

Mao, Zedong, *Mao Zedong xuanji [Selected Works of Mao Zedong]* (Beijing: Renmin chubanshe, 1964).

Merli, M. Giovanna, and Herbert L. Smith, "Has the Chinese Family Planning Policy Been Successful in Changing Fertility Preferences?," *Demography*, 39 (August 2002), pp. 557–72.

Merli, M. Giovanna, Zhenchao Qian, and Herbert L. Smith, "Prospects for Change in the Chinese Family Planning Program: Notes from the Field," Unpublished manuscript, 2001.

Mosher, Steven W., *Broken Earth: The Rural Chinese* (New York: Free Press, 1983).

NFRB, *Nanfang ribao [Nanfang Daily]*. Guangzhou, China.

Nixon, Richard M., *The Memoirs of Richard Nixon* (New York: Grosset & Dunlap, 1978).

NYT, New York Times. New York.

Oi, Jean C., "Fiscal Reform and the Economic Foundations of Local State Corporatism in China," *World Politics*, 45 (October 1992), pp. 99–126.

Putnam, Robert O., *Making Democracy Work: Civic Traditions in Modern Italy* (Princeton, NJ: Princeton University Press, 1993).

RMRB, Renmin ribao [People's Daily]. Beijing.

SCMP (South China Morning Post). Hong Kong.

Short, Susan E., and Zhai Fengying, "Looking Locally at China's One-Child Policy," *Studies in Family Planning*, 29 (1998), pp. 373–85.

Shue, Vivienne, *The Reach of the State* (Stanford, CA: Stanford University Press, 1988).

Sichuan ribao [Sichuan daily]. Sichuan.

Siu, Helen F., *Agents and Victims in South China: Accomplices in Rural Revolution* (New Haven, CT: Yale University Press, 1989).

Solnick, Steven L., "The Breakdown of Hierarchies in the Soviet Union and China: A Neo-Institutional Perspective," *World Politics*, 48 (1996), pp. 209–38.

Tang Yan, *Zhongguo renkou chao [China's Population Tide]* (Guangzhou: Jinan daxue chubanshe, 1994).

Tian Xueyuan, *Daguo zhinan [The Difficulties Faced by a Great Country]* (Beijing: Jinri zhongguo chubanshe, 1997).

Tsou, Tang, "Interpreting the Revolution in China: Macrohistory and Micromechanisms," *Modern China*, 26 (April 2000), pp. 205–38.

Tuljapurkar, Shripad, Li Nan, and Marcus W. Feldman, "High Sex Ratios in China's Future," *Science*, 267 (1995), pp. 874–76.

Unger, Jonathan, "State and Peasant in Post-Revolution China," *Journal of Peasant Studies*, 17 (1989), pp. 114–36.

Unger, Roberto Mangabeira, *Plasticity into Power: Comparative-Historical Studies on the International Conditions of Economics and Military Success* (Cambridge, England: Cambridge University Press, 1987).

Walder, Andrew G., *The Waning of the Communist State: Economic Origins of Political Decline in China and Hungary* (Berkeley, CA: University of California Press, 1995).

Wang, Ying, *Xin jiti zhuyi: xiangcun shehui de zaizuzhi [New Collectivism: The Reorganization of Rural Society]* (Beijing: Jingji guanli chubanshe, 1996).

Wasserstrom, Jeffery, "Resistance to the One-Child Family," *Modern China*, 10 (1984), pp. 345–74.

Weisskopf, Michael, "China's Birth Control Policy Drives Some to Kill Baby Girls," *Washington Post*, January 8, 1985.

White, Tyrene, "Domination, resistance and accommodation in China's one-child campaign," in Elizabeth J. Perry and Mark Seldon, eds., *Chinese Society: Change, conflict and resistance* (New York: Routledge, 2000), pp. 102–119.

"Postrevolutionary Mobilization in China," *World Politics* 43 (1990), pp. 53–76.

Winckler, Edwin A., "Re-enforcing State Birth Planning," In Edward Winckler, ed., *Transition from Communism in China: Institutional and Comparative Analyses* (Boulder, CO: Lynne Rienner, 1999), pp. 181–204.

World Bank, *World Development Report 1997: The State in a Changing World* (New York: Oxford University Press, 1997).

Xiao Zhenyu, "Zhongguo de renkou jihua yu shengyu kongzhi" [China's Population Planning and Birth Control]. In Ma Bing, ed., *Zhongguo renkou kongzhi: shijian yu duiche [China's Population Control: Practice and Strategy]* (Beijing: Zhongguo guoji guangbo chubanshe, 1990), pp. 80–82.

Xu Dixin, ed., *Dangdai zhongguo de renkou [China Today: Population]* (Beijing: Zhongguo shehui kexue chubanshe, 1988).

Yang, Dali L., *Calamity and Reform in China: State, Rural Society, and Institutional Change Since the Great Leap Famine* (Stanford, CA: Stanford University Press, 1996).

Yang Zihui, ed., *Zhongguo lidai renkou tongji ziliao yanjiu [China Historical Population Data and the Relevant Studies]* (Beijing: Gaige chubanshe, 1996).

ZGJSNJ, Zhongguo jihuashengyu nianjian [China Birth Planning Yearbook] (Beijing: Kepu chubanshe, various years).

ZGRKNJ, Zhongguo renkou nianjian [China Population Yearbook] (Beijing: Zhongguo shehui kexue chubanshe, 1985).

ZGRKTJNJ, Zhongguo renkou tongji nianjian [China Population Statistics Yearbook] (Beijing: Zhongguo tongji chubanshe, various years).

ZGWSNJ, Zhongguo weisheng tongji nianjian [China Public Health Yearbook] (Beijing: Renmin weisheng chubanshe, various years).

Zhang, Junsen, "Socioeconomic Determinants of Fertility in Hebei Province, China: An Application of the Sequential Logit Model," *Economic Development and Cultural Change*, 43 (October 1994), pp. 67–90.

Zhang, Weiguo, "Implementation of State Family Planning Programmes in a Northern Chinese Village," *China Quarterly*, 157 (1999), pp. 202–30.

7

The Political Economy of Industrial Restructuring in China's Coal Industry, 1992–1999

Fubing Su

After 10 years of reform, China had gradually grown out of the planned economy and, in most sectors, the market had replaced bureaucracies as the main mechanism for coordinating economic transactions.[1] By the beginning of the 1990s, shortages had already become a thing of the past and industrial products flooded markets, manifesting the power of the market economy. Moreover, most markets were populated by a large number of small- and medium-sized firms. With small market shares and low capitalization, these firms were incapable of investing in advanced technologies and developing new products; they had to resort to cutthroat competition at the low end of production. Industrial restructuring was clearly needed if the competitiveness of Chinese industries were to be improved in the long run. With the massive entry of multinational corporations at the beginning of the 1990s, the very survival of many Chinese indigenous industries was called into question and generated heated debates within policy circles.[2] Instead of erecting barriers and warding off international competition, the new central leadership under Jiang Zemin and Zhu Rongji decided to actively intervene in this process and help readjust industrial structures in a more rational manner so that domestic firms could meet challenges from the outside. Through economic

---

[1] Barry Naughton, *Growing Out of the Plan: Chinese Economic Reform, 1978–1993* (Cambridge University Press, 1995).

[2] For a more general analysis of Chinese government's policy toward multinational corporations and politics behind it during this period, see Dali Yang and Fubing Su, "Taming the Market: China and the forces of globalization," in Aseem Prakash and Jeffrey A. Hart, eds., *Responding to Globalization* (London: Routledge, 2000), pp. 33–64.

incentives and administrative coercion, the central government tried to encourage (sometimes force) some inefficient industrial firms to diversify into other businesses and leave market shares to more competitive ones.

For the coal industry, market saturation set in during the early 1990s and the central government responded very promptly. As the next section shows in detail, the first policy choice of the central government was to push state key coal mines (Guoyou Tongpei Meikuang) to the market by liberalizing coal prices and hardening their budget constraints. Billions of Chinese yuan in zero-interest loans were also provided so some inefficient state key coal mines could be shut down or diversify into other businesses. According to the central government's plan, this transition was to be completed in three years.

By the end of 1994, however, this policy basically came to a standstill and a new policy was pushed to the front by the central government. It targeted instead small coal mines for closure or restructuring, leaving more of the market for state key coal mines. Even though this policy was justified by the central government on the grounds of resource conservation and environmental protection, it faced tremendous resistance during the implementation stage. As a result of the property rights arrangement in the coal industry, bureaucrats at various local governments did not share the preferences of the central government. They would rather keep those small coal mines running and therefore shirked their responsibilities whenever it was possible. In response, the central government tightened its monitoring efforts and resorted to traditional policy tools such as campaigning, quota assigning, inspecting, and designing positive and negative incentives. Moreover, as this study shows, the central government was finally able to readjust the institutional structure in a way that could accommodate the interests of the local governments, and it turned the zero-sum game into a win–win scenario. This strategic move has facilitated a smoother implementation of this policy.

Closing down small coal mines has not been easy, but, after five years of effort, the central government has, by and large, achieved its targets. Initially, it set the targets of closing 25,000 small coal mines and cutting coal production by 250 million tons. According to latest official statistics, more than 33,000 small coal mines have been closed and coal output has

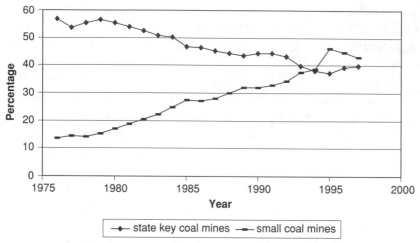

Figure 7.1. Share of coal production by ownership, 1976–1997.

decreased by 300 million tons.[3] In contrast, state key coal mines have indeed clinched more market shares from small coal mines.

As Figure 7.1 shows, after the initiation of the policy in 1995, the market share of the state key coal mines climbed continuously in 1996 and 1997. These gains came at the direct expense of small coal mines. After the 1995 peak of 47 percent of the coal market, more and more small coal mines were forced out of the market and met their fate of closure. At the same time, state key coal mines were able to keep their mining machines running to their full capacities and fill in the gap. Before this policy, it was estimated that only about 60 percent of the mining capacity of state key coal mines was actually utilized.

Given the strong resistance of local bureaucrats, we may wonder how the central government managed to (largely) obtain its goals. This chapter sets out to answer this question. The analysis can contribute to our understanding of policy making and implementation in one of the most important industries in China. Moreover, it offers some insights with regard to changes in the Chinese state. Since the economic reform, the Chinese economy and society have gone through dramatic changes. As a result, the Chinese state has been under tremendous pressure to make adjustments and accommodate the new environment. Scholars are debating whether

---

[3] "Readjusting effective in China's coal sector," Xinhua News Agency-Ceis, Woodside, July 28, 2000.

these adjustments have seriously undermined the ability of the Chinese state to govern the country. Particularly contentious is whether or not the central government can control more assertive local governments. To anticipate my conclusion, this study demonstrates that economic changes have indeed posed some serious challenges to the central leadership. But, in the end, the central government has managed to achieve its policy goals. What is more interesting is that this improved effectiveness in governance was obtained through mutual adjustments by both the central government and local governments. Moreover, the central government seemed to be willing to reform institutions to accommodate the interest of various local governments.

The first section provides a brief overview of the coal industry over the past several decades, highlighting the origin of the current problem. The central government's two policy choices in the early 1990s are also analyzed. The next section describes how the property rights arrangement in the coal industry has driven the preferences of the central government and local bureaucrats apart, which in turn underlies the problem of implementation. The central government's attempt to deal with this problem is the topic of the third section. Finally, the last section summarizes the findings and lists implications of this study for the general question of Chinese central–local relations.

THE COAL INDUSTRY AND EARLY ECONOMIC REFORMS

The importance of coal to the Chinese economy cannot be overstated. As Figure 7.2 shows, coal has been a significant source of energy throughout the past fifty years. In the 1950s, it supplied more than 90 percent of the energy in China. Despite a gradual decline in the 1960s and 1970s, it has never dropped below the 70 percent level. In fact, coal consumption in the 1980s even experienced a steady increase in the aftermath of the oil crisis in the world market. In comparison with the trend in other parts of the world, China's energy consumption pattern is quite distinctive among major economies (Table 7.1).

Most countries have opted to rely more heavily on oil and natural gas, with no more than 30 percent of their energy supply coming from coal. This choice is partly a response to rising environmental concerns in domestic politics on the one hand and the availability of cheap oil in the world market on the other. The reasons for China's heavy reliance

Table 7.1. *Energy Comparison Between China and the World*

	Year	Solid	Liquid	Gas	Hydropower and Nuclear Power
World	1970	34.9	42.9	19.8	2.4
	1990	32.3	38.7	23.5	5.1
	1996	26.9	39.6	23.5	10
United States	1970	25.3	36.5	36.6	1.6
	1990	27.9	42.3	25.4	4.4
	1996	24.2	39.1	26.7	10
China	1970	80.9	14.7	0.9	3.5
	1990	76.2	16.6	2.1	5.1
	1995	75.0	17.3	1.8	5.9

Source: Figures for the world are from *Chinese Coal Industry Yearbook* (1996, 1998); figures for China are from *China Energy Development Report* (1997) (Beijing: Economic Management Publisher).

on coal are multiple. Besides a poor endowment of oil resources and a lack of environmental concern in China, the higher technology barrier to exploring and extracting oil and natural gas is largely to blame. This was actually the rationale for developing coal at the beginning of the Chinese Communist Party (CCP) rule. With capital in severe shortage at the beginning of the CCP rule, targeting less capital-intensive coal extraction became a natural choice. Another episode was the oil crisis in

Figure 7.2. *Energy Consumption in China, 1953–1996*

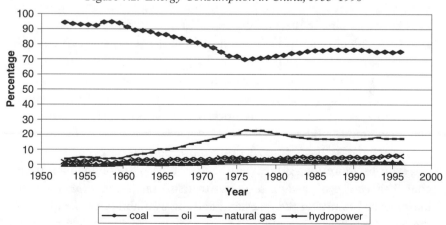

the late 1970s, which convinced Chinese leaders that it was too risky to rely on the world market.[4]

As the backbone of the energy supply for Chinese industrialization, coal was among the handful of materials that remained subject to central government planning into the 1990s. Moreover, the government set coal prices below the market-clearing price until the early 1990s.[5] Partly because of governmental price policy, the demand for coal consistently exceeded supply by a large margin for most of the time before the economic reform. Shortages of coal constantly challenged central planners, and the problem assumed even greater urgency in the early 1980s. The new generation of CCP leadership sought to regain legitimacy through economic revival. In the 12th CCP Party Congress in 1982, Hu Yaobang, then the CCP General Secretary, set the grand target of quadrupling the gross national product by the year of 2000. To achieve this goal, the coal industry was under tremendous pressure to meet the industrial demand for energy.[6]

The central government had been quite generous in meeting state key coal mines' demands for more investments and more employees. According to one survey in the mid-1980s, thirty state key coal mines were among the top fifty enterprises that had the largest number of employees. At the same time, thirteen of them were also among the top fifty enterprises that had the largest fixed assets in China.[7] However, because of bureaucratic management and soft budget constraints, there were clear signs that the state key coal mines would not be able to make ambitious government-set

---

[4] An editorial in the *People's Daily* (March 20, 1980, p. 1) reads that "the world is currently suffering from an oil crisis, which makes all countries turn their eyes back to coal again. The second golden time for coal is coming in the 80s. For the foreseeable future, coal should be the basis of our energy supply, as oil is too costly and not economical. We must fundamentally change the situation of the coal industry to meet the demands of the four-modernizations. The four-modernizations determine the future of our nation, and coal determines the future of the four-modernizations."

[5] One caveat is that, as a result of the incentive policy for coal production in early 1983, coal from nonstate key coal mines could be marketed freely. However, these mines did not have the privileged access to low-interest loans, underpriced production materials input, and rail transportation that state key coal mines did.

[6] In an interview, Minister of the Coal Industry Gao Yangwen commented that "the 1980s is a critical period for the four-modernizations, and the progress of the four-modernizations depends on the progress of energy, mainly coal. We want to be the promoters of the four-modernizations. Therefore, the development of coal can't slow down; instead we must speed up" (*Worker's Daily*, March 22, 1980, p. 3).

[7] *China Coal News (CCN)*, May 27, 1987.

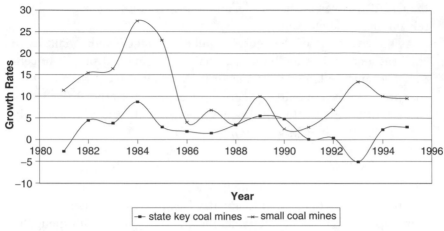

Figure 7.3. Growth rates of coal mines in China, 1981–1996.

targets by themselves.[8] In this urgent situation, a new policy was pushed to the front in 1983, which in effect broke the ideological barrier and allowed nonstate and private ownership in the coal industry.[9] This policy, known as "speeding up resource flows" (*youshui kuailiu*), called on collectives and individuals from all walks of life to invest their money in coal production. In return, they were allowed to control their products and market them freely. This is a quite powerful reward in an economy that had suffered from serious shortages of coal. As a result, many township and village governments as well as private entrepreneurs poured resources into coal production. In less than one year, the number of small coal mines doubled,

[8] In 1981, a national meeting for state key coal mines was convened. The reason for the meeting was that coal production had fallen short of the state plan, and Minister Gao Yangwen attributed this nonperformance to the poor morale of the leaders and workers. He was forced to make a self-criticism. The state key coal mines actually registered a negative growth rate in 1981 (see the *Chinese Coal Industry Yearbook*, 1982, pp. 156, 157, 172, 173; *China Finance & Trade News*, August 29, 1981).

[9] This policy was first publicized by the Ministry of the Coal Industry on April 27, 1983. The document, "Eight measures for speeding up local coal mine development," can be found in the *Chinese Coal Industry Yearbook*, 1984, p. 79. Zhao Ziyang pushed this idea even further and criticized the state-led development strategy; he said that "we must combine the best coal deposit with our rich endowment of cheap labor in developing this coal field. We will rely mostly on collective and private investments. We need to liberate our mind, and change the old thinking of relying on huge investments from the state and use high tech to extract coal. We should instead extract easy coal, then reinvest in road and machinery, and develop mechanized extraction step by step. This way coal will be obtained with the least state investment" (*Shaanxi Daily*, July 15, 1986, p. 1).

Table 7.2. *Losses of State Key Coal Mines in China, 1962–1998*

	State Key Coal Mines	
Year	Loss (billion yuan)	Percentage in the Red
1962	−0.45	80.0
1963	—	NA
1964	—	NA
1965	+	NA
NA	NA	NA
1971	NA	NA
NA	NA	NA
1977	−0.18	72.8
NA	NA	NA
1982	−0.09	NA
1983	NA	63.0
1984	−0.13	61.0*
1985	−0.56	70.0*
1986	−1.12	NA
1987	−1.52	NA
1988	−1.68	93.0*
1989	−3.00	95.5*
1990	−7.90	NA
1991	−6.25	NA
1992	−5.75	90.3
1993	−4.00	81.0
1994	−1.95	68.8
1995	−1.40	72.0
1996	−0.60	41.0
1997	+0.20	30.0
1998	−3.71	80.8

* From Wang Xiaoqi and Yang Zhigang, "Thoughts on Further Reforming Coal Prices," *Coal Economics Research [Meitan Jingji Yanjiu]*, No. 2 (1990), pp. 23–27.

Notes: Figures for 1991 to 1998 are from annual reports of the Ministry of the Coal Industry. Those before 1991 are from Liu Guanwen, Wu Dechun, and Dong Jibing, eds. *Coal Prices in China* (Beijing: China Plan Publishing House, 1990), pp. 290, 300, 318. The number for 1990 is from *Coal Economics Research [Meitan Jingji Yanjiu]*, No. 11 (1991), p. 2. The plus sign means surplus and the minus sign means in red. NA indicates that data are not available.

and their output shot up to more than 27 percent (Figure 7.3). After several years of rapid expansion, by the end of the 1980s, the small coal mines had produced more than 30 percent of the coal in the entire country, and they had gradually taken over more market share from state key coal mines (see Figure 7.1). This was totally beyond the initial intention of the policy makers.[10]

With the massive entry of small coal mines in the 1980s, the coal market quickly became saturated. In less than ten years, the long-standing problem of coal shortage disappeared. Another problem, however, arose: overproduction and the excessive competition associated with it. Small coal mines took advantage of their low production costs and fought a cutthroat price war with state key coal mines. As a result, more and more state key coal mines were losing money at the turn of the 1990s (Table 7.2), and many faced heavy debt burdens.[11]

THE ONSET OF INDUSTRIAL POLICIES

In the face of a troubled industry, politicians have basically three policy options. They can take a hands-off stance and let the market sort out the winners and losers. They can also positively intervene in this process by either nurturing the winners or helping the losers to diversify and exit. Lastly, they may choose to continue subsidizing the losers and slow down the industrial restructuring. In response to the crisis in the coal industry, the central government finally decided to step in and actively intervene in 1992. By helping less efficient firms diversify into other businesses, the central government hoped to rationalize the structure of the coal industry in a relatively short period of time. This would free up resources for more productive uses and have a positive effect on the national economy.

In 1992, the central government began to tackle the root problem and targeted the inefficient state key coal mines. In March 1992, (then) Vice Premier Zhu Rongji made this comment:

[I]f only the irrational prices are stressed, the coal industry [state key coal mines] will not have an improvement . . . there are huge wastes in the coal industry. . . . We have to make the determination, and there is no alternative. It is estimated that there are three million [employees in the coal industry] and at least one million workers are redundant.[12]

---

[10] Gao Yangwen, Minister of the Coal Industry, remarked that the success of small coal mines was a surprise to the central leadership (*Chinese Coal Industry Yearbook*, 1986).

[11] Massive entry coupled with central government price control made state key coal mines, as a whole, the least profitable sector among 37 major industrial sectors in China. See Naughton, *Growing Out of the Plan*, p. 238.

[12] An abstract can be found in the *Chinese Coal Industry Yearbook*, 1992, pp. 97–9. Zhu reiterated the same message during his trip to state key coal mines in Shaanxi province on August 21, 1992 (*Chinese Coal Industry Yearbook*, 1993, pp. 92–4).

A consensus seemed to be emerging among the top decision makers: heavy capitalization and high employment together simply do not make good business sense. The best way to restructure the coal industry was to nourish a few competitive state key coal mines by hardening their budget constraint and diversifying surplus workers to service industries. At the same time, money-losing state key coal mines should be allowed to go bankrupt and exit the market. This new policy, dubbed "liberalizing coal prices and withdrawing subsidies in three years," aimed to push the state key coal mines to the market by liberalizing the coal price, giving them more autonomy, and withdrawing the annual subsidies of 2 billion yuan.[13] The central government would also earmark 2 billion yuan zero-interest loans to aid this transition, and diversification into other businesses was especially encouraged to absorb their excess workers. At the same time, some of the coal mines, which had incurred heavy losses in the past, would be closed down.[14]

This government-led liberalization policy in the coal industry, however upbeat and promising it sounded at the beginning, came to a silent end without much accomplishment. By the end of the third year (1995), the state key coal mines still ran a loss of 1.4 billion yuan.[15] The price liberalization was in place, but the central government had backtracked from its earlier promise of withdrawing subsidies and had continued to pour money into the state key coal mines. This in effect softened the budget constraint of state key coal mines again and sounded the death knell for the positive intervention policy. The coal industry was basically back to the situation of three years before, and the problem of oversupply still baffled the politicians.

The reasons for this unsuccessful policy intervention are basically twofold. First, the central decision makers did not anticipate the reaction from the small coal mines. Encouraged by the liberal orientation of the government policy, hundreds and thousands of small coal mines decided to take advantage of their low costs and entered coal production or simply raised their output level. As shown in Figure 7.3, the output of small coal mines in 1993 increased to approximately 13 percent. What

---

[13] Wang Shenhao, "Achieving the historical change in the coal industry," *Management World*, No. 1, 1993.

[14] See the annual report of the Minister in 1993 in the *Chinese Coal Industry Yearbook*, 1994.

[15] Considering the misreporting of figures, the losses are definitely higher than that. One sign of this misinformation is the huge losses reported in 1998 and 1999.

was more important was that, unlike in the 1980s when both state key coal mines and small coal mines could expand simultaneously, the increase in small coal mines in 1993 came directly at the expense of state key coal mines. What was also alarming was the rapid increase in market share by small coal mines in these three years. Figure 7.1 graphs market shares of different players. The period from 1993 to 1995 witnessed the fastest surge for small coal mines and the steepest plunge for state key coal mines. They simply could not keep pace with these naturally profit-seeking market actors. For the first time, small coal mines overtook state key coal mines as the largest producers in the coal market in 1994. The significance of this takeover was probably more symbolic than substantive. It struck a sense of crisis among state key coal mines and invited unwanted attention from the latter party.

Second, the diversification program sponsored by the central government failed miserably. The coal industry is a sector with low barriers to entry but high costs of exit. The industry typically employs unskilled labor for production, mostly peasants in Chinese coal mines. Given their low skills, the peasants have a hard time finding other new employment opportunities once they are laid off. When the diversification program was announced in 1993, state key coal mines rushed in and set up various enterprises, most of which lay at the low end of the industrial ladder. According to one survey, among 879 enterprises sampled, 93 were coal dressing, sales, and transportation enterprises; 105 were machinery repair shops; 120 were construction materials factories (47 were cement factories); and 74 were construction teams.[16] These were already saturated industries by the middle of the 1990s, and, instead of relieving the pressure, many of them soon became new burdens of debt-stricken state key coal mines. They applied for new loans from the central government every year but only to keep those new enterprises afloat.[17] Clearly, diversification wouldn't help them very much.

Declining market shares, together with the failed diversification attempt, forced leaders of state key coal mines to reevaluate their initial support of the government's restructuring policy, and they concluded that this policy would not do them good in the long term. To protect their incomes and employment opportunities, both managers and workers in

---

[16] Survey of diversification business in the coal industry (personal interview, on condition of anonymity, July 15, 1998).

[17] Personal interview, on condition of anonymity, July 15, 1998.

state key coal mines chose to press for a political solution. They lobbied the top decision makers intensively to terminate the liberalization policy and keep the government's commitment to protection. Moreover, seeing this as a zero-sum game, they persuaded the central government to adopt new regulatory policies and force small coal mines to shoulder the burden of adjustment.[18]

After more than one year's deliberation, a new policy, called "regulating the coal industry according to laws," gradually formed. It first emerged in 1995 when two pieces of regulatory policy with regard to small coal mines were published by the State Council, namely *Administrative Rules for Township Coal Mines* and *Administrative Methods for Coal Production Permits*. This policy was finally pushed to the front of national politics in 1997. It gained full momentum in a national teleconference on May 22, 1997, attended by Vice Premier Wu Bangguo and various departments of the central government. On November 11, 1998, the State Council hosted another national meeting and reasserted the policy.[19] It maintained the government's protection over state key coal mines. Small coal mines became the target for adjustment instead. Because many small coal mines were charged with wasting coal resources and damaging the environment and because they had no legal mining certificates, they were required to be shut down.[20] This was done under the name of regulating the coal industry according to the Law of Coal and other national regulations, but politicians were also very explicit about their intention of protecting market shares for state key coal mines at the expense of small coal mines. Zhu, by that time Premier, made the goal of this policy very clear: "we must reform and adjust the order in the coal industry, close down illegal and irrationally located coal mines. We should make full use of the state key coal mines and let the modern mining equipment run to full capacity."[21]

---

[18] This political process has been thoroughly analyzed in another paper, "Private Interests and Public Policy Making in Transitional China: The Coal Mining Case" (working paper).

[19] *CCN*, December 29, 1998.

[20] According to government statistics, there are around 60,000 small coal mines, 51,200 of which are illegal (accessed on November 13, 1998 at http://www.chinadaily.com.cn/cndydb/1998/11/d5-2caol.k13.html). The truth is that the government licensing regulation has been very poorly designed and irregular in its execution since 1995. Even government officials have to admit that it has been largely ignored in practice.

[21] *CCN*, September 8, 1998, p. 1. Zhang Baoming, director of the State Coal Industry Bureau, also commented that "bringing state-owned enterprises into the black in three years is not only an economic task but also a political one . . . closing down illegal and irrational coal mines is the root of reaching this goal" (*CCN*, June 3, 1999, p. 1).

This new policy, however, faced serious problems during the implementation stage. Resistance from local bureaucrats was strong and the central government had to commit more and more resources to monitoring them. The most important reason, as discussed in the next section, can be found in the great divergence in the preferences of the central leadership and local bureaucrats. One important institution in the coal industry, that is, property rights arrangement, explains why policy implementation in this issue area is particularly problematic.

PROPERTY RIGHTS AND INCENTIVES: ONE INDUSTRY AND TWO WORLDS

According to Chinese laws, all natural resources belong to the state. As the incarnation of the state, the central government monopolizes all these resources in the country.[22] It will normally assign monopolistic rights to certain giant state-run enterprises and put them directly under various ministries of the central government. In the coal industry, however, because of the speeding up resource flows or *youshui kuailiu* policy in the early 1980s, a dual structure had been created.

By the mid-1990s, two groups of coal producers dominated the industry.[23] The first group included 100 or so mammoth state key coal mines. They were entitled to own the vast majority of the coal reserves in any major coal field. Before the policy change in 1998, they were owned by the central government and directly managed by the Ministry of the Coal Industry (MCI). With huge state investments from the central government, these state key coal mines imported a lot of modern mining equipment, thus operating the most technically sophisticated coal colliers in the country. At the same time, they also employed more than 3 million workers, making them one of the industries with the largest number of state employees. Because of their ownership relationship with the central

---

[22] For a discussion of the property rights in coal resources, see Zhang Yunzhang, "Lun Meitan Ziyuan Chanquan de Guanli" ["On the Management of Property Rights in Coal Resources"], *Coal Economics Research*, 9 (2002), pp. 58–62. Also see Pan Weier, "Guanyu Meitan Hangye Jiegou Tiaozheng de Fenxi" ["Analysis of Structural Adjustment in the Coal Industry"], *Energy of China*, 1 (2002); pp. 2–10.

[23] For completeness, there was also a third group, i.e., state coal mines owned by various local governments. This chapter focuses on only the first two groups. The market share by these local state coal mines was small. What was more important was that their impact on the industrial readjustment policy was marginal.

government, these coal mines basically existed in pockets of administrative enclaves and were largely isolated from local societies and authorities. Their leaders were appointed by the MCI and products were distributed through central government plans. Of course, these enterprises would submit all profits to and receive subsidies from the central government.

The second group of coal producers was tens of thousands of small coal mines owned by various local governments and private entrepreneurs. To boost coal production in the early 1980s, the central government decided to allocate small pockets of coal reserves or margins of major reserves to small coal mines. This policy in fact enabled local governments and private businessmen to establish some de facto rights over parts of the coal resources. What was more important was that, for various levels of local governments, these small coal mines were under their jurisdiction, so they could legitimately tap into the wealth through taxation or regulatory fees.

As we can see now, this dual structure created the potential of preference divergence between the central government and local bureaucrats. Whereas the central government wanted to protect more modern state key coal mines and close down backward small coal mines, local bureaucrats held the opposite view. From the perspective of the latter, state key coal mines were "foreign colonizers."[24] They were profiteering from local resources yet making no local contributions. The development of small coal mines, in contrast, was viewed as a redress of this injustice of resource allocation. Moreover, the interests of local bureaucrats could and had been enhanced directly by these small coal mines. To get promoted, local bureaucrats needed to oversee a rapidly growing economy or have deep pockets. On both accounts, small coal mines had become indispensable for ambitious local officials.

As a matter of fact, most of China's coal reserves are distributed in less developed and mountainous western and southwestern regions. With little opportunity for development in those areas, local bureaucrats attached great importance to the development of small coal mines. Coal mining and coal-related businesses have carried heavy weight in local economies. For example, in 1994, small coal mines contributed about 80 percent of the local budget in Xiaoyi City of Shanxi Province, and 80 percent of peasants'

---

[24] Personal interview, on August 3, 1998. Also see CCN, December 29, 1998.

income came from coal-related businesses. For Huangling County of Shanxi Province, that figure was about 85 percent.[25] For 112 key coal-producing counties in China, revenues from coal reached 18.4 billion yuan in 1996, taxes reached 1.2 billion yuan, and profits reached 1.4 billion yuan. More than 1.2 million peasants were employed in those small coal mines.[26]

More interesting is the way in which this wealth has been transferred from small coal mines to local government budgets and local bureaucrats' pockets. Contrary to the benevolent-local-state hypothesis some scholars have developed,[27] local governments in reality bore no resemblance to a market-preserving dictator at all. Small coal mines were not convinced of the nonpredatory nature of local governments either. Instead, local governments behaved as predicted in the public choice literature: Economic opportunities and profits invited government regulation and opportunities for bureaucrats to engage in rent seeking. With the boom of small coal mines in the 1980s, local laws and regulations regarding these coal mines also proliferated. Government bureaucracies tried to tap into this newly discovered source of revenue by creating various certificates, licenses, and fees. To illustrate the extent of this overregulation, I assembled a list of the coal revenue breakdowns for small coal mines. These numbers were collected during a trip to Shanxi Province in 1999. One thing to note is that local regulations are ad hoc, and the items included in the list vary from year to year and from place to place. For example, during an interview, one owner of several small coal mines complained that he was charged a "family planning fee" even though none of his employees were female.[28] This item does not appear in the list shown here. However, the

---

[25] *CCN*, February 14, 1995.

[26] *CCN*, December 29, 1998. Another estimate shows that, in 1985, about 2 million peasant workers were employed in various small coal mines and their income amounted to 2.5 billion yuan; see "A Survey of Local Coal Mines Development," MCI Survey Team, in *Industrial Economics Management Gazette*, 3 (1987), pp. 30–4.

[27] The idea of economic growth-friendly political institutions comes from the original theorization in Douglass North and Barry Weingast, "Constitutions and Commitment: The Evolution of Institutions Governing Public Choice in 17th Century England," in *Journal of Economic History*, 49 (December 1989), pp. 803–832. It was applied to explain the successful economic development of the Chinese economy in the 1980s by Montinola, Qian, and Weingast, "Federalism, Chinese Style," in *World Politics*, 48 (October 1995), pp. 50–81. The argument is that decentralization and competition have forced local governments in China to preserve the market system notwithstanding their autocratic governance.

[28] Personal interview, on June 26, 1999.

general trend is that the proliferation of various fees on small coal mines was rapid in the 1990s, as confirmed by personal interviews during my field trips.

As shown in Table 7.3, all levels of local governments and all kinds of government agencies have tapped into the wealth created by small coal mines. Despite the outcries over rampant fees that appeared in the public media, the extent of overregulation on small coal mines is still shocking. Of the market price of 115.2 yuan/ton, small coal mines ended up with only approximately 40 percent of that value in 1996, which squeezed their profit to only 2.91 yuan/ton. One small coal mine was designated a "unit for preferential support" by the local government. The owner alleged that "my coal mine turns over more than 300,000 yuan every year to the government. Otherwise, it will be closed."[29] These fees were only applicable to small coal mines, and state-owned coal mines were immune from these fees. As a result, despite the low production costs of small coal mines, their comparative advantages have been eroded through heavy local government regulations.[30]

Besides various fees, other local government agencies also ratchet up the regulation by issuing all sorts of permits. One prominent example is again found in Shanxi Province. The Shanxi Transportation & Sales Corporation – a government trading company not affiliated with the coal industry – took over a great deal of coal business from the provincial Shanxi Department of Coal Industry (DCI). The Shanxi DCI tried to reclaim their turf by issuing a Coal Sales Permit in 1995. This new regulation required all small coal mines to obtain a Coal Sales Permit from the DCI at various levels of local government.[31] Only those small coal mines that carried these permits were allowed to sell their products on the market. To ensure compliance, the Shanxi DCI also financed a Coal Safety Inspection Team for this purpose.

The formal rules of regulations partly explain why small coal mines became so important for the budgets of all local governments in coal-producing areas. What is equally important, however, is that small coal

---

[29] *CCN*, February 4, 1999, p. 3.
[30] One industrial insider claimed that this was a deliberate policy of the local governments to protect their inefficient state-owned coal mines and level the playing field.
[31] Personal interview, on June 17, 1999. When I visited the headquarters of the inspection team in Taiyuan, they were drafting a proposal to write the Coal Sales Permit into the Shanxi Provincial Coal Administration Rules.

Table 7.3. *Revenue Breakdown of Small Coal Mines in Ningwu County, Shanxi Province, 1996*

Items	Yuan/ton	% of Total
Energy development funds	17.22	15.2
Various taxes and fees	23.04	20.3
Value added tax	13	
Resource tax	1.5	
Income tax	1.43	
City construction tax	0.12	
Printing tax	0.01	
Education addition	0.36	
Water fee	2	
Resource compensation fee	0.49	
Water and soil loss fee	0.15	
Pollution fee	0.04	
Auditing fee	0.01	
Price controlling fund	0.18	
Forestation fee	0.25	
City fee	1	
Self-owned vehicle (etc.) fee	2.5	
Provincial and prefectural regulating organization fees	26.42	23.38
Provincial service fee	2.28	
Production subsidy fee	8.71	
Coal sales administration fee	9.23	
Simple production	6.2	
Coal mines earnings	48.52	42.05
Production cost	26.38	
Sales cost	9.93	
Administration fee	5.3	
Finance fee	4	
Profits	2.91	
Total coal price	115.2	100

Notes: Data were collected during the author's field trips. Another source reports some figures for coal mines in Yu County in Shanxi Province. The coal price in 1995 was reported to be 106 yuan/ton with 45 yuan as costs and 2 yuan as profits for small coal mines. Various fees added up to 58% of the income from coal sales (CCN, August 13, 1996). These numbers correspond well with those in the table.

mines also contributed handsomely to those bureaucrats in charge of these regulations. One purpose of the regulation is for the government agency to increase their budgetary income from new sources. The other purpose is that, by creating rent-seeking opportunities, self-interested bureaucrats invite briberies to their personal pockets. Facing numerous fees and regulations, most, if not all, small coal mines had to bribe bureaucrats and enforcers at the checkpoints in order to avoid them. One owner of a small coal mine claimed that, "there are about 400 small coal mines in my area. I dare to say that none of them have paid all their fees. How can anyone earn money without escaping those fees!"[32] To escape the fees safely, they had to preempt the bureaucrats by giving money and gifts beforehand. Given the covert nature of these transactions, it is very hard to gauge the extent of the bribery. One typical example may suffice to convey the idea. Shanxi is the largest base for exporting coke to other countries and other parts of the country. A 20 yuan/ton energy fund fee was charged for coke exiting the provincial borders. In 1994, 14 million tons of coke were shipped out of Shanxi Province, and accordingly the government should have received 280 million yuan in energy fund fees. In reality, only 15 million yuan was collected. Almost 95 percent of the fee was lost during this process, either to bureaucrats at various levels or to the hands of small coal mine owners.[33]

In short, at both macro and micro levels, small coal mines have contributed very positively to the interests of local bureaucrats. Most small coal mine owners considered these rent-seeking bureaucrats "annoying," and they hated inconsistent local regulations that caused uncertainties and drained their profits.[34] They felt obligated to cater to those bureaucrats in order to survive. Ironically, precisely because of these "annoying" rent-seeking activities, small coal mines were able to forge an alliance with the local bureaucrats and drive the latter's preferences farther away from that of the central government.

As demonstrated in the analysis given herein, the central government and local bureaucrats held almost diametrically opposed views regarding the closure of small coal mines. Whereas the central government favored closing small coal mines and leaving market space for more modern state

---

[32] "Looking at flowers in the fog," *CCN*, August 4, 1998.
[33] *Shanxi Daily*, March 21, 1995.
[34] Personal interview, on August 3, 1998.

key coal mines, local bureaucrats saw themselves as losers from this industrial readjustment. Although state key coal mines might turn profitable after closing down small coal mines, because of the dual structure, local bureaucrats would not be able to reap these gains through taxation and fees. In contrast, closure of small mines would immediately cut one crucial source of economic growth, job opportunities, revenues, and rents for them. With interests as divergent as this, local bureaucrats could not be expected to implement the central policy faithfully and close down small coal mines.

INDUCING COMPLIANCE: POSITIVE AND NEGATIVE INCENTIVES

As discussed in the previous section, the institutional structure of the property rights arrangement in the coal industry drove a wedge between the central government and local bureaucrats regarding the closure of small coal mines. Most local bureaucrats did not share the preference of the central government. A local bureaucrat was quoted as saying that "our region has experienced a fast growing economy in the past few years and small coal mines have made important contributions. It is very hard for us to close them down."[35] In Shanxi, one leading official overseeing the implementation of this policy in the province confessed privately that "publicly we have to say what the central government says, but, to be honest, I have reservations. And when I travel to local governments and persuade them to close down small coal mines, I can sense the strong resistance among the local cadres."[36]

Being pushed by orders from above, local bureaucrats dragged out the closing process and hoped that this policy campaign would end quickly. Some bureaucrats took advantage of their superior local information and fooled the central government. In many incidences, local governments were found to shut down depleted mines used for storage or small coal mines that ceased production as a result of flooding, whereas really competitive ones actually increased their outputs.[37] In other cases, they would dynamite the entrances of small coal mines in front of the central inspectors and then dig them out again after the inspectors left.

[35] *CCN*, June 9, 1998.
[36] Personal interview, on August 12, 1998.
[37] *CCN*, April 20, 1999 and *CCN*, May 6, 1999.

The central government knew very well the preferences of local bureaucrats and understood the widespread problem of noncompliance. To induce compliance, it resorted to a host of policy tools to shape the incentives of the local bureaucrats.

Campaigning

The root cause of noncompliance is the divergence of preferences between the central government and local bureaucrats. The most straightforward solution, of course, is to persuade the local bureaucrats to share the central government's preference. On many occasions, this has been done through national campaigns. During these campaigns, the central government will typically summon major leaders from all levels of local government to Beijing and drum its policy goals into these bureaucrats. By carefully framing the choice as a dichotomy between broad national interests and narrow local interests, the central government puts the latter at a morally unjustifiable position. Therefore, local bureaucrats have the moral obligation to fully implement the central government's policy and subdue their interests for the good of the nation. Just as strong ideological conviction can dissuade people from individual self-interest, this moral argument also has the effect of aligning local bureaucrats' interests with the central one. Since the inception of this policy in 1995, six rounds of national campaigns have been launched to publicize the policy of closing down small coal mines.

These included the National Coal Conference in Henan on December 26, 1996; Four Ministries, One Commission, and One Union[38] National Teleconference on May 22, 1997; another Four Ministries, One Commission, and One Union Conference on November 18, 1997; the Datong Conference on February 17, 1998; the Closing Down Working Conference on November 11, 1998; and the Closing Down National Teleconference on February 4, 1999. After the national conference, provincial governments would conduct their own conferences. This was especially true after the delegation of state key coal mines to local governments in 1998. For example, after the national convention on November 11, 1998, the Shanxi

---

[38] They are the Ministry of the Coal Industry, the Ministry of Labor, the Ministry of Geography & Minerals, the Ministry of Inspection, the State Economic and Trade Commission, and the Chinese National Labor Union.

Province convened its working conference on November 30 of the same
year, during which the first party secretary emphasized that "we must
understand the closing-down policy from the perspective of conforming
to the central decision, . . . and have the big picture in mind."[39]

Inspecting

In addition to aligning interests, the central government can also induce
compliance by inflicting higher costs on noncompliance. One way is to
increase the probability of detecting deviant behavior, and the central
government has, through repeated interaction with local governments,
figured out that frequent inspection did just that. During these campaigns,
the central government routinely dispatched armies of inspectors across
the country, and it monitored the performance in various local regions.
By reporting directly to the central government, these teams facilitated
information flows and enabled the central government to discipline deviant local bureaucrats more promptly. This in turn tended to induce a
higher level of compliance. For instance, after the Four Ministries, One
Commission, and One Union National Teleconference on May 22, 1997,
eight teams of 108 inspectors were sent to nineteen major coal-producing
provinces to investigate the implementation of the central policy. In less
than ten days, they visited closed coal mines and listened to reports by
local bureaucrats.[40] In some instances, officials from rival provinces have
been recruited to cross-inspect the implementation of the policy. With
their own interests at stake, inspectors would be more attentive to uncov-
ering frauds.[41]

The monitoring efforts at the provincial level were equally impressive.
After the provincial convention on November 30, 1998, Shanxi Province
sent forty high-ranking officials on January 25, 1999 to monitor the implementation. They inspected eight cities, twenty-three key coal-producing
counties, and 129 coal mines, and they reported directly to the provincial
governor. On March 22, 1999, another 100-member inspection team was
again on its way to eleven cities, thirty-five key coal-producing counties,

[39]   Shanxi Coal Administration, 1999, "Closing down, coordinating well, and guaranteeing
       the healthy development of state key coal mines," (internal material), pp. 2–3.
[40]   *CCN*, December 29, 1998.
[41]   Personal interview, on July 21, 1999.

and 103 coal mines. They evaluated the closure and corrected wrongdoing in various locations.[42]

Punishing

As discussed in previous paragraphs, the central government can induce compliance by imposing higher costs on noncompliance, and one way to do this is to increase the frequency of inspection. Another way of doing it is simply to increase the severity of punishment for deviant behavior. Being rational, local bureaucrats would react to this change and become less likely to shirk duties during implementation. In particular, the central government has instituted a "responsibility system" in the government hierarchy. Leading officials at each level of government, such as governor, mayor, county magistrate, township leader, village head, and party secretaries, were held personally responsible for the effectiveness of the closure in their respective regions. In Changzhi city, Shanxi Province, every county-level leader has been assigned to be responsible for several villages, every township leader for some coal mines, and every village cadre for certain coal colliers. All local bureaucrats were personally tied to some measurable targets.[43] In some areas, this responsibility chain has taken the form of written contracts between superiors and their subordinates. It has also been factored into the cadre evaluation system. In addition to other criteria, whether or not the cadres have accomplished their targets would affect their career future: promotion, status quo, or demotion. According to the official document, during the campaigns, this criterion would carry a heavy weight in cadres' overall "political achievements" (Zhengji). Cadres who have made little progress in closure or faked numbers would be punished severely, demoted, or even thrown into jail.[44]

Delegating

These policy tools can be effective if used consistently, but they are very costly in terms of the amount of monetary and administrative resources

---

[42] Yang Zhiming, 1999, "Ensuring a successful completion of closure and downsizing in our province" (internal material), pp. 4–5.

[43] Ibid, p. 3.

[44] Leading Group of Shanxi Closing Coal Mines Campaign, 1998, "Implementation Plan for Shanxi Closing Coal Mines Campaign" (internal material), p. 9.

involved. Because of the incongruence of preferences between the central government and local bureaucrats, shirking has become something that constantly baffled the central government and therefore demanded its endless monitoring. Small coal mines could easily resume production under protective local governments if monitoring was relaxed. From the perspective of the central government, keeping constant vigil was really costly. Just imagine that all local bureaucrats were periodically summoned for conventions and central government officials were sent down routinely to discipline deviants for the policy of closing down small coal mines. This would obviously crowd out other more important issues on the administrative agenda. After several rounds of national campaigns, the central government was finally motivated to seek an institutional solution to this problem and decided to delegate all state key coal mines to various local governments.

As discussed in the incentive section, the root cause of diverging interests is the dual structure of the coal industry. Any institutional change that can demolish or weaken such duality will narrow the interest gap. If the interests of local bureaucrats could be realigned with that of the central government, it would be in the local bureaucrats' interests to close down small coal mines and protect market shares for state key coal mines. Being permanently present in the local areas, these bureaucrats would be able to deter small coal mines from resuming production. In the summer of 1998, the central government finally decided to undertake an institutional readjustment and delegate state key coal mines to local governments.[45] In only about one month, 94 state key coal mines and 176 affiliated enterprises were transferred to various local governments, with total assets of 240 billion yuan and 3.2 million employees.[46] Compared with the dual structure, this new property rights arrangement put both state key coal mines and small coal mines under the jurisdiction of local governments. Instead of protecting small coal mines, which provided major sources of revenue, local governments had more incentive to crack down on them.[47] In fact, the central government was not shy about its intention and touted

---

[45] *CCN*, August 18, 1998.

[46] *CCN*, September 12, 1998.

[47] Even with both state key coal mines and small coal mines, local governments would still prefer other regions to close their small coal mines first. I have analyzed this collective action problem in my dissertation, "Agency, Incentive, and Institutional Design: Bureaucracy Control and Evolution of Governance in Contemporary China" (Ph.D.

that this new institutional arrangement created better conditions for closing down small coal mines in the future.[48] One editorial in the *Zhongguo
Meitan Bao (China Coal News)* made this consideration very clear:

"[T]he work of consolidating township and village coal mines has been conducted
for several years, including a few large scale campaigns. While there are some
positive results, the prominent issue is that [the campaigns] are incomplete and
not consistent. The situation gets better for a while, then becomes chaotic again.
Cleaning illegal small coal mines is like harvesting leeks. Some are cut but others soon grow back. One of the reasons is the lack of unity in the management
system.... Local governments administrate township and village coal mines, and
demand industrial output, taxes, and political achievements from them. They don't
care much about the well being of coal mines under the central government's budget.... Now, delegating the management authority to local governments creates
the conditions for solving the problem."[49]

Seeing central leaders' determination, provincial governments had to
take up this responsibility and work hard to turn the situation around. For
the first time, local bureaucrats were willing to break down the administrative isolation and regard the old "colonizers" as part of their own.
Many provincial leaders visited the troubled state coal mines and listened
to their demands.[50] This was not a common occurrence before the decentralization. With regard to the regulation policy at the end of 1998, all
major provincial officials also started to defend it from the perspective of
state coal mines. For example, Vice Governor of Henan Province, Zhang
Yixiang, talked about the new campaign with great enthusiasm and made
his argument from the perspective of state coal mines. "Closing small
coal mines is our own need, and we fully support it.... Some people think
that small coal mines have employed many workers, [and] closing them
will make many unemployed. What they do not know is that, because of
small coal mines, state coal mines cannot operate to their full capacity,
and many workers have been laid off (*xiagang*). It is clear to calculate this
way."[51]

dissertation, the University of Chicago). This chapter focuses mainly on the distributive
aspect of the industrial policy.
[48] The director of the State Coal Industry Bureau made this comment in an interview
(*CCN*, September 12, 1998), p. 1.
[49] *CCN*, August 22, 1998, p. 1.
[50] *CCN*, November 21, 1998; December 19, 1998.
[51] *CCN*, November 17, 1998, p. 1.

In addition to pushing lower-level bureaucrats harder to implement the regulation policy, provincial leaders were also willing to take advice from state coal mines and use political power to intervene in the coal market. In China, approximately 40 percent of all coal was purchased by power plants. To increase profitability, many of them had jettisoned the high-priced coal from state coal mines and bought coal from small coal mines, including illegal mines. This market demand created a powerful force against the regulation campaign. State coal mines had complained about this matter to the central government and provincial governments, but, before the decentralization, provincial governments had not bothered to heed the complaint. Now, with the change of institutions, state coal mines lobbied again for provincial intervention.[52] Many provinces did then adopt policies along this line. For example, Vice Governor of Guizhou Province, Liu Changgui, ordered all power plants in Guizhou Province to buy 60 percent of their coal from state coal mines and 40 percent from small coal mines. Moreover, the coal price from small mines was fixed at a minimum of 20 yuan/ton. Otherwise, even legal small coal mines would be shut down.[53] Shanxi Province also issued "coal sales tickets" to enforce this policy. Only coal mines that had passed the proper examination could get the tickets. All power plants were ordered to reject coal without the tickets. Provincial inspectors were stationed around power plants to enforce this rule.[54] By restricting small coal mines' access to market, this intervention complemented the regulation campaign and forced illegal small coal mines to exit the market.

CONCLUSION

Like land reform in rural areas, the development of the coal industry in the 1980s demonstrates again the power of institutional change. With the relaxation of ideological constraints in the early 1980s, tens of thousands of small coal mines entered coal production. In less than ten years, coal

---

[52] *CCN*, October 29, 1998. During my visit to Hebei and Inner Mongolia, state coal mines also allegedly sent reports to provincial governments and asked provincial leaders to order nearby power plants to purchase coal from them.

[53] *CCN*, December 31, 1998. The ratio varied in other provinces. Sichuan Province Party Secretary Xie Shijie demanded that power plants in Sichuan buy 70% of their coal from state coal mines (*CCN*, November 17, 1998).

[54] Personal interview, on July 21, 1999.

production had exceeded the demand, a remarkable achievement for an economy that was constantly baffled by coal shortages. The saturation of the coal market, however, turned against these naturally profit-seeking market players. When the central government's attempt to restructure the state key coal mines came to a halt, small coal mines became the target for closure so that market shares could be squeezed out for state key coal mines. This new policy, as discussed herein, faced tremendous problems during implementation. As a result of the dual structure of the coal industry, local bureaucrats did not share the preference of the central government. For them, small coal mines were their main sources of revenue, whereas the health of state key coal mines did not bear much on the local economies and government budgets.

To achieve its policy goals, the central government has devoted a lot of administrative resources and adopted an impressive array of policy tools to rein in disobedient bureaucrats. To date, six rounds of national campaigns have been launched to propagate the central government's policy goals and persuade local bureaucrats to share its preference. The central government has also introduced more negative incentives by increasing the frequency of inspections and elevating the severity of punishment for noncompliance. Moreover, as the monitoring became costly, the central government managed to initiate an institutional reorganization and tried to accommodate the interests of local governments.

This study of restructuring in the coal industry can shed some light on the ongoing debate about the relationship between the central government and local governments. As indicated in the policy implementation of closing down small coal mines in the latter half of the 1990s, the central government clearly still commands policy tools that can achieve its goals. Despite the many changes in Chinese politics and societies since the economic reform, national campaigns and administrative disciplines have remained a salient feature in Chinese politics. Other authors in this volume also draw similar conclusions in their studies of different policy issues. What is interesting from the research in this chapter is that, instead of imposing its preference on local governments, the central government seems to be willing and able to accommodate the latter's interests. By adjusting the governance structure, the central government tries to turn a zero-sum game into a win–win situation for both parties. In the face of challenges from rapid economic changes and development, the central government will continue to seek institutional designs that can align its own interests and those of local governments in a more smooth and productive fashion. Therefore, future research should focus on how these institutions have been chosen as a result of bargaining and how these changes shape the governance structure in China.

ACKNOWLEDGMENT

This research was supported by Smith Richardson Foundation. I thank Dali Yang for his advice and timely encouragement. I also benefited from discussions with Zhiyue Bo, Richard Carson, Mark Hansen, Yanzhong Huang, Cheng Li, Barry Naughton, Duncan Snidal, Dorothy Solinger, Susan Whiting, and Dingxin Zhao. Participants of the East Asia Workshop at the University of Chicago also contributed tremendously to this project. Finally, I also thank four anonymous reviewers for their helpful advice. Any errors are, of course, mine.

8

The Western Development Program

Barry J. Naughton

The Western Development Program has been featured prominently in government media since it was first proclaimed by President Jiang Zemin in June 1999. The program is the centerpiece of the Chinese government's effort to strengthen national unity and integration. By initiating the Western Development Program (WDP), the government of China has acknowledged the strength of the centrifugal forces tugging China apart, and it has undertaken a highly visible and symbolically important program designed to offset those forces. In a sense, the WDP is the Chinese government's response to the trends that are the main themes of this volume, and an attempt to demonstrate the government's commitment to national unity.

The first half of this chapter describes the emergence of the WDP. The concerns that led to a priority western development plan grew during the late 1980s and 1990s along with changes in the patterns of China's regional economic development, and with increasing recognition of the problem of poverty. The fiscal position of the government improved dramatically at the end of the 1990s, after the fiscal reform of 1994, and this made it possible for the government to devote substantial new resources to regional development. Thus there is a simple story at the heart of the WDP: Economic reform brought rapid growth to China's coastal regions, exacerbating regional inequality; and after the government gained adequate control of its finances, it began to make an effort to correct these regional imbalances. But the overall story of the WDP is also more complex than this, because Chinese politicians recognized in the WDP an opportunity to bundle together a number of preexisting concerns and government policies in ingenious ways. The ultimate impact of the WDP will be extremely complex because of the many different objectives and interests incorporated into the program.

The second half of the chapter shifts gears; it adopts a critical approach to the WDP, essentially trying to deconstruct the premises and policies of the program. This deconstruction begins with the geographic realities that define the western regions, arguing that the West should be divided into a Northwest and a Southwest, with very different problems, possibilities, and economic trajectories. It then proceeds to examine the legacy of past state investments in industry and infrastructure in the West. Contrary to an easy presumption, China's West has *not* suffered from neglect from the central government – quite the contrary. In addition, past experience shows clearly that economic development in the West will not be fostered by simply throwing money into an accelerated investment program. The framers of the WDP have recognized this, and they have emphasized the need for further market reforms, designed in part to bring in nonstate investment as well. Reforms are designed to substantially liberalize labor markets and increase the availability of human skills in the West. However, these policies run up against serious practical constraints, and there is reason to question the design and effectiveness of the policies.

The paper concludes with a preliminary assessment of the WDP. The WDP is an omnibus package, including many different provisions that seek to achieve different goals and please different constituencies. It is the outcome of a complex political process and, as such, naturally reflects diverse interests and objectives. However, the complexity also reflects a serious effort to adopt and combine innovative approaches and avoid mistakes of the past. Despite these efforts, there are significant dangers that the bandwagon effects associated with the WDP, and the rapid increase in spending, will end up creating significant waste and new liabilities and problems for the future. In the medium run, the incentives created for local government officials and the process of local implementation will probably determine the effectiveness of the program.

The long-term significance of the WDP probably does *not* lie in its ability to correct regional differences in economic development. In fact, it is likely to have a very modest impact on those differentials. Recent research indicates that World Trade Organization (WTO) membership will significantly worsen regional economic inequality (Li and Zhai, 2002). It is unlikely that the WDP would do anything more than modestly ameliorate the worsening of inequality caused by increased integration with the global economy. Instead, the WDP is a public demonstration of the government's concern with national unity, inequality, and poverty; one strand of an energy policy; an environmental program; and a catalyst for further measures of economic liberalization. The WDP is not a single thing, then, but a cluster of initiatives that tells us much about China's current political and economic reality.

SECTION I: THE EMERGENCE AND REALIZATION OF THE WDP

The announcement of the WDP in 1999 was not a sudden shift of policy, but rather a realignment of existing policies into a more visible and prominent policy package. Most of the elements that were to make up the WDP had been steadily gaining prominence during the 1990s, but the act of packaging discrete policies into an overall program gave those policies more impetus. As the rhetoric of western development has ratcheted up, so inevitably the concentration of policy and financial resources on western China has increased.

In one sense, the WDP represents a return to the traditional preoccupations of Chinese policy makers. For decades after 1949, China's planners pursued policies designed to achieve "regionally balanced growth," by which they meant the development of industries inland, to replace the legacy of coastal development that the People's Republic of China (PRC) inherited in 1949. The WDP simply resumes this traditional preoccupation and focuses it on twelve western provinces (including Inner Mongolia and Guangxi along with the ten provinces traditionally classified as "western"; see map, Figure 8.1). The WDP provinces are home to 358 million people, 29 percent of China's total, a quarter of whom are in Sichuan. The western focus excludes eight inland central and northeastern provinces. These nonwestern, noncoastal provinces are themselves home to 420 million people and have significant populations in poverty.

The resumption of the traditional interest in inland development stands in sharp contrast to the preferential policies for coastal provinces that prevailed through the 1980s. The 1980s were unusual in PRC history in that the traditional concern for regional "balance" evaporated, at least insofar as practical policy making was concerned. The orientation was symbolized by Deng Xiaoping's 1983 injunction to "let some people, and some regions, get rich first." It is not that China simply abandoned equality and adopted the single-minded pursuit of economic growth as the national

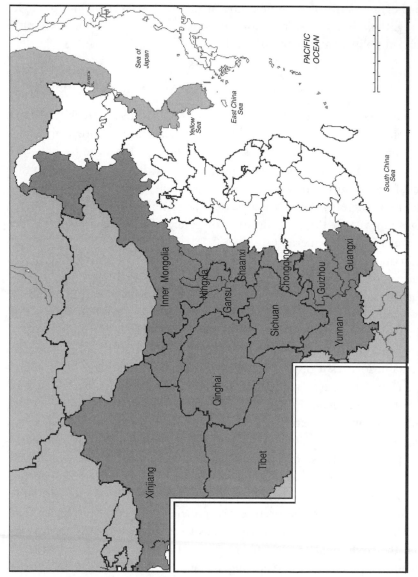

Figure 8.1. Western Development Program.

goal in the 1980s. Rather the shift in development strategy was the result of a realistic assessment of the economic situation facing China, and the need to open to the world economy. In the first place, it was by no means clear in the early 1980s that China could be competitive in the global economy: in order to participate it was necessary to build infrastructure and shift industrial investment and policy resources to coastal areas well situated for international trade. The challenge in the 1980s was for the government to fashion workable policies of economic opening, and make a credible commitment to their success. It was inevitable that coastal regions would lead the charge to internationalization, and therefore that inland regions would drop in the priority rankings.

Second, the shift in development strategy was accompanied by – and indeed was partially motivated by – a critical reassessment of past efforts at regional redistribution. Three points were essential: First, past inland investments had been extremely expensive and the resulting projects were often unsustainable. Second, the spillover effects from inland development – and especially from the massive "Third Front" Program from 1964 through 1973 – were seen to have been remarkably small (Naughton, 1988). One Chinese source described Third Front projects as "flying carpets" because they seemed to have so little economic interaction with their immediate hinterland. In theory the relatively high-income workers brought to Third Front projects should have generated demand for food and sideline products from nearby farmers, raising their incomes, but in practice this rarely happened. Finally, infrastructure and industrial plants developed inland were underutilized, whereas acute bottlenecks were emerging in the developed eastern areas (e.g., in railroads). Redistributive investment had clearly gotten too far ahead of economic activity.

Finally, interregional inequality was perceived very differently in the early 1980s than it came to be seen subsequently. Although the differential in per capita gross domestic product between the most developed coastal province (Shanghai) and the least developed inland province (Guizhou) was enormous – of the order of 13:1 – there was no clear pattern by which all inland provinces were backward and all coastal provinces advanced. Urban household incomes were fairly equal across provinces. Moreover, the first decade of economic reform eased concerns about regional inequalities. By most measures, interprovincial disparities declined during the 1980s, in part because of increased agricultural prices and rapid rural growth in the early 1980s. For a while, it seemed possible

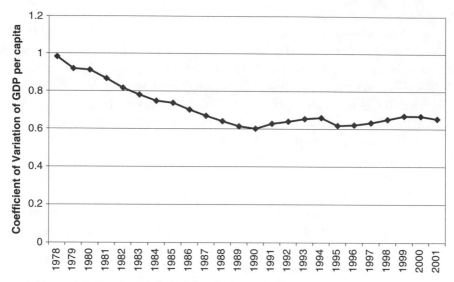

Figure 8.2. Provincial disparities: GDP per capita coefficient of variation.

to achieve greater regional equity through the reform process, without paying a price in foregone growth. Figure 8.2 shows a standard measure of interregional inequality, the coefficient of variation of provincial per capita gross domestic product (GDP). This measure declined until 1991, before stabilizing and beginning to rise again. For all these reasons, the regional distribution of growth was allowed to fade as an issue during the 1980s.[1]

Increasing Concern

The beginnings of the shift in regional policy can be traced to an increased concern with poverty during the latter part of the 1980s. Early rural reforms had initially led to rapid increases in rural incomes and an exceptionally rapid reduction in the number of people living in absolute

[1] Western development remained a national objective, but the issues were resolved by pushing western development back to a later stage of growth, after the Coast had reach a moderate level of prosperity. Even Deng Xiaoping, in 1988, called for western development, but later. This has been cited repeatedly as a legitimation and foreshadowing of the WDP (Development Research Centre, 2000, pp. 3–4.) For analysis of regional strategies and realities during the 1980s and early 90s, see Liu 1993, Naughton 1999; Tian 2000, and Yang, 1997.

poverty. However, as rural growth slowed in the second half of the 1980s, the number of people living in poverty proved stubbornly resistant to further reductions. Prompted by the World Bank and the United Nations, China began to develop an antipoverty program that could be more effectively focused on regions with a high incidence of poverty. In 1986, China began to designate certain counties as poor counties, revealing a strong presumption that poverty could be explained by geographic factors. Three main instruments were developed: budgetary grants; a subsidized loan program; and a food-for-work program of public works. Funding for this program started out strong, at 0.4 percent of GDP in 1986, but gradually fell victim to China's steadily worsening budget crisis in the late 1980s. In 1993, the government began to restore the poverty program; it increased the number of designated poor counties from 328 to 592 in that year, and it gradually restored funding to the real level of 1986. Poverty alleviation is de facto a regional policy, because 62 percent of designated poor counties are in the twelve WDP provinces. In the West, 37 percent of the rural population lives in designated poor counties, compared with 17 percent in the rest of China.[2]

Meanwhile, perceptions of regional inequality were changing. Through the 1980s, the coastal provinces had been growing more rapidly than the inland provinces, and by the end of the decade this growth had begun to align China's provinces into two opposite groups: a rich, rapidly growing coast versus a more poor, less rapidly growing inland. Overall, regional disparities were not larger than before, but the persistent regional differences could increasingly be explained as a coastal–inland gap.[2a] The renewed focus on the coastal–inland gap began to be reflected in policy pronouncements, such as the injunction to increase poverty alleviation work in central and western China that was part of the Eighth Five Year Plan for 1991–1995. However, little was actually done to change development priorities. In fact, the enormous surge of incoming foreign investment that began in 1992 lifted growth rates of the coastal provinces, and it began to increase regional disparities (see Figure 8.2). However, as we have already seen with the poverty program, concern with these issues

[2] Park, Wang, and Wu, 2002, p. 127. Funding increases roughly restored the original amounted of spending in real terms, although this amounted to 0.2% of China's much larger GDP in 1997.

[2a] The literature on China's income distribution is enormous. See, in particular Hare 1994, Khan and Riskin 1998, Knight and Song 1993, 1999 and World Bank 1997.

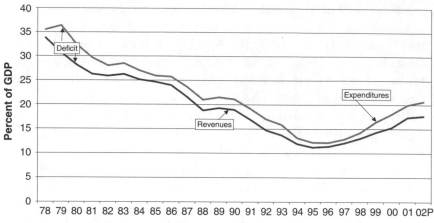

Figure 8.3. Budgetary revenues and expenditures.

in itself was insufficient if budgetary resources were not available to support the programs. The next milestone, then, was the resolution of fiscal problems that had previously hobbled attempts to generate a sustained antipoverty program.

PRECONDITION FOR THE WDP: INCREASING FISCAL CAPABILITY

The fiscal reform of January 1, 1994 was a fundamental milestone along China's economic development path. Fiscal reform halted the erosion of fiscal revenues that had been underway since 1978, and, after a two-year lag, budgetary revenues began to increase as a share of GDP (Figure 8.3). Moreover, fiscal reforms sharply increased the share of budgetary revenues initially collected by central government tax collectors. The central government itself had more to spend, and, although the bulk of expenditures continued to be made at the local level, the central government first collected and then redistributed to localities an increased share of total resources. Inevitably, this gave the center more leeway for redistribution and more influence over local government spending.

Increasing fiscal capacity intersected with an important shift in macroeconomic policy. From 1998 onward, China began to abandon its traditional aversion to fiscal deficits (Table 8.1). The external trigger was the export slowdown induced by the Asian financial crisis, beginning in 1997. Equally important was a change in domestic economic conditions. From

Table 8.1. *Budgetary Revenues, Expenditures, and Balance*

Year	Revenues %	Expenditures %	Central %	Local %	Balance %
1994	11.2	12.4	3.8	8.7	−1.2
1995	10.8	11.8	3.5	8.4	−1.0
1996	10.9	11.7	3.2	8.5	−0.8
1997	11.6	12.4	3.4	9.0	−0.8
1998	12.6	13.8	4.0	9.8	−1.2
1999	13.9	16.1	5.1	11.0	−2.1
2000	15.0	17.8	6.2	11.6	−2.8
2001	17.1	19.7	6.0	13.7	−2.6
2002p	17.4	20.4	6.2	14.2	−3.0

Note: Values are shown as a percentage of the GDP.
Source: NBS (2001), pp. 245, 246, 258; Xiang Huaicheng, "Report in 2001 Budget."

about 1996, a massive downsizing of the state enterprise sector began in China, with a dramatic rise in unemployment, including registered unemployment and "off-post" or "laid-off" (*xiagang*) workers. China experienced an adverse shock, a contraction in domestic demand that was due to state enterprise downsizing and increased unemployment – China's delayed and muted version of the transitional recession experienced in other transforming socialist economies. Chinese policy makers developed a consensus on the need to stimulate domestic demand, which was in favor of an expansionary fiscal policy. Thus, in a sense, a fiscal deficit "became available" for the WDP. Resources had to be spent to pump up the economy, and the search was on for a plausible justification for the specific policies of deficit spending. The WDP provided a political popular framework for maintaining this fiscal stimulus. Growing concerns and increasing capability soon produced a response.

THE DECLARATION OF A NATIONAL POLICY

When Jiang Zemin announced the WDP in June 1999, he set off a scramble among government planners to make the idea of a program into a reality. Although state media immediately began touting the program, it took quite a while longer to actually assemble a concrete set of projects and policies. The 1999 year-end economics and planning work conferences formally endorsed the concept; at the beginning of the year 2000, a Western Development Leadership Small Group was established, headed by Premier Zhu Rongji. The Western Development Leadership Small Group formally established its own Western Development Office in March 2000 – headed by Zeng Peiyan, concurrently Chairman of the State Development and Planning Commission – and the WDP officially began in 2000.

But now that the leaders had committed to a large-scale effort to assist the western regions, what should that effort consist of? Policy makers were under pressure to demonstrate action quickly, but at the same time they needed to give researchers time to develop a more effective overall program.[3] There were reasons for caution. China, after all, has had extensive experience with hastily proclaimed campaigns that ended up spiraling out of control, generating huge waste, and in some cases leading to disaster. Moreover, regional differentials in development are among the most intractable and difficult of all problems. International experience is full of expensive programs that achieved little: Italy's effort to reduce the gap between the North and South is most well known, but many other countries have had similar experiences. The last thing that China needed was a hasty and ill-conceived program to throw money at the western half of the country.

There was plenty of ongoing activity that the WDP Office could immediately associate with the WDP. Quickly, ten large-scale investment projects were grouped together as the WDP 2000 Big Ten. The list of projects in the top ten has not always been consistent, showing that the purpose of the list was to signal commitment, not to guide actual planning.[4] The list also signals that increased infrastructure investment has, from the beginning, been at the core of the WDP. After the initial fanfare, policy makers came up with a programmatic document, issued by

---

[3]   Western Development Program Office, "Beijing Ziliao ["Background Material"], May 8, 2002 (at www.chinawest.gov.cn/chinese/doc/XBJCSD/200205080873.htm). Feng Lun, "Fazhan Zhanlue de Zhongda Tiaozheng: Qidong Xibu Dakaifa Zhengce ["An Important Shift in Development Strategy: Starting the Western Development Program"], in City University of Hong Kong Public Management and Comparative Social Policy Center and Chinese Academy of Sciences Public Policy Research Center, eds., *Zhongguo Gonggong Zhengce Fenxi 2002* (Hong Kong: Xianggang Chengshi Daxue Chubanshe, 2002), pp. 141–2.

[4]   Compare Zeng Peiyan, *Beijing Review*, May 29, 2000, with the updated account of the ten projects on-line (at www.chinawest.gov.cn). However, perhaps the inconsistency demonstrates that such lists are no longer taken very seriously by China's planners and economists.

the State Council in October 2000.[5] The document outlined the basic principles of the WDP, including increased central funding of investment and government activity in the West; an improved investment climate; further opening of the western economy to foreign firms and to firms in the rest of China; and greater investment in education, skills, and technology. The first two strategic objectives of the WDP were to dramatically improve infrastructure and the natural environment within five to ten years, thereby preparing for a prosperous and stable West by midcentury. Specific WDP policies were to go into effect in 2001 and be valid for ten years.

As the WDP was elaborated, planners bundled into the program concerns that originated in rather different policy arenas. Some of this was sheer opportunism, stuffing into the WDP anything that involved government activity in western China. However, some of the bundling was motivated by a desire to balance against an excessive emphasis on increasing investment that would lead to wasteful expenditure. From an early stage, concerns from four different policy arenas were incorporated into the WDP: environment, energy, market reform, and minority nationalities. These concerns were outside – but not necessarily incompatible with – the core WDP agenda of fostering more rapid development in the West itself and thereby reducing regional differentials.

The first area was environment. Of course, the problems of western China and of rural poverty have always been "environmental" problems, simply because so many people live in water-short, degraded, and overpopulated locales that frequently seem to be near or beyond their carrying capacity. However, these multiple "local" environmental problems were suddenly raised into a consciousness of common national environmental problems by a series of water-related events in the late 1990s.

The first was an especially severe drought in the upper reaches of the Yellow River. It is common for the flow of water in the lower reaches of the Yellow River to be interrupted during the dry season, but concern had mounted with the increasing frequency of such interruptions. During 1997, the flow of water in the Yellow River was interrupted for a particularly

---

5   State Council, "Guowuyuan Guanyu Shishi Xibu Dakaifa Ruogan Zhengce Cuoshi de Tongzhi ["State Council Notice Promulgating 'Several Policy Measures of the Western Development Program,'"], October 2000, *Guofa [2000] No. 33* (at www.taaas.org/ NYZC/3-15.htm).

long time in its upper and middle reaches. Huge expensive dams were idled; farmers were cut off from water supplies. Moreover, the realization grew that the emerging problems were not just the result of one year's bad weather; they instead reflected a long-term trend of depleting upstream water resources following overexploitation of grass and forest land, spread of the desert, and global warming that could be depleting the reservoir of ice and snow stored in the Himalayas. Then, in 1998, devastating floods occurred on the Yangtze that were linked to deforestation around the river's upper reaches. Although the symptoms – drought versus flood – were opposite, the root cause was the same: Overexploitation that seriously degraded the environment's capacity to store water and release it in a moderate, sustainable manner. If the West is to develop, it is clear that its development must be accompanied by a reduction in overexploitation of resources and by a restoration of the vigor of grass and forest lands. Environmental needs could thus exert a claim over the investment resources coming to the western regions. This recognition was quickly bundled into the WDP outline.

The second formerly separate area was energy policy. Energy policy has traditionally been linked to regional policy in China, and western China has been seen as a supplier of hydropower and other forms of energy to the rest of China. Energy policy has taken on a new urgency since 1993, when China became a net importer of oil. Imports have grown rapidly and are projected to continue to increase. Currently, all oil import is by tanker to the coastal provinces. Since the mid-1990s, China has been attempting to diversify its sources of energy supply. Oil reserves in the West – and particularly in Xinjiang's Tarim basin – are the most promising in China, but the costs of transporting this oil to markets in eastern China are prohibitive. An improved pipeline and electricity grid would allow China to bring energy from West to East China, and perhaps even tap into gas and oil reserves in central Asian countries.

Third, policy makers were cognizant of the need to advance market reforms in West China. Traditionally, market reforms have proceeded furthest and most quickly in coastal China, because of the responsiveness of the small-scale sector (especially township and village enterprises) and the concessionary policies adopted to attract foreign investment. Enterprise reforms had lagged behind in the West, as the state sector proved resistant to change and nonstate enterprises grew less robustly. Moreover, market reforms had led to burgeoning labor markets, so workers could no longer simply be assigned to work in the West; skilled workers had to take up jobs in the West voluntarily. Solutions that would increase the human skills available in the West would have to be consistent with newly emerging labor markets. Clearly, reforms had to be accelerated in western China if that region were to successfully develop. The WDP could thus be turned into an excellent opportunity to push market reforms forward; at the same time, a WDP without a significant reform component was much more likely to deteriorate into a big spending boondoggle or, worse, a new Leap Forward.

Finally, minority policy is deeply entwined with the WDP. Minority policy clearly influenced the selection of provinces to be included in the WDP. Inner Mongolia and Guangxi are both outside the standard list of western provinces but included in the WDP, presumably because of their large minority populations. In addition, three predominantly minority prefectures in Hunan, Hubei, and Jilin – all of which are outside the WDP – are to be granted preferential policies similar to those of WDP provinces. Xinjiang, also heavily minority, is of course always Western, but it would not necessarily have been included in a needs-based development program, because it is relatively prosperous. Certainly the WDP is in part a response to the development of self-conscious ethnic identities and political movements in Tibet and Xinjiang. Justifications of the program are quite explicit:

For many years, enemy forces at home and abroad... have used the nationality and religious issues of the Western regions to carry out subversive and 'splitist' movements. In order to... defeat the plots of the enemy forces... the most important measure is to accelerate the economic development and social progress of these regions.[6]

Enhanced national unity is to be achieved both through the direct affect of knitting the nation more closely together through improved communications and transportation and by the indirect impact of improving the economic position of ethnic minorities and other dispersed and backward groups.

Thus, from an early stage, these multiple agendas and objectives were interwoven in the development of the WDP. Though initial priority is

---

[6] Western Development Program Office, "Beijing Ziliao ["Background Materials"] (at www.chinawest.gov.cn/chinese/bjzl.htm).

to infrastructure and environmental restoration, other objectives are incorporated into the program. Through much of 2000 and 2001, the WDP Office was engaged in search and research, looking for ways to elaborate a meaningful program. Development of the WDP was intertwined with the drafting of the Tenth Five Year Plan (2001–2005), and significant revisions were made in both. It was not until August 2001 that the Western Development Office came out with a more concrete and comprehensive document, the "Opinions on Implementation," which followed the outline of the October 2000 State Council document.[7] The "Opinions" primarily describe policies; a concrete description of the projects and geographic distribution of the WDP had to wait until the public release of the overall provisions for western development in the Tenth Plan, which did not occur until July 2002.[8] Along with other recent reports, these two documents can serve as the basis for analysis of the WDP.

MAIN PROVISIONS OF THE WDP

The "Opinions" document represents a great deal of thoughtful work on the meaning of a regional development program. It is unusually detailed and concrete and frequently sets specific central government commitments and policy parameters, although, as is usual in China, a considerable amount of implementation is left up to the locals. It seeks to lock in the government's general commitment to western development with a series of specific measures, and it also gives priority to western provinces in a huge range of ordinary government policies.

The document has 70 paragraphs, which are generally – but not always – grouped into sections that correspond to the main programs within the WDP. The most important sections discussed here are those that call for increased investment and central government fiscal and credit support; an improved investment environment through deregulation and

---

[7] State Council Western Development Office, "Guanyu Xibu Dakaifa Ruogan Zhengce Cuoshi to Shishi Yijian ["Opinions on Implementation of Several Policy Measures for Western Development"], August 28, 2001 (at www.chinawest.gov.cn/chinese/doc/xbzc/200112252632.htm).

[8] Western Development Office, "'Shiwu' Xibu Kaifa Zongti Guihua," July 10, 2002 (at www.chinawest.gov.cn/chinese/asp/showinfo.asp?name=200207100032);   English version, "Overall Plan of Western Region Development During the 10th Five Year Plan Period" (available at www.chinawest.gov.cn/english/asp/showinfo.asp?name=200207100002).

accelerated enterprise reforms, with both domestic private and foreign-invested firms to enjoy increased access; human capital and labor market programs; and conversion of agricultural land to forest and range.

The "Opinions" document clearly describes a major increase in the commitment of central government budgetary resources to the western provinces. This is evidence first in infrastructure investment: Funding for major infrastructure projects is to be provided primarily by the central government, with no shortfalls in financing left to be covered by local government matching funds (Section 3). Priority in approval of *new* central government infrastructure projects is to go to the West (Section 5). Even more striking is the wide range of ordinary fiscal expenditure categories for which preference is to be granted to western regions. This includes general purpose intergovernmental fiscal transfers (Section 6), special budgetary transfers to pay for increased government wages and welfare payments (Section 7), antipoverty funds (Section 8), research and development funds (Section 61), education (Section 65), and health (Section 69). In essence, the program seeks to make Chinese fiscal expenditure much more redistributive, by specifying that each of the major components of expenditure should become more redistributive.

Moreover, increased fiscal expenditure in the West is only part of the picture. The document calls for increased bank credit for western provinces, both through government development banks and commercial banks. It outlines a series of measures – extended repayment terms, expanded definition of collateral, and exemption of certain kinds of lending from bank evaluation criteria – designed to make it easier for commercial banks to lend to WDP projects (Sections 12–15). There are also a series of tax breaks associated with the WDP, including income tax reductions for foreign-invested enterprises and minority firms and expanded tax credits for research and development. The cumulative impact of these multiple commitments is likely to be large, particularly given the over ten-year time frame of the program.

How Big Is the WDP?

During the first two years of the WDP (2000–2001), more than 20 large-scale investment projects were begun in the western region, with a total budgeted investment of over 400 billion yuan, almost 5 percent of national GDP. Actual investment on new projects amounted to 130 billion yuan during the two years. These figures are difficult to interpret, though, because most of these projects had been in the pipeline already and would have been built as part of China's large ongoing investment effort anyway. Subject to that qualification, and not limiting the calculation to new projects, one can determine the rough scale of the investment effort. Estimates for investment in 2001 in the WDP include highways, 70 billion; railroads, 27 billion; and water conservancy, 14 billion.[9] Unfortunately, no separate estimate for energy-related projects was found.

However, how much of this effort represents *incremental* financial commitment made as part of the WDP? One approach is to estimate the scale of the two main elements of the WDP in 2001 that can be most directly attributed to the new policies. First, the expansionary fiscal policy described herein has been accompanied by the issuance of long-term infrastructure bonds. Central government bond-financed infrastructure in the West increased from less than 40 billion in 1998–1999, to 43 billion in 2000, and then to 60 billion in 2001 and 2002.[10] Second, according to one official estimate, all the ordinary fiscal transfers and preferential allocations through the fiscal system amounted to another 54 billion renminbi (RMB) in 2001.[11] When these two elements are put together, the total cost of the WDP in 2001 was 114 billion yuan, around 1.2 percent of the GDP.

---

[9] Western Development Office, "Xibu Diqu Jichu Sheshi Jianshe Maichu Shizhixing Bufa ["Major Steps Have been Taken in Infrastructure in the West"], April 2, 2002 (at www.chinawest.gov.cn/chinese/asp/showinfo.asp?name=200204020004). Western Development Office, "Xibu Dakaifa Zongshu Zhi'er ["General Description of Western Development, No. 2"] (at www.chinawest.gov.cn/chinese/doc/ XBGZ/200203052476.htm).

[10] "Guozhai Touzi: Ladong Jingji Gongbukemo" ["State Bonds: Indispensable Role in Powering the Economy"], *Renmin Ribao*, February 21, 2002 (at www.sdpc.gov.cn/ zt3/200202212.htm); "Guowuyuan Xibu Kaifa ban youguan Fuzeren Fantan zhiwu" ["Visiting With a Responsible Person at the State Council Western Development Office (No. 5)"] (at www.chinawest.gov.cn/chinese/doc/XBGZ/200203052471.htm); and Xiang Huaicheng, "Report on the Implementation of the Central and Local Budgets for 2001 and on the Draft Central and Local Budgets for 2002," March 6, 2002, Fifth Session of the Ninth National People's Congress. WDP projects made up a third of the total 120 billion yuan per year of bonds during 1998–2000 and over 40% of the 150 billion yuan in 2001 and 2002. In turn, infrastructure bonds financed 58% of the total 2001 deficit of 260 billion.

[11] Western Development Office, "2002 Nian Xibukaifa Gongzuo de Zhuyao Renwu he Cuoshi" ["Main Responsibilities and Measures for Western Development Work in 2002"], June 6, 2002 (at www.chinawest.gov.cn/chinese/doc/XBGZ/200206063870. htm).

These figures are subject to more than the usual uncertainty, however. In the short run, they are probably too high, because bureaucrats throughout China are hastening to reclassify things they would be doing anyway as WDP expenditures. Projects and programs that would have happened anyway are now attributed to the WDP and are not really incremental resources. However, in the long run, these figures could give a misleadingly low impression of WDP resources. As bandwagon effects kick in and more and more new expenditures are authorized on the grounds that they support the WDP, the real total cost could expand significantly. Already budgetary authorities appear inclined to approve other programs not formally part of the WDP but that appear justified by the same economic and political concerns that legitimate it. For example, the accounting of the aforementioned WDP costs explicitly includes subsidies to social security funds in the West, but no mention is made of subsidies to civil servant wages. In fact, the central government has authorized large ad hoc transfers to fill the gaps in local government wage accounts, caused by civil servant wage hikes mandated by the central government. This policy is already very expensive: at 89 billion yuan in 2001 and a budgeted 118 billion in 2002, it is already almost as costly as the entire WDP, and over 1 percent of GDP. The bulk of these payments almost certainly go to western provinces.[12] Recorded outlays in 2001 may be just the opening wedge in the commitment of resources to the West.

WDP Infrastructure Projects

At the core of the WDP is infrastructure. The infrastructure projects funded under the WDP are in a broad range of sectors – including irrigation, urban construction, and environmental restoration – but by far the largest share are transport or energy related. The transport priority is highways, and it is claimed that 20,000 kilometers of usable western highways were built in 2000–2001. There has been an attempt to strike a balance in highway construction between interregional and local construction. Important links between western and central China are included, including a new highway between Sichuan and Hunan. However, there is also a focus on extending local paved roads: 281 western county seats are scheduled

---

[12]   Xiang Huaicheng, "Report."

to be linked to the road network during 2002.[13] Transport projects also include three interprovincial rail lines, of which the most prominent and expensive is the Qinghai–Tibet link. Finally approved in 2001, 1 billion yuan was spent in the first year, and a further 5 billion is budgeted for 2002.[14]

Energy projects include five big dams (already under construction), several thermal power plants, and significant additions to the electricity grid. The WDP fits into the ongoing plan to tie together China's fragmented electricity grids: a first batch of projects to "send western electricity East" began in November 2000, and a second batch began during 2001: both batches are incorporated into the WDP. The objective is to tie western energy resources into the (mostly) eastern electricity grids at three points: South into Guangdong; the midsection from the Three Gorges Dam to Shanghai; and North from the coal mines of Shanxi and Inner Mongolia to Beijing and Tianjin.[15] However, by far the largest and most ambitious of the energy projects is the East–West gas pipeline, which will ship natural gas from the Tarim basin in Xinjiang all the way to Shanghai and the east coast. Thus, the WDP is not just a series of disconnected projects; it is rather a systematic, large-scale effort to integrate West China into national transport and energy grids.

The 4,200-kilometer East–West pipeline project exemplifies on a grand scale many of the themes of the WDP. It is a major infrastructure project

---

[13] State Development and Planning Commission, "Guojia Jiwei Zhuren Zeng Peiyan Zai Quanguo Jihua Huiyishang Tichu Yonghao Guozhai, Jixu Fahui Guozhai Touzi de Jiji Zuoyong," December 3, 2001 (at www.sdpc.gov.cn/a/news/0112031.htm). The highway projects are part of a national grid of limited access highways, five North–South and seven East–West, plus an additional eight national highways in the western provinces. Western Development Office, "Xibu Dakaifa Zongshu 2" ["General Account of Western Development Program, No. 2"], March 5, 2002 (at www.chinawest.gov.cn/chinese/doc/XBGZ/200203052476.htm). On intrastructure investment in China's regional development generally, see Démurger 2001.

[14] Western Development Office, "Overall No. 2," Xinhua, "Qingzang Tielu Jianshe Jinnian Jiang Wancheng Touzi 50 Yiyuan" ["5 billion will be spent on the Qinghai-Tibet line this year"], May 8, 2002 (at www.chinawest.gov.cn/chinese/doc/XBJCSD/200205080873.htm). The project is controversial: "Many Tibetans fear that building a railway linking the [Tibetan Autonomous Region] to the rest of the PRC will increase central control and accelerate Chinese domination and assimilation." Tibet Information Network, *China's Great Leap West* (London: Tibet Information Network, 2001), p. 44.

[15] "China to Build Three Channels for West-East Electricity Transmission," March 20, 2002 (at www.chinawest.gov.cn/english/asp/showinfo.asp?name=200203200001); Western Development Office, "Xibu Diqu Jichu Sheshi Jianshe Maichu Shizhixing Bufa" ["Major Steps Have been Taken in Infrastructure in the West"], April 2, 2002 (at www.chinawest.gov.cn/chinese/asp/showinfo.asp?name=200204020004).

of enormous cost; it is a major initiative in China's overall energy strategy; and it also represents an important step in market opening. Never before have foreign multinational corporations been allowed to participate in exploitation of oil and gas resources on the Chinese mainland (only off-shore). For the pipeline, though, three foreign firms – Shell, ExxonMobil, and Russia's Gazprom – will each take a 15 percent stake in the pipeline (China's PetroChina will hold 50 percent and Sinopec an additional 5 percent). In return, these firms will invest upstream in the exploration and production of natural gas through production-sharing contracts. The cost of the pipeline itself is estimated at 70 billion RMB, with another 70 billion estimated required for downstream distribution facilities.[16] The WDP provides a framework for investment in infrastructure that will lower transport costs and facilitate bringing western oil to the East. The international implications may extend beyond involvement of the major transnational oil companies. China has signed an agreement to develop oilfields in Kazakhstan and transport the oil by pipeline to Xinjiang. Chinese planners clearly wish to work toward a long-term option in which China might emerge at the center of a distribution grid for Central Asian oil and gas, with Korea and Japan participating as investors and consumers. In that way, all the East Asian economies would have reduced their dependence on Middle Eastern oil delivered by tanker. The WDP will facilitate a part of this grand vision.

Improving the Investment Environment

The pipeline project also exemplifies the stress throughout the WDP on improving the investment environment for both foreign and domestic firms. In part, this represents a decision that the West should take the lead in the continuing gradual privatization of the Chinese economy. Indeed, the principles for western development incorporated in the Tenth Five Year Plan include a "dramatic increase in the share of non-public enterprise in output and capital stock."[17]

---

[16] Christine Chan and Denise Tsang, "Historic Gas Deal Signed in Beijing," *South China Morning Post*, July 5, 2002; Denise Tsang and Eric Ng, "Gas Pipelines Shareholding Settled," *South China Morning Post*, July 2, 2002 (accessed on-line).

[17] Western Development Office, "'Shiwu' Xibukaia Zongti Guihua" ["Long-range Plan for Western Development in the 10th Five Year Plan"], July 10, 2002 (at www.chinawest.gov.cn/chinese/doc/XBGH/200207101669.htm).

The WDP makes explicit the policy that "domestic firms" (*neizi qiye*) are to be subject to most of the same preferential policies and permissions that are available to foreign-invested firms. The definition of domestic firms includes publicly owned firms from East China, but the emphasis is clearly on private businesses. In this respect, the WDP follows up a December, 2001 declaration by the State Development and Planning Commission that sectors open to foreign investors nationwide are to be opened to domestic private investors as well.[18] One of the most critical implementation measures is that all firms in sectors favored by (the 2000 version of) national industrial policy are to pay income tax at the rate of only 15 percent, half of the usual rate (Sections 21 and 51). There are some slight differences between the list of preferred sectors for foreign and domestic firms, but the general principle is that the government designates sectors – rather than ownership forms – and extends preferential policies to all ownership types.

There is a significant emphasis on deregulation in the "Opinions" document. Permissions required are to be reduced (and the Western Development Office web site has many news reports declaring that localities have reduced permits required by 30 percent or more). Localities are given streamlined powers to approve foreign investment, and capital requirements for foreign investment are relaxed. Foreign technicians can be awarded multiple-entry visas (Sections 5, 19, 43, and 59). Like any top-down deregulation process, these measures sometimes produce an unintentionally comic effect, leaving the reader wondering: If these restrictions hold back economic growth, why are they being left in place in other parts of the country?

Efforts to improve the investment climate also have an important sectoral component. There are a number of measures that expand access to mineral resources and that allow prospectors and exploiters of new mineral resources to include the value of the resource in the registered capital of the firms they establish. Mineral rights achieved by discovery can be amortized and bought and sold (Sections 30–34). Opening of the service sector, especially to foreign firms, is to be accelerated (Section 39). In this sense, the WDP turns China's WTO commitments upside down: In many service sectors, the WTO agreement envisages gradual liberalization

---

[18] State Development and Planning Commission, "Opinions on Encouraging and Guiding Civil Investment (*Guanyu Cujin he Yindao Minjian Touzi de Ruogan Yijian*)," December 11, 2001 (at www.sdpc.gov.cn/b/b200202061.htm).

beginning with advanced coastal cities. The WDP allows western provinces to quickly catch up with coastal provinces in allowing foreign investment in these previously closed sectors.

Grain for Green

Although it does not have a separate section, the "Opinions" document is extremely clear on the most important environmental policy, that of removing land from cultivation in order to restore natural forests and grasslands ("grain for green"). Farmers who remove grain land from cultivation are to be compensated both in state-supplied grain and in cash. Farmers in the North receive 1,500 kilograms of unhusked grain plus 300 yuan cash per hectare taken out of grain cultivation; another 750 yuan per hectare planted in grass or forest. Farmers in the South receive a 50 percent larger grain payment, but the same amount of cash. The subsidies are to continue for five to eight years, plus the farmer retains property rights over the land for fifty years. This amount of compensation is reasonable. Valuing grain at 1.4 yuan per kilogram, the program provides annual compensation of 3,000–4,000 yuan per hectare (if the land is successfully replanted), compared with a national average gross output value of around 6,700 yuan per hectare. However, this average gross output includes input costs and is on substantially better land than the marginal plots that will be taken out of production. For the program to be successful, the farmers will have to have been able to find workable alternative occupations by the end of the five- to eight-year period.

China's grain prices peaked in 1995 – along with world food prices – at a record high of 2.16 yuan per kilogram. Since that time, grain prices have been falling, and the government has tried to slow that fall with a price-support program at around 1.4 yuan per kilogram. The price-support program has been very costly and not entirely successful, and grain has piled up in government granaries.[19] The WDP represents a welcome recognition that China's objective should not be to prop up grain production at any cost. Worldwide trends are toward a low and probably declining price of grain, as genetic technologies push down food prices,

[19] Feng Lu, "Three Grain Surpluses: Evolution of China's Grain Price and Marketing Policies (1978–1999)," papers presented at the Symposium on China's Agricultural Trade and Policy: Issues, Analysis, and Global Consequences, San Francisco, CA, June 25–26, 1999.

and China's membership in the WTO will strengthen the linkage between world and domestic grain prices. The WDP represents a recognition that grain prices are likely to be low for a long time, and that there is relative surplus of grain stocks in China: The government can take advantage of the situation by ensuring that the land taken out of cultivation is marginal agricultural land that can be more socially productive as forest or grass land.

The overall scale of the program is substantial. The three provinces of Sichuan, Shaanxi, and Gansu (all WDP provinces) began pilot implementation in October 1999. Through the end of 2001, 1.24 million hectares were removed from grain production, and an additional 1.09 million hectares of forest were planted on wasteland, for a total of 2.3 million hectares. (China's total cultivated area is 130 million hectares.) The program is scheduled to accelerate, with the amount removed from cultivation jumping from under half a million hectares in 2001 to a planned 2.27 million hectares in 2002. Since 1999, the central government has paid 7.6 billion yuan for the program.[20]

Labor and Education

The WDP gives extensive attention to the fact that the West is short on human skills compared with other regions in China. Education levels are significantly lower here than in the rest of China, and the West has lost skilled workers through emigration. The WDP addresses this from the bottom up: poor and minority areas of the West are to receive central government funds to spread universal compulsory elementary education; all WDP regions are to receive generalized preferential treatment in educational allocations. Western colleges are to expand, recruit additional students, receive more money, and be aided by counterpart teams from eastern universities.

[20] "Implementation Opinions," item 10. Xinhua, "Woguo zhengfu 'yiliangshi huan sheng-tai' Quanmian Qidong Tuigeng Huanlin Gongcheng" ["The National Policy of 'Exchanging Grain for Natural Environment' Has Begun Full-Scale Implementation of the Project to Return Grainland to Forest"] (at new.sina.com.cn/c/2002-06-20/2056611824.html; Western Development Office, "Xibu Diqu Shengtai Huanjing Baohu yu Jianshe Dedao Jiaqiang" ["Protection and Construction of the Natural Environment in the West has been Strengthened"], April 2, 2002 (at www.chinawest.gov.cn/chinese/asp/showinfo.asp?name=200204020005).

In addition, much attention is paid to supporting skilled personnel in the West. Central government officials are to rotate West for temporary assignments, whereas western officials are to receive special training (in 2001, 6,000 trained domestically and 2,500 were send abroad).[21] A series of arrangements encourages Eastern professionals to come to the West for short-term employment, including second jobs, service contracts, and provisions to grant equity in start-up firms for entrepreneurial or technological contributions. Procedures are to be deregulated and liberalized. The central government will also guarantee that wage supplements in hardship posts – not the whole western region – will be paid by the central government and take total salaries of approximately national average levels.

The document recognizes that one of the keys to such an approach is to greatly liberalize controls on population movement. People will not come to the West if they are not confident they will be able to leave. More generally, accelerated development in the West requires that migration restrictions within the West be eased. The "Opinions" document says that urban residence permits will be freely available for all prefecture-level cities and below. However, for province-level cities, localities are merely told that they may liberalize urban residence permits.[22] In addition, investors and businessmen coming to West China both from abroad and from the remainder of China are to have easy access to temporary residence arrangements.

SECTION II: DECONSTRUCTING THE WDP

The WDP and Geography

Any discussion of the WDP must start with a consideration of geographic factors. All of the Western provinces have disadvantageous geographic

---

[21] Western Development Office, "2002 Nian Xibukaifa Gongzuo de Zhuyao Renwu he Cuoshi" ["Main Responsibilities and Measures for Western Development in 2002"], June 6, 2002 (at www.chinawest.gov.cn/chinese/doc/XBGZ/200206063870.htm); and "Xibu Diqu Keji Jiaoyu he Rencai Kaifa Gongzuo Lidu Jiada" ["The Effort Put Into Technical Education and Human Resource Development in the West Has Been Increased"], April 2, 2002 (at www.chinawest.gov.cn/chinese/asp/showinfo.asp?name=200204020003).

[22] "Opinions on Implementation," item 60. Cities between provincial and prefectural rank are included with provincial cities.

features. All suffer from remoteness, rugged terrain, fragmented and dispersed economic activity, and shortages of usable water. In cross-national comparisons, the importance, and intractable character, of such disadvantageous geographic endowment has recently been stressed (Gallup and Sachs, 1999). These problems are hard to address effectively because their economic implications are multidimensional. Endowments of good agricultural land are low because of water shortages, and so initial local incomes are low. Remoteness means that costs of investing in infrastructure are higher, and operation and maintenance is more expensive once it is completed. Local market potential is limited because the population is dispersed over a large area, and high transport costs limit access to both local and distant markets. Indirect effects can also be debilitating: inhabitants of remote areas are less likely to observe new products and processes they can imitate; communication and education lag behind; and absorption of new ideas is hampered.

Despite their common geographic problems, the western provinces fall into two very different groups. One group, in the West and Northwest, consists of predominantly large, arid, sparsely settled regions. Water availability is clearly an immediate, binding constraint on the development of many districts in this broad region. Five provinces clearly fit into this group – Tibet, Qinghai, Gansu, Ningxia, and Xinjiang – and all have around ten persons per square kilometer or fewer.[23] (Inner Mongolia has generally similar features but also some distinctive characteristics.) Altogether, these five provinces have a total population of 56 million, only 4.5 percent of China's total. Almost half of those are in Gansu (25 million). In the paragraphs that follow, I refer to this group of five provinces as the "Northwest."

The second group consists of the rugged, densely settled regions of the Southwest. Population densities range from 10 to 40 persons per square kilometer. Although these densities are less than those in the fertile, well-endowed regions of eastern China, they are still very high given the poorly endowed, mountainous landscape. Four provinces clearly fit into this group – Sichuan, Chongqing, Guizhou, and Yunnan – and together they hold 200 million people, almost 16 percent of China's total

---

[23] Xinjiang's geographic endowment is much superior to the others, because there are numerous "oases," ecological niches with productive potential and relatively pleasant climates. Xinjiang also has opportunities for trade with neighboring central Asian economies. Xinjiang is the only western province with a per capita GDP (slightly) above the national median.

population. I label this group of five provinces the "Southwest." (In addition, the impoverished parts of Guangxi fit into this geographical region.)[24] For simplicity, I focus on the two most clearly demarcated groups – the five-province Northwest and the four-province Southwest.

These two groups have had dramatically different development trajectories over the past twenty years. Surprisingly, the Northwest was reasonably prosperous in 1978, but the economy there has collapsed relative to the rest of China in the two decades since. The Southwest started poor and has remained poor, but it has not changed much in relative position. In 1978, the five provinces in the Northwest had an average per capita GDP equal to 97 percent of the national average (365 yuan). Qinghai, in fact, had a per capita GDP equal to that of the wealthy coastal province of Jiangsu, so that the two were tied for sixth place in the rankings. By contrast, the four provinces in the Southwest had an average per capita GDP of only 216 yuan, a mere 57 percent of the national average.[25] Since 1978, the western provinces in general have had GDP growth rates below the Chinese average. However, the northwestern provinces have – in relative terms – collapsed. They dropped from 97 percent of the national average in 1978 to only 66 percent in the 1996–99 period. The southwestern provinces have grown at rates near the national-average, which of course means that they have been unable to close the gap with national-average development levels. They have remained roughly constant at 57 percent of national averages both in 1978 and in 1996.[26]

What accounts for these differences? Data on urbanization reveal some of the answers (Column one of Table 8.2). The northwestern provinces have *higher* urbanization rates than China as a whole (urbanization is

---

[24] The other western province, Shaanxi, a populous province with 36 million, has three distinctive ecological zones: the southern counties are clearly "Southwestern," densely populated well-watered hills; the northern region is rugged and short of water, basically "Northwest," although more densely populated; and the central Wei river valley is quite well endowed and fairly highly developed.

[25] These comparisons are slightly less stark if we take the weighted average of each region. In that case, the per capita GDP in the Northwest was 92% of the national average, and the per capita GDP in the Southwest was 61% of the national average.

[26] Data are from National Bureau of Statistics 2002. The statistical relationship between provincial GDP and national GDP changes after 1996, as all provincial economies begin reporting growth rates above the national average! Correcting for this, and assuming roughly constant degrees of overstatement across provinces, we see that the southwestern GDP actually declines three or four percentage points compared with the national average in 1996–1999, whereas the northwestern GDP per capita inches up a point or two.

Table 8.2. *Composition of Labor Force*

Area	Of Total: Registered Urban (%)	Of Rural: Working Away from Home		In Private Firm or Self-Employed (%)	In TVEs (%)
		Outside Province (%)	Within Province (%)		
Northwest					
Inner	38.9	2.7	2.2	11.8	62.0
Mongolia					
Tibet	17.5	—	—	—	—
Gansu	22.4	10.1	13.2	6.7	16.2
Qinghai	28.2	3.6	5.0	3.2	13.0
Ningxia	29.1	11.9	9.6	5.3	25.5
Xinjiang	48.8	—	—	8.0	21.9
Shanxi	25.5	7.7	5.0	11.2	29.5
Southwest					
Guangxi	16.2	7.8	1.6	4.7	16.5
Chongqing	18.1	13.9	3.4	6.0	10.7
Sichuan	15.2	10.9	6.2	4.9	15.4
Guizhou	12.5	7.5	1.8	2.7	7.4
Yunnan	15.9	0.5	1.3	4.7	12.3
China	23.9	5.8	3.1	9.7	25.6

Note: Urban, private, and TVEs are for 1999; rural working away from home, 1998. Two-thirds of Inner Mongolia TVE employment is in private enterprises.
Source: Statistical Yearbook (2000), pp. 119–20; *Labor Statistics* (1999), pp. 128–31.

proxied in Table 8.2 by percentage of the provincial labor force in the formal urban sectors). Because agricultural development in the Northwest is constrained by the scarcity of water, urban centers develop based on interregional functions and appear "large" relative to their rural hinterlands. (In this respect, the Northwest is like the western United States, which, largely because of its small agricultural sector, is the most urbanized region of the United States). Back in 1978, large urban work forces were primarily in state-owned factories, and they enjoyed a wage and living standard similar to that of all other state workers, while the national government propped up the region with high levels of industrial investment and support. When government support for the state-run economy was reduced, these high-cost and uncompetitive industrial systems crumbled. By contrast, southwestern provinces have urbanization rates far below national averages. Guizhou has only 12.5 percent of its labor force in the formal urban sector, which is only half the national average. Moreover, there are significantly fewer rural workers employed locally in nonagricultural occupations (township and village enterprises, or TVEs; private businesses; or within-province migrants) in the Southwest. With large, poor agricultural populations, the average GDP in the Southwest is correspondingly low. The Southwest never had a particularly large state sector, so it did not decline in relative terms when support for the state sector was reduced.

The fundamental challenges faced by people in the Southwest are very different from those of the Northwest. In the Southwest, a dense population, overwhelmingly engaged in agriculture, is pushed by force of numbers onto steep slopes and high elevations, not well suited for human cultivation. Both groups face potential geographically given poverty traps created by overexploitation of the natural environment. In the Northwest, the most crucial issues are overgrazing of pasture land and conversion of pasture to cropland, both leading to desertification. Absolute shortages of water inhibit agricultural and industrial development projects. In the Southwest, the most crucial issue is deforestation, leading to erosion. Although the problems are similar in kind, the physical environment is quite different, and the nature of effective solutions might be different as well. It is extremely unlikely that a program of activities that was well suited to one group would also be appropriate for the other.

The collapse of the Northwest has been balanced, to a certain extent, by the rapid rise of southern and central China. Coastal provinces, of course, have grown rapidly, but so have many of the central inland provinces, including Henan and Anhui. Remarkably, the ten southern and central provinces (ranging from Henan in the North to Hainan in the South, including Guangdong but excluding the lower Yangtze) were significantly *below* the national average in 1978, with per capita GDP at only 76 percent of the national average. Twenty years later, this entire group had caught up and was equal to 102 percent of the national average. What this means is that individual provinces and entire large regions have traded places. The Northwest used to be at the national average and is now far below; the southern central area used to be well below national averages and is now at the national average. As Table 8.3 shows, there have been huge changes in relative rankings. Fujian has moved up an astonishing 17 places (out of 30) in the provincial rankings. Four of the northwestern provinces have dropped more than ten places in the rankings. In international experience,

Table 8.3. *Change in Provincial per Capita GDP Rankings*

Province	Rank in 1978	Rank in 2001	Change in Rank
Fujian	24	7	17
Zhejiang	16	4	12
Shandong	19	9	10
Henan	27	18	9
Xinjiang	*18*	*12*	*6*
Guangdong	11	5	6
Hunan	22	17	5
Hainan	20	15	5
Sichuan	*25*	*22*	*3*
Anhui	26	23	3
Yunnan	*28*	*26*	*2*
Hubei	15	13	2
Hebei	13	11	2
Inner Mongolia	*17*	*16*	*1*
Guangxi	*29*	*28*	*1*
Tianjin	3	3	0
Shanghai	1	1	0
Jiangsu	6	6	0
Guizhou	*30*	*30*	*0*
Beijing	2	2	0
Jiangxi	23	24	−1
Shaanxi	*21*	*25*	*−4*
Liaoning	4	8	−4
Heilongjiang	5	10	−5
Jilin	8	14	−6
Shanxi	12	20	−8
Ningxia	*10*	*21*	*−11*
Qinghai	*7*	*19*	*−12*
Gansu	*14*	*29*	*−15*
Xizang	*9*	*27*	*−18*

Note: WDP provinces are shown in bold italics. Chongqing is included with Sichuan.
Source: NBS (2002), pp. 20, 36. Xizang 2001 data are not yet available. Xizang's 2000 ranking has been imputed for 2001.

such large relative shifts are extremely unusual: Within the United States, for example, the rank ordering of states has been stable for a century (i.e., Connecticut at the top and Mississippi at the bottom). Two lessons may be drawn from the different experiences of the Northwest and South-west. First, China's "West" is a vast diverse area, and it is inconceivable that one set of national policies can be crafted that is appropriate to all regions. Second, the experience of the Northwest shows that economic backwardness in the West is not just the result of natural and geographic forces. Under the planned economy, the Northwest, in particular, was a beneficiary of central government investments, whereas the southern central provinces were neglected. When policies shifted to market-oriented development, the southern central provinces were much better placed both to take advantage of their initially better endowments and to leverage the opening policies that of course affected coastal provinces most positively. Critical reassessment of government policy is an ongoing need if western development is to succeed.

The WDP and Economics

The Transportation Infrastructure Legacy

The western provinces are less densely populated than those of eastern China, and their transport network is less dense as well. Overall, however, the lagging regions are not strikingly underserved by the transportation infrastructure. The twelve provinces contain 37 percent of China's national railway mileage and also 37 percent of China's paved roads, well above the 29 percent of China's population that lives there, but spread over 71 percent of China's land area. Again, there are significant differences between subregions. The Northwest (six provinces, including Inner Mongolia), with its low-density population, has a sparse transport network per surface area, but it has approximately three times as much railroad track per capita, and twice as much road per capita, as the national average. The railroad network in the Northwest is utilized at a lower intensity than the national average: freight throughput per kilometer of track is approximately two-thirds of the national average, and so freight shipped per capita is approximately twice national average. Highways, in contrast, are utilized nearly as intensively as the national average.

The Southwest has 74 percent as much railway per capita as the national average, but near-national-average highways per capita. However, the utilization of this network is lower across the board – approximately 70 percent as much freight per capita on the railroads and only 60 percent on the highways. Thus, rail freight per capita is only about half the national average, and highway freight per capita is approximately three-fourths the national average.

When regional variation is taken into account, the transport infrastructure of the lagging regions is roughly equivalent to that in eastern China.

Indeed, the integration of these regions into the national transport network was a major achievement of the development strategy followed in the 1950s through the 1970s. Of course, it is not easy to determine what the levels of transport infrastructure ought to be. We might expect economic activity in dispersed population regions to use transport more intensively than in concentrated regions, but in rugged and inaccessible regions, expectations are less certain because transport is more costly. It may be that demand for transport as a share of economic activity might be higher in rugged areas as well. However, when we keep in mind that the per capita GDP in most western provinces is less than half the national average, it is clear that transport activity per unit of economic activity is *not* comparatively low in the lagging regions. Indeed, there are many local areas where infrastructure construction has run far ahead of demand and is very lightly utilized, leading to substantial waste. Zhou (2000) discusses examples of underutilized highways in western China.

The WDP is not a program to ease transport bottlenecks; rather, it is a program to lead economic development with transport investment ahead of market demand. The historical record shows that the impact of large-scale investment in the West in advance of economic development demands is bleak. Though today's program is much better conceived than past programs, it might still turn out that transport-led economic growth will fail. Does it make sense for China to concentrate new transport investment in areas where the existing network is utilized less intensively than the national average? Wouldn't it make sense to increase the share of transport investment going to regions where the existing network is used intensively and is already close to capacity?

Industrial Ownership

Until 1978, state industry was the driving force of Chinese growth, and state industry remains important today, nowhere more so than in the West. The West produced only 11 percent of China's industrial output in 1988, but 19 percent of state-owned industrial output. State-owned industry, with all its attendant liabilities, is a larger part of the urban economy in the West than in the rest of China. Table 8.4 shows the 1998 industrial output divided into three simple ownership aggregates: state, nonstate with an output above 5 million yuan, and small-scale nonstate (output below 5 million yuan gross). The composition of industrial output differs systematically: In the West the state share is larger, but the small-scale

Table 8.4. *Composition of Industrial Output, 1998*

Province	State (%)	Nonstate Above Scale (%)	Small-Scale Sector (%)
Inner Mongolia	42	8	49
Guangxi	37	18	45
Chongqing	45	16	38
Sichuan	34	18	48
Guizhou	53	11	36
Yunnan	56	12	32
Tibet	83	17	0
Shaanxi	55	16	28
Gansu	50	11	39
Qinghai	73	9	18
Ningxia	67	13	20
Xinjiang	76	10	14
National	28	29	43
WDP	46	15	39
Non-WDP	26	30	44

Notes: Table shows percent of total output. "State" includes state-controlled joint stock corporations.
Source: Statistical Yearbook (1999), pp. 425–26.

sector is quite robust. The state sector accounts for fully 46 percent of output in the western regions, compared with only 26 percent in the eastern regions. However, small-scale output accounts for 39 percent of western output, not too far short of its 44 percent share of eastern output. The large-scale, nonstate sector is, however, much smaller in the West, accounting for only 15 percent of output, compared to 30 percent in the East. The composition of the industrial sector is much more *dualistic* in the western regions than it is in eastern China (Rozelle 1994; Tsui 1991).

The difference in industrial growth in the West, over the past twenty years, has been largely due to the slower growth of TVEs and foreign-invested firms. State-sector growth and small-scale private sector growth have both been as robust in the West as in the rest of China. We might say that the economic reform strategy that worked so well in the rest of China did not work very well in the lagging regions. In the remainder of China, liberalization of the economic system encouraged new entrants, particularly into industry. New entrants created competition and a more diverse economy, and this drove the development process. In the West, entry by large firms was much weaker, and the resulting industrial structure is much more dualistic. It is only a slight oversimplification to say that the lagging region industrial sector consists of a large state sector, and a large fringe of small-scale firms that are often private.

It is perhaps in recognition of this fact that the WDP places so much stress on attracting investment to the West from both foreign companies and from firms in eastern China. No doubt, this is seen as the easiest way to make up the missing middle in the industrial distribution in the West. Nevertheless, it will certainly be true that the bulk of the growth of middle-sized firms in the West will come from the expansion of existing and new small-scale firms. The WDP is relatively less explicit about fostering the growth of these existing small-scale, predominantly private firms. There is room here to do more.

Industrial Structure

From the 1950s through the 1970s, the Chinese government poured massive amounts of heavy industrial investment into the West, targeting sectors with strategic importance, which were also almost invariably capital and technology intensive. The legacy of past industrial investment decisions is particularly evident in the northwestern provinces. The 1995 Industrial Census reveals that the industrial output structure of these provinces is dominated by energy production and refining, ferrous and nonferrous metallurgy, and electricity. These heavy industrial sectors on average account for 23.7 percent of the national output value; in the five northwestern provinces, they account for 46.8 percent, twice as much. Development of these industries has been shaped by strategic concerns. The extensive nonferrous metallurgy sectors in Gansu and Qinghai, with their voracious demands for electricity, combined with significant energy resources in the region, explain much of the resulting structure. It should be kept in mind, however, that these provinces account for only 2.1 percent of the national industrial output.

In the Southwest, the industrial structure is less distorted by past development decisions, but it more clearly shows the imprint of economic backwardness. The food processing and products sector (including tobacco and beverages) is larger than national averages (17.3 percent of output vs. 10.7 percent nationally). It is expected that these early developing sectors would have a larger weight in southwestern output, particularly given the large rural population. More striking is the fact that light, labor-intensive manufactures are substantially underdeveloped.[27] Nationally, these account for 18.2 percent of output, but in the Southwest, only 11.3 percent. Because China's exports are strongly concentrated on labor-intensive manufactures, the lower share of these products in the Southwest is related to the low levels of foreign investment and low foreign trade intensity of these provinces.

These data once again demonstrate the different challenges faced by the Northwest and Southwest. In the Northwest, existing industrial structures severely limit the diffusion of industrial skills and opportunities. Production is capital intensive and with substantial scale economies. Partly as a result, government monopolies and barriers to entry are much more common in these sectors. Demonstration effects for new start-up businesses are weaker. Opportunities for subcontracting, imitation, and learning by doing are correspondingly fewer. Information about new products and new market opportunities is more scarce. What is most important is that the projects proposed for the Northwest are unlikely to change this picture much. Interregional gas pipelines may be justified on the grounds of national energy policy, but they will do relatively little to facilitate the development of local economies in the Northwest. Much of the development foreseen for the Northwest should in fact be seen as subordinate to national economic needs.

In the Southwest, the key problem is the development of labor-intensive manufacturing that can take advantage of the Southwest's low labor costs. In the Southwest, again, the problem is less the legacy of past development choices and more the simple fact of failed development efforts and persistent poverty. In the Southwest, a good investment climate and policies that keep the cost of doing business to a minimum are likely to be most effective in fostering industrial growth.

Labor and Migration

The emphasis in the WDP on skills and education is laudable, as is the recognition that individual choice will be the main determinant of whether skilled workers remain in or relocate to the West. But much of the emphasis in the "Opinions on Implementation" is on providing high incomes to government functionaries and technicians who work in the West. This

---

[27] Labor-intensive manufactures are defined as textiles, garments, leather products, sporting goods and other miscellaneous products, rubber products, and plastic products

is perhaps an essential strand of WDP policy, but it stands in contrast to an alternative policy emphasis on deregulation of labor markets and decontrol of population movement. Table 8.2 showed that migration is already more important to the rural population in the West than in the remainder of the country (see also West and Zhao, 1999). To be sure, deregulation and decontrol is included in the WDP, but the actual measures decreed are somewhat disappointing – opening of provincial and above-prefectural level cities to new migrants is made a matter of local discretion, rather than national policy. Migration is encouraged, but rather weakly and passively, in the program. In contrast, a more activist policy might seek to foster rural-to-urban migration and the movement of labor-intensive manufacturing from China's booming coast to the Southwest in particular.

Impact of the Fiscal System

The fiscal policy reforms of 1994 did not merely give the central government enough money to fund a WDP. They also changed the rules according to which revenues were raised and disbursed across provinces. The most fundamental principle of the fiscal reform was that tax rates should be lowered but spread more evenly across different activities and regions. As we have seen, such a policy was effective in broadening the tax base and increasing overall revenues. It did so, in part, by releasing previously high-tax manufacturing from the constraint of high and uncertain taxes. Moreover, in order to improve the incentive effect of taxes, the adopted tax-sharing formulas implied that provinces were able to retain a large share of the increase in tax revenues, once the transition to the new system was fully in place.

Inevitably these policies implied that the relative tax burden would decline in high income, previously high-tax provinces (such as Shanghai), and, in relative terms, increase in lower income, low-tax (or subsidized) provinces (such as those in the Northwest). To buffer the impact of this change, the government promised to protect the financial resources of poorer provinces, but the central government has never fully made good on its promises to the poorer provinces. Indeed, careful studies have shown that the overall impact of intergovernmental transfers within the Chinese fiscal system is *disequalizing* – net of all effects, intergovernmental transfers tend to favor more developed provinces (Wong 1997, World Bank 2002). This implies that the WDP is a highly visible, tangible compensation for the mostly invisible operation of the budgetary system. The WDP brings publicity to all the activities the central government undertakes to the benefit of the Western regions, and it draws attention away from the systemic transfers that work to the disadvantage of the West. On equity grounds, the effort to shift resources to the less developed West is commendable. But in a sense, the WDP represents an alternative to an effort to reconstruct the fiscal system more thoroughly in a way that provides more resources to less developed provinces reliably and over the long term. Such an effort would involve clear, credible, multiyear rules governing local government resources and intergovernmental transfers. Instead of undertaking this difficult – but now overdue – effort, the WDP represents a kind of ad hoc increase in resources, committed to the West somewhat in the spirit of an old-fashioned development campaign. Such a campaign is clearly less desirable than a thorough restructuring of the budgetary system, and it defers many budgetary problems for resolution in the future.

The WDP can partially compensate for the systemic effects of the existing Chinese fiscal system, but it does so at some cost. The "Opinions" document describes a number of areas where central government allocations will guarantee completion of certain tasks and cover shortfalls in local government spending. By their nature, such policies create perverse incentives. Local governments that fail to cover wages and pensions can reasonably expect to be bailed out. Expectations are reinforced if local officials are in western China or in other poor rural areas. Over the long run, these perverse incentives will erode the predictability and authoritativeness of central government budget policy.

The WDP and Politics

The WDP is a highly visible, symbolically charged policy that sends messages to political audiences about the leadership's commitment to national unity, to economic fairness, and to healthy and sustainable long-term development. The program clearly has resonance with the Chinese public, even among those who are cynical about the Chinese government and about the economic prospects of the program. The "winners" in China's reform process – concentrated in the booming coastal cities – seem willing to support a program that benefits areas that have missed out on some or all of the benefits, as long as the cost does not become excessive.

Moreover, the bundling of agendas implies that the WDP has some policy component that appeals to just about everyone.

But another side of the WDP is of equal or perhaps greater importance. The WDP is an enormous opportunity to distribute particularistic benefits to a network of political clients. Since 1995, Chinese fiscal capacity has expended steadily, and the WDP represents one of the ways in which that expansion in state spending capacity is being spread through the political system. All the major central government ministries are represented in the WDP Leadership Small Group, and all of them have set up Western Development offices or sections, designed to increase their spending and operation in the West. Existing interests are nearly all being given a stake in the WDP. One telling example of this buy-in comes in the way that stepped-up technology and renovation investments were allocated in 2001. A peculiarity of the relatively primitive Chinese fiscal system is that budgetary spending is divided into four macrochannels, controlled respectively by the Ministry of Finance, the Science and Technology Ministry, the State Planning and Development Commission (SDPC), and the State Economics and Trade Commission (SETC). Each one of these has a separate fund to channel specialized investments to the western regions.[28] To a remarkable extent, virtually every existing institution gets a cut of WDP largesse.

It is not accidental that the WDP was ramped up in 2002, which was an "election year" in the Chinese political system. The 16th Communist Party Congress, in the fall of 2002, determined the configuration of China's new leadership. The WDP is part of a sustained effort by the existing leadership – dominated by Jiang Zemin as Party Secretary and Zhu Rongji as Premier – to buy support, ensure stability, and discourage challenges to their leadership and transition strategy. All the top leaders are linked to the WDP – Jiang is hailed as the visionary and creator, whereas Zhu Rongji heads the Leadership Small Group. Wen Jiabao, Zhu's successor as Premier, plays an important role in the Leadership Small Group. Zeng Peiyan, head of the Planning Commission and a close associate of Jiang Zemin, headed the office that staffed the actual work, and he became Vice Premier in 2003. The WDP is clearly part of the effort by the Jiang–Zhu leadership to solidify their legacy and ensure a smooth transition.

---

[28] Western Development Office, "2002 Nian Xibukaifa Gongzuo de Zhuyao Renwu he Cuoshi," June 6, 2002 (at www.chinawest.gov.cn/chinese/doc/XBGZ/200206063870.htm).

SECTION III: EVALUATION – WHAT DIFFERENCE
WILL THE WDP MAKE?

How successful is the WDP likely to be over its more than ten-year life span? The preceding discussion has made clear that the WDP serves multiple objectives and multiple constituencies. It will not be surprising, therefore, to find that the WDP is not the optimal solution to any one of the problems it addresses. On the contrary, the WDP is full of contradictions and compromises, and some of its more ambitious goals will not be attained. The WDP is a hybrid beast, the offspring of a complex political system in which many interests and opinions can claim a voice. It would be unreasonable to evaluate it by any single criterion.

At the same time, the very complexity of the WDP should be seen as a serious effort to avoid past mistakes, to blend competing objectives in order to end up with reasonable and balanced policies. Increased government investment is the core content of the WDP, but other principles have been introduced in tandem with increased investment in order to guard against past problems with "big pushes" and "leaps forward," trying to ensure a market-conforming investment surge. Government investment is confined primarily to infrastructure, with only a few noninfrastructure industrial projects on central government lists, such as a potassium fertilizer mine in Qinghai. The emphasis on infrastructure goes along with a more limited and clearly defined role for government than had been traditional in PRC policy. A government-created infrastructure may facilitate activities – including service development and even emigration from lagging regions – that improve local well-being without increasing the government role.

How much will the WDP do to reduce regional income gaps and fight poverty in the West? First, it is important to emphasize that many of the specific projects and programs of the WDP are really directed at national – rather than regional – goals. This is most obviously true of the big energy projects, which are designed to ensure diverse and stable energy supplies to (primarily) eastern China. However, it is also true of the main environmental initiative, exchanging grain for green. The benefits to that program, if it is carried out well, will accrue to the whole country, not specifically to the western regions. Indeed, individual farmers who surrender their grain land, even for orchards and other economically productive uses, will exchange a low but certain return for an uncertain and potentially difficult future. None of the really big, signature projects of the WDP is likely to significantly benefit the West, compared with China as a whole.

At the opposite extreme to these big-ticket items is the ongoing Poverty Alleviation Program (PAP), which relates to the origins of the WDP. The largest of the three main parts of the PAP, the subsidized loan program, was initially focused on lending directly to agricultural households. After 1989, guidelines were relaxed to permit more lending to nonagricultural projects, including township and villages enterprises. During the 1991–1995 period, 56 percent of subsidized loans went to industrial projects, and 35 percent went to agriculture.[29] This gradual shift in the orientation of the PAP may reflect institutional pressures, and it relates to the criticism to which the PAP has frequently been subject. Many of the criticisms are related to the fact that the program targets poor counties, rather than poor households. The majority of households in designated counties are not poor, and many poor people do not live in designated counties. Funds are channeled through county governments, which has swelled administrative expenses and led to diversion of funds. Incentives of government officials are not fully aligned with the objectives of the PAP. Officials have very strong incentives to support the development of TVEs. The marginal tax rate on TVEs is much higher than that on agricultural households. Moreover, local officials undergo professional evaluation in which TVE output, TVE profit and budgetary revenue collection, and their rates of increase count as major success indicators. As a result, local officials have strong incentives to direct funds toward industrial projects, even if those may not make the greatest contribution to growth or poverty alleviation.[30]

Despite these criticisms, the few attempts made to rigorously evaluate the impact of the PAP have generally been positive. Three rigorous independent studies have found that the PAP made a moderate but positive and significant difference to economic growth in the designated counties. There was some evidence of declining success in later years, a finding

---

[29] Rozelle et al., 1998; Park, Wang, and Wu, 2001; "Xibu Dinghui Zouchu Pinkun" ["The West Will Certainly be Able to Eliminate Poverty"], *Jingji Ribao*, August 17, 2001 (at www.sdpc.gov.cn/e/e200108172.htm).

[30] For critiques, see Ah, 1994 and Riskin, 1994. More generally, see Morduch, 2000. Riskin, working with the earlier smaller group of 328, found that only 37 percent of poor households were in designated counties. "Xibu Dinghui" (see previous note) asserts that 57 percent of impoverished households live in the 592 currently designated poor counties. On incentives of local officials, see Chapter 3 of this volume and Whiting, 2001.

that might be related to the shift of focus in the subsidized loan program from agricultural households to industrial enterprises.[31] The WDP will complement the existing PAP in a number of ways. First, it will provide central government subsidies to expand universal elementary education in western designated counties. Second, it will accelerate the construction of the local infrastructure, especially the local road network (including those built through food-for-work programs). Finally, an interesting emphasis has been placed on the program of "restructuring" that is included in the WDP. A large effort is to be made to foster "agriculture with local characteristics," meaning specialized products, suited to local conditions, that can be sold to distant markets in China or abroad. Examples include high-quality fruits in Northwest China's oases, flowers in Yunnan, and traditional medicinal herbs. These efforts depend on an improved infrastructure, and they may make a significant difference for a few selected agricultural areas.

The single factor most likely to reduce poverty in the West is outmigration. Already, migrants from Sichuan, Guizhou, and Shaanxi receive higher incomes in coastal jobs, and they remit tens of billions of yuan home every year. As Table 8.2 showed, interregional (including cross-county, within-province) migration is relatively more prominent in the West than elsewhere. The policies of the WDP are generally sympathetic to emigration: local road construction is sometimes justified as "providing a road out." However, actual implementation of promigration policies falls somewhat short. There are currently many barriers to migration, and the WDP makes a rather lukewarm effort to relax restrictions on moving to smaller cities in the West itself. Clearly, a much broader liberalization of population controls – and one that extended to migrant destinations in East China as well – would make an important contribution to poverty alleviation in the West.

The complex situation described previously by deconstructing the WDP reveals what we might call the paradox of the WDP. Those resources that the government could directly provide to the western regions are in fact already fairly abundantly provided; the resources that the West lacks are precisely those that the government is unable to provide directly. As we have seen, when we examine the West's endowment of productive

[31] Ravallion and Jalan 1999; Park et al., 2002; and Rozelle et al., 1998.

resources, we find that the West is reasonably well supplied with infrastructure – especially transportation infrastructure – and still has a relatively large state-owned industrial sector. Nor is money lacking: A comprehensive study of China's financial institutions revealed that western provinces have much more money available to lend, compared with their deposit base, than do other regions of the country.[32] In a few cases, stepped-up investment in infrastructure that can lead to expanded private activity will be effective in accelerating western growth; in other cases, however, increased investment in low-productivity publicly managed assets will simply be wasted.

How would the WDP fail? Note at the outset that the WDP is a campaign-style program that is implicitly an alternative to a more systemic approach. For example, the WDP provides more budgetary resources to local governments in the West, but it does so without carrying out more systematic restructuring of the fiscal system. As a result, it tends to resolve resource problems but does not resolve incentive problems. Indeed, the WDP may make incentive problems worse. Local governments in the West have much stronger incentives now to plead poverty and to divert existing funds into non-WDP programs (so that the need for central government support to carry out the WDP becomes more obvious). There are very few formulas or clear regulations to divide funds and responsibilities under the WDP. Incentive problems may also worsen in the financial system. As the government urges policy banks and commercial banks to loan to the West, it provides implicit guarantees on these projects, and many of these projects will turn out to be low return. This will undermine China's push toward commercial criteria and strict accountability in the banking system.

Moreover, the WDP is most likely to fail if the patronage nature of the program becomes predominant. Local governments will sign on to the program as they see potential benefits. Resources will tend to be scattered in projects that are below economic scale. In the early phases, the main investments are huge, national projects that have been in the pipeline for years, but as more new projects come on stream, we can expect to see a diversification of projects and a trend toward smaller sizes. Local governments may be attached to their own industrial projects

[32] Park and Sehrt, 2000. See also Brandt, Giles and Park 1997.

(including TVEs) that generate tax revenues and jobs, even when they are not competitive and profitable. The more the WDP degenerates into a pure patronage-type program, the greater is the danger that the scope of the program will become inflated. If local governments enthusiastically promote their own projects, the total government commitment to the program may snowball. In this scenario, we would see a bigger, bloated, and more dispersed WDP, one that brought few benefits to the most needy areas. Paradoxically, it would also be a WDP that was less successful in concentrating resources in productive agglomerations, or growth poles, that could help pull the region out of poverty.

If the Chinese government is successful in restraining these negative aspects of the WDP, it could provide some significant benefits. The WDP will succeed in tying the West into rapidly expanding communication, transport, and energy grids (Naughton 2003). It will increase coverage of forest and grassland in some proportion of the acreage covered by the Grain for Green Program. It will contribute to an ongoing liberalization and deregulation that will ameliorate some of the disadvantages of the western regions. And certainly, in many local areas, the impact of local road construction, support for entrepreneurship, increased financial resources, and new business opportunities will accelerate local economic growth. Whether these success stories will be cumulatively sufficient to overcome some of the negative characteristics of the WDP remains to be seen. It is extremely unlikely, though, that after ten years of the WDP, we will see a reduced gap between East and West in China. The disadvantages of the West are too deeply rooted, and too many of the programs of the WDP are not really designed to foster western growth. Moreover, the overwhelming economic advantages of China's East are already being intensified by China's WTO membership (Li and Zhai 2002). The WDP will play itself out in a complex institutional environment, as a variety of actors try to reach multiple and, on occasion, conflicting, goals. Those goals will be symbolic and political, as well as economic.

REFERENCES

Ah, Xiang. "How Peculiar! Some People Cheer for Poverty," *Kaifachu Daokan*, 9 (1994), pp. 56–60.
Brandt, Loren, John Giles, and Albert Park. *Giving Credit Where Credit Is Due: The Changing Role of Rural Financial Institutions in China* (Toronto: University of Toronto, 1997).

Démurger, Sylvie, "Infrastructure Development and Economic Growth: An Explanation for Regional Disparities in China?," *Journal of Comparative Economics*, 29 (2001), pp. 95–117.

Development Research Center, State Council. *Xibu Dakaifa Zhinan [Guide to the Development of the West]* (Beijing: Zhongguo Shehui).

Gallup, John Luke, and Jeffrey Sachs, "Geography and Economic Growth," *Annual World Bank Conference on Development Economics* (Washington, DC: World Bank, 1999).

Hare, Denise, "Rural Nonagricultural Activities and Their Impact on the Distribution of Income: Evidence from Farm Households in Southern China," *China Economic Review*, 41 (1994), pp. 59–82.

Khan, Azizur, and Carl Riskin, "Income and Inequality in China: Composition, Distribution and Growth of Household Income, 1988 to 1995," *China Quarterly*, 154 (1998), pp. 221–51.

Knight, John, and Lina Song, "The Spatial Contribution to Income Inequality in Rural China," *Cambridge Journal of Economics*, 17 (1993), pp. 195–213.

Knight, John, and Lina Song, *The Rural-Urban Divide: Economic Disparities and Interactions in China* (Oxford: Oxford University Press, 1999).

Li, Shantong, and Zhai, Fan, "China's WTO Accession and Implications for Its Regional Economies," *Economie International*, 92 (2002), p. 4.

Liu, Jiang, *Zhongguo Xibu Diqu Kaifa Nianjian [Yearbook of China's Western Region Development]* (Beijing: Gaige).

Morduch, Jonathan, "Reforming Poverty Alleviation Policies," in Anne Krueger, ed., *Economic Policy Reform: The Second Stage* (Chicago: University of Chicago Press, 2000), pp. 342–389.

Naughton, Barry, "The Third Front: Defense Industrialization in the Chinese Interior," *The China Quarterly*, 115 (1988), pp. 351–86.

Naughton, Barry, "Causes et Consequences des Disparites dans la Croissance Economique des Provinces Chinoises," *Revue d'economie du developpement*, 1–2 (1999), pp. 33–70.

Naughton, Barry, "How Much Can Regional Integration do to Unify China's Markets?", in Nicholas Hope, Dennis Yang and Mu Yang Li eds., *How Far Across the River? Chinese Policy Reform at the Millennium Completing China's Transition to the Market* (Stanford, CA: Stanford University Press, 2003).

National Bureau of Statistics, *Zhongguo Tongji Nianjian* (Beijing: Zhongguo Tongji, 2002.

Park, Albert, and Kaja Sehrt, *Tests of Financial Intermediation and Banking Reform in China* (Ann Arbor, MI: University of Michigan, 2000).

Park, Albert, Sangui Wang, and Guobao Wu, "Regional Poverty Targeting in China," *Journal of Public Economics*, Vol. 86 Issue 1, (2002), pp. 123–153.

Ravallion, Martin, and Jyotsna Jalan, "China's Lagging Poor Areas," *American Economic Review*, 89 (1999), pp. 301–5.

Riskin, Carl, "Chinese Rural Poverty: Marginalized or Dispersed?" *American Economic Review* 84: 2 (1994), pp. 281–84.

Rozelle, Scott, "Rural Industrialization and Increasing Inequality: Emerging Patterns in China's Reforming Economy," *Journal of Comparative Economics*, 1 (1994), pp. 362–91.

Rozelle, Scott, Albert Park, Vince Benziger, and Changqing Ren, "Targeted Poverty Investments and Economic Growth in China," *World Development*, Vol. 26, No. 12 (1998), pp. 2137–51.

State Council, *Zhongguo Xibu Dakaifa Tongyi Zhengce Chutai [Unified Policies Released for China's Western Development]* (Beijing: Huashengbao, 2000).

Tian, Qiushang, "Basic Constraints and Appropriate Countermeasures for Economic Development in China's Western Regions [in Chinese]," *Gaige*, 2 (2000), pp. 73–7.

Tsui, Kai-Yuen, "China's Regional Inequality, 1952–1985," *Journal of Comparative Economics*, 15 (1991), pp. 1–21.

West, Lorraine, and Yaohui Zhao, eds., *The Flow of Rural Labor in China* (Berkeley, CA: University of California Press, 1999).

Whiting, Susan. *Power and Wealth in Rural China: The Political Economy of Institutional Change*. (New York: Cambridge University Press, 2001).

Wong, Christine, ed., *Financing Local Government in the People's Republic of China* (New York: Oxford University Press, 1997).

World Bank, *Sharing Rising Incomes: Disparities in China* (Washington, DC: World Bank, 1997).

World Bank, *China: National Development and Sub-National Finance*. (Washington, DC: World Bank, 2002).

Yang, Dali, *Beyond Beijing: Liberalization and the Regions in China* (New York: Routledge, 1997).

Zhou, Minliang, "Changes in the Chinese Regional Economic Structure and Western Development [in Chinese]," *Gaige*, 3 (2000), pp. 51–7.

Index

administrative systems, 8
  bureaucratization, 81
  cadres and. *See* cadre system
  centralized. *See* centralized government
  elites and. *See* elites, system of
  hierarchies and, 11, 13, 71–73
  institutionalization of, 14
  national unity and, 11
  personnel systems and. *See* personnel
    systems
  vertical, 17
  See also specific organizations
agriculture, 108–109
  arable acreage, 163
  dams, 264
  drought vs. flood, 264
  famines and, 194
  farmers, 149, 151
  food processing, 284
  grain, 273, 289–290
  grasslands, 273
  Three Gorges Dam, 270
  See also environment
Anti-Japanese War, 34
Asian financial crisis, 4, 17, 149
  fiscal policies and, 260–261
  Guangzhou and, 153, 166, 177–178
  regulation/supervision and, 129–130
  Shenyang and, 153, 166
autocracy, 8
avoidance rule, 15
  interest-conflicts and, 84–85
  origins of, 49
  provincial heads and, 62
  reform era and, 49–50

bandwagoners, 86
banking system, 17, 126–127, 267
bureaucratism, 81
Burns, J., 52–53

cadre system, 81, 101, 116
  appointment/promotion in, 82
  cadres, defined, 109
  Central Committees and, 102–103
  evaluation for, 101–103, 106
  exchange regulations, 62
  experimental basis for, 102–103
  Interim Regulations, 77–78
  local level and, 106
  movement within, 85
  Organization Department, 104
  performance criteria for, 106
  policy implementation and, 112
  principle-agent theory, 101
  reform of, 102
  Shanghai and, 106
Cantonese separatists, 65
Cao Jianming, 41
Cao Zhi, 51–52
CCA. *See* China Consumer's Association
Central Committees, 31–32, 38, 75
  evaluation system for, 102–103
  Organization Department, 51
  quota for, 59
  representation in, 36–38, 59
  Shanghai Gang and, 45
Chen Liangyu, 34–35
Chen Xitong, 97
Chen Zhili, 40, 59, 66–67
Cheng Li, ix, 11–13

Cheung, Peter T.Y., 86
China Construction Bank, 133
China Consumer's Association (CCA), 142
China Deconstructs (Goodman and Segal), 3
China Directory, 55
China Securities Regulatory Commission (CSRC), 132, 134
China-threat literature, 7
Chinese Communist Party (CCP)
  autocratic nature of, 8
  cadre management, 99, 116. *See* cadre system
  Central Committees. *See* Central Committees
  Central Party School, 62, 68
  changes in, 25
  checks/balances and, 15, 62
  Constitution of, 75
  control of, 83
  decentralization and, 99. *See* decentralization
  democratization and, 24. *See* democratization
  dominance by, 15, 99
  durability of, 101, 116
  economic reform and, 10
  elections and, 15–16
  favoritism and, 31
  15th Congress, 32, 77, 149–150, 156, 158, 160, 165, 171, 180
  hierarchical systems and, 11, 13, 71–73
  institutionalization of, 70, 99. *See* institutionalization
  leaders of, 39
  Mao era, 39. *See also* Mao Zedong
  mass line, 218–219
  national unity and, 23
  nepotism and, 31
  nomenklatura, 12
  Organization Department of, 40, 51, 59, 62, 71–73, 75, 83, 104
  origins of, 39
  paradox of rule, 101
  party goals, 16
  People's Congresses, 13–14, 73–74, 76, 81
  personnel appointments, 10, 51, 76
  Politburo, 33, 38
  political commitment in, 117
  principal-agent models, 7–8
  Propaganda Department, 40–41
  Secretariat of, 33
  16th Party Congress, 288
  tongxiang and, 30
  trends during 1990s, 8
  See specific groups, policies, persons
Chinese Communist Youth League, 45
Chinese People's Political Consultative Conference (CPPCC), 98
coal industry, 226
  decentralization and, 250
  diversification program, 236
  four modernizations and, 231
  industrialization and, 231, 248
  inspection and, 246–247
  land reform and, 250
  Law of Coal, 237
  liberalization and, 235
  Ministry of, 238
  oil crisis and, 231
  peasant workers and, 240
  safety and, 138
  shortages and, 232–233
coastal regions, 257, 279, 287–288. *See also* Western Development Program
coercion, state, 193
collectives
  decollectivization and, 215–216
  leadership of, 69, 110
  rural, 215–216
conservatism, 86
Constitution, of PRC, 72, 85
corruption, 97–98, 129–130
CPPCC. *See* Chinese People's Political Consultative Conference
credentials, revolution of, 34
CSRC. *See* China Securities Regulatory Commission
Cultural Revolution, 104, 195

Dali Yang, i, x, 15, 17, 19
decentralization, 1
  authoritative state and, 1–2
  banking system and, 126–127
  CCP and, 99
  coal industry and, 250
  disintegration thesis and, 3
  excessive, 1–2
  incentives for, 121
  political tensions and, 35

Soviet Union and, 9
  tax policies and, 125
decision-making procedures, 81
democratization, 14, 24, 79
  media and, 79–80
  reforms and, 8, 13
  Tiananmen crisis and, 1–2, 121
Deng Xiaoping
  economic liberalization and, 255–257
  elite-management system, 71
  Jiang and, 29. *See also* Jiang Zemin
  political reform and, 13, 69
  population growth and, 196
  post-Deng era and, 77, 130
direct foreign investment, 150, 162, 264,
  271, 285
disintegration/fragmentation thesis, 2–7
Du Qinglin, 63

East-West pipeline, 270–271
Eastern provinces, 68
economics, 229
  agricultural output, 108
  Asian financial crisis. *See* Asian financial
    crisis
  balanced growth, 255
  banking, 17, 126–127, 267
  coal. *See* coal industry
  competitiveness, 152, 167
  domestic firms, 272
  financial system, 17, 126–127. *See also*
    banking
  fiscal system, 122, 286
  foreign exchange reserve, 129
  foreign investment, 150, 162, 264, 271,
    285
  GDP, 160, 258, 280, 282
  global economy, 151, 162, 257
  IMF and, 4
  industrial output, 106, 110, 113, 160,
    283–284. *See also* industries
  institutions and, 8
  Keynesian theory, 153, 167, 171, 175, 190
  labor markets. *See* labor markets
  liberalization, 1, 142, 235–236, 283–284
  marketization, 149
  multinational corporations, 226
  municipal economies, 160
  Party and, 10
  performance and, 111

price stability, 122, 129
  protectionism, 121, 135–136
  rebuilding and, 120
  reforms, 10, 86, 129, 229, 253, 264
  regional, 150, 255
  rent-seeking and, 117, 240
  stabilization and, 122
  sunset industries, 171
  textiles sector, 180–181
  WDP and, 21, 253, 264, 272
  See also specific organizations, topics
education
  birth control and, 211
  cadre-evaluation system and, 108
  provincial leadership requirements and,
    82
  skilled labor and, 274
Eggertsson, S., 112–113
elites, system of
  candidates for, 81–82, 84
  demotion procedures, 98
  disciplinary problems, 40
  geographical distribution, 68–69
  institutionalization of, 70, 77, 83–84, 99
  Jiang era, 29
  localism and, 53
  mobility and, 83
  no-permits policies, 82–83
  nomination process, 78
  promotion and, 53, 68
  recruitment of, 29, 68
energy
  coal. *See* coal industry
  consumption of, 230
  electrical, 270, 284
  global comparisons, 230
  industrialization and, 231
  oil, 229–231, 264, 270–271
  projects for, 270
  resources. *See* natural resources
  supply of, 229–230
  thermal, 270
  WDP and, 264
  See also environment
environment, 17, 263
  deforestation, 264
  desertification, 279
  forests, 273
  protection of, 139
  WDP and, 264

factionalism, 12
favoritism, 12, 29, 31, 53, 67–68
federalist system, 10, 123
fiscal contracting system, 114
Foucault, Michel, 203, 211
Four modernizations, 231
Fourth Generation leaders, 25
Fubing Su, x, 20

gaming, of system, 112–113
geography, of provinces, 276
globalization, 151, 162, 257
Goldstone, Jack, 3–4
Gong Xueping, 46
grass-roots leadership, 63
grass-roots organizations, 214
Guangdong province
    Central Committees and, 38, 59, 68
    International Trust & Investment Corp.,
        131–133
    labor markets and, 164
    officials from, 39
    outside leadership and, 53
    performance criteria and, 24–25
    separatist movement and, 65
    unemployment in, 178
Guangzhou municipality, 19, 157–158, 168,
    180
    Asian crisis and, 153, 166, 177–178
    exports from, 162
    foreign enterprises and, 177
    imports to, 162
    international competition and, 166
    marketist bias in, 177
    reemployment, 168–169
    Shenyang and, 159–160
    surplus rural labor, 185
    Thatcherism and, 176
    unemployment in, 159, 163,
        168–170
    Wuhan and, 174–175
Guizhou province, 250

Han Zheng, 57, 59
Han Zhubin, 40
He Guoqiang, 33–35
hierarchical systems
    adaptation of, 8, 22
    congressional system and, 72
    measurement of, 10

national unity and, 11
    political institutions and, 71
horizontal/vertical dimensions, 8–9, 17,
    124–126, 138–139, 141
Hu Angang, 59–61
Hu Jintao, 25, 29, 34
Hu Yaobang, 13, 231
Hua Guofeng, 102, 121
Huang Huahua, 34–35
Huang Ju, 33–35, 40
Huang Liman, 66
Hubei province, 39, 164
Hui Liangyu, 33
Hunan province, 39

identification cards, 179
incentive systems, 9
    decentralization and, 121
    high-powered, 109
    property rights and, 238
Indonesia, 4
industries
    coal industry. *See* coal industry
    composition of, 283
    economics and. *See* economics
    energy supply for, 231
    industrialization process, 120, 231
    liberalization and, 283–284
    output of, 283
    ownership of, 282
    policies for, 234
    profits from, 106, 111, 114
    restructuring of, 226
    state-ownership of, 282
    structure of, 284
    See also specific groups, topics
institutionalization, 8, 14, 31, 71, 201
    administrative systems, 14
    Chinese Communist Party, 70
    Deng Xiaoping and, 71
    elite-management. *See*
        elite-management systems
    hierarchical systems and, 71
    horizontal/vertical dimensions, 8–9, 17,
        124–126, 138–139, 141
    ideology and, 71
    institutional restraints, 29
    Jiang Zemin and, 71
    localism and, 29
    Mao Zedong and, 71

intellectual property rights, 17
Islam, 205
Italy, 262

Jia Qinglin, 32–35
Jiading county, 107, 118
Jiang Zemin, 12, 16, 25, 39–40,
    77, 121, 220, 226–227, 253, 261,
    288
  Deng Xiaoping and, 29, 40
  elite recruitment and, 30
  era of, 29, 35–38, 69
  institutionalization and, 71
  promotions by, 41
  WDP and, 288
Jiangsu province, 35–38, 40, 68
judicial systems, 71–72

Kenichi Ohmae, 3

labor markets, 19, 274
  building of, 186
  central policy toward, 154
  deregulation of, 286
  employment and, 152
  Food-for-Work programs, 259, 291
  formation of, 155
  labor force composition, 278
  migration. *See* migration
  policies for, 19
  productivity and, 152
  Reemployment Project, 155–156,
      168–169, 171–172
  rural workers, 154–155, 164
  urban workers, 154–155
land reform, 250
leadership. *See* provincial leaders
Leninism, 81
Li Changchun, 33, 52–53
Li Cheng, 12–13
Li Keqiang, 35
Li Lanqing, 39–40
Li Yuanchao, 35, 45, 57
Liaoning province, 162–164, 172,
    181
Liaowang journal, 52
Lindblom, Charles, 22
Liu Changgui, 250
Liu Qi, 34–35
Liu Yunshan, 33

localism, 15, 49–50, 68
  avoidance rule and, 49
  central domination and, 31
  defined, 29
  elite promotion and, 53
  favoritism/nepotism and, 53
  hometowns and, 84
  institutional restraints, 29
  inter-provincial transfers, 90
  non-native leaders, 52
  political, 29
  provincial leaders, 35
  restraint on, 34, 53
  Shanghai Gang and, 30–31
  WDP and, 21
Long March, 34
Lu Zhangong, 57

Mao Zedong, 39, 69, 71, 81, 197
Marxism, 81
mechanization, 120
media
  democracy and, 79–80
  Ministry of Communications, 138
  propaganda and, 40–41
Meng Jianzhu, 45
Meng Xuenong, 35, 59
metallurgy, 284
migration, 164, 285
  peasants and, 151–152, 176
  poverty and, 291
  restrictions on, 275
  rural-to-urban migration, 19
  WDP and, 286
military, 71–72
Ming Xia, 74
minority populations, 57, 212, 265
mishu system, 45, 67–68
moral hazard, 112–113

national government, 120
  administrative system and, 11
  checks and balances within, 72
  Communist Party and, 23
  decentralization and, 1, 15, 31
  nomenklatura system and, 9
  rebuilding and, 7
  regional autonomy and, 31
  stepped-up, 17
  WDP and, 21

National People's Congress, 13–14, 30, 38–39, 73, 76, 81
  chairmanship of, 76–77
  favoritism/nepotism and, 31
  15th Congress, 149–150, 156, 158, 160, 165, 171, 180
  Party congresses and, 77
  retirement transfers, 98
  16th Congress, 288
  Standing Committee of, 72–73, 98
  See specific congress, groups
National Statistical Bureau, 218
natural resources, 238
  coal. *See* coal industry
  industry and. *See* industrialization
  mineral rights, 272
  Ministry of, 138
  natural gas, 229–230
  oil. *See* oil
Naughton, Barry, i, ix, 18, 21
Nee-Lian model, 117–118
neo-conservatives, 2
nepotism, 12, 29, 31, 53, 67–68
network building, 74
Nixon, Richard, 197
nomenklatura system, 9, 12, 51, 68
Northwest provinces, 277, 279, 285

O'Brien, Kevin, 74
oil, 229–231, 264, 270–271
opportunism, commitment vs., 117–118
Organic Law, 73, 75

Peng Zhen, 72, 74
People Daily website, 79–80
People's Bank of China, 41, 126–133
performance criteria, 106
  government leaders and, 105
  local party leaders and, 105
  multi-tasking and, 115
  township executives and, 107
personnel systems, 11, 14, 79. *See also* elites, system of
Polanyi, Karl, 142
policy implementation, 201
  cadre system and, 112
  case studies of, 18
  grassroots level and, 101
  principle-agent models, 113
Politburo, 32, 38
  provincial leaders in, 32, 39
  representation in, 38

population growth policies, 211
  de-control of, 286
  Deng Xiaoping and, 196
  evolution of, 194
  Family Planning Commission, 194–195, 201–202
  GDP per capita and, 19
  implementation of, 197
  natural rate of, 199
  persistence of, 219–220
  state coercion and, 20, 193
  urbanization and, 157
  western migration and, 275
  women's quality of life and, 194
poverty, 289
  migration and, 291
  poverty alleviation program, 290–291
  WDP and, 290–291
princelings, 16, 30, 65–67
principal-agent models, 7, 20, 101, 113
Product Quality Law, 141
professionalization, 12
promotion/transfer patterns, 35, 54–55, 61, 63–64, 87–96
property rights, 17, 238
provincial leaders, 33
  ages of, 57–58
  avoidance rule, 49–50, 62
  CPPCC and, 98
  favoritism/nepotism and, 67–68
  fourth generation leadership, 63
  full/alternative memberships, 60
  generational change and, 58
  importance of, 34, 67–68
  laggards, 86
  localism and, 35, 84
  mobility/reshuffling of, 34, 62
  national political system and, 12
  natives/non-natives, 50, 62–63, 84
  NPC and, 98
  pioneers and, 86
  Politburo members and, 32
  previous service of, 65
  promotion/transfer patterns, 35, 54–55, 61, 63–64, 87–96
  qualifications for, 34
  retirement of, 57
  rise of, 34
  role of, 32
  term limits, 54–55
  types of, 86

Qian Yunlu, 63
Quality Administration, 137–138, 141
quality standards, 136

Reemployment Project (REP), 155–156,
    168–169, 171–172
reforms, 130
    avoidance rule and, 49–50
    cadre evaluation system and, 102
    coastal cities and, 287–288
    democratization and, 13
    era of, 49–50
    process of, 258–259, 287–288
    regional policy, 258–259
    WDP and, 287–288
    See also specific institutions
regionalism, 2–3
    autonomy and, 31
    definition of, 131
    leadership and. *See* provincial leaders
    reform and, 258–259
    tongxiang and, 30
regulatory institutions, 134, 137–138, 141
REP. *See* Reemployment Project
resignation, 98
responsibility system, 247
retirement, 57, 98
revenue collection, 17
revolutionary credentials, 34
Rousseau, J.-J., 218
Ruan Chongwu, 97

SARS epidemic, 24, 35
screening, 80
Securities Law, 134
separatist movements, 65
Shandong province, 35–38, 59, 68
Shanghai Gang, 30–31, 40, 42–45, 67–68
Shanghai municipality, 46
    cadre evaluation system and, 106
    Jiading County, 107
    leaders from, 49
    reemployment and, 156
    suburban counties of, 106
    top officials in, 47–48
Shanxi province, 241, 243
Shenyang municipality, 158
    Asian crisis and, 153, 166
    employment problems in, 171
    exports from, 162
    foreign investment in, 159–160
    Guangzhou and, 159–160

imports to, 162
investment in, 160–161
Japanese investment in, 159
labor market in, 186
labor markets and, 159, 162–164,
    170–173, 175, 180
population of, 157
Reemployment Project and, 171–172
Soviet aid to, 159
Thatcherism and, 176
welfare policies, 19
Wuhan and, 174–175
Shirk, Susan, 112
Sichuan province, 38, 68
socialism, 22, 81, 117
Solinger, Dorothy J., ix–x, 19, 77
Song Fatang, 64–65
Songjiang county, 114–115
Southwest provinces, 277–279, 281, 285
Soviet Union, 9, 121, 194
Suharto regime, 130
Sun Weiben, 76
system, 101

taizi system, 30
taxation, 114–115, 122–124
    decentralization and, 125
    rates of, 286
    reforms and, 18
    State Bureaus, 124–125
    WDP and, 286
term limits, 53–55
Thatcher, Margaret, 153, 175, 190
Third Front projects, 257
Tian Jiyun, 141
Tiananmen crisis, 1–2, 121
Tibet, 57, 59
tongxiang, 30, 68
township and village enterprises (TVEs),
    290
township government, 107
transfers. *See* promotion/transfer patterns
transportation systems, 281–282
TVEs. *See* township and village enterprises

U.N. Population Fund (UNFPA), 215
unemployment, 156, 167
    Guangzhou and, 163, 168–170
    hiring policies and, 179
    REP. *See* Reemployment Project
    Shenyang and, 162–163, 170–171, 175
    Wuhan and, 162–163, 174–175

United States, 3, 120, 128
urban centers, 278
  migrant labor in, 182
  population, 157
  residence permits, 275
  rural workers in, 154–155
  unemployment in, 154, 180. *See*
    unemployment
  urbanization process, 120, 277
  See also specific urban areas

village leaders, 110–111
  income, 110
  incomes of, 112
  remuneration, 111
voting procedures, 81

Walder, Andrew, 117
Wang Hai, 141
Wang Huning, 41
Wang Sanyun, 34–35
Wang Xiaofeng, 63
Wang Xuebing, 133
water supplies, 264
Weberian instruments, 23
welfare objectives, 19
Wen Jiabao, 34, 288
Western Development Program (WDP),
    18, 21, 253
  areas of, 256
  central government, 21
  domestic firms, 272
  economics and, 21, 253, 281
  emergence of, 255
  emigration, 291
  energy policy, 264
  environmental needs, 264
  evaluation of, 289
  geography and, 275
  infrastructure projects, 269
  Leadership Small Group, 288
  local government officials, 21
  main provisions of, 266
  migration and, 286
  minorities and, 265
  national unity and, 21
  negative aspects of, 293
  politics and, 287
  poverty and, 290–291

  reforms and, 264, 287–288
  size of, 267
  taxation and, 286
Western provinces, 276
Whiting, Susan, x, 16–17
Wiebe, Robert H., 120
women's rights, 194, 211
World Bank, 4, 211
Wu Bangguo, 40, 237
Wuhan municipality, 19, 157–158, 161, 167,
    186
  exports from, 162
  flexibility toward outsiders, 183
  Guangzhou and, 174–175
  imports to, 162
  investment in, 160–161
  labor market in, 187–188
  outside labor, 182
  reemployment policies, 174–175
  Shenyang and, 174–175
  study of, 49
  Thatcherism and, 176
  unemployment, 162–163, 174–175

Xiang Nan, 76
Xinjiang, 59
Xu Guangchun, 40–41
Xu Jiatun, 76

Yang Xiaodu, 46
Yanzhong Huang, ix, 19
Ye Xuanping, 65, 97–98
Yellow River, 263–264
Ying-mao Kau, 49
You Xigui, 66
Yunnan, 59

Zeng Peiyan, 288
Zeng Qinghong, 34, 40, 67
Zhang Dejiang, 33–34
Zhang Quanjing, 72
Zhang Xuezhong, 35
Zhang Yixiang, 249
Zhao Ziyang, 13, 232
Zhiyue Bo, ix, 13
Zhou Mingwei, 41
ZhouYongkang, 33
Zhu Rongji, 17, 41, 226–227, 234, 262, 288
Zhu Xiaohua, 41